Passport
to the
Cosmos

Commemorative Edition

Human Transformation
and Alien Encounters

Also by John E. Mack, M.D.

Nightmares and Human Conflict

Borderline States in Psychiatry
(Edited)

A Prince of Our Disorder:
The Life of T. E. Lawrence
(Pulitzer Prize in Biography 1977)

Vivienne: The Life and Suicide of an Adolescent Girl
(with Holly Hickler)

Last Aid
(Edited with E. Chivian, S. Chivian, and R. J. Lifton)

The Development and Sustaining of Self-Esteem in Childhood
(Edited with Steven Ablon)

The Alchemy of Survival: One Woman's Journey
(with Rita S. Rogers)

Human Feelings: Explorations in Affect Development and Meaning
(Edited with Steven Ablon, Daniel Brown, and Edward J. Khantzian)

Abduction: Human Encounters With Aliens

The Psychospiritual Clinician's Handbook
Sharon G. Mijares and Gurucharan Singh Khalsa (eds.)
(contributor)

Mind Before Matter
(Edited with Trish Pfeiffer and Paul Devereux)

Passport
to the
Cosmos
Commemorative Edition

Human Transformation
and Alien Encounters

John E. Mack, M.D.
Pulitzer Prize-Winning Author
of the Bestselling *Abduction*

To the experiencers,

who have been my teachers

Review From *Publishers Weekly*

Here is a fascinating foray into an exotic world. From Harvard psychiatry professor and Pulitzer prize-winning author John Mack comes a second book (after *Abduction*) based on accounts by people who claim to have been abducted by aliens. While he fudges the question of whether the aliens are "real in a strictly material sense," he insists that the experience is "real" for the abductees, in the way that shamans' spiritual journeys are real to them; indeed, a couple of his interviewees are shamans. He focuses on the newly emerging spiritual importance of the alleged abductees' message. Their reports, Mack believes, reveal much about human culture and the future of the human race. In extensive interviews with Mack, those who claim to have been abducted report that the aliens are especially motivated by questions of ecological destruction, and that they may even be survivors of a destroyed civilization seeking to breed hybrid children with humans to ensure the survival of both the human race and their own. Overwhelmingly, the abductees state that the aliens visit Earth to warn us that our cavalier tree-cutting, water-polluting, trash-dumping habits will have dire consequences if we do not change our ways. Abductees are left with not only a profound caring for the environment, but with a sense that they have encountered creatures sent by whatever power rules the universe. They particularly find that their experiences resonate with Native American religions. This discussion leads into what is possibly the most intriguing section of the book, the examination of sex between humans and aliens—great sex, by numerous accounts. But as a serious investigation into a mystifying experience, Mack's account poses questions begging for answers.

Review From *Library Journal*

Mack, a Harvard University psychiatrist and Pulitzer Prize-winning biographer of T.E. Lawrence, created an academic stir with the publication of *Abduction: Human Encounters with Aliens* (1994), in which he argued that tales of alien abduction were true. As a result, Harvard warned him to adhere to its standards of conduct for clinical research. In this follow-up, Mack, still undaunted, argues that our knowledge of reality needs to change and that scientific rationalism alone cannot explain the alien abduction syndrome. He examines traditional views of reality, the implications for humanity in light of the abduction phenomenon, and the traumatic effects on "experiencers" or abductees. Mack's work with indigenous people—shamans and medicine men and women—suggests that the phenomenon is not simply a product of Western imagination. This veritable handbook of New Age philosophy will find a readership in most public libraries.

NAME—NOM
JOHN EDWARD MACK

SEX—SEXE | BIRTHPLACE—LIEU DE NAISSANCE
M | **NEW YORK, U.S.A.**

BIRTH DATE—DATE DE NAISSANCE
OCT. 4, 1929

ISSUE DATE—DATE DE DELIVRANCE
APRIL 9, 1985

NATIONALITY—NATIONALITÉ
UNITED STATES OF AMERICA

EXPIRES ON—EXPIRE LE
➧ **APRIL 8, 1995**

SIGNATURE OF BEARER—SIGNATURE DU TITULAIRE

NOT VALID UNTIL SIGNED

John E. Mack, MD: A Tribute

By Michael H. Cohen, Esq.

This is a tribute to John E. Mack, MD, who has transitioned from his physical body to the next plane of consciousness. He was a colleague and explorer of the human experience who modeled insight, humor, and courage.

Grieving John's Bodily Transition

When someone you love suddenly passes, a series of shocks ripple through the system: waves of grief, tenderness, memories, combined with a sense of your own finitude, and at the same time, this paradoxical analytical process of combing through the associations and trying to understand the enormity of what this person meant in your life.

When I learned from a friend last night that John Mack had suddenly died, I found these waves of emotions rising and subsiding. I felt deeply connected to John, though I knew him professionally only in passing, and personally hardly at all. I realized that we had connected beyond time and space, through a shared bond, a passion for truth; I admired John, and felt that I was able to travel further simply knowing he was there.

The details of John Mack's legacy are now coming to light in tributes from around the world, both from academics and institutions of great learning—including Harvard, which once put him through what might have seemed an inquisition—and the many individuals whose lives he touched. John was a pioneer, a Pulitzer-prize winning author, a dedicated psychiatrist and a humanitarian deeply committed to improving his community. John was committed to his local community in Cambridge, the community of mental healthcare, and the larger community of all beings everywhere. Whether specifically a Buddhist or maybe a bit of everything, he seemed to me to embody the Buddhist ideal of aspiring to help uplift the entire creation. John held the space for many to open up to their felt experiences, not judging them but allowing, and in our time together, I experienced his wisdom, his compassion, and his humanness. Both in his intellectual triumphs and in the stillness we shared—the contact in-between the words—I felt his essence as a marvel.

John Mack: A Freedom-Fighter for Consciousness

John was a freedom-fighter, working toward liberation of human consciousness. That meant a lot to many people—particularly those "experiencers," people who had experienced extraordinary planes of consciousness, tried to express their inner (and sometimes tormenting) adventures, and found only scorn (and further abuse) on most other doorsteps within the scientific and mental health care communities. Many of these individuals finally found a measure of acceptance (and self-acceptance) through John's work, a way to reflect on and integrate their intense experiences. And John's openness to spiritual experience, combined with his prominence in academe, meant a lot personally and professionally to me.

John Opened the Way for People to Trust their Inner Experience

I had first heard of John Mack while I was a sophomore at the Barbara Brennan School of Healing. The year was 1994; I was a new law professor teaching in the Midwest; "alternative medicine" was just barely on the map. Professionally, I was teaching a seminar on the emerging legal framework surrounding alternative medicine, using whatever crumbs of medical literature were available to validate my interest in the field and counter any possible objections within the law school that my interests might be on the lunatic fringe.

Personally, I was learning about energy healing—skeptical and distant at first, but increasingly releasing a hard-edged denial of my own gifts in this arena. While at the Brennan school, we were studying the "astral levels of the [human energy] field," the places where, according to Brennan's energy healing theory and practice, our consciousness could encounter beings from other planes, past-life memories, traumas and triumphs from other dimensions of existence, and other things seemingly out of fantasy or science fiction, and certainly not then supported by prevailing scientific theory other than, perhaps, notions of the "holographic universe" developed by physicist David Bohm. All these things were real to me—or became real, not by virtue of any indoctrination by Brennan, but because of my own research—I call it that—an experiential dive into planes of consciousness that increasingly opened as I let my heart and spirit soften.

Having traversed mystical experience in a variety of ways prior to enrolling in the school—some through Judaism, others through Christianity, Buddhism, Hinduism, and various forms of meditation—I had moved beyond a rigid intellectualization to a place of increasing receptivity. But still, it was difficult to reconcile the professional identities of lawyer and healer. Simply learning about John Mack and his work, even from afar, opened me to trust my inner experience.

A friend from Brennan's school had happened to meet John while traveling to receive 'darshan' with Mother Meera, a purported Indian avatar, in Germany. Just knowing about that encounter with John helped further heal the split between the 'scientific' (or 'legal') and the inner, mystical that my personal and professional path seemed to be increasingly embodying.

John: A Pioneering Advocate for a Broader Worldview

Our work on the "astral planes" in the Brennan school opened me to the possibility that "ET" (extraterrestrial) encounters were real: not fictive, delusional, or otherwise phantasmagorical imagining. Nor were these products of distorted, deceptive or false memories by a self-perceived victim. For me, the notion of ET's pointed toward transcendence, not only and always abuse recapitulated. Since in healing school we were having regular experiences of spirit guides, angels (as well as demons), and spiritual forces both benevolent and sinister, extending that experience to 'brothers and sisters' from other planets—whose bodies did not necessarily have to be physical, like ours, but rather could exist solely on other levels of the energy field—seemed reasonable.

Of course, one has to take the leap and actually experience oneself as inhabiting more than what current biology takes as real; it helps to experience oneself on the higher levels of the human energy field, rather than as a "just" a body and a mind. That leap is impossible if one uses skepticism, an otherwise valuable tool, to intellectualize away or otherwise distance oneself from inner experience. It takes a rare soul who can not only include critical intellectual faculties in the quest for clarity but also lead other critical thinkers past limited conceptualizations to new paradigmatic possibilities.

Indeed, continuing his pioneering efforts along these lines, and combining his skills as a psychiatrist and biographer, John was working on a new manuscript about communications from a healer after her death. He was exploring how a field of love can literally create a bridge between worlds: reiterating the perennial wisdom in the psychologically rich, biographical vein that had won him the Pulitzer.

John's exploration, while controversial to some, has resonances in epistemology and other branches of philosophy, and may inspire colleagues in other fields, including a new scientific discipline known as astrobiology. I believe his work will stand the test of time and be recognized as a great contribution to human knowledge. But I want to turn more specifically to John's influence and how that filtered into my own life through the worldwide web of auspicious connections that ultimately brought me zero degrees of separation from him.

One of my teachers at Barbara Brennan's school was Peter, an "experiencer" (the preferred term to "abductee") who had explored his memories of the ET experience through hypnosis with John, and served as subject for a main chapter in John's book, *Abduction: Human Encounters with Aliens*. Peter described his experiences to a group at the school; that same year he appeared, with John and others, on Oprah.

Peter's experiences frightened even many of my classmates at Barbara Brennan's school, perhaps because they suggested a loss of control or invasion. I felt safe in the ET territory, perhaps because I conceptualized ETs as dwelling on a continuum of consciousness, together with many other mystical and "extraordinary experiences," as John would come to denote these inner adventures. But for many, the ET experience, particularly its "abduction" aspects, connoted trauma; abuse; being out-of-control. To help dispel the fears (and hostility) that seemed to permeate response to descriptions from experiencers, Peter explained that there were several distinct races of ETs that others had identified, and only one—the so-called Grays—were involved in the abduction phenomena.

According to Peter, the abduction phenomenon, the defining modus operandi of the Grays, reified the classic mind-body split that arguably has been responsible for so much evil in human history: a runaway intellect divorced from the heart, technology gone wild. This, indeed, was a theme in John's work—to quote the John E. Mack Institute's tribute to John, "Mack advocates that Western culture requires a shift away from a purely materialist worldview (which he feels is responsible for the Cold War, the global ecological crisis, ethnonationalism and regional conflict) towards a transpersonal worldview which embraces certain elements of Eastern spiritual and philosophical traditions." Whether one took the Grays as metaphysics or metaphor, the archetype of gray consciousness had power: head separated from heart, a mutant Cartesian dualism massively distorting the connectivity of love, resulting in sick and sense-less experimentation.

In a larger context, though, the flipside of the abduction encounter was the possibility for transcendence and a heart encounter with all-that-is. That was the theme of John's subsequent book, *Passport to the Cosmos*. Some parts of the alien encounter experience included the alienness (from the perspective of mundane human emotions) of exalted states, feelings of cosmic unity, an end to the separation that Alan Watts had characterized as leaving us "an ego encased in a bag of skin." Following this line of inquiry, John advocated a broader worldview than the species-centric, human-dominated view of the cosmos. John's spacious mind allowed a broader conceptualization of our place in the omni-verse, a place in which we humans might coexist with other species and, indeed, intelligently converse with them. But to do so, if one followed the line of John's work, required more than radio signals and scientific intelligence—it required emotional and spiritual intelligence, including a capacity to deepen our opening to inner experience.

In this way, John was a pioneering advocate for a broader view of consciousness, and of our relatedness to the entire creation. John moved us past the marriage to our own intellectual constructs, and into an awareness of our soul bond with something more unrestricted.

In a sense, I had 'met' John Mack in 1994, through Peter, the Barbara Brennan School, and my own unfolding spiritual life. John's presence on this Earth, and his contribution to human awareness, scholarly discourse, and "the literature," was as much a part of my spiritual opening as my encounter with different religions.

Meeting John

I had linked my consciousness with John's in 1994, but it took until 2003 to meet him in person. Oddly, it happened at a men's group organized by a physician friend and held at the New England School for Acupuncture. Around the circle, John introduced himself to the group casually, humbly, without any pretense or ego. There he was, another man, like each of us: gifted, charged with desire for contribution, and also riddled with the complexities of modern life. I recognized him and went up and introduced myself after the meeting, mentioning briefly my friendship with Peter and the fact that I, too, had had experiences, though not of the abduction kind. John peered down his half-glasses and warmly asked: "Spiritual experiences?" I nodded, and we arranged to meet.

In truth, my ET experience had occurred (back in 1994) in what seemed an unlikely—though in one sense, deeply spiritual—space: at the Cleveland Clinic. I was at the Medical Institute for Law Faculty, visiting the Clinic with about a dozen law professors in a scholarly exchange between the professions of law and medicine. Our visit included the operating rooms during surgery and the intensive care unit. One evening while drifting off in my hotel room, I experienced a being in my room. She—for femaleness described her—wore a headpiece, had intelligent eyes, and communicated telepathically. I felt a great kinship with her. I had a sense of her compassionate awareness and presence during the states of nonverbal connection I had experienced with anesthetized patients, with individuals on life support, and with others in the twilight zone of life and death. She might have been Mary, or Kwan Yin, or some other being identified from any religious tradition, but I identified her as ET because of an otherness about her that cannot be described—a sense of different kind of intelligence, with its own world, customs, cultures, languages, even energetic (nonphysical) bodies and modes of transportation.

For I was experiencing a dual reality during the Medical Institute—the world of the doctors, the nurses, the bleeping machines, the families laboring under grief and stress; and the inner world, a silent one in which all sorts of—for lack of a better word—energies were exchanged.

Yet who, in my academic community, could validate or even sanction such an experience? I could be ridiculed for claiming to speak with an ET in my hotel room at the Cleveland Clinic. Yet, paradoxically, the same community that might launch a witch hunt for an admission of 'ET contact' could laud an admission of conversing privately with Jesus, Yahweh, or any recognized figure from a mainstream religion. Beliefs are strange creatures, some accepted, others scandalized. It would be perfectly acceptable for me to believe that Mary physically ascended to heaven or that Moses parted the Red Sea or that Arjuna had entered a chariot driven by Krishna, but ludicrous, in the minds of many, to believe that a being from another planet could speak to me telepathically in a hotel room. The former likely would be called, religious impulse; the second labeled fantasy or delusion. My ET experience was spiritual, not the abduction experience— but even if were in that other category, the shaming aspects of contemporary judgment might make it feel unsafe to describe. Yet I was having experiences as real to me— perhaps more—than discussions with peer attorneys and doctors; indeed, many of those conversations were intellectualized abstractions, coated with thick denial of the palpable suffering around us, while my inner experiences allowed no room to deflect from genuine, authentic emotions. And yet to keep myself professionally safe, I wrote about the experience in a scholarly journal, but from a detached perspective—hinting but ultimately concealing the fact that it was my experience.

John Mack offered a gift to all with extraordinary experiences who might otherwise have felt shamed by the judgment of many segments within contemporary society, who may have hesitated coming open with the truth of their psychic receptivity to other parts of the cosmos than those accepted in what psychologist Charles Tart has called "consensus trance." John's gift was unconditional acceptance of the possibility for transcendence. It was a gift to meet John personally and say to him that I, too, had had close encounters of a kind not usually admitted in academic—or any professional— circles. These encounters were held with care and recognition in the heart and mind of a great being like John.

Being able to acknowledge my ET connection and locate its reality within the context of John Mack's work made it somehow safer to be fully myself. Meeting John in person at the men's group brought yet another level of solidity to imbibing his life's work. My verbal interaction with John there lasted only a few minutes, but being with him, knowing he was there, making that heart and mind and soul connection, in an instant made a shift.

John Mack himself was a passport to the cosmos.

An Interview with John Mack

My next physical encounter with John was professional. He was building an institute at the intersection of psychology and spirituality, a subject of deep interest given my involvement in complementary medicine law and policy, and we were looking for ways to form a professional bridge. But, while much of complementary medicine at least could be scientifically validated (or, alternatively, debunked) through conventional scientific process, the objective reality of subjective mystical experience could not. On one level, John's professional inquiry seemed more radical than mine, because he delved into realms of the mind that lacked tangible expression, capable of receiving objective consensus. Yet we were both spiritual warriors, trying to give expression to our interest in the sublime through our mundane (in the world) positions as academics.

In a sense, we were coming at the same problem—tackling a lot of fear and limitation of consciousness—from opposite directions: complementary medicine had gained a foothold in academic circles. But John had been excoriated by some within his academic community, even if ultimately vindicated. And I was coming from law, John from psychiatry.

The John E. Mack Institute's website summarizes John's Harvard trials as follows: "In 1994 the Dean of Harvard Medical School appointed a committee of peers to review Mack's clinical care and clinical investigation of the people who had shared their alien encounters with him (some of their cases were written of in Mack's 1994 book *Abduction*). After fourteen months of inquiry and amid growing questions from the academic community (including Harvard Professor of Law Alan Dershowitz) regarding the validity of Harvard's investigation of a tenured professor, Harvard issued a statement stating that the Dean had 'reaffirmed Dr. Mack's academic freedom to study what he wishes and to state his opinions without impediment,' concluding 'Dr. Mack remains a member in good standing of the Harvard Faculty of Medicine.'"

It seemed to me that John had come through the experience with wisdom and even humor. But we also discussed our dislike for the bias, bigotry, hostility, and rigid ideological stance that some—not all—within our community could hold against openness to inner experience.

In many ways I, too, had experienced the sting of enemy fire against freedom of consciousness in various academic affiliations. Noting this fact is not a tirade against Harvard—as indeed in many ways it has been a welcome academic home—but rather a memoir of the deep connection I felt with John in our brief association. We were both faculty members at the same institution—he far more senior and deeply rooted, and having withstood an assault on his scholarly reputation and line of inquiry, but both sharing a maverick's eye from within the citadel of science. Knowing he was there; that he had faced challenge, defended himself, and come through; that he, too, respected mystical experience yet could stand, shoulder-to-shoulder, with colleagues committed to compassionate clinical care and dispassionate scientific inquiry; all this gave me a warm feeling of fellowship unavailable in many quarters.

In fact, simply having a kind of job interview with John freed me from the shackles—the "mind-forg'd manacles," as Blake would call them—of fear-based thinking, keeping who I was under wraps. I had been admonished by some—not all—peers to avoid being "perceived as an advocate" for therapies that could be considered 'unproven.' To be so perceived could, according to some, mean falling from professional grace, perhaps even being run out of the institution. John Mack served as the 'bad boy' example of what might happen were I to be truly myself—as he courageously was. Because of this professional pressure to avoid anything that might possibly be perceived as 'unscientific', and concomitant pressure to dissociate myself from John, I joked with John that I could not be seen with him in the parking lot. He smiled at the old joke that "just because you're paranoid doesn't mean they're not out to get you." Several times he picked up on and repeated the joke about having to disguise our appearing together—we spoke of institutional spies; this was a kind of humorous, self-referential way to reflect our shared distaste for the abundance of judgment that some quarters heaped upon our shared interest in psychology and spirituality.

Perhaps that was one reason I cried when I learned he had passed. I was proud of my association with John, and longed for it to deepen. To me he was a kind, generous, thoughtful man, full of beguiling vulnerability alongside his penetrating and boundary-breaking brilliance. What we shared in our encounters was not merely kinship around interest in alien experiences—it was our humanness. There was a deep tenderness about and within him and a mutual empathy between us for our shared battle against ideological stifling and control. And, I might say, a kind of divine love passed—certainly an appreciation flowed for his contribution as well as his struggles. I miss him.

Working with John

As I grieved John's death, I told my wife: "I had hoped to work closely with him." My wife wisely and sweetly responded: "You still will. That work will continue." I miss John being here physically, and continue to feel him on subtle levels. And I am sure many of us will be supporting John and feel supported by John as he continues his work alongside ours in the new dimensions of body and consciousness in which he resides.

I was gratified to read that one of John's spiritual friends and teachers will be saying prayers at a holy place in New Mexico. I dedicate today's yoga practice to him; may it bring blessings, peace, and wholeness in worlds to come.

I will also echo this tribute to John from songwriter Stuart Davis, as it is absolutely true: "as anyone who's had the pleasure of meeting John knows, he was a total sweet heart of a human being, instantly lovable. each time i was with him, i was struck by his transparency, humility, and curiousity. he was 64 when i met him, he sparkled like a diamond, and he was every bit as glowing when i had dinner with him for the last time about a year ago....john, it is with much love and gratitude that i thank you for your amazing presence in our lives, for your gifts to humanity, and indeed all beings-everywhere. may your radiant soul be received by its source and continue to illuminate us from the point of all places."

A few months ago, I ran into John on a train ride to New York. It was wonderful to be in contact with his keen mind, wry humor, and generous heart. John could be intellectually critical and skeptical—as he was when the notion of "karma" was raised—yet as a person he was simultaneously embracing, tolerant, and full of wisdom.

John Gave Permission

At the end of our interview, John stood and shared with me some very personal book projects on which he was working. After that, he stood close and softly asked: "is there anything more; is there anything more you wish to share?"

Of course there was; I could have gone on for days. There was a book, for example, I was writing on my experience in Byelorussia, in a visit that involved trying to help children radiation victims of Chernobyl through energy healing. John had been involved in the physicians' movement for nuclear disarmament. He was a link in the legacy of psychiatrists (such as Robert Jay Lifton, MD) who had written about the mass dissociation known as 'psychic numbing;' who had catalogued the splits and distortions in our collective response to 'nuclear absurdity;' who had bared witness to the human capacity for shutting off feeling the immensity of a shared horror.

I sent my book manuscript about the children of Chernobyl to John for review. Simply knowing John was there—the enormity of his knowledge base, understanding, and interests—provided a touchstone for further creativity. The fact that he understood the issues, that he was caring, that he had a spiritual as well as a clinical and academic side, that he did not judge—gave room for exploration.

By asking "is there anything more," John was compassionately offering to elicit anything personal I might share such as the split between the scholarly and the spiritual. But John was my senior colleague and friend. I made the decision not to go into my own experiences, as our meeting was professionally exploratory and it was important for me to stay in the role of lawyer and legal scholar. But John gave permission and took a kind interest in me as a whole being. He was neither all head nor all heart, but rather a compassionate, wise old soul who, in his crowded schedule, made room for everything.

What John did as a psychiatrist and scholar he embodied, and modeled, during our moments together: he gave permission for the full authentic expression of self to be.

Contents

Acknowledgments

As the time has come for me to thank the people who have helped me with this book, I realize just how many there have been.

Many people have read parts or all of the manuscript and have given me invaluable feedback. I want to give each my heartfelt thanks. These include Michael Baldwin, Paul Bernstein, Joan Bird, Dennis Briefer, Ron Bryan, Pat Carr, Anne Carter, Laurel Chiten, Roberta Colasanti, Linda Gerber, Stanislav Grof, Michael Harner, Pam Kasey, Jonathan Katz, Steve Larsen, Amy Lawrence, Joe Lewels, Sergio Lub, Richmond Mayo-Smith and the board members of the Center for Psychology and Social Change, Caroline McLeod, Ralph Metzner, Edgar Mitchell, Gilda Moura, Brian O'Leary, Trish Pfeiffer, Andy Pritchard, David Pritchard, Jeff Rediger, Ted Roszak, Rudolph Schild, Elaine Seiler, Larry Shainberg, Richard Tarnas, Angela Thompson-Smith, Roger Walsh, Karen Wesolowski, and Michael Zimmerman.

Others who provided helpful support, ideas, papers, references, and advice include Robert Bigelow and his advisors at NIDS, Ron Bryan, John Gutfreund, Charles Laughlin, Howard Levine, Christopher Lydon, Ruth Mack, Barbara and Charles Overby and the Lifebridge Foundation, Laurance Rockefeller, and Arthur Zajonc.

I want to express my special appreciation to Dominique Callimanopulos for her inspiration throughout the project and especially for realizing the central importance of a cross-cultural perspective. For several years she was my associate in the research, and many of the book's insights came out of our collaboration. Roberta Colasanti was my clinical partner through all the years of this project, and the opportunity to discuss what we were learning from this work has been essential from its beginning. Paul Bernstein's painstaking efforts in exploring relevant literature and organizing the book's references have been extraordinarily important. Karen Speerstra, with her customary generosity, gave the manuscript a thorough editing at a crucial time.

Leslie Hansen worked devotedly in shepherding the manuscript through its various versions. My assistant, Pat Carr, was with me throughout its creation, as she has been in so many projects, and helped to bring it to completion.

Karen Wesolowski and the staff at PEER have shared ideas and offered useful criticism from the start. In addition they have given the kind of steady support without which the book would not have become a reality.

A special thank-you goes to my editor, Kristin Kiser, whose upbeat encouragement and thoughtful way of helping to shape the manuscript have meant a lot to me, and to my indomitable agent, Timothy Seldes, who has helped me so much for more years than either of us might care to say.

I wish to give great thanks for the kindness of Mu Soeng, Katherine Diehl, and the staff at the Buddhist Study Center in Barre, Massachusetts, who provided a place of respite, peace, and understanding where much of this book was written.

Finally, it is to the experiencers themselves, pioneers of the unknown, to whom I owe the most. Some are represented in this book and some are not. The book is dedicated to them.

Preface

When you see the Earth like this, and the cosmos like this, and ten times more stars, ten times as bright because of no intervening atmosphere, in the full 180-degree view, if you put your face to the windows, it's magnificent, it's overwhelming. . . . What happened was a sudden recognition of heart.... It made me realize that the answers to the ancient questions, "Who are we? How did we get here? Where are we going?" within science were certainly incomplete and perhaps flawed. This feeling of unity and connectedness was an ecstatic, blissful experience. When I came back, I knew my life had changed. I knew that I had to go find out what was this experience I had had.

Astronaut Edgar Mitchell
Remarks at PEER's Star Wisdom conference May 8, 1998

During the nearly ten years that I have studied the alien abduction phenomenon, its potential implications have continued to broaden and deepen. At first the phenomenon seemed to be a strange, unpleasant intrusion by an unknown force into the bodies, minds, and lives of a large number of people, seemingly selected at random. Surely, to a certain extent, it remains just that. But over time my work with the courageous individuals called abductees or experiencers has made me see how these experiences can actually lead to the kind of ancient questions of which Edgar Mitchell spoke: Who are we? How did we get here? Where are we going?

I wish to stress at the outset that I am not in this book seeking to establish the material reality of the alien abduction phenomenon, that is, people's reports of being taken by humanoid beings into some sort of enclosure where a variety of procedures and communications are said to take place. Rather, I am more concerned with the meaning of these experiences for the so-called abductees and for humankind more generally. In that sense this book is not simply about abductions but has to do with what such anomalous experiences and related phenomena can tell us about ourselves and our evolving knowledge of the nature of reality.

Looking back at the path that brought me to my present viewpoint, I realize that one cannot begin to consider seriously something so preposterous without at least a minimal willingness to look at the possibility that our view of the universe and ways of knowing about it have indeed been incomplete and perhaps flawed. This worldview would require that for something to be real, its behavior must be consistent with the laws of nature we already know, and it should yield its secrets to a way of knowing that relies primarily on the five senses, rational analysis, and a virtually complete separation of subject and object, of the explorer and what is being explored.

Having this in mind, I would like to make a plea that my readers begin with an attitude of *not* knowing, including not knowing about how we know about anything, especially what is most important to us. I would also ask that they suspend the natural tendency to form questions according to the logic that is characteristic of the human mind as it applies itself to the human world, such as, "If the aliens are X, then why don't they do Y?"

My own approach has been largely that of a clinician, allowing the abduction experiencers to tell their stories without initial judgments or interpretations, knowing there is always time to assess the messenger and the message later. In this regard clinicians have a certain advantage. For in working with other human beings, we have always relied heavily on empathy and intuition, on the use of ourselves as the instruments of knowing. We are accustomed to uncertainty and to immersing ourselves in the varieties and mysteries of human experience.

John E. Mack, M.D.
Boulder, Colorado

John E. Mack, M.D. © Judy Dater

little "baby"

"My ego rebels against this," Karin says, but "in my higher self-consciousness, I'm in complete agreement with the whole process.... It's creating life. It's just creation. It's what God does." (from p. 130). Illustration by Karin.

Part One

"One tentative step on the end of my bed and I found my familiar panic. It was now fully on the bed and I was fully awake ...Then it let me open my eyes. 'Jesus Christ! You look like a fucking bug!'" Illustrations by Karin.

Chapter 1

Abduction: The Next Generation

The power of the encounters comes from acknowledging your helplessness and keeping the whole matter in question, because the deeper the question goes, the more you attempt to come to some kind of resolution. If you keep asking them [the beings] questions, they keep reforming the thing in such a way that the questions get more provocative but can't quite be answered. . . . If you start saying, "Well, they are aliens and they're from this planet," you're lost. . . . I've often been in situations where the question has been impossible to live with. You can't not answer it, and you can't answer it either. And there you have it. You sit in a situation where you can't bear to be—and you grow.

Whitley Strieber
Interview with author
Wagner, South Dakota June 16, 1996

Background

In the years since the publication of *Abduction* (Mack 1994), I have worked with more than one hundred additional people in the United States and other countries who report encounters with strange beings. These individuals are called "abductees," "experiencers" or "anomalous experiencers"—finding appropriate language, as we shall see, has become an increasingly difficult problem.

The alien abduction phenomenon can be defined as the experience of being taken by humanoid beings, usually but not always against the person's will, into some sort of enclosure where a variety of procedures and communications occur. Not all of the encounters described in this book are typical or classical in the sense of being intrusive and/or traumatic. As you will see, the experiences of Carlos Diaz, Jean, Sequoyah and Gary, for example, are not typical, and I do not have evidence that Bernardo or the children at the Ariel School were actually abducted by the beings they saw, although their encounters affected them profoundly. I believe that including a somewhat wider range of experiences is likely to add to our understanding. In this book I will tell what I have learned from my further explorations. My understanding of the meaning and power of this extraordinary phenomenon, especially its relationship to the planet's ecological crisis, is continuously evolving. I will set forth the consistent patterns that seem to be emerging as well as the contradictions and paradoxes that persist. The implications of these experiences for our understanding of ourselves in this universe will, I think, be reflected in each chapter of the book.

Before telling of the findings that have led me to my present viewpoint, I thought it might be useful to share with the reader where I have arrived, or have been taken, philosophically speaking, by my immersion in this fascinating and compelling work. There has been a continuing evolution of my perspective regarding the data itself, the most effective method of bringing it forth, and the most useful way of interpreting the material. I have tried to be scrupulous in my observations and analysis, but I recognize that in the end what I have done will always to some degree remain idiosyncratic; that is, it is the product of the interplay of my own psyche or consciousness with the experiences of others.

I was raised in a secular American family of German Jewish heritage. The idea of a great bearded figure suspended somehow in the heavens was the only representation of God I remember being taught, and my logical, rational mind rejected this notion as impossible and absurd. Spirituality was a vaguely pleasant but unrealistic concept. My father, a professor of English at New York's City College, read the Bible to my sister and me as culture and literature. In medical school any thought that the complex life-forms we were studying were created by purpose or intelligent design rather than simply through Darwinian selection was disparagingly labeled "teleology," a kind of academic expletive. The experiences of native peoples with spirits, and the religious beliefs of the faithful, I looked upon, with Freud (another secular Jewish rationalist), as animism, primitivism, and illusion. Psychoanalysis and psychiatry, while expressly addressing the inner life, at the same time fit well into my materialist worldview, offering mechanistic explanations for human behavior, feelings, and experiences.

When I first heard of the alien abduction phenomenon, I tried to fit it into my knowledge of psychopathology. But no consistent psychiatric disturbance has been found that could account for these reports, nor has a major psychological study of this population demonstrated more psychopathology than a matched comparison group (McLeod et al. forthcoming). I soon realized, therefore, that no plausible fit was emerging. A purely intrapsychic or psychosocial explanation—that is, one that did not include the possibility of another intelligence or force entering the experiencers' lives, as if from outside—was not consistent with my diagnostic assessment of what these clients were presenting.

I was then faced with the choice of either trying to fit these individuals' reports into a framework that fit my worldview—they were having fantasies, strange dreams, delusions, or some other distortion of reality—or of modifying my worldview to include the possibility that entities, beings, energies—*something*—could be reaching my clients from another realm. The first choice was compatible with my worldview but did not fit the clinical data. The second was inconsistent with my philosophical grounding, and with conventional assumptions about reality, but appeared to fit better what I was finding. It seemed to me to be more logical, and intellectually more honest, to modify my cosmology than to continue trying to force my clients into molds that clearly did not suit them.

In 1995 a close friend, a psychologist who is herself a pioneer in working with nonordinary states of consciousness, challenged me with the question, "John, where do you think you are on the weakest ground in this work?" I assumed correctly that what she had in mind was my crediting the possibility that beings, spirits, or anything at all could "cross over" from the unseen or "other" world into our material reality. This crossover seems to be regarded as a regular occurrence in many if not most indigenous cultures, but in our Western or scientific/materialist society, the domains of spirit and matter have been kept separate and distinct, and the possibility of traffic between them is looked upon as doubtful if not altogether impossible. When I pointed out to her that in other cultures in which I have tried to investigate the abduction phenomenon, such interchange is "no big deal," she replied that in our culture it is indeed a big deal.

Worldviews and Other Cultures

Just how deeply held is the worldview that separates radically the material world from the realms of spirit, unseen agency, "daimonic reality" in the words of English writer Patrick Harpur (1994, p. 37), or what are called the subtle realms in Eastern spiritual traditions, was brought home to me a few weeks after the publication of my book in the spring of 1994, when one of the deans at the Harvard Medical School handed me a letter that called for the establishment of a small committee to investigate my work.* After explaining vaguely that "concerns" had been expressed to the university about what I was doing (although he told of no specific complaint, nor was any offered in the letter), he added pleasantly—for he had been a friend and colleague—that I would not have gotten into trouble if I had not suggested in the book that my findings might require a change in our view of reality rather than saying that I had found a new psychiatric syndrome whose cause had not yet been established.†

Some of the subjects of my recent interviews have come from indigenous cultures in the United States and other countries. Frequently these informants will tell me that, according to tribal legends, their people came from the sky and that their cultures were founded by "star people," arriving sometimes in what they call UFOs or something like them. I have found it difficult to interpret such communications, primarily because of the different relationship between the spirit or unseen and the material

* The word "daimonic" as used by Harpur is not to be confused with "demonic." Harpur uses this word simply to refer to unseen realities or forces that may, nevertheless, manifest in the physical world.

† One of the recommendations of this committee was that I involve more colleagues in the work. This had not been easy, but with this encouragement the Program for Extraordinary Experience Research (PEER) in affiliation with the Cambridge Hospital Department of Psychiatry convened a multidisciplinary group to study anomalous phenomena. The first meeting of this group took place at Harvard University on April 10 and 11, 1999. At the meeting distinguished colleagues from inside and outside the university discussed fruitfully the challenges of exploring the alien abduction phenomenon and other anomalies. Disciplines represented included astrophysics, optical physics, history of science, history of psychology, anthropology, philosophy, theology, neurophysiology, and of course, psychiatry and psychology. This meeting will be referred to in the text as the "multidisciplinary study group conference" or "study group conference" or just "study group."

worlds in native cultures. For example, according to Bernardo Peixoto, a shaman who was raised by the Ipixuma tribe of the Brazilian rain forest, "our legends say that a long time ago a flying saucer landed in the Amazon basin" and that men emerged from this spaceship. He said there were even cave drawings, made hundreds if not thousands of years ago, that showed some kind of craft. These beings were *makuras,* or spirits that "came from high up in the sky." When I asked him if among his people this legend was to be regarded literally as referring to the material world, or should be seen rather as metaphoric, or a crossing over from the unseen or spirit realms into the material world, he replied succinctly that among his people "this makes no difference."[1]

Similarly, Malidoma Somé, a shaman of the Dagara people of Burkina Faso in West Africa, with advanced degrees from the Sorbonne and Brandeis University, has written, "In Western reality, there is a clear split between the spiritual and the material, between religious life and secular life. This concept is alien to the Dagara. For us, as for many indigenous cultures, the supernatural is part of our everyday lives. To a Dagara man or woman, the material is just the spiritual taking on form" (Somé 1995, p. 8). I have heard similar statements frequently from native people in North America. Sequoyah Trueblood (see Chapter 9), for example, says that for him whether the physical body is taken during an abduction is not important, for "we are spirit." Native people, he adds, live in a world of "spirit and meaning," while whites live in a world of "science and facts" (personal communication to author, May 6, 1998).

Among native peoples, at least those who have maintained a connection with the traditional ways, direct communication with the Creator may be part of everyday life, and UFOs, or something like them, seem to play a part in this contact. Wallace Black Elk, an esteemed Lakota elder and shaman, has said, "We don't need a piece of paper" to contact the spirits. ". . . We send a voice to the Creator—'Yo-ho'—and somebody responds and comes in." Someone might say, "'Yo-ho, I'm lost. I need help.' Then a spirit comes and takes me some place. They'll fly you there. They'll take you any place. If you want to visit the moon, they'll take you up there. They'll put you in one of those little flying saucers, and they'll zoom you up there in no time. Then, they'll bring you back" (Black Elk and Lyon 1991, p. 32).

It is hard to know how the scientifically raised mind could regard this passage. I have since spoken with Black Elk, and he appears to mean it quite literally (among other meanings), in spite of the fact that what he describes is absurd from a materialist point of view. I am sometimes told that my interviewees tend to tell me this sort of thing because they know I am with them to talk of UFOs, abductions, and such matters. So this passage from the story of Black Elk's life is interesting, as it records words told—rather casually, it would appear—in the 1980s to anthropologist William Lyon several years before I was studying these things. Lyon seems to have had no particular interest in UFOs.

If one is to communicate effectively about something so controversial and complex as the alien abduction phenomenon, then it is important to be as clear and specific as possible about one's own worldview and how it may have changed. Failing to do so can result in leaving the reader at the post, philosophically speaking, wondering just how the author is regarding the reality of what is being described. For example, a reader who is generally open-minded but whose worldview cannot accept literally the possibility of alien abductions in a purely material sense might say something like "Well, something is going on here. The question is what?" A less ontologically—"ontology" refers in philosophy to the nature of being, reality or existence—open-minded person might reject the whole matter out of hand. I cannot, of course, ask anyone to share the philosophical perspective at which I have arrived, but I believe the chance of having my observations and arguments taken seriously is greater if this point of view is made clear.

In the world in which I was raised and schooled, the idea of life, beings, energy—really anything at all—emanating from an unseen reality and manifesting materially was just not possible. Yet something precisely like this seems to be what is occurring in the case of the alien abduction phenomenon. I have been repeatedly reminded of the story Patrick Harpur tells of the British scientist Sir William Crookes, who was sent by his colleagues to debunk the nineteenth-century star spiritualist D. D. Home. When instead he was himself "converted" and reported this to his colleagues, they were outraged and told him that what Home was doing was impossible. Crookes said, "I never said it was possible. I said it was true" (Harpur 1994, p. 64). What I have been finding has been, according to my own background, not "possible." Yet from the standpoint of my clinical experience and judgment, it does indeed appear in some way to be true. In that sense the phenomenon might be described as an anomaly—that is, an occurrence that is—as the bizarre reports of rocks we now call meteorites falling from the sky seemed in the eighteenth century (Westrum 1978)— not possible according to the science of the times but may nevertheless turn out to be real in some way that we do not yet understand.[2]

What Kind of Phenomenon Is This, and What Can It Tell Us?

It will be apparent by now that my purpose in this book is not to establish that alien abductions are real purely in a literal, physical sense, although there may be physical manifestations. Whether or not alien beings and the phenomena associated with them exist in a form that can be observed, measured, and replicated may have great interest for science and our view of the world. But marshaling the sorts of evidence that might conceivably satisfy the requirements of the physical sciences on their "own turf" has proved to be a formidable and elusive task. I will document experiencers' reports with physical evidence where applicable, but my principal interest is in the experiences themselves, their pattern, meaning, and potential implications for our understanding of reality and our knowledge of ourselves in the universe.

I have come to regard the alien abduction phenomenon as one among a number of occurrences currently confronting human consciousness, like near-death and out-of-body experiences (Ring 1984; Ring and Valarino 1998; Monroe 1971 and 1996; Buhlman 1996), strange animal mutilations, the complex crop formations that appear mysteriously in a few seconds in fields of rape and other grains, apparitions of the Virgin Mary, and spontaneous shamanic experiences, which might be described as crossover phenomena (events of various sorts that appear to manifest *in* the material world but seem not to be *of* it). These phenomena seem to violate that barrier, so sacred to the rationalist mind, between the forces of the unseen world and the material realm, giving us "glimpses," in researcher Linda Howe's words, "of other realities" (Howe 1993 and 1998).

In a certain sense, any cosmic mystery might at least theoretically be thought of as simply a reflection of laws of the universe or subtler energies that we do not yet comprehend or know how to measure, rather than as "paranormal" or "supernatural." But the alien abduction phenomenon and the other anomalies named above seem to operate so far outside of the laws of physics (as traditionally understood) that they may require a new paradigm of reality to include them as real and an expansion of our ways of knowing to explore them (see chapter 2).

It seems to me possible that the matters under consideration here will not yield their secrets to the methodologies of science that were evolved to explore phenomena that were accepted as existing entirely within the material world. This is not to say that careful methods of observation and analysis should not be applied to the physical aspects of the alien abduction phenomenon. Yet the investigations of UFO photographs, radar records, missing persons and pregnancies following abductions, reported observations of strange beings, burned earth patches where UFOs presumably landed, bodily lesions and so-called implants removed from experiencers' bodies after abductions, and all the other physical signs associated with the phenomenon, have been relentlessly accompanied by such discrepancies and difficulties in finding certainty or proof that even the most committed explorers have frequently turned against each other with revelations or accusations of insufficient or bogus credentials and cries of hoax, while the doubtful have tended to dismiss the whole matter as hallucination or the paranoid delusion of true believers.

It is as if the agent or intelligence at work here were parodying, mocking, tricking, and deceiving the investigators, providing just enough physical evidence to win over those who are prepared to believe in the phenomenon but not enough to convince the skeptic. In this apparently frustrating situation, there may lie a deeper truth and possibility. It is as if the phenomenon were inviting us to change our ways, to expand our consciousness and ways of learning, to use, in addition to our conventional ways of knowing and observing, methodologies more appropriate to its own complex, subtle, and perhaps ultimately unknowable nature.

Wallace Black Elk, who, like many native American elders, has had experiences with "disks," "these little people," and telepathic communication with them, mocks the literalness and limited knowing power of scientific materialism. "The scientists call that a UFO," he told Lyon, "but that's a joke, see? Because they are not trained; they lost contact with the wisdom, knowledge, power, and gift. So they have to see everything first with their naked eye. They have to catch one first. They have to shoot it down and see what all it is made of, how it was shaped and formed. But their intention is wrong, so *somebody* is misleading those scientists that way. . . . But the biggest joke is on those scientists, because they lost contact with those star-nation people" (Black Elk and Lyon 1991, p. 91, emphasis mine).

We are just beginning to learn how to understand and explore phenomena that might be called intrusions from the unseen or "subtle" realms (Mack 1996). What appears to yield the best results, as measured by a steady emergence of information or knowledge, falling short of conventional demands for proof, is a combination of meticulous empirical observation together with carefully recorded narratives of firsthand experiences, matching, sorting, and comparing accounts from many individuals from different locations and cultures. An attitude of not knowing, a kind of Buddhist-like "empty mind," is essential, a willingness to hear and record observations and reports that "do not fit" established schemes or frameworks.

In the case of the alien abduction phenomenon—and perhaps this is true of all "daimonic realities"—the source is unseen. The encounters penetrate into the material world, but these manifestations are elusive, sporadic, and difficult to document convincingly. The greatest source of information is the reports of the experiencers themselves. Here the investigator, if not a mental health professional by training, must become in some sense a clinician, opening himself or herself to information that may threaten intensely any established worldview. Much can be learned just from listening to consciously recollected experience. The use of a nonordinary state of consciousness, however—a relaxation exercise or modified hypnosis—can penetrate more deeply into the mystery of the experiences and help therapeutically to release the powerful emotions held within that seem almost always to be left in the wake of the experiences. The method of investigation process used will be discussed in more detail in the next chapter.

The Primacy of Experience

In doing this work, I am reminded of the dilemma facing the astronomer Ellie Arroway in the film *Contact* upon her return from her "flight" into space. Strapped into her shaking interstellar pod, she has presumably been launched into the heavens, hurtling toward the star Vega. In what seems like hours to her, Ellie passes through vortices of spectacular power and beauty, opening into cosmic vistas of such transcendent glory that she is overwhelmed with awe and reverence, feeling as if she were in the presence of the magnificence of God. She lands on a luminescent seashore, where the fabric of divine nature seems virtually palpable. In this spirit-realm-made-real, Ellie meets her long-dead father. Then she abruptly finds herself back at the launch site, where she is told that the system malfunctioned, that she and her space pod did not go anywhere, and that only a few minutes of time on Earth have passed. Scientists try to tell her that her belief in her experiences represents delusion or hallucination, as she has no artifacts from space or other evidence to back up her story. But everything about her as a sane and, heretofore at least, rational person tells her that what occurred was altogether real.

Her little spaceship's videotape shows that, in "its" time perspective, eighteen hours have passed, tending to corroborate Ellie's story, while opening a new mystery of differential time perception. But that is not the most important point. *She* has had an experience that is unequivocally real and of transcendent power and meaning to her, challenging, if not shattering, her secular worldview.

Ellie's dilemma is similar to the one that I and the abduction experiencers with whom I work must face. It is the experiences themselves, and our—the experiencers' and my—estimate of their reality that is our principal source of data in determining the truth of what has taken place. It is, for example, the conviction of the children about their experiences that gives the 1994 incident at the Ariel School in Zimbabwe (see page 42) such credibility. "It's definitely reality," twelve-year-old Emily said, "and anybody can think that it's not true or that we're making things up. But we know what we've seen, and we believe it." I asked eleven-year-old Nathaniel what he would say to someone who suggested the children imagined or dreamed the incident. "I would say that most of the other kids in my class saw it as well," he replied a little indignantly.

Physical evidence, if it is present, may seem to confirm the material or objective fact of the experience. But the most powerful evidence is subjective, or intersubjective (see page 25), insofar as the experience is told to an interviewer who must be willing to enter to a degree into the narrative to learn of it. We must make what is, in effect, a clinical as well as an ontological judgment. We need a certain courage, a willingness to say that from what we know of this person, at this time and in this context what they are telling or reliving appears to be real (or not, as the case may be), however much it may violate our beliefs about what is possible. The validity of our findings is reinforced when other observers discover the same or similar things.

Beyond Ethnocentrism

As Whitley Strieber expresses in the epigraph to this chapter, part of the power of the abduction experiences to bring about personal change derives from the essentially unanswerable nature of the questions the encounters pose. The matter of whether we are "alone" in the universe or are accompanied by other beings, even in this world, carries a lot of weight for those of us who have been raised in the scientifically oriented Western culture. Possible evidence of bacteria from Mars or of the former existence of water on that planet's surface is communicated excitedly in the national media.

For the native peoples I have interviewed, including many who are close-encounter experiencers themselves, the universe is filled with life, or entities of various sorts, and some of them have the capacity to show up on the material plane. But for abductees with a Western scientific background, it is often the mind-shattering terror of these encounters that forces them to acknowledge the reality of the beings. As one young woman wrote, after she was forced by the terror of her abduction experiences to realize their actuality, she became aware that "such a profound and beautiful existence is this world we live in, and how much more wondrous to truly know that not only are we not alone, we're *really* not alone" (letter from Karin to author, August 14, 1996).*

Basic Elements of the Abduction Phenomenon

Overview

Having set forth the framework in which I approach the abduction phenomenon, I wish now to set down what seem to me to be its fundamental elements. The orientation and ideology of the investigator, and the questions he or she asks or does not ask, will determine to some degree what data can be enabled or allowed to come forth and will affect profoundly the interpretation of the experiences. Furthermore, abductees select consciously and unconsciously to whom they turn to tell their stories. And to make matters still more complex, the phenomenon itself seems to change

---

* There is a section at the end of chapter 2 that provides brief biographies of the experiencer participants.

and evolve according to the stage or level of consciousness of the experiencer and the facilitator with whom he or she is working. But allowing for these variabilities, it does nevertheless seem possible to distinguish certain essential elements. For me, a more or less consistent picture is emerging, which I will summarize here and elaborate further in later chapters. The emphasis will be more upon the informational and transformative aspects than in my 1994 book *Abduction*. Whether this is because the phenomenon itself has changed or my orientation toward it has evolved—or both—is not altogether clear to me.

Medical- and Surgical-like Aspects and the Hybrid "Project"

First are the now-familiar elements of the abduction experience itself. A person of virtually any age (though the concentration appears to be in young adulthood) is in bed at home, in a car, or out of doors, when his or her consciousness is disturbed by a bright light, a humming sound, strange bodily vibrations or paralysis, the close-up sighting of an odd craft, or the appearance of one or more humanoid or even human-appearing strange beings in their environment. Experiencing varying degrees of anxiety, depending on the status of their relationship to the phenomenon, the experiencers describe being taken, usually against their will, to be floated through walls, doors, or windows into a curved enclosure that appears to contain computerlike and other technical equipment. There may be several rooms in the craft, or whatever it is, and more strange beings are seen busily moving around doing tasks the experiencers do not really understand.

In one or another room, the experiencers undergo a variety of medical- or surgical-like examinations and procedures, which are more or less traumatic, depending on what is done, the experiencer's current relationship to what they have been undergoing, and other incompletely understood factors. A central feature of the experience appears to be a complex sexual/reproductive "project" that, after a sequence of experiences, may result in the apparent creation of hybrid beings, toward whom the experiencers, especially young women, feel a poignantly troubled relationship. On the one hand, they feel that the creatures, which look like a cross between the aliens and humans, need their love and nurturance and that they themselves are part of some life-creating evolutionary venture. On the other hand, they realize that they have no control over when, if ever, they can see the hybrid "baby" or "child" again, and they may resent being used as "breeders."

To the abductees themselves, as well as to some investigators, these hybrids exist quite materially and literally. The experiences may be altogether real from the standpoint of consciousness, but the hybrid offspring might not exist in material reality as we know it, especially as no clear physical evidence for their literal existence in this dimension has been found (see chapter 6). Although the beings may communicate to the experiencers that the hybrid creatures are to be the future inheritors of the Earth after we have completed our destruction of its capacity to support advanced life-forms, this also does not mean that they exist in a literal, physical sense, however certain the experiencers may be that they do.

But the hybrid "project" is by no means all that happens in the craft. According to the experiencers' reports, they may be gazed at closely by the compelling large eyes of the beings and otherwise examined, probed, and monitored. Sometimes the experiencers feel that their health is being followed, especially through ano-rectal and colonic examinations ("checkups"), and they even report healings of a vast array of minor and sometimes major conditions (Dennett 1996). They may gain a sense that they have been selected and are being protected for some sort of important cosmic enterprise or mission, though this is not talked of in an egoistic way. On other occasions the experiencers report probes being inserted into their brains through the nose, ears, and eyes, and they may feel that their psyche has been transformed, primarily in the sense that they have become more humanly tolerant and intuitively connected with others and the Earth itself.

Clearly these experiences have a physical as well as a psychological dimension. The probes abductees experience appear to be correlated with nosebleeds, and the examinations with skin lesions (sometimes, as in the case of multiple abductions, in symmetrical patterns on more than one experiencer at the same time). The abductee may be witnessed to be actually missing for varying periods of time, although this is not common. Independent corroboration, in my experience, especially on the part of someone not directly involved in the encounter, is quite rare. The experiencers sometimes report that during the abduction implants are inserted under the skin or into one or another orifice, and they may feel certain that these represent some sort of tracking or monitoring devices. Several of these have been recovered surgically and analyzed. But the evidence regarding the composition of the implants—whether or not they have bizarre physical or chemical characteristics suggesting nonearthly origins—has been inconsistent (David Pritchard 1994, pp. 279–95; Strieber 1998; Leir 1998).

The fact that the abduction experiences are accompanied by physical manifestations should not necessarily lead to the conclusion that the phenomenon itself exists entirely in the material world. In fact, as previously noted, this penetration into the material world may be thought of as a kind of small iceberg-tip of a phenomenon of great depth, breadth, and meaning that extends far beyond the literal, physical realm. That this might indeed be the case is evidenced by the fact that the abductees themselves may report great variation in the degree to which they are literally physically "taken." It may range from the apparent physical removal of their bodies into space, through out-of-body-like experiences where the physical body is witnessed to be still in place, to encounters where there is little or nothing more than the appearance of strange lights or a vague sense that "they" are present in the abductee's environment.

Information: Protecting the Earth

The second important dimension of the abduction phenomenon is the transmission of information from the beings to the experiencers (see chapter 5). The communication occurs through telepathic transmission, by images shown on televisionlike monitors, by contact with the large compelling eyes of the beings, and through the beings "taking" the experiencers to earthly environments that demonstrate one or another aspect of the Earth's beauty and threatened ecology. Scenes of apocalyptic destruction may be juxtaposed with images of beauty so exquisite that it seems at times as if a cosmic teacher were trying to reach the experiencers in the depths of their soul.

The information conveyed can cover a wide range, including skills of all sorts; spiritual truths; and knowledge of healing, art, science, technology, and ecology. Above all the information concerns the status of the Earth and our relationship to it. The experiencers may be unclear as to just what they are to do with this knowledge but feel that it is of profound, even sacred, meaning and importance, that they are privileged to be receiving it, and that they must act in some way to bring about change. Taken together, this communication, which may have a powerful impact on the experiencers, constitutes a confrontation with their own sense of themselves, raising questions of individual and collective identity.

Some abduction researchers argue that this information is given by the beings to test the experiencers' reactions. Indeed, the beings may be seen to be gazing intently to observe the response to what the experiencers have been shown. Furthermore, the argument goes, if the aliens are so concerned with the environment, why don't they help us fix things.[3] The impact, however, upon the consciousness and lives of the experiencers is sometimes so profound and transformative that something more purposeful and vital than testing or deception seems to be at work. Many experiencers develop a deep, heartbreaking relationship to the Earth's plight and subsequently strive intensely to fulfill a sense of mission, although having at times to fight a sense of despair.

Credo Mutwa, a leading African *sanusi* or high medicine man, who told me of his own abduction experiences (see chapter 10), said urgently, "I am shown that the world is dying. . . . These creatures are trying to warn us about danger. . . . The thing that you are looking into is real. It is not a figment of anybody's imagination. . . ." It would appear that no direct intervention or "problem solving" is offered by the beings or whatever intelligence lies behind this phenomenon; it seems to operate through changing the consciousness of the experiencers and others who may open themselves to its meaning.

Transformation and Spirituality

The third dimension of the abduction phenomenon might variously be defined as "consciousness expanding," "growth engendering," or "spiritual." One of the most intense debates in this field occurs around the question of whether these changes in the psyche of the experiencers—no researchers seem to deny that such change, even transformation, does in fact occur in some cases—is an intrinsic aspect of the phenomenon, even its "purpose" or "intention," or is instead a kind of by-product, reflecting human creativity, resilience, and adaptability in the face of traumatic challenge, or is even the result of alien trickery or deception.

There is a good deal of confusion in the abduction research field surrounding the word *spiritual*. How, some argue, can a phenomenon that is so clearly traumatic for many people, one that seems to disregard human wishes, feelings, and morality, be spiritual in the sense of coming from a higher source? Some experiencers are even left with external and possibly internal organ scarring, as well as lasting conscious and unconscious fears and phobias. Should not spiritual experiences be benign, largely uplifting, or directly enlightening? Yet we know that some experiences, such as life-threatening illnesses, tragic losses, and other personal crises, are often catalysts for profound personal growth and transformation.

Furthermore, many spiritual disciplines, such as Zen Buddhism and shamanic initiations, include harsh practices that confront the student with disturbing aspects of internal and external reality. Some abduction experiencers describe openings and connections to what they variously describe as the other world, Divine Light, Home, Source, or God, that leave little doubt in the minds of the people who talk with them that something important has occurred. Whitley Strieber had been on a path of transformation through the Gurdjieff Foundation before he became aware of his encounters with the "visitors," as he calls them. When he told his Gurdjieff teacher about his experiences with the beings, which had initially been intensely terrifying, the teacher said, "Fifteen seconds with those people; fifteen years of meditation. You're very lucky" (Strieber 1987 and 1996b).

The apparent expansion of psychic or intuitive abilities, a heightened reverence for nature with the feeling of having a life-preserving mission, the collapse of space/time perception, a sense of entering other dimensions of reality or universes, the conviction of possessing a dual human/alien identity, a feeling of connection with all of creation, and related transpersonal experiences—all are such frequent features of the abduction phenomenon that I have come to feel that they are, at least potentially, basic elements of the process. Indeed, the experiences of abductees may bring them to something very much akin to shamanic or mystical states of mind (see chapter 7), although for the most part the experiencers remain deeply rooted in everyday "three-dimensional" life, a dilemma that sometimes causes them a good deal of pain.

Even when abductees initially experience the beings themselves, especially the now well-known small gray figures with huge black eyes, as instigators of great fear and trauma, over time they may come to see them as odd spirit guides, closer to the ultimate creative principle or Source than humans, even as emissaries from the Divine. Abductees also commonly experience a poignant sense that they have themselves become too separated from Home, Source, or God and will cry and rage against the fact that they have been incarnated or reincarnated back on Earth. As one man said, crying, "I just want to go Home. They will get me there. It's a gate, and I will go through it." Reluctantly, experiencers will accept that they have made some sort of agreement with the beings or the Creator itself to fulfill a human mission.

Relationships

The fourth basic dimension of the abduction phenomenon concerns the evolution of the human/alien relationship(s) (see chapter 13). The experience of connection between one or more of the alien beings and the abductees with whom they relate is such a powerful and consistent aspect of the phenomenon that I have come to perceive it as one of its basic elements. The relationships vary, of course, according to the sort of alien (and probably human) being involved. The gray reptilian beings seem to be more trauma-inducing, at least initially, than the light or human-appearing beings. Nevertheless, some generalization seems possible.

It seems as if transdimensional or interspecies relationship is itself a fundamental part of this whole process. Sometimes the beings may be perceived by small children or recalled by adults as friendly childhood playmates or even protectors, but such memories may come later, after the recall of other sorts of experiences. Even recalled, pleasant childhood experiences tend to shift in later childhood or adolescence into more businesslike encounters with an apparently serious reproductive, educational, or other agenda.

Commonly the initial memories of abduction experiences are of cold, indifferent contacts in which the aliens (especially the gray reptilian or praying mantis–like beings) render the person altogether helpless and then proceed with their agendas without apparent regard for the feelings of the experiencer. But over time the relationship seems to evolve into something quite different, especially if the experiencer can be helped to face and go through the terror that so often accompanies these seemingly bizarre encounters. A deep familiarity and sense of meaningful connection develops between the experiencer and one or more of the beings, which can reach heights of love so profound as to be felt to be incompatible with earthly love. This connection is experienced especially through contact with the eyes of the beings. The abductee may feel enveloped, engulfed, or swallowed up in the fathomless depths of these black voids. Jealousies and other disturbances in marriages and in various earthly relationships occur and are most commonly resolved by the tolerance of erotic and other intense emotional connection, as long as it is occurring in another realm or domain.

Some abductees report that the beings come from a civilization destroyed by greed, war, or other technology-wrought devastation and have come here like colonists to replenish their biological stock. Whether or not this is literally true, the beings do seem to be involved in some sort of breeding program that they have initiated for the purpose of creating a hybrid race, whose physical actuality again must be questioned, however powerful or vivid the experiences themselves may be (see chapter 6).

Experiencers report that the beings appear to be greatly interested in our physicality and emotionality, seeming, as is said of angels, to envy our embodiment. They seem to be enthralled with sexuality, maternal love, and other expressions of sensuality or dense physicality, as if this were a new or lost possibility for them. They encourage human mothers to nurture the hybrid beings, seeming to realize in a puzzled way that they need something that only human love can provide. The beings' knowledge of the requirements of human parenting appears to be rudimentary. They may stage acts of sexual intercourse between humans so they can watch this primal, earthy expression of love and pleasure. When they do participate directly in sexual acts with humans, the experience seems curiously odd or new to the alien creatures, and they may act awkwardly or like students needing to learn. At the same time, for the human beings involved, the experience can range from cold and bodiless to ecstatic, beyond what is known to them in earthly love (see chapter 13).

In the chapters that follow, I have drawn upon extensive case material to discover and illustrate these patterns within the broad framework set forth above. Each chapter documents a part of a whole, whose shape and form seems in some respects to be increasingly discernible. Yet in the end there remain uncharted terrains and, as it were, anomalies within the anomalous that do not "fit" the emerging patterns. Our ontological and linguistic categories seem at times to fall so short as to leave us gasping for new words. The boundaries of fantasy, metaphor, and actuality seem at times to blur, making us eager for newer descriptive words for the subtleties of consciousness, reality, and experience. I may have some claim, if not to objectivity, at least to a relative lack of preconception. For nothing in the first sixty years of my life quite prepared me for where this exploratory journey would lead.

Organization

The book is organized into an introductory chapter followed by four parts and some concluding thoughts. In this introductory chapter, I have written about where my thinking and approach have come to in the years since the publication of *Abduction* in 1994 and have provided an overview of what appear to me to be the basic elements of the abduction phenomenon.

The chapters in part I are concerned with how we might look at a phenomenon that seems to violate what, in a world so influenced by scientific materialism, we have come to think of as real. Chapter 2, "How Do We Study Something Like This?" takes up the question of what ways of knowing might be most useful for a phenomenon that seems to exist both in the material and in the invisible worlds. I write here also about how Roberta Colasanti, the psychiatric social worker who is with me during most of the sessions, and I have been working with abduction experiencers and the particular challenges that this work provides for us as clinicians. Chapter 3, "Is It 'Real' and If So, How?" looks at the problem of reality itself, and the way in which this phenomenon is or is not real depending on our perspective or worldview. Chapter 4, "Light, Energy, and Vibration," examines the extraordinary, intense energetic elements that accompany the phenomenon and what they may tell us about its reality and implications.

Part II looks at the implications of the abduction phenomenon for the fate of the Earth and our life on this planet. Chapter 5, "Protecting the Earth," examines the information that abductees have been receiving in their experiences, especially powerful communications about the condition of this planet and our responsibility for it. In chapter 6, "The Hybrid 'Project,'" I look at this central aspect of the abduction phenomenon and its relationship to the current ecological crisis that humankind and other species are now facing.

In part III, I consider the deep symbolic structures of thought and meaning that appear to be a regular and important aspect of the abduction phenomenon for experiencers and how the experiences are reported by three native healers. These elements are familiar to us from the study of shamanism, and indeed abductees seem often to be drawn to the worlds of indigenous peoples. Chapter 7, "Shamans, Symbols, and Archetypes," reviews the symbolic and archetypal dimensions of the phenomenon and draws on my work with indigenous healers and medicine men. Chapters

8, 9, and 10 tell about three native shamans who have had alien encounters: a Brazilian, Bernardo Peixoto; a Native American, Sequoyah Trueblood; and a South African, Credo Mutwa.

Part IV is about the further meaning and power of the encounters for the experiencers and their implications for human consciousness. The traumatic dimensions are considered in relation to the spiritual elements, and I also look at the role that the relationships of experiencers with the beings themselves plays in this evolutionary process. In chapter 11, "Trauma and Transformation," I discuss the traumatic aspect of the phenomenon and how it affects the consciousness and emotional development of individual abductees. Chapter 12, "Returning to Source," looks specifically at the powerful spiritual yearnings that seem often to accompany the experiences and the conflicts that they create for the everyday lives of abductees. In chapter 13, "Relationships: Contact Through the Eyes," I take up the unexpected intensity, power and meaning that connection with the beings may have for the experiencers and the implications that it may hold for identity—theirs and ours.

Chapter 2

How Do We Study Something Like This?

I wouldn't try to publish a scientific paper about these things, because I can't do any experiments. I can't make glowing raccoons appear. I can't buy them from a scientific supply house to study. I can't cause myself to be lost again for several hours. But I don't deny what happened. It's what science calls anecdotal, because it only happened in a way that you can't reproduce. But it happened.

Nobel Prize laureate Kary Mullis,
with regard to an unusual experience that
occurred one night in 1985

"All Knowledge of Reality Starts From Experience"

In the fall of 1997, a distinguished scientific panel, chaired by Peter A. Sturrock of Stanford University, spent four days studying the UFO phenomenon and concluded that the number of intriguing and inexplicable observations is sufficient to warrant careful research. "Whenever there are unexplained observations," the panel wrote in its summary report, "there is the possibility that scientists will learn something new by studying those observations.""The history of earth science," the panel noted, "includes several examples of the final success of phenomena originally dismissed as folk tales: two centuries ago meteorites (then regarded as stones falling from the sky) were in this category" (Sturrock et al. 1998, pp. 183, 184).

The report was welcomed by the UFO community, as much as it was met with outrage by the debunkers, since now for the first time the subject of UFO studies was given some mainstream legitimacy. But for someone like myself, who examines testimonies of people who report encounters with the presumed occupants of these craft, the question remains as to what sort of study is suitable for the subject matter at hand. In this chapter I will consider the methodological questions that I have confronted in trying to explore the alien abduction phenomenon, and the way I have actually worked with my clients in trying to learn about it.

Although there has been within science some "craving for generality" (Monk 1990, p. 338), it is clear that methods of study will vary depending on what is being examined. As philosopher of science Paul Feyerabend wrote in the early 1990s, "the events, procedures and results that constitute the sciences have no common structure," and "successful research does not obey general standards." Even "'Facts' come from negotiations between different parties" (Feyerabend 1993, pp. 1, xi). Physicists and other "natural" scientists use measurement, experimentation, and quantification to establish the validity of hypotheses and ensure objectivity, but even physics "is but a scattered collection of subjects," each requiring its own methodologies (p. x). In the case of the abduction phenomenon, it is hard even to know in what territory or territories of knowledge we are working. Perhaps it is characteristic of certain anomalies that they refuse to locate themselves in any of our established disciplines, thus forcing us to use a multidisciplinary approach or requiring the creation of a new discipline altogether.

There has been a presumption in science that with sufficient scrupulosity and attention to method, true objectivity—a radical separation of subject from object—may somehow be attained. In April 1998, for example, I shared with one of the Harvard Medical School professors who had been most critical of my 1994 book a quote from Einstein that "all knowledge of reality starts from experience and ends in it." He wrote to me that I had misunderstood the quote, for he believed that "the kind of 'experience'" to which Einstein was referring to was "objective, not subjective" (letter to author, April 9, 1998).

Quite a few decades ago, philosopher Alfred North Whitehead noted that all knowledge that human beings gain grows out of a complex "interplay of subject with object," of knower and known, and that "subject and object are relative terms" (Whitehead 1933, pp. 177, 176). Increasingly, scientists and philosophers are questioning the extent to which research in any field is free of the biases introduced by ambitions, expectations, preconceptions, and worldviews (Sheldrake 1995, 1998; Wilber 1998). All research, as philosopher Henryk Skolimowski has demonstrated, is participatory and relies on "the art of communion with the object of enquiry" (Skolimowski 1994, p. 160).

Philosopher Ken Wilber, with his proclivity for useful but rather rigid categorizations, has defined three "eyes" of knowing: the eye of flesh (empiricism), the eye of mind (rationalism), and the eye of contemplation (mysticism) (Wilber 1983 and 1998). Whatever instrument of knowing we use, knowledge begins with experience. As Ludwig Wittgenstein said in one of his lectures on ethics in the early 1930s, experiences themselves "seem to those who have had them, for instance to me, to have in some sense an intrinsic, absolute value" (Wittgenstein 1965, p. 10), and "cannot be captured by factual language because their value lies beyond the world of facts" (Monk 1990, p. 277). It is not surprising that Wittgenstein broke with Bertrand Russell and the other positivistic philosophers of his day.

Wilber has noted that empirical and positivistic science has always been "spooked" by inner reality ("interiors"), perhaps by experiences themselves, because they are so difficult to pin down or objectify (Wilber 1998, p. 151). The Sturrock report calls for a concentration on cases that "include as much physical evidence as possible" (Sturrock et al. 1998, p. 184). This recommendation may apply to the study of the UFOs themselves, but the understanding of what has happened to the experiencers of UFO contact requires much more than the search for physical evidence.

In psychiatry, psychoanalysis, or any psychologically oriented endeavor, in which the principal investigative instrument is oneself and the data consist of memories of human experiences, the differentiation of subject and object is even less clear than in the physical sciences. Psychoanalytic theorists (Levine and Friedman 2000; Stolorow et al. 1994; Brenneis 1997) are increasingly using the term *intersubjective* to characterize the patient/therapist connection. Psychoanalyst Howard Levine writes of an "irreducible subjectivity" in the therapeutic encounter and challenges the classical notion that "the analyst has the potential to be an objective (non-distorting) observer of reality." In actual fact memory is continually being "constructed rather than retrieved from storage in its original, pristine form" (Levine and Friedman 2000, pp. 67, 77).*

---

* Eastern psychology uses the idea of "neutral mind," neither purely objective nor subjective. It is present, mindful, and tough-minded but not attached, including both observation and feeling in the process of knowing. Perhaps it is with our neutral minds that the work with abductees should be conducted.

The best the interviewer can achieve, Levine concludes, is "to follow along with the observation and experience of the patient's subjectivity in interaction with one's own subjectivity, trying to understand how the two interact and are related" (p. 77). This does not, of course, mean that meaningful reconstruction of the past is impossible. But it disposes of the notion that it can occur with precision and places a special responsibility upon the investigator to note points where subtle, unacknowledged pressures to bring forth particular memories, and other sources of possible conscious and unconscious distortion of the investigative process, may be present. Philosopher Michael Zimmerman suggests that in the alien abduction phenomenon, something complex is going on that requires us to move beyond the "dualistic conception of subjective psychology vs. objective matter-energy" (Zimmerman 1993, p. 24).

Having said all that, we must ask what kind of a matter *is* the so-called alien abduction phenomenon, and what is the appropriate method of studying it? To begin with (as I have discussed on pages 9–10), it seems to belong to that particular class of phenomena, not even generally accepted as existing by mainstream Western science, that seem not to be *of* this visible, known material universe and yet appear to manifest *in* it. These are phenomena like mysterious crop formations, unexplained animal mutilations, and apparitions of the Virgin Mary, that seem to "cross over," or to violate the radical separation of the spirit or unseen realms from the material world that is at the center of the scientific materialist worldview.

Physical Evidence and Its Limitations

Insofar as the abduction phenomenon does enter the physical world, it can be studied by the traditional methods of science—photographs and videos of UFOs; analysis of soil samples where craft appear to have landed (Phillips, 1975), medical examination of skin lesions, possible alien pregnancies, and various health problems that appear to be related to abduction experiences; physical/chemical analysis of subcutaneous "implants" that seem abduction related; and careful examination of witnesses who may have reported someone missing during the time an abduction was presumably taking place, or of neighbors who say they observed a UFO close to a place where an abduction was reported to have happened.

But even here it has been difficult to obtain data that would satisfy the scientific community that something extraterrestrial or otherwise strange has taken place (Sturrock et al. 1998). Good, even spectacular photos and videos exist, but somehow doubt and uncertainty seem inevitably to arise as to their authenticity, even within the UFO community itself (Walters and Walters 1990; Hyzer 1992; Hufford 1993; Diaz 1995). Skin lesions have been repeatedly documented, yet it is almost impossible to prove that they are UFO or abduction related. No alien pregnancy has ever, to my knowledge, been convincingly documented by physical examination or pregnancy testing. Implants when studied may turn out to be of conventional terrestrial or foreign-body nature (David Pritchard 1994, pp. 279–95; Leir 1998, pp. 213–29), or when they do seem to be truly strange, their "pedigree" (physicist David Pritchard's word for the capacity to establish the history of an object taken from someone's body that is clearly abduction related) cannot be established with certainty.

There are a smattering of reports of people said to be missing by relatives and friends (especially, in my experience, parents and children who cannot find each other during the night) at the time of an abduction, or even witnessing part of an actual abduction (Hopkins 1996). But just as often, it seems, a person has not gone anywhere while they were experiencing an abduction. A non-Western observer could argue here that it is not the physical but the astral, ethereal, or subtle body that has traveled, but this would hardly satisfy the desire for proof and scientific affirmation that ufologists have been seeking.

What are we to make of this consistent elusiveness of the sort of physical evidence that would satisfy scientists that people are truly being taken up into spacecraft in the sky by alien beings? Is it that the aliens themselves are so subtle, clever, and deceptive that they cover their footprints? Are people not actually being abducted? Is it "all in the mind"? Is *nothing* really happening at all? This last seems highly unlikely, given the power, frequency, and consistency of the reported experiences. Is it that the phenomenon itself is redolent of a kind of tricksterism that mocks our technology and the literalness of minds, which require material proof before they believe anything really exists (Jung 1959; Nisker 1990; Radin 1956)? There may be something to this idea. Finally, it appears that we are dealing with a class of phenomena, Patrick Harpur's "daimonic realities" (Harpur 1994), that by their very nature elude efforts to prove or pin them down.

UFOs and phenomena related to them are, for Harpur, the ultimate "daimonic realities." The physical evidence, though quite real, "is as ambiguous as the phenomena themselves, just enough to convince those people who want to believe in their literal reality—just too little to win over the unbeliever" (Harpur 1994, p. 148). In Harpur's view—and surely this has been borne out by all our efforts to date—"all attempts to imagine a cause which is not quite material but is able to act as a mechanism," all attempts, "that is, to bridge the age-old gap between spirit and matter, between the invisible and the visible," have been unsuccessful. "There is always," Harpur notes, "a point of *discontinuity* at which the spiritual ceases to be spiritual and becomes material and vice versa" (p. 154).

Does this mean that we should give up the search for more physical evidence of the material reality of abduction experiences? Although I share Harpur's doubt that we will ever fully bridge the gap between the visible and the invisible worlds, I think not, for several reasons. First, the physical evidence is strongly *corroborative* in conjunction with careful reports of abduction experiences. Second, the sheer mass of detail relating to the physical evidence, even though it does not meet scientific standards of proof, becomes part of the case for the reality of the phenomenon. Third, it is in a sense built into our natures in this culture to seek physical evidence for the things that matter to us. My only concern is that the determination to find or rely on physical proof in order to convince the skeptical elite that the abduction phenomenon is worthy of study should not distract us from appreciating and exploring in ever greater depth the meaning that these extraordinary experiences may hold.

The Messiness of Consciousness: Filling in the Tapestry

Toward the end of a conference on the abduction phenomenon at MIT in June 1992, David Pritchard, cochair of the gathering, arranged to have several of his physicist colleagues from MIT and Harvard critique our work and present the findings of the Search for Extra-terrestrial Intelligence (SETI) program, which seeks to discover life in the cosmos by listening for patterned radio waves.[1] Favoring a more holistic approach, I leaned forward in my chair and asked Philip Morrison, a distinguished MIT physicist whom I had known slightly from my anti-nuclear-weapons-activist days, why, given the uncertain nature of the problem, SETI was not using some form of altered state of consciousness as well as radio waves to discover and communicate with extraterrestrial beings. After all, consciousness may not be limited by the constraints of space/time that plague the search for extraterrestrial intelligence. Morrison replied honestly that they were having enough trouble with their instruments as it was, and consciousness was so "messy." Another eminent MIT physics professor, Victor Weisskoff, once remarked to theologian Huston Smith, "We know there's more. We just don't know how to get at it" (quoted in Smith 1992, p. 275).

It is the very messiness, I suppose, that attracts people like me, and causes scientists like Nobel Prize–winner Kary Mullis to call reports of anomalous experiences like his own encounter with "glowing raccoons" "anecdotal." Pritchard himself, at the Star Wisdom conference held by the Program for Extraordinary Experience Research (PEER) in May 1998, created a polarity—somewhat facetiously, I must admit—between "quantifiability" on the one hand and "it's like that" or "I feel good about that" on the other. Consistency in reported personal experience, he proclaimed, is hard to come by, and therefore only physical evidence "withstands scientific scrutiny" (Pritchard 1998).

When I began my psychiatric residency at the Massachusetts Mental Health Center in July 1956, Elvin Semrad, one of the great humanitarian teachers in this field, counseled the new residents, who were fresh from medical internships, that in this work we would no longer be able to rely so heavily on instruments and physical tests. Our principal tool now would be ourselves, he said, and our success would depend upon our ability to enter empathically into the patient's world, to gain trust so that matters of intense personal sensitivity and importance could be shared. Together we would explore the source of the patients' pain, and healing could come about—in part, at least—from our ability to be with the powerful emotions that they were holding inside. We would need to use not just our intellects but our hearts and souls, our whole selves, in order to enable our patients to trust us with what mattered so much to them. We did not then use words and phrases like intersubjectivity and consciousness as an instrument of knowing, but that was what it was.

Semrad's method has proved to be invaluable in working with abduction experiencers, for there seems to be no experiment we can conduct that will replicate an abduction encounter, despite various efforts to do so (Lawson 1980; Persinger 1989 and 1992). Although abductees have been studied at some length, there does not appear to be a great deal that can be physically measured. Norman Don and Gilda Moura have shown that when an abduction is being relived or remembered, a frontal-lobe hyper-arousal pattern is found by electroencephalogram (EEG) similar to that seen only in advanced spiritual meditators (Don and Moura 1997, pp. 435-53). But to my knowledge there has been no other finding that con-sistently distinguishes this group physiologically from the general popula-tion. Caroline McLeod and her colleagues at PEER compared forty abduction experiencers with forty matched controls using a great range of psychopathology and personality measures (McLeod et al. forthcoming). Their results confirmed what previous psychometric studies have shown (summarized in Mack 1995, pp. 4-5): no findings of personality disorder or other psychopathology that might explain the abduction phenomenon distinguished the experiencer from the control group.[2]

So we proceed, case by case, looking for consistencies and inconsisten-cies between our clients' reports and those of others, while being as careful as we can to notice subtle cues that we or they might be signaling that could distort the exploration. In no work that I have done has Semrad's training been so relevant. For reliving the powerful energies associated with an apparent abduction experience is a mind-shattering event both for the client and the facilitator. Although the sheer number of cases reporting similar experiences helps to fill out the tapestry, multiple witnesses to an abduction experience provide additional evidence that we are not dealing with an entirely subjective or internally generated experience (Hopkins 1996; Carpenter 1991; Randles 1988). Outside "character witnesses" who can attest to the integrity and honesty of the experiencer, especially with regard to any tendency to embellish or distort experience, also helps us to establish the authenticity of the reports.

How Do We Actually Work With Experiencers?

Since the first publication of *Abduction* in 1994, I have continued to work intensively with individuals who contact me or PEER because they suspect that they may have had an abduction encounter. This population is self-selected by virtue of the fact that by now my general orientation toward the abduction phenomenon is fairly well known. First, I do not consider that abduction reports necessarily reflect a literal, physical taking of the human body (see page 8), nor do I look upon experiencers as victims, although I strive to be empathic in relation to the pain and trauma that they may have undergone. Also, it is known that in my work I have come to regard the phenomenon not merely as a negative and cruel intrusion, which it can be, but also as one that can bring about new understanding of ourselves and our identity in the cosmos.

Psychiatric social worker Roberta Colasanti, who is present during most of the meetings with experiencers, helps to select those with whom we will meet. We can see only a small fraction of those who contact us, but we use no fixed criteria to select them. Generally, we look for people who seem quite clearly to have had anomalous experiences, as suggested by apparent contact during waking hours with an unexplained "presence" (interpreted sometimes as an angel, ghost, spirit guide, or other entity known within the belief structure of a particular culture), or with a nonhuman entity, and/or a close encounter with a UFO, strange unexplained bright lights, periods of missing time, and odd small lesions on the body that seem to have appeared in conjunction with the above indicators.

Individuals contact us primarily by letter or phone. Roberta, as the clinical director of PEER, screens individuals with the use of a structured telephone interview. The intention of this screening tool is to help rule out gross mental illness, substance abuse, and suicidality.[3] If the individuals need psychiatric help, Roberta will refer them to an appropriate therapist or clinical facility. Once the individual has been appropriately screened, he or she is asked to write a brief letter specifying the reason for contacting us and providing basic biological information. The individual is offered an initial appointment, so that we may determine the benefit from the contact and gain knowledge that will further our understanding. There are occasions when we decide, after meeting with an individual, that the person is not an experiencer or that even if he or she is experiencing anomalous events, it is not in the individual's best interest to pursue further investigations at that time. In 1996 we received funding to work with cases where there was more than one witness to a particular abduction experience, so we are currently guided by this requirement.[4]

The initial interview usually takes at least two hours, for we must establish trust, take a full personal history, examine the individual for possible psychiatric symptoms that may or may not relate to the presenting reason for coming, and of course review in detail the story of the possible abduction encounters or other anomalous experiences. Sometimes a relative or other individual is present, who may serve as a support person or corroborating witness. Because of the importance, in the multiple-witness project, of keeping reports uncontaminated, we usually interview relatives and other possible witnesses separately.

A modified hypnosis or relaxation exercise may be used to help focus the client's attention upon their inner experience and memories, but it should be emphasized that about 80 percent of the information is obtained through conscious recollection. In this slightly altered state of mind, it is easier for the individual to recall more fully their experiences, which are usually not deeply repressed, and to begin to discharge the intense energies that seem to be held as if in the very tissues of the body (see chapter 4). We are careful not to lead individuals or to encourage them to "produce" an abduction story— we use neutral, encouraging comments and questions. But we must enter deeply into the experiencer's world in order to create trust and to help them tell their story and "hold" the power of the experiences as they relive them. Sometimes the recall appears to be so emotionally intense that it seems as if each experience is being relived in the present moment.

Psychiatrist C. Brooks Brenneis has framed well the dilemma clinicians face in doing any sort of exploration that seeks to recover memories. "Leaning in the direction of doubt," he writes, "threatens betrayal," while "leaning in the direction of belief" promotes fabrication. "If one does not believe, no memory can be tolerated; and if one does believe, whatever memory appears is suspect" (Brenneis 1997, p. 59).[5] Our clients will return to us as often as seems to be needed to integrate their experiences emotionally, and also for help living in a society that does not even recognize, at least among its elite, the vast realms of being to which they have been opened. Needless to say, this integration is never altogether satisfactory.

What I have written so far might apply *fundamentally* to any sort of psychological study or exploration of emotionally powerful experiences. But working with abduction experiencers requires something different from working with any other patients, clients, or research populations. This is difficult to express clearly, but it has to do with the capacity to let go more fully of one's ego boundaries in order to follow the experiencers into whatever energy field or nonordinary state of consciousness they may take us to as they remember or relive an encounter (see also chapter 4).

At the same time, we must provide a holding container for the intense emotions and energies that come forth (experiencers may sweat, sob, shake, or scream during these sessions), while retaining an observing, mindful presence that maintains appropriate control of the process. Psychologist Shelley Tanenbaum comes close to describing this process when she writes of "an intuitive way of knowing based on the body as experienced during moment-to-moment self-observation or mindfulness" (Tanenbaum 1995, p. 3).[6]

After we had been working together for more than two years, Will (see biographical sketch on page 52) was asked to write a brief article for PEER's newsletter about his understanding of our way of learning together. He wrote of "another way" of knowing that is "not rational, not irrational" but is based on "direct perception." This is a different "frequency setting," an inner or intuitive way, "another voice" to which we often do not listen. This voice, Will writes, is itself a state of remembering that has always been within us, but to discover or rediscover it, our minds must choose "to open this window" (Maney 1998).

And there are other challenges. For what we hear may seem so bizarre or impossible from the standpoint of the worldview in which we were brought up that our minds rebel and want to intervene with the reality-testing confrontations that psychiatrists know so well. But to do this would abort communication and destroy trust. We are, of course, aided in this curious "suspension of disbelief" by the fact that we are concerned only with the authenticity and honesty of the client's report, and the presence or absence of psychopathology or another biographical experience that might account for it. There is no injunction to establish the literal or material actuality of the reported experiences.

Our conviction of the truthfulness of what is being witnessed comes from the sheer intensity of feeling and its appropriateness to what is being reported; the consistency of the narrative with work with other clients; the absence of apparent secondary gain or other motive; and finally a judgment, which may be quite subtle and not always correct, that the individual is being as truthful as he or she is able to be. Surely, as the poet Rainer Maria Rilke wrote, we must be prepared "for the most strange, the most singular and most inexplicable that we may encounter" (Rilke 1987).

Working Cross-Culturally

As we will see in part three, working with experiencers in other cultures, especially with indigenous people who have radically different notions of reality and the human place in the universe, presents particular challenges. In the first place, medicine men and women and other native people are usually meeting with me precisely because they, or someone else, believes that they have had experiences of the sort that I am investigating. In addition they are usually pleased with what I am doing, for my work is seen as affirming tribal myths, legends, and experiences. It is an example of a "white man" crediting matters that are sacred for them, that have been known in their cultures for centuries. Thus there may be built-in pressures, conscious and unconscious, upon these individuals to come up with stories that will satisfy me, to make sure that I do not go away "empty handed."

Another major problem is knowing how to interpret communications when I am unfamiliar with a particular culture's language, myths, and traditions. How, for example, am I to know what to make of a statement that a particular tribe is descended from "star people"? It does little good, I have found, to explore whether this is meant literally or metaphorically. For among the native peoples with whom I have worked, this distinction, insofar as it does exist, is not one that they seem to know how to discuss with me. How am I to sort out what may have been actual, individual experiences from the proxy participation of the person in the knowledge of tribal stories, legends, and ceremonies? Problems also come from the fact that I lack anthropological training and do not immerse myself in the culture of the people I interview, so that those I have come to know are usually people who have, to some degree, lived in the white world. They may even, like the three medicine men discussed in part III, have grown up in both native and white societies, and their communications contain elements of the two ways of life mingled together.

Despite all of these difficulties, it has, I believe, been possible for me to learn a great deal from native people, keeping in mind the uncertainties that derive from these problems. Most helpful in distinguishing actual personal experience from tribal belief and legend has been my ability to recognize elements that are identical or similar in the reports of tribal people to those of Americans and other Westerners. In addition, there seems to be a language of words and bodily expressions of intense feeling that is similar and relatively unmistakable across cultures. As Whitehead has written, "The basis of experience is emotional" (Whitehead 1933, p. 176). Intense personal fear, excitement, anger, and grief have a universal language that points to actual events in someone's life, thus suggesting, in Whitehead's term, that there has been a "Provoker." The interpretation by the experiencer of what has happened (as we shall see in chapters 8, 9, and 10) will vary greatly from culture to culture.

When Worldviews Clash

I wish to consider here the part that resistance to knowing, particularly of matters that conflict with a fully internalized worldview, can play in how we think about something like the alien abduction phenomenon. Scrupulosity of attention to method will not in itself result in getting through anything new to others if their minds are sealed off by virtue of the need, conscious or unconscious, to defend a particular view of what the universe contains and how it works.

I am particularly indebted to Tulane University philosopher Michael Zimmerman for his insightful discussion of the power and meaning of worldviews for human consciousness and security, and the ideological basis of resistance to the UFO and UFO abduction phenomena by academics and other cultural elites. In a series of papers, discussions, and letters, Zimmerman (1993, 1997, 1998, and 2002) has probed searchingly the social and psychological roots of the intense, sometimes even vicious, attacks that members of these groups have leveled at those who have chosen to study, and thus possibly legitimate, the UFO and UFO abduction phenomena. Zimmerman relates these intense reactions to the challenge that the UFO abduction phenomenon presents to our culture's dominant worldview. He uses the terms "anthropocentric rationalism" and "anthropocentric humanism" to characterize the dominant zeitgeist or worldview of our scientific culture. *Rationalism* in this context means not only the use of reason and the intellect to gain knowledge or to apply appropriate skepticism, but also the use of the mind to preempt or exclude, a priori, information that might challenge the prevailing worldview. Above all, this worldview underscores a fear of the unknown and keeps at bay for a time the knowledge of invisible realms.

According to the anthropocentric rationalistic or humanistic worldview, humankind is the most advanced intelligence we know of in the cosmos and stands at the peak of the Great Chain of Being in a universe otherwise without sentience, meaning, or intelligence. The Creator Itself has been gradually removed, leaving us alone in a universe of dead matter and energy from which the gods have fled. In this universe only man has ultimate value and purpose, and nature is but raw material or a "marketplace" that exists for the satisfaction of our species (see p. 215 for Credo Mutwa's blunt remarks about the arrogance of the dominant Western worldview). Without a higher power to affirm our value, and without an overriding sense of the sacred that might derive therefrom, our chief pleasures come from self-assertion, conquest, and the acquisition of material goods. From the anthropocentric perspective, religious belief or conviction serves a fundamental human need for security or transcendence, but it is not about anything that exists apart from our hungers or wishes.*

A worldview functions at both individual and institutional levels. It is a source of security and a compass to guide us. For an individual it holds the psyche together. To destroy someone's worldview is virtually to destroy that person. A complex network of institutions, an edifice of power and money, supports a worldview and gives it legitimacy. People who present ideas that seriously challenge a worldview are punished—by death for heresy in the past, and now by ridicule, debunking, and efforts to destroy their reputation. Catholic theologian Thomas Berry has written, "For peoples generally, their story of the universe and the human role in the universe is their primary source of intelligibility and value . . . the deepest crises experienced by any society are those moments of change when the story becomes inadequate for meeting the survival demands of the present situation" (Berry 1990, p. xi). In the Zen tradition, the collapse of a worldview is called *daishigyo*, which means "the great death." This occurs when there is a melting away of our images of self, the world, and culture—the loss of the sense of who we are in the cosmos that a worldview provides (Zen master George Bowman, personal communication to author, June 25, 1998).[7]

The UFO abduction phenomenon seems especially well suited to challenge the anthropocentric humanistic worldview. It suggests that we are but one of the higher forms of intelligence that have evolved in the cosmos, and not the brightest one at that. It reveals technologically superior beings whom we do not understand, who confront us with the fact of our lack of autonomy, power, and control, and who may even be mating with us without our permission. These beings seem even to have the gall to

---

* Anthropologist Jeremy Narby notes that the most important thing he has learned from his researches is that "we see what we believe, and not just the contrary; and to change what we see, it is sometimes necessary to change what we believe" (Narby 1998, p. 139).

confront us with the dangers of ecological devastation that are the inevitable consequence of the scientific materialistic enterprise.

It is not surprising that those who have studied UFO and abduction phenomena and given them legitimacy have been met with ridicule and attacked as irrational, or condemned for not following the scientific methodologies evolved for studying phenomena circumscribed by the Newtonian/Cartesian worldview. Perhaps this will change some now because of the Sturrock report. Zimmerman has called UFOs "ultra-terrestrial agents of cultural deconstruction" (Zimmerman 1997, p. 247). I suspect that dire warnings of societal collapse, should the alien reality ever be officially affirmed, reflect more the conscious and unconscious fear on the part of cultural elites that the perquisites that the status quo provides will be severely challenged than any actual danger of social disorder. For the general public, it seems to me, appears quite ready to accept the reality of an alien presence, if they do not already know that it has come about.

In thinking about how some academics may defend a strictly materialist worldview, consider the resistance to accepting the contemporary findings of parapsychology. Distinguished scientists like Dean Radin and Rupert Sheldrake, after extensive reviews, have shown that the standards of research in this field—the percentage, for example, of blind experiments and controlled studies—exceeds that of other branches of science (Tart 1997; Radin 1997; Sheldrake 1995 and 1998). But we should not be surprised that otherwise-renowned scientists are still making ad hominem statements to the effect that no convincing research establishes the reality of parapsychology or psi phenomena (Radin 1997, pp. 221–24). For the findings of parapsychology challenge the idea of a mechanistic universe operating by established causal principles, suggesting a world in which unseen connections work mysteriously according to principles we do not yet understand and certainly do not control.

In his later years (the 1940s), having seen the devastation wrought in two world wars by the abuse of science and technology, Ludwig Wittgenstein wanted to "change everything," philosophically speaking. But he was pessimistic, knowing that "the way we look at things is determined, not by our philosophical beliefs, but by our culture, by the way we are brought up." "What can one man do alone?" he asked another philosopher (quoted in Monk 1990, p. 533). Wittgenstein appears to have been right that "the way we look at things" is much more than a matter of philosophical belief. He, like Berry, seems to have understood how a worldview may be what holds the psyche together—at least, people feel and act that way. For we have seen in our own time the lengths to which people have been willing to go to defend a particular worldview or ideology against information that appears to threaten it.

The popular movie *The Truman Show* can be seen as a metaphor for how a worldview limits what is possible for a person to perceive or know. Locked literally inside an apparently seamless bubble, Truman's life is scripted by television corporate executives who profit from the limitation of his horizon, both in the literal and figurative senses. After many years in the bubble, Truman, with the help of someone who loves him and who breaks courageously from the commercial script, is able finally to put clues together that suggest he has been criminally reality-deprived. Then and only then can he "break out" of the bubble, both literally and metaphorically, to discover that there is a great world outside it of which he has had no inkling. Abduction experiencers might be thought of as ontological pioneers who, like Truman, are helping us to break out of the bubble of a constricting worldview.

I felt I was up against something similar to Truman's problem several years ago, when I asked a distinguished physicist colleague what might have preceded the Big Bang. He replied that in the mathematical system that underlay the physics in which he worked, the question had no meaning (see also Easterbrook 1998, pp. 24–29). Apparently not all physicists—or at least not all cosmologists—would agree with this perspective. According to another renowned physicist, Michio Kaku, the positing of parallel universes and the matter of "what happened before the big bang," far from being without meaning, are the *dominant* questions within cosmology. Our universe, Kaku suggests, is itself like a "bubble," and universes are being created all the time within a kind of "multiverse" (Kaku 1998 and 1994, pp. 191, 254). Perhaps someday, he speculates, we may have enough energy to leave the bubble of this universe and enter other universes, where the laws of physics could be quite different. Several abductees with no background in physics have, like Catherine (see biographical sketch on page 46 and Mack 1995, chap. 7), also tried to explain to me, when I have seemed incredulous about one or another aspect of her experience, that "there are slightly different physical laws there."

Once we permit ourselves to question the laws of physics that appear to us as given, science seems to cross into or merge with the territory of religion. For Kaku "what happened just before the big bang is also the moment when God said, 'Let there be light'" (Kaku 1998). Theologian Huston Smith considers the same questions but from what he calls a religious perspective. Instead of thinking of multiple universes, he proposes "ontological levels" or foci of reality. He suggests four levels: everyday world, the spirit realm, God, and the ultimate creative principle or "Godhead." We can, Smith says, for the sake of simplicity, reduce these four to two, the world and an invisible domain that "exceeds us" (Smith 1992, pp. 275–76).

Interestingly, "dark" or "invisible" matter, which seems to constitute most of our universe, becomes a possible meeting ground for physicist and theologian. According to Kaku, what can be seen through the largest telescope is but "a tiny little saucer," surrounded by dark matter that is vastly greater. Smith, noting too that perhaps ninety-nine percent of the matter in this universe does not "impact" any of our instruments, postulates an "invisible order with its own *population* and ways of behaving" that may not even "need physical underpinnings" (Smith 1992, p. 276, italics mine).

The central point for this study concerns the appropriate way to seek to know about the invisible domain in this universe and the other postulated universes that appear to be inaccessible to our instruments. Natural science seems to balk at the edge of these mysterious realms. Kaku suggests no ways of knowing about them, except perhaps to pass somehow from one universe or dimension to another via cosmic "wormholes" that might connect them, rather like Alice going through the looking glass. For a civilization that has mastered the power of the stars, Kaku suggests, "this kind of fantastic maneuvering between dimensions" may indeed seem like "child's play" (1998).

Astrophysicist Rudolf Schild has said that he has no problem with the idea of parallel universes per se, but that he is rather at a loss to know what a physicist who relies on telescopes and mathematics is supposed to do with the idea (Schild 1994). But for theologian Smith, it is precisely the "messy" meditational, mediational, and other consciousness-expanding and spiritual exercises known to indigenous cultures and to all the "wisdom traditions"—and, I would add, more recently developed forms of nonordinary consciousness, such as hypnosis-related exercises, Holotropic Breathwork,* remote viewing (Puthoff 1996, Radin 1997), and focused out-of-body techniques (Buhlman 1996)—that may at least allow

---

* Holotropic Breathwork is a method developed by Stanislav and Christina Grof to achieve a nonordinary state of consciousness (Grof 1988).

us to initiate access to these hidden realms (Smith 1992). In the case of the abduction phenomenon, which appears to be a bridge (that is, to exist in both the visible and the invisible domains), the methods of traditional science, psychology, and the spiritual traditions may all apply to one or another of its aspects.

Even Wittgenstein in his darkest time could acknowledge that frameworks do change, and "what was once dismissed as absurd may now be accepted" (quoted in Monk 1990, p. 571). But we understand very little about what combination of new information, persuasion, leadership, social crisis, and terrible failures of old ideas and ways brings this about. My own view of a secular universe, devoid of consciousness and intelligence "beyond the brain" (Grof 1985), gave way little by little over several decades and now seems quite absurd. But it happened because I had what was, for me, incontrovertible experiential evidence of a transcendent reality, and I also received a huge amount of data from clients that was contrary to my worldview and for which I have been unable to find a conventional material or psychological explanation. So convincing has this evidence seemed that I have, at times, been slow to realize that others have not traveled the same road and are not so ready to accept as true what sometimes appears clear or even obvious to me.

My colleague Paul Bernstein wrote in a note to me that "perhaps the greater weakness in the field of abduction research is not inadequacies in its methodology so much as the paucity of courage motivating a sufficient number of people to enter and explore its risky territory" (personal communication, October 1998). I do not share Bernstein's notion of courage in this regard, for I believe that a "calling," the choice of what we undertake, may seem virtually to be forced upon us. I would, however, welcome more qualified people to explore the subject of abductions and related matters, and I hope that this book will stimulate some to do so. Finally, I can only agree with Whitehead that "the doctrines which best repay critical examination are those which for the longest period have remained unquestioned." As he wrote, in what seems like a rare moment of passionate abandon, "the creativity of the world is the throbbing emotion of the past hurling itself into a new transcendent fact" (Whitehead 1933, p. 177).

All the ways of knowing considered in this chapter—direct, meditative, intuitive, contemplative, intersubjective, bodily, and nonsensory—may, in addition to empirical and experimental methods, lead us to dimensions of reality with which we may not be familiar. These are the realms of being that abductees describe in their journeys. It is to a consideration of these possible realities that we now turn. But before considering them, I provide here brief biographical sketches of the experiencers whose reports constitute the principal data of this book.

Experiencer Participants

When it came time to identify the people I have written about in this book, it was immediately apparent that I did not know what to call them. Not all are *abductees*, and I do not like that word anyway, with its implication that capture by force occurs all or most of the time. They are not *clients* in the usual professional sense, and certainly not principally *patients* whom I take care of as a doctor. *Subjects*, as in research subjects, will not do, for we work together as coinvestigators or joint explorers. Each person has had some sort of encounter or experience with strange beings, so I have settled on *experiencer participants*, knowing that it sounds a bit awkward.

Although I write about some forty of the more than 200 people I have interviewed in the past nine years, I draw particularly heavily on the experiences of a few individuals whom I have gotten to know well enough to be able to explore their stories in some depth. In most cases I have used pseudonyms indicated by an asterisk before their names; a few individuals have given me permission to use their own first names. In some cases I have changed minor details in order to protect the confidentiality of the experiencers or those close to them without, I hope, altering the important elements of the stories.

I expect that in some instances readers might wish to know more details of particular experiencers' lives. But because this is not primarily a book of case studies, such biographical information must of necessity be limited. I have tried, however, not to omit information that could shed light on the experiences themselves. Other people may, of course, disagree with the judgments I have made about what data to include.

When I quote from interviews with experiencers, usually no date is given. I do, however, provide a reference when I quote from statements they made at a conference or in a letter, in an interview with someone else, in an article or paper.

*Abby** was a thirty-year-old married hairstylist, living on the West Coast, when she called me to see if I could help her remember more about several incidents that had occurred in 1991, culminating in an encounter in Mexico where she and her husband-to-be had been camping. She recalled consciously seeing intense light fill her tent, strange large heads lean over her, and being stuck in the arm with needles. She came to Cambridge for a weekend in November 1997, accompanied by her employer, a television producer who was personally supportive and had been interested in my work. We met for about ten hours over three days, which included a two-hour relaxation session.

*Andrea** is a forty-five-year-old married mother of two daughters living in the northeastern United States. She has a degenerative eye disorder that has left her legally blind. She originally contacted PEER to seek help regarding several very disturbing images of herself and a family member being contacted by nonhuman entities. Andrea is participating in a multiple-witness research project at PEER in which several of her family members—husband, sister-in-law, and sister—have also been interviewed. As a result of remembering her experiences, Andrea has decided to return to school in order to train as an alternative medicine practitioner. She has been working successfully with clients as a diagnostic intuitive in order to help facilitate their healing.

Children at the Ariel School in Ruwa, Zimbabwe. On September 16, 1994, about sixty children at the Ariel School, a private elementary school in Ruwa, near Harare, the capital of Zimbabwe, saw several UFOs and one or more "strange beings" in the schoolyard during the morning recess. The older children (ages eleven and twelve), while supervising the younger ones (ages nine and ten), noticed that they had moved beyond the perimeter of the schoolyard. When they followed the younger children to bring them back, the older children too saw what the younger ones had seen. The children ran excitedly back to the school to tell the teachers, who were in a meeting, what had happened, but the teachers initially dismissed it as a prank or the imagination of the children, and when they finally went out to look, there was nothing to be seen. Eventually, because the children were so unswerving and consistent in their stories and in the drawings they were asked to make of what they saw, the teachers and headmaster came to the conclusion, as one teacher put it, that the children had seen something that was "not of this world."

At the recommendation of Cynthia Hind, a respected and experienced UFO investigator in Harare, Timothy Leach, the BBC bureau chief there who had been investigating the story, faxed a number of the children's drawings to my associate Dominique Callimanopulos and me and asked us to investigate the incident. Allowing for variations in the children's perceptions and artistic style, the images in the drawings were remarkably consistent. As it happened, we had already scheduled a trip to southern Africa, unrelated to this incident. We came to the school on December 2 and 3. By then some of the children had already been interviewed two or three times, giving consistent accounts each time.

Dominique and I met with twelve of the children, and I also interviewed the headmaster, Colin Mackie. In addition we met with most of the teachers in a group and attended a fourth-grade class where the incident was discussed. A number of the children had had persistent fears and troubling dreams since the episode, and we encouraged the faculty to speak openly with the students and give them the opportunity to say what they thought about what had happened. The school was of the strict British postcolonial sort, and the children conveyed a sense of disciplined conscientiousness in replying to our questions.

Each of the children with whom we met told more or less the same story, namely that at 10:15 a.m. on that Friday morning, a large spacecraft and several smaller ones, from which one or more "strange beings" had emerged, were seen hovering just above the ground or had "landed" in their schoolyard. When I played the devil's advocate with one of the children and offered the possibility that a child had made up the story and got the others to tell it to the teachers as a prank, she thought this over carefully and replied that she could see how an adult might think that, but "that's not what happened." Except for the odd, difficult-to-believe nature of the episode, there was nothing about the way the children talked about it to suggest that anything had happened other than what they said.

Portions of the interviews of seven of the children are included in this book. *Emily* was twelve, *Emma, Lisel, Nathaniel,* and *Francis* were eleven at the time of our interviews; *Kay Leigh* was ten, and *Olivia* nine. Another account of the Ariel School incident can be found in Callimanopulos (1995).

Bernardo Peixoto is a Brazilian shaman, anthropologist, and ethnobotanist. His biographical details are in chapter 8.

Carlos Diaz is a Mexican photographer who has become internationally well known, at least in UFO circles, for the impressive still photographs and videos he has taken of luminous yellow, orange, and red oval objects that have appeared in the sky near his home in Tepoztlan and in other places near Mexico City.* Carlos was thirty-seven when we first met in October 1995 in Düsseldorf, Germany, where we were both presenting at a UFO conference organized by researcher Michael Hesemann. I was impressed then by Carlos's sincerity, passion, and caring for the Earth's beauty and precious life. He told me through his wife Margarita, who has lived in the United States and speaks English fluently (Carlos himself speaks very little English), about his encounters, including experiences in which he was taken inside the object by human-appearing beings. Because of his genuineness, the spiritual power of the experiences, and the spectacular nature of his photographs, I resolved to meet further with him should the opportunity arise.

I was privileged to spend three days in February 1997 with Carlos, Margarita, and their two children, Carlitos and Alessandro (then twelve and nine), at their home. I was accompanied by Marc Barasch, who was then working on a film related to my work; abduction researcher Joe Lewels; Jim Boyer, a young journalist (who decided he did not know enough about the subject to write an article); and Michael Hesemann. Tepoztlan is a large town, spectacularly set in a valley with high cliff walls, an hour and a half drive south of Mexico City in the state of Morelos. The town is named after Tepoztco, the son of the Aztec god Quetzalcoatl, who brought knowledge to the people. There are a number of sacred sites nearby, including a pyramid built on the side of a cliff, and many tourists come to the area for its beauty and spiritual importance.

---

* Because of their extraordinary nature, Carlos's photos and videos have been subjected to numerous analyses by photo experts to rule out the possibility of fraud. To the best of my knowledge, none of these experts have found evidence to challenge their authenticity. The matter is perhaps moot inasmuch as several of the townspeople of Tepoztlan when shown Carlos's photos say that they have seen similar objects. Having spent the better part of three days with Carlos and his family, it seems virtually inconceivable to me that he would have tried to fake the photos and videos.

Carlos and his family welcomed us all warmly, and Margarita trans-lated what he and her sons had to say, except for a brief period in which Joe Lewels, who has a Mexican-American background, was able to inter-view Carlos directly. Again I was struck by Carlos's sincerity and his eager-ness to share his experiences and have his ideas, especially about the need to protect the Earth's life and beauty (see chapter 5), more widely known and appreciated. The family seemed to all of us to be a warm and loving one, although in one poignant moment in our meetings, Carlitos told his father directly through his tears that he felt his father's absorption with his experiences had taken him away from the family and he wanted to be able to be with him more.

We were impressed with how well respected Carlos is by the towns-people of Tepoztlan for his integrity and truthfulness. They accept the authenticity of his sensational photographs because so many of them told us they have seen objects like the one he has photographed. In January 1999 I learned from Margarita that the Diazes and a local partner are creating a center in Tepoztlan in order to further knowledge and understanding of "the UFO reality" (personal communication, January 9). In addition, officials of Morelos have asked Carlos to contribute an article on UFOs and related matters for a book setting forth the worthy things about the state. Throughout his adult life, Carlos has suffered from a seizure disorder, now well controlled with medication. It is interesting to speculate about what relevance this neurological condition might have to the consciousness or perceptual ability and direction that enables the experiences to occur.

*Carol is a forty-year-old married woman with two teenage children. She resides in the northeastern United States and has been working as a regis-tered nurse for the past twenty years. She reports an unexplainable event that occurred when she was a young adult driving home with a friend late one afternoon. She recalls exiting off a highway and within seconds realiz-ing that the sun had set and they were ten miles down the road, having exited off on an incorrect ramp. She felt dazed and worried about how she could be missing several hours of time. Her friend was also confused, but to her amazement they never spoke about what had occurred. To this day her friend continues to refuse any discussion of the incident.

***Catherine** was a twenty-two-year-old single music student and nightclub receptionist when we first met in 1991. Her story was told in *Abduction* (Mack 1995). Since we stopped working together in 1993, Catherine has completed a master's degree in psychology and was married in October 1998.

***Celeste** is a thirty-eight-year-old homemaker with four children who resides in British Columbia. She wrote to PEER several years ago detailing a puzzling and upsetting event that she had experienced as an undergraduate in 1980. While a student in an Italian-immersion program in Rome, she and her roommate both experienced thirty-six hours of missing time. Upon further investigation Celeste vividly recalled being taken by nonhuman entities into an enclosed and unfamiliar place in which she was the subject of intrusive medical-like procedures. Her roommate confirmed that they had both experienced thirty-six hours of missing time, yet she did not have any abduction-oriented memories associated with their missing time.

Credo Mutwa is a South African *sanusi* or high medicine man. His biographical details are in chapter 10.

Dave was forty-one, a well-established health care administrator (not to be confused with the Dave in *Abduction*) and divorced father of four children, living and working in South Bend, Indiana, when a psychologist encouraged him to call me in July 1992. Memories had been flooding back to him of encounters he had had with strange beings or "presences" as a child, especially one episode at age five or six when he saw a frightening face against a barn on the family farm in Missouri. Despite the fear associated with them, Dave felt certain that his experiences, which continued into his adult life, had brought him a great spiritual openness. This view contrasted sharply with the fundamentalist Christian attitude in which he had grown up, and which he was still encountering, that interpreted his experiences as demon possession or the work of Satan.

Dave came to Massachusetts to see me in September 1992, and we met for many hours. I saw him off and on for the next few years when he could come to Cambridge and sometimes at UFO conferences. In 1994 he courageously permitted a relaxation session to be filmed for NBC's *Dateline*, but this powerful and revealing interview was greatly cut and a banally debunking presentation was produced. I spoke with Dave several times in early 1999. More than ever he feels certain that these encounters are part of a "dimensional shift" in human consciousness, "toward the light." One of Dave's sons has said openly to him, "I've seen them, Dad," and attributes his openness of mind to this contact.

*Eva is a married mother of two children, now in their teens. Her story, based on our meetings in 1992 and 1993, is told in Abduction. Over the next few years, she would call me when she wanted to explore additional experiences or share with me what was going on in her life. Although she has continued to work in an administrative job, the focus of her life has been increasingly her search for spiritual realization. In connection with this purpose, she attended the Barbara Brennan School of Healing and in 1997 wrote a thesis, Communion, that tells of her journey of self-discovery and her exploration of the Kabbalistic healing traditions and her Jewish roots.

Gary is a close friend of Credo Mutwa's (chapter 10) who lived alone about an hour outside of Johannesburg. It was he who first took Dominique Callimanopulos, television filmmaker Nicky Carter, and me to see Credo in his village in Bophatswana in November 1994. (Gary has a background in the film industry.) He is in his midforties and describes himself as a white medicine man or shaman. He is trusted by black healers and has pioneered quite successfully to have traditional healing methods included in the national health care program, working to reconcile African and Western approaches to health and medicine. In December 1995, during my second trip to South Africa, Gary asked to do a relaxation session with me to get in touch with UFO-related encounters, of which he already had considerable awareness. The mystical state Gary entered during the regression persisted intensely for many hours afterward.

*Greg was forty-nine, a successful physician in a southern U.S. city, when he contacted me in November 1996 after reading Abduction. He was aware of lifelong encounters and wanted especially to explore with me some of his earliest experiences with alien beings. Greg came to Boston for four one-and-a-half-to-two-hour sessions in December 1996 and March 1997. In these meetings he struggled in particular with fears of threatening reptilian beings that, though real to him, seemed at the same time to represent the dark elements of his own nature. When we spoke in January 1999, Greg said that as a result of confronting the shadow side of his nature, the experiences had become richer and more varied and multidimensional. In his view the nature of alien encounters is reflective of the consciousness of the individual. Whatever remains unintegrated in a person's nature, Greg suggested, may show up in the experiences.

*Isabel was thirty-three, a recently divorced Honduran-born mother of three children, when she contacted me in November 1994. She felt a sense of urgency about the fate of the planet and about frightening experiences of her own that she could not understand. Isabel was raised by her mother and stepfather, who brought her and her siblings to the United States when she was six. She was brought up amid a confusing welter of religious sects and beliefs, which included Pentecostalism (mother) and Catholicism (maternal grandmother). Both her mother and grandmother were deeply affected by their Haitian spiritual heritage. Her biological father, whom she never knew, was of Mesquita and Mayan descent. Whatever the source of the abduction experiences, Isabel has always believed that they had something to do with religion. As a child she thought of the "little men" who came around her bed at night as demons, and it was many years before she realized that she could not explain her lifelong encounters with strange beings within the framework of the family's religious belief-system.

When I first met her, Isabel had had conscious memories of experiences in which she was paralyzed and dragged through walls by beings she came to call the "blue baldies." "I have gone with them many times," she told me in our first interview. She grew up feeling terribly lonely and that she belonged more with the beings than here on earth, a feeling that has persisted. She even recalled working with the beings to abduct people from the Earth. Over the first four years that we have known each other, I met with Isabel more than thirty times. Our meetings have, for both of us I believe, been a journey into the unknown, an exploration of the possibilities of human consciousness. About a year after I met Isabel, her oldest son, a boy then in his mid teens, was killed tragically in an automobile accident. I believe that the strength that she has derived from her deep connection with the invisible realms has helped her come to terms with this terrible loss.

*Jean, a divorced mother living in the western United States, was in her late forties when she was encouraged by a mutual friend to contact me regarding episodes with light "presences" that she had experienced for several years.

Jean is a social scientist and spiritual leader, a writer who lectures widely. She came with her friend to my home for an overnight visit in 1993, during which we talked for several hours and did a relaxation session that brought back additional memories of her encounters. The beings with whom she has had contact both on the Earth plane and in the ships have, in her case, always been beneficent. She attributes much of her creative power and insights to the encounters themselves, which, she believes, brought about a kind of neuropsychological "reprogramming."

Jim Sparks was a forty-year-old residential real estate contractor of Italian-American background when we first got together in March 1996 at a meeting arranged by a friend of his. The purpose of this and subsequent meetings was primarily for Jim to help me to learn about the abduction phenomenon from his experiences (about which he has spoken publicly) and to discuss their possible significance. For without hypnosis or any other relaxation exercises, Jim has had quite full recall of alien encounters since 1989. For him these experiences have been a major learning process, resulting in his becoming a political activist on behalf of the survival of the planet's life, including a project to obtain amnesty for government officials who have concealed information about UFO or abduction phenomena. Jim's book about his experiences, which was well under way before we first met, will be published soon.

*Joseph is a married psychotherapist in his late thirties living in New York City. He first contacted me in 1993 to explore strange episodes that had occurred several years earlier, when he was living in Europe. He had conscious memories of terrifying experiences during that period in which his room was flooded with intense light, he could not move, and he felt the presence of odd beings around him. Resentment and fear had persisted from that time, and when Joseph heard about my work, he contacted me to see if I could help him allay his fears and understand what had happened to him.

*Julie was thirty-four, a married homemaker and the mother of a seven-year-old girl and a two-year-old boy, when she called me in June 1990 to explore "strange experiences," including two UFO incidents and a period of missing time while on an automobile trip with a friend. Julie was one of my first cases, and she taught me the basic elements of the abduction phenomenon. We had many meetings in 1990 and 1991, including five regressions. As she became reconciled with the shattering fact that the experiences that she had once dismissed as ghosts were in some way real, we met less often, although she would keep me fairly well informed as to what was occurring for her and her family. Both of her children have had encounters; the two-year-old boy, when I met him, was afraid of the men from space who bit his nose, while the girl never wanted to talk about her visitations.

Julie is the kind of person that I like to have on the podium with me when I speak on this subject, for she comes across as a quite straightforward, capable housewife and mother, utterly plausible and normal. Indeed, the chief of psychology in our department concluded his battery of psychological tests with the diagnosis of a "high functioning woman within a healthy neurotic [*neurotic* is a kind of compliment in mental health circles] level of development," ending his report with the statement, "The exact nature and status of her anxiety remains a mystery even after the testing." Indeed. When I spoke with Julie in January 1999, she had "put it all behind me." Her experiences had left her more open-minded and less judgmental, she believed, but she could not really integrate her day-to-day life, with which she was now fully occupied, and the encounter history. The world of her experiences Julie now holds as a separate though "absolute" reality.

Karin was twenty-seven, single, and working as a waitress in Boston when she was referred to me by a therapist she had known in Florida. Her given first name was Deborah, which she changed to Karin in the course of her experiences. In a letter dated August 14, 1996, she provided details of many alien encounters of which she had conscious memories, including a "dream" in which she was brought in contact with a hybrid child she estimated to be about nine years old. In spite of the disturbing, sometimes terrifying aspects of her experiences, an attitude of wonder and appreciation was always evident throughout the more than thirty meetings and many informal conversations Karin had with me and other members of the PEER staff over the next two years. In these meetings we explored a great range of abduction and abduction-related experiences.

During the time that I have known her, Karin's personal growth has been remarkable. She is a teacher who brings her transformational messages to whomever is able to listen, including the clientele of several restaurants and pubs in which she has worked. She is an unusually passionate and effective public speaker, who has come to appreciate the spiritual power and implications of her experiences.

*Matthew is a fifty-year-old science writer living on the East Coast. He has a strong interest in astronomy and astrophysics and has been studying and investigating the subject of extraterrestrial life for over fifteen years. He and his wife Teri contacted PEER due to a shared anomalous experience they witnessed while vacationing on Cape Cod several years ago.

*Nona was in her late thirties in the summer of 1992, when I first was told about her case by one of her friends. I had given a lecture on the abduction phenomenon in a village in northern New England, near to the rural community where Nona lives. She is married to a home builder and is the mother of five children, four of whom appear to have had some sort of encounter. We did not actually meet to discuss her experiences in detail until February 1996, when she decided to consult me in order to find out if the strange occurrences she had undergone over the past few years "really happened." Over the next three years, we had more than twenty meetings, which included several relaxation sessions and many telephone conversations. I also met in their home with two of Nona's daughters, Nancy and Elizabeth, ages seven and nine at the time, concerning their encounters. Nona is a thin, energetic, and appealing person with piercing blue eyes.

Rusty was one of my first teachers about the abduction phenomenon. We first met in Budd Hopkins's apartment in February 1990, when he was a thirty-four-year-old musician. I was struck then by his sincerity and soundness of mind and was astounded to learn about the abduction encounters he had had throughout most of his life. Terrified initially by his experiences, as he explored them he soon came to see their potential importance for personal and cultural transformation of consciousness. Rusty has spoken openly in public about his experiences and has appeared several times on television. He is one of the most articulate educators regarding the abduction phenomenon. Over the past decade, Rusty has become an expert on the Enneagram and has authored or coauthored several books on this subject.

Sequoyah Trueblood is a Native American medicine man and teacher. His biographical details are in chapter 9.

Sharon was forty-three, a highly functioning practicing psychologist and a divorced mother of a teenage girl, when she came to see me in 1993 because of terrifying memories of abduction experiences that had emerged during Holotropic Breathwork sessions. After two meetings, including one regression, Sharon felt she could deal with her experiences through the supports available in her community. In December 1998 she gave a very effective presentation about her experiences and their meaning to a large college audience in her home city.

Sue was a forty-year-old homemaker, married to a physician, and mother of a fourteen-year-old girl and twelve-year-old boy at the time of our two-hour meeting in 1994. Although she was trained and has worked as a dental hygienist, Sue thinks of herself as a kind of jack-of-all-trades, interested in creative activities of many kinds. She first consulted another abduction investigator in 1987 because of a disturbing nighttime visitation that she could not explain. She was invited to the 1992 MIT conference on the abduction phenomenon, and in her remarks there she spoke of her growing concern for the environment and the relationship of this to her UFO abduction encounters. I asked her to meet with me in order to understand this relationship better.

Will is a forty-five-year-old divorced father of a teenage son. He makes his living as an intuitive, working with both individuals and corporations. At the age of fifteen, he lost his left arm after being electrocuted by a high-voltage tension wire he had grabbed while climbing a tree. He asserts he had an out-of-body experience in those moments and that nonhuman entities encouraged him to return to his body. He contacted PEER to address the ongoing grief reaction he experiences from being "touched" and then "abandoned" by the beings. He is also taking part in PEER's multiple-witness research project regarding an anomalous experience he shared with his ex-wife while on a sailing trip in 1980. Sometimes Will refers to himself as "Billy," the frightened totally physical part of himself that has no experience of a positive connection with the beings.

Chapter 3

Is It "Real," And If So, How?

Oh my God, this is really happening.
This isn't a dream.
This is really happening.

Sue
January 20, 1994

Experientially Real*

The abduction phenomenon virtually forces us to consider profound philosophical questions about the nature of reality and how as a society we decide what is real. For the experiencers themselves, what they have undergone is altogether real, "as real as my five kids," Nona told me. After one of her encounters, in which she experienced being taken through a closed window, Nona got up the next morning to check and see if it was broken (it was not). "It definitely happened," Isabel said of one of her experiences. But the experiencers, like most of us raised in this scientific culture, usually have a good deal of appropriate doubt and resistance to accepting their own perceptions.

It is not just the experiencers' conviction that what they have undergone is in some way real that has made me take them seriously. The richly detailed narratives they provide, the appropriate surprise, the convincing incredulity, and above all the genuine distress or other feelings they

---

* Interestingly, at the Multidisciplinary Study Group Conference on anomalous experiences several of the participants remarked that we seem not really to have a "science of experience."

report, together with the observable emotion and intense bodily reactions they exhibit when their experiences are recalled—all these elements combined can give any witness the sense that something powerful has happened to these individuals, however impossible this may seem from the standpoint of our traditional worldview.

Sue reported to me an experience she had had several years before I first saw her. She remembered "floating down my stairs from my bedroom in a blue light, a beautiful blue light. I felt I was with someone who I'd known forever. I just don't ever recall not knowing this person. I was extremely excited. I said, 'I can't believe I've been waiting so long. You finally came. I thought you weren't coming.' I don't know who this was, but I was just really happy. This person brought me to the back door. . . . The next thing I saw was him standing on the hill outside my kitchen door. I go through my kitchen and realize, 'Oh my God, this is really happening. This isn't a dream. This is really happening.'"

However powerful and vivid their encounters may be, these events are contrary to what most abductees have grown up to believe is possible. For Andrea, her experiences "totally shook my belief system," while Isabel found her abduction "disturbing" because "it shatters everything that I was raised up to believe." Some remain doubtful, even when they have satisfied themselves that they were not dreaming and have exhausted, to their own satisfaction, alternative possibilities. British-born psychologist and researcher of consciousness Angela Thompson Smith, herself an abduction experiencer, has had "wide swings" in how she views her experiences. Sometimes she is certain that she has been brought to another environment, while at other times she wonders if it is not "all imagination" (personal communication, May 11, 1998). After we had worked together for several months, I asked Carol, a nurse with a strong scholarly bent, if to her the experiences were "totally real." "Absolutely," she said, "[but] I'm certainly not gonna get on television and say it." Six months later she could still say, "I can't tell you this is what is happening. I can tell you images that I'm seeing."

The fact, as is frequently reported, that not everyone around them seems to perceive what they do understandably reinforces doubt for abductees about the reality of their experiences. Karin "knows" that she has been abducted, but she believes others are unaware of what was happening to her. Andrea vividly recalled seeing many UFOs close to her home, which is near an air force base. "I'm constantly judging what's happening," she said. "If what I saw is real, why isn't anyone else seeing these ships? . . . They have all kinds of radar." As far as we have been able to tell, no UFO sightings were reported in that vicinity during the period in question. It is also possible, of course, that Andrea was seeing airplanes, though some of her descriptions (see chapter 4) did not seem to have to do with airplanes.

Ontological Shock

I have used the term *ontological shock* to describe the experience that many abductees go through at the moment when they can no longer deny that what they have undergone is in some way real. For Sharon, as she came to feel she could no longer "disown" her experiences, it felt like "a sledgehammer's been taken against it all. It's all been shattered. It's like I've got a five-thousand-piece puzzle of the blue sky to try to put together."

Abby screamed in a relaxation session as she relived the shock of seeing the alien beings before her in ordinary consciousness. "I know what it is, and I'm not ready for that," she cried. "Ready for what?" I asked. "Seeing them clearly like that." It was a "huge" shock, she said, "because I was awake, in the here and now." I asked what was so horrible about that. "Dealing with the acceptance," she said, "acceptance of a reality that's been happening to me." The part of her mind that had questioned the reality of the memories was "destroyed."

Celeste experienced a day of missing time but dared not speak about it. Many years later she described in a letter to us the way the experience had affected her life and the isolation she had felt.

Isolation. That was the term that [in our first meeting] reassured me the most. It was akin to hitting the nail on the head. Years and years have passed since losing the day in Italy. My concept of life and reality had been challenged by the experience, and I could only expose this momentary flaw in an otherwise ordered sense of life with a few people (none were professionals in a helping capacity). You know that the minute you even broach the topic in any really sincere way, you will be met with laughter. You do not mention such unexplained experiences, and you also laugh about what is not understood. The experience remained unexplored and hidden (letter to Roberta Colasanti, October 20, 1998).

Four months later Celeste spoke of this experience as causing a "fracture" or a "cutting through" of her sense of time, space, and reality. Reflecting further on the reasons for her own incredulity she wrote, "Events like this cannot be understood within the structures that we live. There are no allowances in society to explain this" (letter to Roberta Colasanti, February 18, 1999).

Greg, a fifty-year-old physician who does not fundamentally doubt the reality of his experiences, knows the terror that can be associated with the breakdown of a worldview. "We can't just put our tradition totally aside, because we're lost. Then you feel like your whole world has gone away, plunging a person into the unknown. The unknown is terrifying to everyone," he said, "no matter how much they have explored pieces of the unknown." Regarding his own experience, he recalled, "As I go to explore deeper into it, I get terrified all over again. But I have a history of knowing that I've taken this small step, and this step, and I'm safe. I can always run back here [to "ordinary" reality] if I want to."

Even though abductees are quite capable of distinguishing their experiences from dreams, they may still call them dreams rather than face more threatening possibilities. But in distinction to a dream, the person realizes he or she was not asleep (some experiences occur in the middle of daytime activities); they feel they have remembered something that actually occurred; the narrative has a logical sequence, however strange its content; and the episode, when recalled or relived, may be accompanied by intense emotions and bodily reactions more usually associated with remembered events than with dreams. Finally, like Ellie Arroway in *Contact*, everything that makes them who they are tells them "this really happened," however contrary the experience may be to what they have heretofore considered possible.

Isabel notes, "*Dream* is like a catchall word. But I don't know what else to call it, so I call it a dream because you know something? I haven't found another word to describe what happens at night, so I call them dreams." But "I know they're not dreams," she asserts. Andrea told me, "I am in another place. I can't describe to you the clarity of what I'm seeing. It's crystal clear.

It's not like a dream." Carol, to help herself with reality testing, distinguishes three types of dreams—ordinary dreams, shamanic or spirit-guided dreams, and "type three" dreams, which are experiences the psyche recalls as events that may have really happened. These, she says, occur in some sort of full waking consciousness and may even seem "hyperreal."

For Credo Mutwa, the abduction phenomenon and the gray beings (called *mantindane* in his culture) are altogether real, and he is impatient and even scornful of those, especially in the West, who doubt it (see chapter 10). "I just get mad," he told me, "because this thing is real. I just get furious because the people from the stars are trying to give us knowledge, but we are too stupid. The thing that you are looking into is one of the oldest things that we have known. The thing that you are talking about, sir, is real. It's not a figment of anyone's imagination. . . . Why is it that people of different races, people of different cultures, see the same thing?" But for Credo, as for many of the indigenous people whom I have met, in "what" reality the phenomenon resides, from whence it comes, or in what sense it is real—questions that are so crucial to us in the West—may not be of such great importance. It is to these questions I will turn next.

Real in What Way? Other Dimensions

Michael Grosso, like Michael Zimmerman, is a philosopher who has grasped the ontological ambiguities of the UFO abduction phenomenon. The sheer number and variety of apparent UFO "visitors" leads Grosso to suggest that something "psychical, mythical, or imaginal" is going on. UFO encounters, he notes, are strange hybrids of mind and matter. They seem to come from both outside and "our inside" and therefore belong, like apparitions of the Virgin Mary, fairies, demons or "other creatures of an elemental, discarnate or excarnate nature," to a "third zone of being" that does not conform to the inside/outside duality by which we conventionally polarize reality (Grosso 2004, p. 204).

If we can allow that the abduction phenomenon is real, at least from the standpoint of the abductees' experiences, the next questions we may ask are, Real how? Real in what sense? In what reality are they occurring? There *are* well-known, frequently described, physical, material accompaniments of abduction experiences (Sturrock et al. 1998; Strieber 1998;

Friedman 1996). But these findings, though providing important corroborative evidence of abduction reports and inviting much more research, are often subtle and elusive, insufficiently robust to satisfy by themselves the requirements of empirical science.

So we are often left with the abductees' reports, narratives of abduction and abduction-related experiences. The fact that these accounts are, much of the time, *not* accompanied by corroborating physical evidence may not diminish their importance for the development of our knowledge and the understanding of the nature of reality, consciousness, and human identity. It means, however, that we need to be more critical and discerning in analyzing their content and not accept the physical reality of UFO-related experiences at face value. To study the abduction phenomenon productively, I believe, the full range of human consciousness, its complex properties and manifold dimensions, need to be considered in their own right.

Abductees usually know that, although their experiences are as real to them as the world experienced in what is called ordinary consciousness, they are occurring, as Carol put it, "in a completely different reality." Eva, in discussing one of her experiences, went so far as to say that although "I had a body, and my body was perceiving . . . that's not it; it's not absolute. It's metaphorical on some level." According to Julie, who has been examining her experiences with me since 1990, "Abduction experiences show you can separate consciousness from the body. What you see is not all there is."

Abductees speak frequently of being taken into another dimension or plane of reality with different properties. The idea of other dimensions that are not detectable by our instruments or knowledge of mathematics has also gained currency among physicists (Kaku 1994; Wolf 1989; Vallee 1988; Bryan 2000). Ron Bryan of Texas A&M University, for example, notes that some physicists have posited more than ten dimensions to explain the existence of subatomic particles, such as, for example, twelve kinds of quarks and leptons (Bryan 2000, p. 258). But according to theoretical physicist Michio Kaku, "We don't have to go to ten dimensions of hyperspace, which I think is fantastic. But we do have to go to higher dimensions. There's not enough room in the three dimensions that we're familiar with to accommodate all of the forces of nature" (Kaku 1998). Since the objective existence of these other realms is difficult to demonstrate empirically, it may seem as if we are dealing with a metaphor that is also real or has become reified—made real—through experience and language. Julie warns that "even the choice of the word *abduction*" is "an interpretation" and "leads us down a certain path." "Boy, it's mind-blowing," she adds, "to not try to construct this in some way, to not put some parameter around it."

Rusty describes his nighttime conscious reality before the beings come in as being like a theater scrim through which they burst, revealing to him another reality of great vividness. Eva, speaking of one of her experiences, said, "I just surrendered" and "woke up in another state, another dimension so to speak." Andrea says of this other reality, "It's crystal clear. I think they're parallel states, and both of them are real." Julie, trying to describe the other realms and her passage into them, says, "I expanded outward, I'm still awake. . . . I can't put it into words. There are fifty dimensions in that other place." For her, the beings and these other realms are right nearby. On that "plane reality folds in on itself," she says. For this reason, the beings "are always around and cohabit space" next to us. Isabel's description is similar. She sees the hybrid babies "in a very real place."

One of the properties of this other reality, or realities, is the different experience of time, space, and dimensionality within them. One of the first things Andrea observed when she began to examine her experiences was that "I went through a tunnel and I lost all conception of time." She stressed what a shock it was to experience that time was collapsing. She has learned to think beyond linear time to feel that the past, present, and future are one.

Eva notes that from the viewpoint of the other reality that she enters during her experiences, the material world is subsumed. "Linear time/space is contained within the greater perspective, but not vice versa," she observes. Similarly, for Karin, in the other realm—what she calls "the fourth dimension"—"everything is always present," and "three-dimensional reality is included within it." Catherine (see Mack 1995, chap. 7) spoke of a kind of "training center" to which she had been taken where it was determined what beings would come to Earth. "It was not a place like we have places here, not in our space/time." Angela Thompson Smith describes a telepathic conversation with an entity she calls the Monitor. He seemed unable to accept our concept of time. When she tried to explain various human ways of measuring time—clocks, sundials, and the like—she says he objected, "But you are just measuring the passage of the sun, not time" (Smith 1998, p. 86). As we shall see, the existence of dimensions of reality in which linear space/time boundaries seem not to apply is familiar to people living in indigenous cultures (see especially chapters 7 to 10).[1]

Altered Perception

Among the most baffling of the many mysteries of the UFO and UFO-abduction phenomena is the fact that witnesses' perceptions may be altered or affected in such a way that some may see or hear what others do not. Physicist Arthur Zajonc has connected such differences to evolving changes in the way human beings perceive: "We are now being called upon to see new things. What this requires is a transformation of self, and the creation of organs of perception which allow us to see new things" (Zajonc 1992, p. 24).

Karin speaks of an "altered state of consciousness" that accompanies her experiences, "a finer, higher vibration" that allows her to be "shown something" she would not otherwise perceive. Andrea is incredulous that the people nearby did not see the many spacecraft she distinguished clearly from the airplanes landing and taking off by the air base near her home. "They couldn't miss it," she said. "There's no way [they] would not see these ships and what's going on." Andrea's sister-in-law and close friend, Sarah, attended two of our sessions and is open to the abduction phenomenon. She knows Andrea as a reliable and credible person. Sarah suggests that "these UFOs can come from different dimensions in and out. In other words they may be perceived by Andrea, who's able to perceive that dimension." Andrea herself concludes with some frustration, "I think there is a choice. They, the ETs, someone, big boss . . . some intelligence is making a choice whether to be seen or not. . . . I think they know the repercussions of being seen fully."

Isabel has had a number of experiences in which her perception seemed odd or significantly altered. One time at the beginning of 1998, when she was riding on the commuter train with a friend who is not an experiencer, she saw another passenger, a man whom she called "a creature," who "looked just frontward like a totally normal human being." But when she looked at him "out of the corner of my eye, I got scared. I got scared shitless." For then "he looked like a bug. He didn't even have hands.

He had these things, like the closest thing to it would be a roach" or "a mantis or something weird like that."

Isabel explained what she had witnessed to her friend, but he did not observe the difference. Thinking to herself, "I'm losing it," she repeated the action, looking at the man "face-on" and then from "the corner of my eye," and each time the same difference of perception occurred. She wondered if the man himself was "somehow creating that type of illusion to the point where no one else could even feel the difference." Taken by itself, an odd incident like this might be seen as an indication of a psychiatric disturbance, but such moments occur so frequently in the lives of experiencers, without other accompanying indication of mental or emotional disturbance, that they call for a different understanding.*

Changes in the perception of time and space in association with the abduction phenomenon are sometimes accompanied by a sense of the existence of, or of moving into, other realities or dimensions. This may be difficult for experiencers to articulate clearly. Here is Karin struggling to express her ontological confusion, the altered perception of space and time during her encounters, and their interdimensional quality:

> It's racking just to go through the window because they have to alter your vibration in order to get a solid object to pass through another solid object, literally. And that happens. You go through the window, or wall—they prefer the window. So on a molecular level it's like everything goes [she makes a noise as if of intense vibration or shaking up] . . . you almost feel separated, and then you go [into] the bottom of this thing that's alive somehow, and then you're on the table, and probably the moment that you're on the table is where they've stopped vibrating you to get you through all the different levels of time and space and everything else so you physically actually manifest in this other dimension.

* Whitley Strieber has told me of similar experiences. Upon reading this passage, educator Richmond Mayo Smith wrote to me that African shaman Malidoma Somé described in a workshop he attended that there were spirits of animals from other dimensions he could identify, but others without his capability saw them as humans (personal communication, February 4, 1999).

Karin calls the other reality she perceives during her experiences the "fourth dimension." "It's what we call illusion, but it's not illusion. It's not illusion. It exists. It's there. That's where they live. . . . You don't use language when you're in this other experience. You use color, and you have vibration and everything else." Space/time in this dimension, she says, is "irrelevant."

Interdimensional Transport: "Delivery"

About six years after we first began to examine her abduction experiences, the word *deliver* came to Julie as a kind of metaphor for the way or mode by which she is brought from one place to another during her encounters. "It's as though, if you want to get from point A to point B, you can take point B and twist it and just wrap it around and make it next to point A. You don't have to 'travel,'" she said. "You just are right there. I don't think it's technology. I think it's more intent. If you're standing on a ship, and it's in the process of moving like that, it is incredible to experience that, the delivery." Mathew too has spoken of the passage to the ship as "a feeling of deliverance." Other experiencers sometimes speak of vortices that are gateways through which they seem to pass from one dimension to another.

Michio Kaku's way of thinking about connection within our universe, or passage from one universe to another via wormholes, sounds rather similar to Julie's notion of "delivery." He also uses the analogy of a curved piece of paper or a doughnut, where "you wind up back to itself again" to capture the proximity of other dimensions of reality. You could "simply go from point A to point B in the same universe," he has suggested (Kaku 1998).[2] (See also Thorne 1994.)

Ron Bryan at Texas A&M is one of the few physicists who has discussed consciousness as a vehicle of interdimensional transport. He conceives of parallel universes as tubes lying very close to each other, "say a millimeter away." Then it might be quite easy for consciousness to "drift over" through a kind of tunnel (he does not use the term *wormhole*) into "another universe in higher dimensional space-time" where it could encounter "the light" and "other consciousnesses" (Bryan 2000, pp. 271). Many abductees speak of "tunnels" or "tubes" filled with light, or containing some sort of energy, through which the beings bring them from one place or dimension to another (see chapters 4 and 7).[3]

Julie has seen houses and land recede when she is abducted, but at the same time she senses that time itself is not relevant to this transport process. Instead she is "delivered," as if instantly, from one dimension to another. Words to describe this sense come with difficulty for Julie, but in the other dimension, polarity or duality itself disappears. Weight and weightlessness, immensity and tininess, form and formlessness all appear to exist simultaneously.

Jim Sparks, like Julie, speaks of "interdimensional travel" and "the ability to go from point A to point B in no time at all" or "to occupy the same space in a different dimension." "I know this to be so," Jim says, "because I have been taken from my home via this 'field' to their ship. Also by the same method I have been transported to different points on the earth's surface" and "across one end of the galaxy to the other." "They call themselves 'star people,'" Jim says. "I know they come from other dimensions . . . this 'field' renders distance inconsequential" (Sparks 2007).

For Jim the capacity to travel between dimensions *is* related to superior technology. "One just needs the tools to tap into these realms," he writes. "With the proper technology, dimensional abilities are limitless" (Sparks 2007). But since he also has observed "thought-activated technology," the aliens' ability to "command their machines with thought," perhaps the distinction is only semantic. Jim's full appreciation of the awesome technological power of the beings grew from his realization that they could find him anywhere—"there was no place to hide." "When one begins to grasp the spellbinding tapestry of the possibilities that lie in other dimensions, it becomes quite clear why I could be found anyplace at any time. It taught me the insignificance of conventional boundaries. The barriers of space and time mean nothing. In this realm there is awesome power and limitless capabilities" (Sparks 2007).

Shifting Worldviews and Other Realms

The abduction phenomenon is not the only contemporary transpersonal experience that challenges our view of reality. Out-of-body (Buhlman 1996) and near-death experiences (NDEs) (Ring 1984), as well as Holotropic Breathwork (Grof 1988) and other practices that bring about a nonordinary state of consciousness, such as various forms of meditation, psychedelic drug experiences, mystical states, and other spiritual epiphanies, all reveal levels of reality and consciousness that are not considered part of the ontological consensus, at least among people who are most powerfully influenced by the materialist worldview.

The abduction phenomenon seems particularly well suited to impact radically the consciousness of our culture, not only because of the compelling quality of the experiences themselves but also because of its apparent ability to manifest in the material world and to appear to take on the forms of recognizable advanced technologies. There are a large number of well-described events that, despite their anomalous nature, contain images that are more or less familiar to a culture preoccupied with space travel, biomedical engineering, and advanced material, communication, and weapons technologies. These include UFOs that seem to defy the laws of gravity, intense energies and vivid lights, floating people through walls, rooms in spacecraft filled with what looks like complex medical and other high-tech equipment, and surgical-like procedures, especially of a sexual and reproductive sort, all under the agency of a variety of humanoid or humanlike beings who communicate telepathically and seem to be able to whisk us in no time from one place to another.

Although abductees are often most concerned with the impact of the experiences on their daily lives and personal well-being, some come to realize the far-reaching implications of what they have experienced, and may still be undergoing, for our view of reality and the evolution of the culture. Greg has had lifelong encounters with alien beings, especially with reptilian-appearing creatures with whom he has engaged in what to him have been struggles of life-and-death proportions. His abduction experiences have, he believes, left him with special sensitivities, which include an ability to intuit the troubled consciousness of particular patients from working with samples of their bodily lesions. Needless to say, he does not usually share these insights with his patients or other people.

One of Greg's purposes in coming to see me has been to further dislodge the grip of the materialist paradigm on *my* psyche. He believes I have looked to him for that. Otherwise I could have put his letter "in the shredder." I may have been around "all this experience of other people already," but in Greg's view, I am still "coming up against" my "own ego structures" that set rigid boundaries around what I can take in. "I wanted to really do it," he told me, "and make it really crack so you could do something with it. If you run round in this tight little circle trying to get certain kinds of proof, you might as well flush it. If you really want to step outside the boundaries, you can."

The way to do it, he says, is to allow the experience and feelings to "gestate inside of you" and let them "roll around in your psyche and in your feelings." "We can talk to brains," he says, "but what's really important is that you get an experiential sense of what I'm saying. The feeling part is so crucial to this whole event." (By *event*, I believe he means both the abduction phenomenon and the process of change.)

Greg appreciates what is at stake in the shifting worldview in which he and I are participating. "What's real," he says, "is so beyond this paradigm. We don't just go there because we're not ready to just go there. It would be a quantum jump." But change, he says, has to be brought about with caring, patience, and love. "We grow lovingly a little bit at a time. We keep expanding." Greg welcomes the future that he has already glimpsed. "It is an 'unbelievable future,'" he says, "and it's very real to me because I've tasted bits of it. It's happened. I just don't tell anybody. There's just stuff that I know is real, and it's about breaking out of this limitation. I think one way that the world is going to pull itself out of the problems is to let in the other realm." Although Greg is one of the more articulate of the experiencers who speak of the ontological shift that is accompanying the abduction phenomenon, he is not the only one who is aware of it. Nona, for example, feels that "a veil is being broken down." "We are coming closer to allowing this within our reality," she says. Her "gut feeling," her perception, is that "we're getting closer."

In summary, much of the debate about the abduction phenomenon has centered upon whether it is real in a material sense. In fact, there are well-described physical manifestations, and much of the phenomenology looks like the aerospace and biomedical technologies with which we are more or less familiar. But the ways of knowing set forth in the previous chapter enable us to learn, with the abduction experiencers, of a greater or deeper reality beyond space and time, in which the material world we know about through the senses appears to be subsumed. Those of us who work with abductees may ourselves be drawn toward an awareness of unseen realms of the infinite, in which the laws of space/time reality as we know them seem not to apply. This can create a dilemma for a mind that would stay in the duality of internal/external, for the phenomenon appears to be both, or now one then the other. Philosopher Michael Grosso calls this reality a "third zone," neither strictly inside nor outside the mind that knows it (Grosso 2004, p. 204). But it is not really a zone at all—how difficult it is not to slip into spatial metaphors—but a realm or realms that appear to be close to the ultimate creative source from which all matter/energy comes (see chapter 12).[4]

Abduction experiences themselves, whatever their source, can be distinguished clinically from dreams and other mental states by both the abductees and those who work with them. They have the properties of real events, however impossible such happenings may appear to be from a consensus reality or scientific standpoint. The other realms that abductees perceive have certain properties that differ from those we generally associate with everyday material reality. For example, distortions of time may occur, or the sense of time may be absent. Modes of transport seem not to follow known physical laws, and perceptions may be altered, even to the point where experiencers may see or hear what others do not.

In some cases the mind itself seems to be opened to such a degree that experiencers may discover they have special psychic abilities, or that their consciousness may seem to separate from the body and travel through space and time to enter or participate in the consciousness of a person from another time or culture. Finally, abductees are sometimes aware of the paradigm-shattering power of what they have experienced and may be continuing to undergo. They may be both terrified and excited by the personal and cultural implications of the ontological shifts in which they are participating.

For me no aspect of the abduction phenomenon affirms that it is, in some way, real more compellingly than the extraordinary energy that experiencers consistently report is associated with it. This energy takes the form of light perceived in relation to the UFOs themselves, or transport to them; in the bodily changes that seem to occur in passing through solid barriers; and in the vibratory sensations that abductees undergo when they recall or relive their experiences. These recollections can reach such intensity that their bodies shake uncontrollably. We turn now to a consideration of these phenomena.

Chapter 4

Light, Energy, Vibration

Imagine this blue beam coming from the depths of the universe.
It's all around us. It's always inside us. It's everything.

Karin
May 9, 1997

Overview

As I have explored the abduction phenomenon, it has become increasingly clear that virtually none of its elements can be appreciated without a consideration of the extraordinary energies involved. These include light or heat from UFOs themselves or transport to them (Vallee 1990; Hill 1995), the means by which UFOs move and the powerful vibratory sensations experienced by the abductees. Indeed, it is this very intensity which often persuades experiencers and those who work with them that something real and important is occurring and also relates to the transformation they undergo. The sense of a higher vibratory "frequency" appears to be directly related to the feeling of a shift of consciousness itself to higher levels. The reported energy phenomena associated with abductions raise many scientific and philosophical questions, which will be addressed toward the end of this chapter.

A great variety of energies or forces are associated with the UFO and abduction phenomena. They include various forms of light, heat, sound, rapid movement, and an acceleration that seems sometimes to overcome the limitations of gravity. Experiencers report various forms of interference with appliances in their vicinity (I have seen this frequently myself), whether or not an abduction experience is taking place, as if they were themselves emanating some sort of strange energy. Electric lights, radios, television sets, toasters, microwave ovens, tape recorders, telephones, answering machines, electric alarm clocks, and automobile starters have all been reported to malfunction or behave strangely. Even streetlights, individually and in rows, are reported to have gone out. I heard recently from an experiencer of an instance in which a whole neighborhood underwent a power failure in conjunction with visitations to him and another abductee. The power returned quickly to all of the houses except the one that they were in. Although these reports are anecdotal, they occur with such frequency and regularity that they should not be ignored.

As I will try to show in this chapter, abduction experiences are associated with a variety of manifestations of light and energy, often of great intensity. Sometimes light is experienced as manifesting the Divine, Source, or God, or it is perceived as that of which everything that exists is formed and from which all that is emanates (see chapter 12). Even a beginning comprehension of the abduction phenomenon must, I think, take into consideration the experiences of energy or vibration that abductees undergo. To know whether these can be interpreted within the framework of our current understanding of light and/or electromagnetic fields, or involve subtler forms of energy that we know less about, will require more study.

Those who have read my book *Abduction* will recall that some of the abductees whose cases I reported there described striking experiences with various forms of these energies (Mack 1995). Sheila spoke of a "very loud noise and flashing lights," preceding experiences that were "full of electricity," while Peter, in the throes of recalling one of his abductions, cried out, "All the cells in my body are vibrating." Edward Carlos, a sensitive visual artist, described in vivid language a great range of light phenomena in connection with his encounters. In some instances working through these experiences, being with or "holding" their power as the experiencers relive their physical, emotional, and spiritual intensity, must count among the most taxing clinical challenges that I have undergone.

I will start with a brief overview of the principal light and energy phenomena that I have noted and then will illustrate these with several case examples. These phenomena often seem interrelated; one may lead into another. I will therefore present these illustrations in sufficient detail to show the apparent interconnections.

As has frequently been observed by anyone associated with the UFO field, the reported craft themselves give off a variety of forms of white and colored light. The yellow-orange-red vessels into which Carlos Diaz experiences being taken seem to be composed of a form of light. "When you are near the ship," he says, "you can see billions of small needles" that seem to have "no real beginning or end." The experiencers, who are more likely than others to report having seen UFOs close up, are struck by the power and range of light phenomena, which may seem to be of blinding intensity.

At the beginning of an encounter, the abductee may or may not see a UFO but will report seeing light in the form of beams, balls, sparks, or simply a flood filling the space or surrounding them. The light may be described as of great intensity, or as if to turn night into day. It is usually said to be blue or bluish but may be white or even red. Before one of his encounters, Matthew saw a huge illuminated object with a strong beam of light extending out from it like an arm that seemed to end abruptly in the sky. His companion, Teri, who was in another room, also saw the light. Seeing light may be preceded or accompanied by hearing a strange hum or other sounds.

Light plays an important role in the "transport" to the craft and may be in the form of a beam, thread, tube, or tunnel, which can seem to protect the experiencer from the cold outside. Here is Andrea's vivid description of being transported to the ship:

> I feel lightness. You lose your body. I'm moving. I'm melting. There's a lot of vibration. . . . Everything's moving all around me. It's like going through a tunnel. It feels like it's going in circles, like it's rolling back, and rolling back, and going forward. I'm like expanding. . . . There's wind all around, and this tremendous energy and activity all around. . . . I know I'm safe and I know I'm protected. It's like waves of energy.... It's totally unbelievable. I'm going through a tunnel. I'm flying. It's like flying through years. It's flying through nothingness.

Inside the craft intense, cool light fills certain rooms. Sometimes a lamp-like object is seen, or the light comes from recessed places—as if "from everywhere," as one man said—but at other times the source is difficult to identify. Andrea recalls being taken to a kind of engine room, where huge spinning magnets seemed to power the spaceship. The beings and the hybrids themselves may seem to be luminous or to glow. This is said especially of the so-called light beings, but even the gray beings may seem to glow. Sometimes the abductees will experience their own bodies as if they were filled with light or simply *were* light. Even elements of the sexual/reproductive cycle that leads to the creation of the hybrids may be associated with light as an instrumental force.

Sometimes, but not always, the light seen during an abduction experience is associated with a vibratory sensation in the body. (This sensation is also often experienced without the apparent presence of light.) The vibration may be quite intense, as if to fill all the experiencers' cells, which feel as if they are separating from each other or coming apart at the "molecular" level, especially when the abductee experiences being taken through a window, wall, or other solid object. Repeated experiences of this kind may leave abductees feeling that their tissues and psyche have been permanently changed. They may feel that their vibratory level has been raised by their encounters, as if to attune them to the vibrations of the beings and the alien environment—"so you're not burned," Karin remarks. On some occasions this heightened vibration is associated with a reported capacity to communicate telepathically with the beings or to connect with a "parallel universe," an otherwise unseen world or different dimension of reality.

Thought, or the mind itself, may be experienced as an energy source with healing powers. The light may be seen as emanating from a divine or sacred Source—from the "depths of the universe"—or the sensation of bodily vibration may be linked to an "awakening" of consciousness, as if at a cellular level. The form in which the light appears may take on a metaphoric meaning. Thread, for example, may be tied to a feeling of spiritual connection, while tunnels or tubes are related to birth or rebirth experiences (see chapter 7). I have used the term *reified metaphor* to capture the idea that these words may express both a literal or instrumental meaning and a metaphoric or symbolic idea.

For some experiencers the light or vibratory energy seems to open them to knowledge of earlier times or other cultures that were more filled with light than ours, in both a literal and spiritual sense. Sometimes they will see or be shown specific objects or symbols that are associated with light, spirituality, or higher consciousness. Some of the abductees develop spiritual practices and may reencounter certain light or other energy phenomena during their meditations. When abductees get together, they often feel an energy resonance that they describe as "infectious." "We all started vibrating," Julie remarked after such a meeting of several experiencers.

Will: A City of Lights

Will told us of a dramatic encounter that had occurred in 1980, when he and his wife were sailing from Bermuda to New England. He was awakened at about three in the morning by a kind of humming sound that he had never heard before. He came up the companionway ladder, he said, and off the starboard side of the boat, he saw a "city of lights." The "thing" looked huge and was "pretty well defined." It had "multiple levels" and "lights around it," appearing as if "the lights are coming from inside, if that's possible." He noticed that the huge object was "not in" nor "on" the water. "So it's somehow above the water, and I'm saying that doesn't make sense."[1]

Then, Will said, "the light changes. There is a different pitch to it. The frequency changes. The vibration actually, I can begin to feel the vibration now, somehow in my body." He was upset as he recalled what followed. "I can feel the tracks of tears on my face. They're very, very cool. All of a sudden I'm in air. I'm not really inside a tunnel, but that would be one way of describing it. There is a differentiation between this column that's around me and surrounding space." He felt around him "a complete immersion in diffuse light, and there's a vibration that I'm aware of. . . . It's completely familiar now. I'm just in a rush to get from here to there. All of a sudden I know that I'm passing through, literally a threshold. Then I'm there. I'm inside. Someone recognizes me."

Inside the craft Will felt that *he* was somehow different, no longer "the guy that left the sailboat." Around him were tall figures, perhaps seven or eight feet in height, that appeared to be translucent. "There's a beauty that doesn't make any sense." He was crying now. "I don't know why they're beautiful, because they don't look like they're beautiful. . . . They have a bluish tint. I guess there are extremities, but I don't see well defined arms and limbs." When he looked into the beings, all he could see was light or "light structures. Luminous is a better word than translucent."

Jean: Beings of Light

Jean told us that she was taken into a spaceship "hundreds of times," to "the same ship" by "the same beings, the same room, for two and a half years, sometimes every night. . . . Sometimes it was like being beamed up. Sometimes it was like being sucked up, sort of like a vacuum cleaner, and all of a sudden just *whoosh!*" In the ship she would be on a large round table "with kind of a huge hole in the middle." There were other human beings there, and at least at first, "we were kind of in a state of shock." The beings that contacted her, she said, were, like those in Will's experience, "very refined energy presences. They were literally beings of light."

For Jean the experiences "with the extraterrestrials on the UFO" were "totally, palpably real," and as she recalled them, there was "just so much light" that she covered her eyes. The beings "were like subtle energies, but they had gross dimensions." They wore "opaque robes or something. But it wasn't fabric in the sense of fabric," and "it wasn't as though their individual presences, their distinctiveness was relevant. What was relevant was the experience of mind or mind transmission." At first she felt an animallike terror and feared that she would not come back—"like kayaking with killer whales. It's bigger than you and you're out of control"—but eventually she overcame her fears.

Jean is a productive writer and a much-valued spiritual teacher, which she attributes in large part to her encounters, although she does not speak of them publicly. She describes her mission to us in grand language, which she does not use when speaking before audiences. Jean "came to understand" that she was "one of a number of people who were being neurologically reprogrammed to be transceivers." These people were to be "instruments for an intergalactic council that was working through us with people here on Earth, with social institutions and with the environment to foment a transformation" that would be "not violent in terms of the destruction of nature."

Jean's personal transformation was also a "physical healing process," an "untying of psychological knots." During her encounters she would "experience the top of my head as molten gold. One of the really important things was to actually influence this energetic process I was in. It was like a hard-drive tune-up, and then new software put in." In the "environment on the ships," she said, "the body in its earthly form can't really function that well. It sort of has to modify."

The result of this "blowing out the nervous system," which Jean likened to "electroconvulsive therapy," was to "activate her energy." This was, she said, "the most erotic experience I've ever had." Then, having been taken through these "energy gates," she would be "freed up" to be "accessible to everything." In this open state, as a "transceiver," she was given "a complex mathematical system" and a new "cosmological system" that enabled her to "plug into Source, or God," a state of "unqualified and unmitigated love" with a "capacity to heal myself and heal other people," a "medium to, if you will, the Divine."

Andrea: "My Whole Body Filling with Light"

Light also played a central role in Andrea's experiences. When she saw light at the start of her experiences, the sensation of bodily vibration would occur immediately or soon after. Her encounters would begin with "a flash of light. I would become extremely aware of everything in the room, like hypersensitive. You can't describe the feeling. It's like when you see an animal looking at its prey, like totally, completely aware. That's what I was like. It was like I was part of the room, and then I would start to vibrate."

In an experience that had occurred about eight years before, a vivid display of white and bluish light came through Andrea's window: "I sat up in bed, and there were incredible amounts of lights in my room, darting all around." It was "wonderful" and "absolutely beautiful," she said. The only part of the room the light illuminated was the bureau below and the window itself. On other occasions Andrea has experienced balls of light in her room or steady beams. Sometimes her two daughters, ages ten and fourteen, also see the lights, and Andrea worries about their participation in the abduction phenomenon.

Andrea attributes to the light itself the energy to float her out of the house up to a spaceship. She recalled in a relaxation session an experience that had happened a week earlier. She was awakened by a humming sound that seemed to surround the house and a flash of bright blue light "like a big headlight on a car." She felt afraid but found that she could not move, and her whole body began to vibrate. She recalled seeing two small thin beings with huge heads, large eyes, and long arms and legs, one of whom was holding a stick or rod that he pressed on the back of her ear. "They're very skinny," she remembered, and "they look like they're made of light. But then underneath there's some physicalness to them like bones. They're not bones though." Then the light seemed to surround her. One of the beings made strong eye contact with her ("his eyes are on my eyes"), and this seemed somehow to get her up out of the bed.

After this Andrea recalled that she "floated" feet first "right through" the glass of the window, which was "just amazing to me." Then she floated, still feet first, high over the trees and could see the road below, which seemed to be illuminated by the same light. The floating power was "in the light," she said. It seemed to form a line or thread that extended from her navel to the beings. It also seemed as if "streamers" of light were coming out from one of the beings to her body. These threads of light seemed to be used to pull her up to the ship.

This light or energy seemed to Andrea to bring about changes in her body. "I'm not a body anymore," she recalled, as she passed through the glass. "My body is expanding completely into the glass. . . . The cells completely explode and expand, and that's how I go through the window . . . because the glass is just nothing. The glass is just like light, just like *going light through light* [sic]." "I'm light," she recalled. "My whole body—they similarly turn my body to light."

When Andrea first began to be conscious of her abductions, or abduction-related experiences, the appearance of light would be immediately accompanied by vibration in her body. It was sometimes so strong that she would wonder how her husband, who usually seemed to be sleeping soundly, could not also feel it. But over the next two years this shifted "from intense vibration to . . . mild to moderate." I asked her what the vibrating feeling was like. Andrea compared it to a child's anticipation, "like you're being given a gift, like a birthday present." Physically it felt as if "your body is finally awake. I believe we walk around in a sleeping condition a lot of us. It's like our bodies, our cells are asleep. They're not as joyful as they could be." Sometimes these feelings and sensations would return in her body during the day: "I know it's not vibrating, but it's a memory."

For several years when she meditated, Andrea experienced internally the presence of bright blue light. "This is like a spiritual experience," she said. Sometimes a "beautiful voice as clear as a bell" said to her, "'Use the light, do it now, love my children.'" Although this was "a really beautiful experience," she did not tell her husband or anyone else about it out of fear she might be thought crazy, as she had "heard a voice that wasn't mine." After a time her experience with the light "wasn't just in meditation. It was there all the time."

Toward the end of one of our sessions, Andrea's consciousness seemed to move through space and time to a period in ancient Egypt, long ago. It appeared to her as if people from that time could be present in our world now. "Oh my God, my whole body turned to light," she exclaimed, as she experienced herself back in that time. The light seemed so intense that she wondered out loud, "Can you see it?" She felt herself to be in the desert with people darker than those she usually associates with ancient Egypt.

"Right now people are living lives in Egypt that are affecting the outcome of where *we* go right now," Andrea said. This was a time when "the planet was filled with light. They came here, and they can come back and forth and help us." Ancient Egypt "is very misunderstood. . . . They [historians] focused on the wrong time. They focused on the time of darkness. It was much more light before then, a period of great expanded consciousness. There is a doorway," Andrea said, through which these people "were able to transfer energy and transfer themselves here." She, in turn, "was in Egypt too. That's why I can feel it. It looks like I'm floating back and forth." People can "live two lives," she asserted. "My eyes are opening. They want me to be a teacher here."

Karin: "A Huge Vibration in My Body"

Karin experiences a vibratory intensification as she feels herself being transported through a solid wall or ceiling into the ship.

"This is where my blackout occurs, because this starts to become more than I can handle. I can't tell you how strong it is. It's like going thirty thousand miles an hour." Another time she said, "This is a speed-of-light movement because you are light. You are moving at light speed. . . . It is a sense of phenomenally unbelievable speed, like white-hot energy. You're basically tucked in a ball. . . . My whole body is close to myself, like my knees are right here [she brings her knees to her chest], and it's orange-red-brown. It's like you could just see these sparks scream off you, you're going so fast. It's like you're burning up in the atmosphere. You think 'God there's no way I'm going to survive this.'" For Karin, these overwhelming energies seem to have a kind of "universal power," as if they emanate from God. When she first became aware of their presence, she thought of the aliens themselves as "very fragile." "But they're not," she said. "They have a very strong soul vibration."

After her experiences Karin feels a great deal of energy still held in her body. One time she recalled "a huge vibration in my body, accompanied by paralysis that I didn't understand, and that was real. I can brush away so many things in this experience, but the one thing I cannot brush away is that it feels like . . . somebody's stuck your finger in a light socket, and you just feel it, and you can't move." Part of our work has been to relieve the residual energy from these experiences through relaxation exercises. "I need to relieve the vibration's tension that's locked, physically—my body remembers it." Her body seems to shake and even vibrate when this occurs, and she may cry out loudly as the tension moves through her.

The power of Karin's experiences remains always with her. "This huge light lives inside me. It doesn't ever leave my body. It resonates in every fiber of every cell. It's always there." She connects the capacity for telepathic communication to these energies.

> Do you know what telepathy is? People say it's the ability to hear somebody's thoughts, like you can hear inside their head. But that's not what telepathy is. It's a resonation. . . . We're so telepathic on a normal everyday basis. . . . This thing [the source of her abduction experiences] sends out this blue energy, this blue emotion, this blue connection to the universe. . . . I'm connected to it. It's as strong as a tree that's been around for a million years, and yet is as malleable as a willow.... If you can imagine this blue beam coming from the depths of the universe. It's all around us. It's always inside us. It's everything.

Nona: Changing Our Vibrations

For Nona experiences of light occur in relation to her encounters, but her most powerful memories are of the energies felt in her body. She, like many of the other abductees with whom I have worked, describes these energies as like a vibration or "an electrical current running through you." They are also directly related for her to changes in consciousness and spiritual growth.

When she meditates, the feelings in her body return. "The deeper I go, the more I vibrate at a finer, just quicker" rate.

In one of our sessions in April 1996, Nona discovered powerful energies that were still held in her body from an abduction experience that had occurred in January 1993. Much of what she went through in the session is omitted, but what follows will, I hope, convey the essence of what occurred. Particular note should be taken of Nona's own appropriate doubt or incredulity. Roberta Colasanti and a friend of Nona's who had accompanied her were present.

In her journal at the time of the experience but before we had met, Nona had written, "I awoke at 1:15. There were many robed hooded beings surrounding me. A shaft of liquid crystalline light was entering through the top of my head. My body began to convulse, shaking and jerking all over. I thought I was going to die. The beings placed their hands on my body until it stopped convulsing, as though they were helping this energy to seat itself in my body. They showed me an ankh [sic] and said, 'This is the magic.' Then they left." At the end of the journal entry, which contained many more details of the encounter, Nona had written, "I woke up the next morning and my body was shaking all over like an electrical current was being run through me. Every cell was vibrating."

Being in the room with Nona as she gave bodily and vocal expression to the release of intense energies was a dramatic experience. For me to be with someone undergoing an experience like this requires a kind of spacious but concentrated "centeredness" (I do not know a better word) that I must struggle to maintain. She recalled sitting on her bed with the beings around her and a light above. "I feel a vibration at the top of my head," she exclaimed. ". . . It's like somebody stuck something up your spine. . . . I'm just feeling energy moving through my body." Moaning a little, breathing heavily, and almost crying, she said, "I feel like it's stuck. It's like every part of my body's waking up." It was difficult for her to talk, but she was able to answer in a halting way my questions about what she was experiencing. "It's in my hands . . . my face. I can feel it in my shoulders. It's all vibrating, all down my back."

In the session, she said, these sensations were not as frightening as when the experience actually occurred. "My legs are starting to vibrate. My knees . . . I can feel it going down. It's in my calves. It's moving through, moving through my entire body, and my body feels very light.

It's getting lighter. My energy in my entire body has been changed. It's like feeling cell against cell against cell against cell." (In a session three weeks later, speaking in a calmer state of reflection, she recalled, "I was just being loosened up, or just coming apart, basically.")

Nona then spoke of feeling "like there's something around me, like a capsule, an energy something, a container but I can see through it. . . . It's holding me." (Three weeks later she called this a "sarcophagus of energy wrapped around me.") "I can see the beings, but I have a sense that they're not right on me. They're not right here." I asked her to move forward a little in time. Then, moaning again, she saw "a being right at my feet." He was holding a gold ankh, an Egyptian symbol of enduring life, and "he tells me 'this is magic.'"

At times Nona would find it difficult to continue, but noting her struggle seemed to enable her to go on. She spoke of a "vibration under my back," and "a sense of being lifted" from "underneath." She was breathing heavily, moaning loudly. I encouraged her to relax further. "I can feel [the energy] at the point where it comes through my hands. . . . It's almost like a cleansing," she said. Then "I go right through the door." Sensing incredulity in her voice, I asked Nona if "your mind has a little trouble with that?" "Uh-huh," she nodded. "My cells are all separated, or I'm separated, or I'm not whole. I'm not solid." Clearly Nona's mind was having further trouble with what she was saying, so I asked her to simply be present to her experience, and we would "figure out the physics, the possibility, the impossibility," later.

"Out the second story of my house," she went on, "I'm surrounded. . . . I can still get the sense that they're around me. They're all around me. I know they're there, but *they're not in form*." I asked where she went then. "I haven't moved any further. I'm just hanging there." I asked what was holding her back from speaking further. "I just need to be a minute." A long pause. "Part of me is saying, 'No, you can't be up here hanging in the air.'" After a further long pause, she said, "It's like I'm sliding down a slide. . . . There's light all around me." She also noticed "shapes" around her, and then she said, "I'm inside the beam of light. I'm going up, and there's a hole above me, and it's dark, but there's light all around it. It's like a blue light." In the meeting three weeks later, she remembered seeing "a ship up in the sky" and "a blue beam of light come down to the ground, and then it was almost like going through a tunnel. . . . They were transporting me, their energy was."

Nona then recalled being "within something," like "being in the room of a house, but I'm in the bottom of something. . . . It's flat where I am, and there's a dome, and this light is coming from the center, the top of it." A long pause. "I get a sense I'm alone right now." What followed was a memory of a quite traumatic experience of lying on her back on a cold surface, "like metal," and feeling pressure and fear but no actual pain as "something" was forced into her ear. She recalled waking up with blood on her pillow and in her ear, and that this had happened "a couple of times before." Doctors have noticed scar tissue in this ear, which until this session had been attributed to her having been near explosives. Nona's friend remarked at the end of the session, "The energy in this room was amazing. My whole body was vibrating with it. . . . There was presence in this room that was very powerful."

Nona feels that her experiences, especially through the intense energies that have been an essential aspect of them, have profoundly changed her mentally and physically. Her "whole being," she says, is "running at a higher vibration, a higher level of frequency." After meeting with Carol, another abductee, she said, "It's overwhelming what happens when we're together. It's just this incredible energy.... I believe we have been shifted or changed in some form. Not just *some* form, a vibratory form, a vibratory way. It is like we're accelerating," she said.

The effect of the experiences depends, Nona says, on "what we bring to it" or "the way we look at things. It can be being abducted in the middle of the night and terrorized and raped. Or it can be spiritually uplifting in that you meet beings who really do care and communicate important information to you. It's like being able to see into a parallel universe." The important information has to do particularly with how "we are not at all in tune with our Earth. We're not at all in tune with other human beings. We're not at all in tune with anything. We keep ourselves as separate entities, not as one. . . . It's all connected. We are all interconnected" (see chapter 5).

Isabel: "It's All Energy"

Isabel also feels that her body has been changed or shifted as a result of the intense energies associated with her encounters. These energies, she feels, contain great powers for healing and creativity—or for destruction, if they are misused. When she first senses the "presence" of the beings in her room, "everything gets really quiet and you hear these tones in your ears. You know that they're coming, and it's almost like the air becomes charged in a way."

On some occasions Isabel will experience the energies that she associates with the beings even when they do not appear to be present. "They don't have to enter the room physically where I am," she says. One time she was home alone sitting in a chair watching television when "my whole body started vibrating. It was like everything inside of me shifted back and forth, like there was an earthquake going on in my body." It "started in my toes. It was a steady move all the way up to every point in my body, and my physical body was actually moving. So it wasn't like just the inside, because I could see my body moving in the chair." It was not as abrupt as an epileptic attack, she recalled, "but it was a shifting like that." "My body warmed up," she continued, "and then when it got to the top of my head, it felt like it was concentrated right here." She pointed to the top of her skull. "Then it started to work its way back down again, and my skin felt like an eggshell, and my whole insides turned like a liquid warm energy. . . . It felt like if I cut my skin, a liquid would have come out."

"It scared the hell out of me," Isabel said, "and I was fighting it." She had tried at the time to relax and keep her breathing steady. Then she heard a voice in her head saying, "'Don't fight it. You always fight it. When you get to a certain point, you always fight. Go with it. It won't hurt you. It has to happen.'" The voice was that of "my friend and guardian" whom she had known since she was twelve. She felt like "the guardian was standing right next to me" and "had been observing me the whole time." The voice and the guardian's "very presence" comforted her. She could not recall this being's face but thought it must be quite tall "because in some of my experiences I remember having to look up."

This experience "just left me really shocked," Isabel said. "To me it was like I had just taken a step. I'm not trying to claim that I reached any point of enlightenment or anything like that. I'm just saying it was a great experience. . . . Something actually changed the energy inside of me, like everything inside of me had suddenly switched over and changed, and my whole insides felt like they were shaking and rearranging." Before this experience occurred, Isabel had been going through a period of intense depression, related to deep mourning as the first anniversary of the death of her oldest child, a fifteen-year-old boy killed in an automobile accident, was approaching. But after the experience "the deep depression that I had felt was totally gone. I felt lighter. I felt happy. I felt positive. I didn't feel at all like I felt before it happened."

One cannot help being curious as to what relationship the timing of this depression-lifting experience had to the death of Isabel's son. Abductees often seem to report visits occurring at times of personal crisis, trauma, and loss, and the experiences may have a healing or mood-shifting power. It is not clear, however, whether the beings "come" to heal the person's trauma, whether the individual is more open to the visitation, or even, as a skeptic might logically think, whether they somehow concoct or invent the experience psychologically to ease their pain.

Isabel herself attributed the lifting of her depression both to the internal energetic shifts and to her renewed connection with the guardian figure. She likened this shift to being placed in a "barren landscape," disconnected "from everything," and "then all of a sudden your friends show up out of nowhere, friends that you always had." In this sense the guardian figures were her "real family." In this state Isabel felt that "everything connects the way it is supposed to be," and she experienced a strong sense of personal power.

Abby: The Body Remembering; Energy That Heals

In November 1991 Abby was twenty-four and camping with her husband-to-be in Mexico when, she recalls, their tent and surroundings were bathed in light, and she saw four luminous beings with large heads and thick necks and arms "float through the side of the tent." Her companion woke her to call her attention to what was occurring, but later could not remember the event. Abby came from the West Coast to see me because she wanted to "remember more." The session reported below was attended by Roberta Colasanti, Karen Wesolowski, and one of Abby's senior colleagues, a television producer she trusted who had taken a special interest in her experiences. She relaxed easily and soon was reliving the experience. "I'm not ready for this," she cried out, remembering her panic upon seeing the beings coming through the sides of the tent and being unable to move. (See page 55 for Abby's struggles with the reality of the experience.)

One of the beings, a female, calmed Abby by touching her on the forehead. Her body shook as she recalled the "energy flow." Then she remembered being lifted from the bed, floated "sideways," and taken "through the side of the tent." "Wow," she said with wonder, as she felt a tingling as if all her cells were "coming apart." "It was so quick and subtle," she said, gasping, "and then you're on the other side. Then you're whole." Laughing in amazement, she remembered the feeling of "going through the tent." Abby seemed to be reliving the intense bodily sensations of this passage, especially in her hands. "It's like the residue of this exchange is exiting through my hands. My fingers are burning right now. The tips of them are like, wild," she said, breathing heavily and deeply.

In a state of awe and fear, Abby continued to relive her experience, speaking in halting phrases and crying about the awesome sense of cellular change, especially in her hands. Her body seemed to remember "how it's done," she said, "becoming separated molecularly" and then "the coming together." "I unbecome and then I become." She relived, gasping and screaming, the energy changes in her arms, feet, legs and head, but it was in her hands that she seemed to carry most intensely the residue of the feeling of coming together. The sensation in her hands became so intense, so far "beyond burning, beyond pins and needles," that Abby felt certain that we could feel it too and asked us to hold them. (We couldn't.)

The beings seemed pleased, Abby recalled, that she had grasped "that you can go through solid things. They knew I was ready to be taught this stuff. They looked at me and said, 'See, you know.'" I asked her to be more specific about what she had learned. "The ability to change matter into nonmatter and vice versa," she said. "That's the lesson that I just lived through. They use no machines to go through matter," she continued. "We have the ability as well, or they wouldn't be able to bring us through matter."

After this, Abby recalled, she was taken in a "cold cylinder" of surrounding white light ("it's the energy that transports us") to the place "where they do their work." This was confusing to her because she thought she was "going up" but felt no "movement in the cylinder. The cylinder opened up, and we walked out," she said, and she found herself "in a big room in their ship, but it's right by the tent. . . . They don't like the word *ship*," she remarked, and she did not either, so we settled on "the place where they do their work." In the room she saw several beings who were "welcoming" her. This was different than other times she had been taken, she said, because "they're not here to do experiments on me—I hate that word and so do they—[but] to show things and explain."

With intense emotion Abby described a process similar to what she had recalled when she was taken through the sides of the tent. One of the beings, the same female who had smiled at her for "getting it" about the molecular or cellular changes that had enabled her to go through the tent, took what "was physical at this stage and made it a nonphysical stage of matter. . . . They made it into energy with their hands. . . . With their hands they can change structure." She gasped and screamed loudly again as she relived this experience. The energy was so powerful, she explained, that she was having trouble breathing.

Coming out of the relaxed state at the end of the session, Abby said, "I've never felt so powerful before, ever. I felt like I could rocket somebody across the room with the energy" by "touching you." Once she recalled that in a healing session, she did "rocket" someone "across the room. I had the same feeling in my hands then." What had been especially startling and profound for Abby was the sense that she could "change physical matter." The session had a particularly powerful impact on Abby's colleague, who said he had been "awakened by the whole experience."

Six months later Abby wrote that after our time together, she had been in a blissful state for several weeks, followed by feeling more grounded than she had before. In the sessions, she wrote, she had had a glimpse of the creative potential human beings had.

In summary it seems increasingly clear that light and other energy manifestations are fundamental aspects not only of UFO activity but also of virtually every part of the abduction experience. Even telepathic communication is felt by the experiencers to be related to subtle forms of energy. Light and certain sounds may be associated with intense subjective and observable vibratory phenomena, whose apparent energies may reach extraordinary levels of intensity. These energies often appear to have been retained somehow in the abductees' bodies since the time of the experience, and relaxation exercises can be very useful in releasing the apparent tensions. Experiencers may shake intensely and cry out with distress and relief when this occurs, which, for the facilitator, may be an experience of awesome power.

Some experiencers have the impression that the changes in their vibratory frequency or "energy fields" are an accommodation or attuning to the higher frequency of the beings themselves, the energies that surround them, and "universal energy fields." This change is also felt in some way to be related to the capacity of the beings to bring the human body through a solid object, an ability the experiencers may be told that we all potentially have. When they relive the memories of moving through solid forms, it is striking how similar are the words they use—"cells separating,""coming apart at the molecular level," and so on. They characteristically evince incredulous disbelief when they relive or recount this part of their experience. Some are left with a strong sense of the interchangeability of matter and energy. Many feel that some sort of permanent change in the vibratory frequency of their bodies occurs as a result of their experiences.

Quite frequently abduction experiencers will relate the energetic changes in their bodies to their own healing or a capacity to heal others, a subject that deserves careful research. Commonly the energy and light experiences that they have undergone become associated with personal transformation, spiritual development, and the evolution of consciousness, both personal and collective. This connection will be explored more fully in chapter 12.

What Is the Nature and Source of These Energies? Some Theoretical Considerations

Efforts to understand the light, energy, and vibratory phenomena that abductees confront take us far beyond this subject and into theoretical questions about the underlying nature of the universe. This is a territory where theoretical physics and spirituality touch each other, if they do not completely converge. In this section I will look at some of these questions, keeping in mind that it is not possible to do justice to their richness and ultimate importance in these few pages.

One of the most fundamental questions is the relationship between light as experienced during abduction encounters, near-death experiences (NDEs), and other "transpersonal journeys" and light as it is observed and studied by physicists. NDE researcher P.M.H. Atwater, for example, has written that "subjective light (present in meditation, otherworld journeys, near-death experiences and visions) behaves in a fashion similar to physical light" (Atwater 1998). But on the other hand, coming from the side of empirical science, MIT physicist David Pritchard (whose specialty *is* optical physics) wrote to me after reading an early draft of this chapter,

"The abductees' light may provide illumination for them, but it doesn't for me. It does not behave like physicists' light that I work with." Furthermore, "the vibratory phenomena have no counterparts in physical reality as I know it." "The language," he noted, "sounds like the stuff I've read on spiritual awakening." Similarly, Arthur Zajonc, another physicist who has made the study of light his specialty and has explored the complex relationship between physical light and light as known in spiritual experiences, asserts that "the light within is of a different order than the objects without" (Zajonc 1995, p. 323).

Both of these scientists, in contrast to Atwater, caution us that in our quest to find ultimate unifying connections between the outer and inner worlds, essential distinctions, an irreducible duality, may in the end remain. The light/vibrational energies related to abduction experiences, even though they may evoke the most vivid analogies and even possibly leave physical traces, may not turn out to be quite like—of the same "order" as—the light and energy manifestations that physicists study and measure.

What then *can* be said about the nature of the extraordinary energies associated with UFOs and especially with the abduction phenomenon? Clearly powerful forces are associated with UFOs themselves related to their propulsion, the light that they give off, their apparent effect on the surrounding environment, the melted hardened earth discovered where they have been seen to have landed (Phillips 1975), and the observations of intense light and the physical and emotional impact of close encounters on the experiencers themselves.

As we have seen in this chapter, abductees observe or feel intense light and vibrational energies during their experiences, which have a lasting effect. Light and energy seem to be at the core of or *are* everything, they try to explain. In a similar vein, consciousness and physics researcher Peter Russell has noted that in both quantum physics and consciousness studies, "light is *in some way* absolutely fundamental" (Russell 1998, p. 7, emphasis mine). This seems intuitively apparent, but what exactly does it mean or imply?

When those who are familiar with Eastern philosophical and spiritual studies learn about abduction encounters, they readily compare aspects of the energy-related experiences to manifestations of chi, prana, kundalini awakenings, and the yogic traditions of India and China (see, for example, Bhajan and Khalsa 1998; Brennan 1987; Bruyere 1994; Eisenberg 1985; Greenwell 1988; Mookerjee 1986; White 1990).[2] All these powerful phenomena are associated with profound spiritual transformations that may even have measurable physical effects (Brennan 1987 and 1993; Rubik 1995). But efforts to reduce them or translate them into the electromagnetic energies with which physicists are familiar have been largely unsuccessful. Former NASA physical scientist Barbara Brennan, who has devoted her life to studying these energies (sometimes referred to as the "human energy field" or the "universal energy field"), has observed that they seem to have great healing properties, and a vast array of alternative therapies based on their application have been developed in recent years.

The human energy field (HEF) and the universal energy field (UEF), experienced vibrationally or observed as auras by energy healers, have qualities that appear to be different from traditionally understood electromagnetic energy in fundamental ways. They are difficult to measure and behave paradoxically. Unlike electromagnetic energy, for example, these energies seem to build on themselves, creating more energy. Most expenditures of physical effort tire you, Dave said at the Multidisciplinary Study Group Conference, but this kind does not. "It boosts you." Also, he noted, this energy contains information and is the vehicle for telepathy. As electromagnetic energies seem to be finite, the human or universal energy fields give intimations of the infinite. They also, Brennan observes, seem to be directly associated with various forms or changes of consciousness and to "evade normal scientific explanations" (Brennan 1987, p. 40).*

For all of the above reasons, researchers who study such matters have joined with Eastern philosophers and practitioners in calling these "subtle energies." They have also in recent years begun to study the healing and other properties of subtle energies and their relation to auras, the chakra system, and the etheric, astral, radiant, and other "subtle" bodies that, in Eastern healing and spiritual traditions, seem to lie at the margin between

---

* A number of studies have sought to measure the human or universal energy fields using one or another kind of instrumentation. Some of these have had positive results (Hunt 1996, pp. 314–48; Brennan 1987, pp. 32–34; Osis and McCormick 1980). This, however, shows only that the subtle energies may, in some instances, have measurable physical manifestations. It does not tell us what they are or from what source they come.

the material and nonmaterial worlds (Collinge 1998; Cooperstein 1996; Hunt 1996; *Bridges* [magazine]; and *Subtle Energies* [journal]; and especially Woolger 1987 and 1988). Physician/scientist Larry Dossey, who has done pioneering studies of the healing power of prayer and the possibility that conscious intent may have helpful effects at a distance (see also Markides 1987, 1989, 1992), questions, however, whether *any* of the known tenets of physiology and physics, or even the concept of "energy" itself, are useful in studying such phenomena (Dossey, 1992 and 1993a).

For abductees a strong physical vibration that seems to affect and even change the cells and molecules of their bodies is a central aspect of the encounters. Anyone who has been present when these experiences are relived is likely to be impressed with the awesome power of such energies. Furthermore, as will be discussed in greater depth in chapter 12, these vibratory experiences appear to be associated with some sort of shift of consciousness, spiritual awakening, and the sense of connecting with other dimensions of reality. In relation to this aspect of the phenomenon, I have been particularly interested in the evolving cosmology that is being brought about by recent discoveries in physics and astrophysics.

The discovery of certain subatomic particles seems mathematically to require the positing of additional dimensions or universes. But of greater significance, perhaps, are the discoveries by physicists that the universe is expanding—that galaxies are flying apart at an *accelerating* rate (Riess et al. 1998)[3]—and that space itself, far from being empty and lifeless, is filled with its own powerful fluctuating energy, called the *vacuum energy field* or *zero point energy* (O'Leary 1996, Mitchell 1996). Physicist Brian O'Leary has documented the controversial results reported by pioneering inventors who have tried to tap into the energies that fill space (O'Leary 1996). Finally, Rudolf Schild suggests that black holes, located at the nuclei of galaxies, seem to function as if they were other universes or connected to other dimensions of reality, especially as we have no way to penetrate them—even laser beams directed at them seem to break up when they reach their margins (Schild 1998).

According to Schild (1998), Bryan (2000), and other scientists, as well as Apollo astronaut Edgar Mitchell (1998), the four-dimensional universe posited by Einstein is not adequate to account for any of these discoveries. Schild wonders if the UFOs and the "aliens" have somehow discovered a way to master the quantum fluctuations of the vacuum

energy field in order to transport themselves and enter the Earth's atmosphere. Perhaps, he speculates, they have found a way of "introducing a
fifth dimension," a principle that would enable them "to organize mass
and energy in our own dimensions that we just haven't encountered yet."
It would not be surprising, he suggests, that abductees would feel such
intense vibrations as they encounter these unusual energies. All of these
discoveries, together with the for him incontrovertible evidence of the
reality of psychic phenomena, has led him to wonder if there might not
be "some larger universal spirit or energies," something like "what gives the
energy its energy," as Catherine puts it, that enables people to communicate telepathically or at great distances.

I am not suggesting that the light or energy phenomena perceived
or experienced by abductees leave no physical traces or have no physical
effects. The intense light that Matthew and his companion saw, and the
nearly overwhelming experience of bodily vibration that Nona and Abby
have gone through, are vividly perceived by them or felt in the body. But
what remains unknown is the precise nature or source of that energy and
how it finds its way into our material world. As adventurous scientists have
done since Wilhelm Reich's experiments with "orgone" energy (Reich 1949,
1951), it may be possible to measure the effects of the "larger universal spirit
or energies" that Schild posited. But this may not bring us much closer to
understanding their nature or origins.

In the end I come back to the apparent fact that the energies (perhaps,
in view of the physical connotation of this word, something like "creative
power" or "source" would be better) associated with the abduction phenomenon seem to contain the possibility of personal growth or spiritual
transformation, and that these changes seem to be related to the vibrational
and emotional intensity of the experiences. But once again we come up
against "the age-old gap between spirit and matter" (Harpur 1994, p. 154)
and the discontinuity between these realms that Patrick Harpur has written
about (see page 28).

This gap may, however, be more apparent than real, growing out of our
limited ways of knowing. It may be a "gap" only if we insist on trying to
close it through physical measurement, or by seeking mechanisms familiar
to us in the physical world, to understand the ways that elements of the
unseen realm(s) can cross over into the material realm, or, in the language
of religion, spirit can become manifest. In making this linkage, we may have

to accept that at this time we can go no further than analogies, concepts, metaphors, and synchronicities, and it may be possible that only intuition, direct knowing, or consciousness itself—Wilber's eye of contemplation—can close the gap.

The experiences of light in abduction encounters may be linked to powerful feelings of love. An Australian man in his early thirties, not quoted elsewhere in this book, spoke during a relaxation session of being surrounded by light and feeling love that was "a thousand times stronger" than ordinary human love. (See also Julie's remarks on page 284.) For Matthew the core cosmic energy is virtually identical to love. "It's been my feeling since I was little," he said to Roberta Colasanti and me, "that physical love, erotic love, the energy of work, the energy of creativity, the blue sky, the spiral galaxies, the spaceships, use this energy. . . . This energy phenomenon is the love phenomenon, is the life energy, is the cosmic energy. Because we don't really feel it, we can't comprehend it."

From the time of the great scientist Michael Faraday, it has been known that some sort of waves, "the vibrations of physical lines of force," are at the core of reality (Zajonc 1995, p. 138). As Rudolf Schild (1998) remarks, "the universe gives us vibrations of all kinds," and light is one of the manifestations of vibration. But *what* exactly is vibrating? It is here, perhaps, that the physical and the nonphysical meet, where spirit and matter intertwine, and where the unknown and the unknowable (at least by the methods of empirical science) touch each other. For light quanta, photons, are without mass, and light appears to exist everywhere with no apparent physical substrate. As Arthur Zajonc has written, light seems to be omnipresent and eternal, existing outside of space and time. "The nature of light cannot be reduced to matter; it is its own thing," a "subtle, entangled" something (Zajonc 1995, pp. 260, 315).

These are the qualities that abductees speak of when they experience the intense light phenomena associated with their encounters, or feel powerful vibrations in their bodies. Words may come with difficulty, but sometimes they know themselves during their experiences to be outside or "beyond" space and time, in an awesome state of being containing both material and nonmaterial elements. The feeling of vibration in the body is intensely physical, yet its effects are as much spiritual as material.[4]

★　　★　　★

The powers associated with the abduction phenomenon may take the form of specific information, especially about the Earth itself, which, like the physical effects, can affect experiencers deeply. Similarly, the coming together of human beings and aliens to form some sort of hybrid race appears to involve strange, intense energies. These seem to derive, abductees sometimes note, from the different "vibrational frequency" of the two species. However we may understand these observations, we will consider these dimensions of the abduction phenomenon in the next two chapters.

Part Two

"*Their minds leak into your mind. Their ideals are able to become ours. ... It is they, sir, who have instilled into our minds at this time in human history a consciousness of the oneness of the whole world.*" (Credo Mutwa interviewed by Dr. John Mack, December 10, 1995). Illustration by Credo Mutwa.

Chapter 5

Protecting The Earth

When they show you these environments, you can actually see the life-force in flowers and in the leaves and the water. It's like colors you've never seen before. . . . In the rain forest you could see the life existing within a leaf, within the tops of these trees. [There] were earth spirits dancing all over the tops of those trees.

Nona

1996

Alien Contact and the Fate of the Earth

I first learned that the UFO abduction phenomenon was in some way connected with the planetary ecology crisis when Julie, one of the first experiencers I came to know, told me, in one of our early meetings in 1990, about disturbing recurring visions of the future she had had, starting about twenty years before. In these visions she was in her midforties—at least ten years older than when she spoke to me. In the visions she is living in a rural area (she was actually living in a suburb of Boston) and is in charge of a section of a food-distribution center in a kind of large greenhouse crowded with old people. There has been a nuclear war or some other planetary cataclysm, causing such disorganization and destruction of the Earth that all food must now be grown hydroponically. It is her job to dish out food to the people in her section, who are jammed in a cafeteria-style line. Julie had also had dreams—which she distinguished from the visions, as they seemed to have less vividness or "weight"—in which she was in a spaceship where she saw alien beings and hydroponic gardens in which the food to supply the people on Earth was being grown.

After this early meeting with Julie, I was astonished to discover that, in case after case, powerful messages about the human threat to the Earth's ecology were being conveyed to the experiencers in vivid, unmistakable words and images. The impact of these communications is often profound and may inspire the experiencer to work actively on behalf of the planet's life. Indeed, it seems to me quite possible that the protection of the Earth's life is at the heart of the abduction phenomenon. Astonishingly, the damage we have been inflicting upon the Earth's life-forms appears not to have gone "unnoticed" by whatever intelligence or creative principle dwells in the cosmos, and it is providing some sort of feedback to us, however strange its form appears to be. In this chapter I will examine how abductees report receiving information from the aliens, the nature of this communication, and its impact on their consciousness and activity. Not all researchers in this field stress the importance of the ecological dimension to the same extent. My conviction of the centrality of the earth-saving dimension of the UFO abduction phenomenon derives from the vividness and power of the messages that experiencers receive and convey about the jeopardy to the planet's life.

Receiving Information for Survival

In order to be able to take in or "access" the information that is being given to them, abductees feel that they must adjust their "vibratory rates." The sense that they are somehow being "reprogrammed" by their experiences so that they can take in knowledge and put it out for others—becoming, in Jean's word, "transceivers"—appears to be directly related to this informational dimension. The information that abductees describe receiving may be of many kinds, but the common element appears to be knowledge that will help in some way with human and planetary survival. They feel that they have learned things through their experiences that they would not otherwise be capable of assimilating.

Abductees report information comes to them in a number of ways, including direct telepathic communication or eye-to-eye contact with the beings themselves, lessons transmitted on televisionlike screens, in classroomlike situations on the ships, and in different sorts of "libraries" where knowledge is contained. The libraries vary from rooms with more or less ordinary-appearing books or knowledge-containing plates, to balls of light that seem to be filled with vast amounts of information. In Mexican photographer Carlos Diaz's experience, information was stored in strange spheres in caves (see page 108).

Balls of light have been important in Andrea's experiences. She was, in her words, "deeply concerned" about her fourteen-year-old daughter Lily's safety, since it appeared that she was being abducted herself and perhaps "used" as a "breeder." Nevertheless, Andrea considered the ball of light that she saw in her experiences to be "so sacred" that she could accept Lily's being in the room with it and learning how to access the information that it contained. The beings, Andrea said, were teaching Lily "how to raise her vibration to the vibration of the ball."

Sue told me that there were two incidents in which she had been shown books. In one of them, "I found myself looking at three bright little white beings with big eyes, and what looked like a black velvet hole, or opening behind them. I approached them. I put my hand out, got a little nervous, and in my concern I found myself on the other side of this black opening with books stacked, piles and piles and piles of books, like you'd find on a bookstore floor." In the other incident she was brought through a tunnel that was dark, and "the higher I went, the lighter it got, and on the way I'm looking at bookshelves after bookshelves after bookshelves of books. What I understood from that was I had to educate myself."

Credo Mutwa calls himself "just an ordinary person," but the "mantindane" have given him knowledge that is sometimes "so advanced that I can't handle it, but it all has to do with the survival of my people." As a schoolboy he had "strange companions who used to tell me things that had to do with schoolwork, and sometimes I found that I knew more than the teacher knew, and yet I had no books to read from." Later, he says, the beings taught him about geography and how to build telescopes ("I did even grind the lenses myself"), jet engines, crossbows, and "an effective gun with which to drive away attackers." Credo was also "given several designs" for constructing ships. "One of the most important designs," he said, was for a tanker that would not "urinate oil into the sea." "Get the world to make such ships, or else the seas are going to die," he says. Credo also believes his healing powers and knowledge of disease, even a procedure that he thought might cure AIDS with the use of ultrasound, and also his abilities as an artist (he is an accomplished painter and sculptor), came, at least in part, from alien beings.

Jim Sparks has written that he was trained aboard the ships in what he calls "alien boot camp" (Sparks 2007). In a classroomlike setting he has been taught many things, including how to communicate telepathically, "alien letters and numbers," the ability (at least on the ships) to move objects with his mind, complex symbols and their meaning, the development of "a sixth sense," and the capacity to think less literally. The method of teaching seems to be rather Socratic or Zen-like. "For the most part," Jim writes, "they don't like to answer direct questions. They answer in riddles." He also writes of the speed with which information is conveyed. One time an older-appearing, wrinkled being with a large head "looked into my eyes and communicated what seemed like over a hundred thoughts. . . . This was done in a split second, which included a separate emotional reaction on my part. I responded in like speed after each transferred statement. This was strange. The speed with which the information was transmitted back and forth overloaded my mind and body."

What Experiencers Are Learning About the Threat to the Earth

Credo Mutwa speaks of this planet as "our Mother Earth," a special "nurturing place" where new species are "allowed to reach maturity and perfection," a "mother world" or "womb world," "a growing place, a garden which we are messing up." "According to African culture and religion," he told us, "there are twenty-four mother worlds in the sky, and our Earth is the twenty-fifth. . . . A mother world is a specially made planet whose purpose is to give birth to life. Now these mother worlds are very, very rare. You can find thousands of worlds without life, and only one mother world." This uniquely created world, he says, is "guarded by ancient entities, such as whales and others, which we kill in our stupidity." The various groups that have an interest in the preservation of our planet, like the *mantindane*, to whom this planet is sacred, are trying now to discuss what to do with us.

The information, education, or training that abductees receive in the course of their encounters may be of many sorts. But it appears most frequently to be related to the ecological threat to the Earth, human responsibility for that threat, and the appropriate actions experiencers, and all of us, must take if we are to preserve life on this planet. Generally speaking, experiencers do not appear, on the basis of their backgrounds, to be particularly likely candidates for becoming environmentalists. Sue, for example, who has become a powerful environmental activist, said at the 1992 conference at M.I.T., "I'd like to make it clear that I have no formal education in environmental sciences. I am self-taught" (Pritchard et al. 1994, p. 153). In our meeting Sue told me, "This was not my personality. I've had a total personality change." Karin too said, "I never was an environmentalist" and learned about the environment by "going to school" on the ships.

Although there is no evidence that the children at the Ariel School were abducted during their encounter, several of the ones I interviewed said that they received information, primarily through the black eyes of the beings, about the danger to the planet's life. Fifth-grader Francis felt drawn to one of the beings. "I think those eyes had something to do with it," he said. He said he learned from the being "about something that's going to happen," and that "pollution mustn't be." There had been some prior discussion in school about what causes pollution, Francis told me, but this was the first time he had thought about it or spoken of it. He felt that his concern came "from him"—from the being he saw outside the craft. "It just popped into my head," he said. Francis got the idea that the being was concerned about pollution from "the way he was staring." When I asked eleven-year-old Emma what she thought these "strange beings" (her words) wanted here, she said, "I think they want people to know that we're actually making harm on this world and we mustn't get too technologed." Eleven-year-old Lisel also received through a being's eyes the message that we are not taking "proper care of the planet."

At the 1992 conference at M.I.T., Sue said that "the most noticeable change" that occurred as a result of her experiences "has been my growing concern for the environment." During one of her experiences, she was shown, on some sort of viewing screen, scenes of land being planted in the Middle East and of a particular hill in South America that had once been covered with forest but was now barren of any plant life. She was told that an ecological "massacre" had occurred here. On a viewing screen, she was shown an artificial environment under several glass domes, complete with people, plants, and animals. "I was then brought down into a large cavern where I was shown and encouraged to handle different kinds of seeds."

"They informed me of the critical condition of our beloved planet," Jim Sparks writes. "Their message is true. It doesn't take a rocket scientist to realize the grave condition of this planet. Nuclear and biological weapons and their waste pollute the air, land, and water. Forests, jungles and trees are being cut down or are dying." Contamination of food, "over-population, disease, and viruses beyond our grasp—these are *just a few* of the problems we have created." Jim is very troubled that "most of us are blind or numb to this reality because we can still go to the grocer and buy food. We can go to work and back and not see this death and dying."

Abductees are left with little doubt about the responsibility of humankind for the critical state of the planet. Carlos Diaz said to us, "The real important thing is the ecological problem we're causing worldwide." Jim Sparks was taught that as a species, "we humans are in the early stages of development" and are "too dangerous to be set free in the universe to do as we please." Often on the ships he has been shown "scene after scene showing mankind's destructive ways and its impact on the environment," accompanied by a telepathic message: "*You Are Killing Your Planet. Your Planet Is Dying.*" "I learned if we can't take care of ourselves and our planet, how can we ever expect to join the galactic neighborhood?"

Credo Mutwa, who has no love for the alien beings, observes with sadly laconic understatement, "We are inflicting unwelcome changes on a world, sir, which is really not ours. . . . Why," he asks, "has man turned into a viruslike animal on this earth? The human race is destroying the Earth, sir. Why? We know it is wrong to cut the forests in the jungle. We know it is wrong to spill oil in the sea. We know it is wrong to make many chimneys and pour smoke into the air. But we are doing it."

Isabel, like Credo, likens the human race to a dangerous virus or cancer that might have "to be removed to preserve the whole body." "The earth has gone through a lot," she says. "It's gone through having to support a whole kindergarten of kids spray-painting it, crayoning it." People poison the planet just with the negative energy they give off, she says. "If we're giving off this negative energy all the time, after a while the Earth looks at us like a harmful bacteria, and it will repel us. It will fight back." She perceives the role of the aliens as "doctors," here to help us heal the Earth and to grow. "These blue baldies [her name for the gray aliens]—I won't say they own this Earth. This is their home. I think this is where they belonged first. They are the keepers, the true keepers of the Earth. . . . They're here to help us with this growth period, to help us mature." For Karin the beings are "monitoring the course of mankind; they're watching over.... It's like the mind of God, or something."

Nona also perceives the beings as intimately connected with the Earth and its fate. She was shown and opened herself to inexpressibly magnificent tropical vistas that appeared to represent the endangered Amazon rain forest. She has seen fairy tale–like gardens on the ships and was told by the beings that there is still the potential to create such beauty on the Earth.

Some experiencers agree that the alien beings are concerned with protecting the Earth but attribute less-than-lofty motives to them. Jim Sparks (1996) sees the "galaxy" as a kind of "playground for business." "Big business on this planet sleeps with aliens," he asserts. "Our destructive path is bad for business to carry on as usual." The beings, according to Sparks, are "serving themselves," and the apparent concern for the planet reflects their effort "to take care of an investment" (Sparks 1996 and 2007).

Credo's negative view of the *mantindane* seems to have more to do with his personal experiences and embitterment than from differences in cultural perspective. The second time I visited with him, we met at the house of one of his friends in Johannesburg. He had just been forced to leave his little village, or *kraal* (see chapter 10). Discouraged and in poor health, he spoke more negatively than he had the year before about the *mantindane*, whom he now called "fearsome little parasites." Like Jim he sees these beings as motivated by "pure selfishness." "The *mantindane*, they don't love us. They need us, have needed us, and will continue needing us until they develop better methods of self-preservation." They warn us about "destroying ourselves as human beings by polluting ourselves" because "how will they get things from us if our bodies are dirtied with drugs and toxins from the air?" "These creatures want the earth alive, they want us alive," like motorists who "don't want a pileup in which your own car will be involved." It seems that when it comes to views about the aliens' purposes in seeking to preserve life on this planet, the truth, as with so many aspects of the alien abduction phenomenon, seems to lie in the perception or consciousness of the beholder.

Apocalypse and Prophecy

Sometimes the images of planetary destruction presented to the experiencers are so dramatic, so utterly bleak or catastrophic, that they reach apocalyptic proportions. These are often taken quite literally by experiencers as a foreseeing of what is to come. Sequoyah calls these changes a "cleansing" by Mother Earth to restore balance. Karin has said that only apocalyptic visions could have affected her deeply enough to evoke her concern for the Earth and cause her to change.[1] The impact of such scenes or visions is profound, evoking intense emotional reactions that include shock, fear, horror, and deep sadness. Most often the abductees believe that they are being shown the actual future, and sometimes they come to feel that they are prophets of a sort (Strieber 1996a). Although they may feel that this future is already determined, they may nevertheless, like biblical prophets, warn that we must change our destructive ways.

Credo Mutwa, who told us of his visions of a dying world, believes "these creatures come from the future. There are terrible prophecies that you find throughout Africa to the effect that as a result of the dirtying of the Earth by human beings, as a result of human beings practicing very bad magic, the sky will become dirty, the animals will vanish, the seas will turn into poisonous mud, water will be even more precious than gold to human beings at that time. Then human beings will change, we are told. They will become smaller"—like the *mantindane*, he suggests.

"Something went terribly wrong someplace," Isabel laments. "I think civilization is eating itself up." She foresees that "there are going to be a lot of ships that are going to come here, and I think that they're going to take us and remove us first. The earth has to be purified." She has dreams of what is to come, "like in the Bible." There will be tidal waves, terrible weather changes, and a lot of sickness. "The Earth is going to be gone," she predicts, and not everyone will be on the "new Earth." Jim Sparks writes of "a sadness I can't seem to shake" when he was shown on monitors "the gravity of the Earth's environmental condition. Why? Because it's truth. *This planet, our home, is dying.* . . . It is taking cultures from God knows where to warn us."

Andrea also has had images of the "cleansing" that will occur and devastation of parts of the Earth. She was awakened in the middle of the night and told by the beings telepathically about a Hawaiian Island that was going to explode, setting off a chain reaction of eruptions. The beings urged her to start telling people about this. She was shown from the ships a picture of the Earth and its magnetic poles and grid lines. There will be "Earth changes," she said, and "static electricity" will cover the planet, "clouds of it," and "at that point they said no one will be let in." She has also seen "a ring of fire to the left of Japan." Beginning in the northern hemisphere, the Earth's axis will shift, she has been told, causing "a lot of depression and chaos" unless people work to become "grounded" and "deeply connected with the Earth."

For Karin, more than any experiencer with whom I have worked, visions of the future are expressed with the hyperbole, agony, and wrath of traditional prophecy. She attributes her apocalyptic fears to the "awakening" that her encounters have brought about, especially the "energy, the vibration" that has come with them. Before that, she says, "I didn't run around thinking about the end of the world. I couldn't have given two shits about the end of the world." In her visions Karin sees an object, or a shower of them, like meteors or possibly nuclear warheads, causing destruction everywhere, "like God's wrath exploding" on the Earth. In an instant "everything changes; everything's being annihilated. Cities are going to be lost in the blink of an eye," and everything will come to an immediate halt. Children will be without parents, "and parents without children, and mates without their mates." Crying now, Karin is "in the future" where there is rubble everywhere, smashed cars and the bodies of dead dogs. The waters are filled with offal and are undrinkable. She likens this crisis to the "tribulation. This is the Second Coming. This is the stuff the Bible is talking about."

Sometimes the scenes of destruction represent what the *aliens* have done to *their* former habitat. Credo told us that he has seen civilizations that have died before. At the international conference in Düsseldorf, Germany, in October 1995, Carlos said that the beings have "lived through" their own history of destruction "but they survived it." Karin has been shown explosions and "strip mining" that caused the destruction of the surface of an alien planet, where they failed to replant and "screwed up the whole balance" so that "they ended up having to go underground because it was so horrible on the surface. . . . They had to create an artificial environment" above because "the atmosphere became unbreathable and everything began to atrophy. Their eyes grew much darker because of lack of light. . . . Their bodies used to be physically much more. . . . They can't breed [presumably because of the genetic changes that resulted], and so now they have to add new blood. In the true sense of the word they need flesh."

During one of Karin's experiences, a being took off his mask and "biomechanical suit" and told her, "'You must make them understand.'" Then the figure seemed to disintegrate before her eyes, and whereas he had looked rather "like a bug" before, now his face became "horrible" with pinpoint-white eyes. "His face looks like he's dead; it looks like he's been rotting." The being insisted she not turn away. "You must understand this. This is what will become of your race. This is what is happening to you."

These apocalyptic visions, no matter how certain abductees may feel that they are literal predictions of what is to come, suggest as much as any aspect of the alien abduction phenomenon that we are dealing with some sort of play of consciousness or cosmic informational process rather than simply events in the material world. Some phenomena, like the hybrid "project" (chapter 6) or the floating of people through windows, walls, and doors, might theoretically at least be comprehended through stretching what we know, or believe we could know, about biology or physics. But the visions of the future that many abductees see, the images they perceive, and the experiences associated with them not only defy our ideas about the physical world but may be logically inconsistent and internally contradictory. Except in a metaphoric sense, the planet's life can be destroyed only in a certain number of ways. Life is not likely to end by plagues, earthquakes, floods, pollution, and nuclear explosions all at once.

One time when she was meditating, Andrea heard a tremendous roar and saw a tidal wave of white water coming toward her, destroying great areas of land in its path. What struck her, she said, was not the water but "the consciousness of what was happening and that it has, in a sense, already happened." It is almost "irrelevant," she added, "what particular thing will happen. Visions of earthquakes, volcanoes, and tidal waves reflect a 'separation from Self' that is more real than an earthquake," she said. For Andrea these visions are "just great schemes" of "God or the Creator or the whole consciousness" to try to deepen our empathic connection with the Earth and "bring us back to who we are."

I am not suggesting that these prophetic images are made up by the experiencers, merely fantasies that reflect their personal fears. On the contrary, what they are experiencing in these instances may be altogether real in the sense that it accurately reflects in vivid symbols the emergent situation that currently afflicts the Earth. It seems reasonable to consider these images as reflecting information, whatever its source, about a compelling reality that is both external and internal, a disaster of both the world and the human psyche, that comes to abductees like Karin who hold the pain, almost like martyrs, for the rest of us. In these experiences time, in effect, collapses, so the reality of the destruction is felt in the present moment as already happening, going to happen, or likely to happen if we do not change our ways. In this regard some abductees seem to embody, like ancient biblical prophets, the archetype of world-ending destruction, except that in our present situation, the danger, as they accurately and viscerally experience, is upon us.

Seeing the Beauty of the Earth

Information conveyed through destructive images that may be of apocalyptic proportions is not the only way that abductees are confronted with the critical importance of the Earth and the danger now confronting its living systems. In addition during their encounters they may be shown nature scenes of breathtaking beauty that sometimes, but not always, are followed by contrasting images of death and destruction.

During one of his experiences, Jim, together with a number of other abductees, says he was shown on a monitor or screen on a ship a series of more than a dozen images that he estimated to last three to five seconds each. The first was a "nature scene in living color, and beautiful it was." There was

> a forest with old-growth trees and mountains in the background. The sky was clear, crisp and blue. The beauty of the scene was emotionally breathtaking, and I could literally feel its majesty. It made me feel good. Then that scene faded away, and with a low hum a few seconds later, the next scene appeared. This time it was a clear blue ocean teeming with fish, and again I felt strong emotions attached to this scene. As that scene faded out, the next one appeared, and it was a gorgeous freshwater lake, pure and clean. The next scene was a beautiful waterfall in a gorgeous mountain setting. Then the rain forest, and so on and so on.

These images left Jim "completely mesmerized."

The same scenes were then shown again in sequence, "only this time they were different. They started to become ugly—in other words, polluted. Each scene started showing mankind's destructive ways" and their impact on the environment.

> For example, the first scene that showed a beautiful old-growth forest, became brown gray and dead-looking instead of healthy

and green. The air was nasty and gray-looking instead of a clear blue sky. This made me feel very sad and depressed. I didn't like at all what I was seeing. The next scene showed dead bloated fish floating on top of the water. Scene after scene, this bleak message continued and saddened me to the point where I couldn't look at it anymore. But it seemed that I had no choice but to look. I couldn't turn away.

Jim tried desperately to take his attention away from "these awful scenes," for "the sorrow of the truth was more than I could bear."

Nona also has been shown scenes of exquisite natural beauty. One of these experiences occurred in the summer of 1996. Incredible as the account was, she insisted she did not dream it. First she told me what she could recall consciously, and then she provided further details in a relaxation exercise.

Nona remembered consciously being taken with another woman to a place that looked the way she imagined the Brazilian rain forest to be. She was "floated . . . over the top of this rain forest with these ships," and there was "a concentration of these balls of light that I've seen in my house" around her. The place seemed well hidden, and Nona speculated that it was a "UFO base," a "very special place," where "many, many gather." Soon she found herself standing on some sort of platform or deck from which she could observe further. The beauty of the scene was magnificent. "Everything was magical, from these balls of light" to "the tops of the trees. It was the most beautiful thing I've ever seen in my life."

We went over the experience again, with Nona now in a more relaxed state. She recalled the scenes in more detail and with greater vividness and emotional power. It was dark, and she guessed that it was perhaps nine or ten o'clock. At the same time, the area was illuminated by "a perfectly even all-natural light," whose source she could not tell. Nona recalled being "pushed up" as if on "an elevator" that came from "very, very deep" inside the Earth, until she found herself in a clearing where it appeared that nothing would grow. Though she herself was on a flat polished metallic surface that felt "like glass," she was surrounded by a conical or trumpet-shaped round shell, made of some sort of very thin strong material, that seemed to fit perfectly inside a section of trees. It seemed to function as a kind of reflector that enhanced what she was seeing.

Nona was inside a bowl, valley, or gorge surrounded by mountains.

The tops of trees were "at my feet," and there were trees everywhere. "At the edge of this bowl," a little above where she was, "was a ship." The sky was "really beautiful," and she felt a sense of safety and protection in the bowl. "There's something very sacred here, very powerful here," she felt, with special light and energy. The forest growth was very thick, wet, and "luscious," and there was dense moss around her too. Although this was a "secluded, very unknown" place, she felt she could recognize it if she were ever to be brought there again. She had a sense that she had been "shown" this "ultimate beauty" so that she would share it with her family, which later she actually did.

Interestingly, four months later, when Nona told of this experience to Bernardo Peixoto (see chapter 8), he readily recognized the bowl as one located in a specific area in the Amazon basin sacred to his people. He and other native people in the area, Peixoto told us, had also "seen those lights swirling over the tops of the trees," which he thought "came from that deep hole in the rain forest" where there was "no vegetation." Peixoto interpreted Nona's experience as a message about the ecological danger threatening the rain forest. Over the next few months she became more deeply involved in the struggles of the indigenous peoples of Brazil to protect the rain forests from the depredations of commercial interests. As a result of her commitment, she was given a special personal invitation by Peixoto to attend a gathering of sixteen hundred medicine men and other native Brazilian people in the jungle itself. At the time of this writing, the meeting has been postponed twice because of flooding in the region.

A few weeks later, Nona and I talked further about this experience and its effect on her. An "incredible" experience like this, she said, "expands me each time. . . . It just changes everything." You realize that "the existence of life" is "so magnificent. . . . We can look at the sky and think there are probably many, many civilizations out there beyond that blue sky." "When they show you these environments," she said, "you can actually see the life-force in flowers and in the leaves and the water. It's like colors you've never seen before. . . . In the rain forest you could see the life existing within a leaf, within the tops of these trees. [There] were earth spirits dancing all over the tops of those trees." At home in her native New Hampshire, she said, she was coming to experience life this way as well.

Feeling the Earth's Pain

"Abductees," Julie says, "have a deep love of the Earth. They truly love their planet." But this love can become filled with anguish when they identify with the Earth's distressed condition. Sue's "absolute feeling of urgency that we have to do something about the environment" began in 1985, about the time she first became aware of her encounters. As she stood on her porch after breakfast one morning, "I suddenly had an overwhelming feeling of illness, of sickness, of poison. I know this sounds weird, but this is the way it was. I felt like I was the planet and that I was suffering." When she looks at plants at the side of the road, Andrea said, they seem to scream to her to help them. "I can feel the plants. I can feel the destruction of what's happening."

In the weeks after a long session in which she was brought in touch with the details of her 1980 abduction experience, Celeste wrote many letters to Roberta and me, pouring out her anguish about the assaults upon the Earth's life in her native Canada, sometimes enclosing articles documenting various environmental problems. She wrote of companies that were ignoring environmental limits on toxic dumping, of the killing of life in Lake Ontario by toxic waste from a nuclear plant, and of the 1.7 tons of waste deposited in the Great Bear Lake region. "We have lost so very much that is precious to us as humans," she lamented. She wrote particularly of her worries about the future. "We cannot waste time. Life is so precious," and "we will be leaving the planet strewn with toxic materials that alter and destroy life. It is a legacy that we should be ashamed of, and do everything in our power to change. The planet was so hospitable for life."[2]

Karin's pain has also been especially intense. "I'm like a babbling brook crying," she says, "about things happening in this city. Every time we tear a street up, it's like ugh! The Earth aches from this. I feel the soil being distressed. How do you feel soil being distressed, and how do you feel plants being distressed? And rocks? I feel like I'm dying a little bit every day. I'm dying with the planet and with all the sorrow and the pain of all of these people that are dying around us." She has "seen the Earth" from a great distance, like "astronauts. It's a jewel and it's unbelievable. It's enough to make you cry."

Although they may have had no special knowledge of indigenous traditions, abduction experiencers seem to be drawn inevitably to native American spirituality and Earth consciousness. "I've never had any interest in Indians," Karin said, but in one of our sessions, she shared an image of "really old Indians being whisked away from their connection to the Earth. They had a connection that was apparently so profound. But now so many of them have lost this connection that was such a direct line to the Earth's vibration. It's a huge wound among their people." Sue said to us, "There are so many parallels between native American spirituality and the UFO phenomenon that you would be amazed." She spoke of an early abduction experience in which she died on a cliff with a medicine man. "I think," she concluded, "I was supposed to ultimately come to Native American spirituality to understand the UFO phenomenon" (see chapter 7).

Carlos Diaz: "The Light of This Life"

The most dramatic example of identification with life and nature was expressed to me by Carlos Diaz, during my several-day visit with him and his family in February 1997.

Carlos's leadership as a teacher of the Earth's ecology began with an encounter that occurred in 1981, two and a half months after he took his first spectacular UFO photographs at Ajusco Park near Mexico City. Seeking further photos, he says, he returned to the same site, where he saw through fog and rain a yellow glow in the midst of the forest. He scrambled up the hillside and came to within what he estimated to be forty to fifty yards of an illuminated domed object with a kind of ring on its top, through which the light had been coming. "Suddenly I felt someone grab my shoulder and I fainted" (Diaz 1995, p. 2). When he awoke some hours later, it was dark and the object was gone. He climbed down to his car and sat in it, trying to overcome his confusion and figure out what had happened. When he started the engine and turned on the headlights he saw a small red car in front of him, and a young man approached him. The man was about Carlos's age (twenty-three at the time) but taller and huskier with lighter hair. The man said that if Carlos wanted to know more about what he had seen at the top of the hill, he should come at noon the next day to a place where the highway to Ajusco divides.

Carlos says that he did go to the designated place, and there he saw this man sitting on the grass and speaking to twenty schoolchildren, with a bus nearby. They were listening raptly as the man talked to them about the relationship of vegetable to animal life, how everything in nature interacts, and how plants and animals have earned their place in nature. The man told Carlos that he was the one who had grabbed his shoulder and spoken to him the night before and that he came from the craft Carlos had seen on the hill. He also told Carlos that he would recover memories of this incident only gradually, as needed, otherwise recalling the encounter would be too much of a shock.

Over the next weeks, detailed memories of the incident came to Carlos. He saw the ship "floating over my head. It was made of millions of small dots of light. I tried to touch the object, but my hand went through the yellow light." It seemed as if he merged with the craft, which brought him a feeling of great tranquillity, like being "deeply in love with someone." Carlos noticed that the craft now appeared to be standing on a platform inside a cave that was lined with stalactites and stalagmites, many of which were carved with what appeared to be Mayan sculptures and other fine works of art.

The man walked with Carlos to another smaller cave. "There was something strange about the illumination," Carlos recalled. "It was everywhere, but I couldn't find a source." It seemed to arise from the rocks themselves. In the cave he was "impressed when I saw seven spheres of light there." The man invited him into one of the spheres, which seemed, like the ship itself, to be made of compressed yellow light. At first Carlos could see nothing but light, but then he found himself surrounded by an image, "as if I were merely an eye. I was in a forest. I could see all over. I could feel the fresh air and hear the singing birds. It was like being there. It was truly amazing. I couldn't touch anything or see my body" (Diaz 1995).

Carlos does not know how long he was inside the sphere, which he had been taken out of "in a twinkle of an eye." He says that the man told him he had been taken into the sphere to receive information, and then he brought Carlos back to the ship. Carlos related his passionate concern for the earth's "ecology" to this and similar encounters. At the international conference in Düsseldorf in October 1995, he said, "All the things I saw in the spheres made me realize about the interaction between the smallest particle to the biggest." Each has "a specific duty."

Carlos's strong sense "of the wonderful whole we are part of," the "wonderful opportunity to be alive" and "enjoy a beautiful living planet," emerged from this and subsequent experiences. He said he learned that the light-haired man was not human, and in later encounters he saw others like him within or in relation to the craft. In the years since that experience, Carlos has tried to share his knowledge in his family, in his local community, and at national and international meetings—"to open as many consciousnesses so we all can preserve life" (Diaz 1995, p. 3).

In Carlos's case the ships seem to serve both as an eye through which he can see nature and as a means of transporting him to different regions or ecosystems such as the forest, desert, jungle, shoreline, or even Arctic areas. Sometimes when he is in the ship he has the desire to know what is outside, and then "all of a sudden the whole ship is my sight." It is as if the ship were "my own eye," and he can see "up, down, side, back—whatever." "With that vision," he says, he can see the jungle, luminous below, the light surrounding and radiating from each living thing.

Carlos's experience of connection with living creatures is so intense that he seems literally to become the thing he is describing. He believes he can actually feel, for example, what it is like to be an insect at night. "When I've been into an ant," he says, he can follow the other ants and seem to work with them in moving eggs to higher places. Different ants have different functions. There seem, for example, to be "guides" and "one that controls all the ants." The ants follow particular odors and a kind of light that emerges from a liquid "that comes out of them" when they walk. Carlos's consciousness of the "being" of ants is so strong that, like an Indian of the Jain sect, when they are in his house, "I take them out. I don't kill them. . . . They come into the house to seek shelter from the rain. The poor things have to have a place to stay overnight."

Sometimes, Carlos told us, he is brought down to the Earth by a beam of light, while at other times the whole ship comes down. He told us of a time when he was brought to a beach, and "eight of us," men and women in casual clothes, "came down with the ship." Before the ship landed he could see around him and "also feel the humidity, the temperature, the pulsating of the earth, the lights." He thought he would focus on what was going on in a specific area of the beach that seemed to radiate a pink color. As the "whole ship would zoom in," Carlos could see turtles putting their eggs in the sand. The sea itself shone, he said, "as if it were millions and millions of diamonds of different colors" that were constantly changing, "a whole show of lights."

Each living thing, Carlos said—plants, trees, and small animals— would be surrounded by its own characteristic "cloud of light," like "its own aura." There were "millions of little dots of light that are pulsating." When an insect, he said, stood on a plant and began to eat from it, "then the light of the plant changes, and the light of the insect also changes." For example, an insect that had started with a blue color would manifest "some violet and some green that it didn't have before," and the color of the plant would also change. "We kept on walking," and "I saw how the little crabs come out as soon as the sand moves. The sand has its own light, and the crabs coming out from the sand bring their own light," like "a small lantern."[3]

Carlos calls the light that he sees during experiences like this, "the light of this life." "Not many of us can see it," he says, "but most of us can feel it."[3] He estimated from the distance that the moon had moved that two hours had elapsed before he walked with the others back along the beach to the ship. After an ecological lesson of this sort, Carlos says, he is brought by the ship back to the football field in front of his home and "put down" to the Earth quickly by a beam of light.

The Web of Life

One effect of the encounters is to leave abductees with a sense of the interdependence of living things and the delicate balance of nature. Those who have read my earlier book, *Abduction*, will recall the case of Catherine, who was shown on a screen beautiful and varied scenes of nature. When asked by the beings if she "understood," she realized that "everything's connected, one cannot exist without the other" (Mack 1995, pp. 160, 162). Isabel says, "Mother Earth to me is like a living organism. It's a living organism. It's a gem, or *was* a gem in the solar system. Mankind is out of balance. . . . Where you have a species leaning toward destruction and not enough creation, then that affects everything else. They [the beings] have to bring about the balance."

Again, among the experiencers with whom I have worked, it is Carlos Diaz who seems to have developed the richest understanding of the interconnected web of nature. The beings speak very little, he says, but when they do, it is to "let me see how all the different kinds of life are interacting." Carlos has seen a "consciousness at work in all the biospheres, where the smallest beings to the biggest ones on the planet are interacting, doing a cooperative job to maintain the planet and also themselves alive." He has been shown how each individual interacts with groups, and then with a bigger group until you get to the whole. He says he has been shown how both complex and simple an ecosystem can be at the same time. As he sees ecosystems connecting with other ecosystems, he realizes that "the Earth is alive." This cooperation in nature has gone on for "millions and millions" of years, he says. "Unfortunately," the dominating forces on the Earth are going against the "natural flow of life." Each creature that has been created in the universe, he says, has "something that is worthwhile to preserve."

Contact with the actual beings that inhabit the ships has itself contributed to Carlos's sense of the interconnection of life. "I've seen an ET," he says, and that experience has made him "certain that life is possible in the universe," and that "one of those manifestations of life is visiting us on our planet and respecting us." Carlos's wife, Margarita, appreciates how pained and alone he feels when those around him are not sensitive to the beauty of nature and the threats to life of which he is so intensely aware. Carlos is not an important "philosophy" teacher but, she says, so much knowledge comes out of him. He wants others to be able to see also that we may be "drowning," but it is difficult for him to convey this. He feels "so alone and impotent," she says, because "nobody feels what he feels."

Awakening and Learning

As they are flooded with information about the perilous state of the Earth's ecology, abductees not only experience great pain, they become increasingly aware that they are being mobilized to play a more active role in the protection of the Earth. They recognize the need for change and that they themselves have a responsibility in this process. "What's happened to me," Andrea says, "is a sadness I cannot shake. I wasn't aware of how much damage we were doing on the planet." She spoke of recycling, and then said, "We should stop buying all these cars. . . . A piece of me is dropping away, a part of that consumerism." One day when she was sitting on the ground, she put her "ear to the grass, and I listened." The Earth seemed to say that "everything is going to turn out perfectly," but she must "talk about this stuff." "We need help in saving the earth" was the message she received.

Jim Sparks, like Credo Mutwa, sees the aliens as protecting their investment in this planet. Nevertheless he sees the need for us to change. "I don't mean to sound like some kid with this elementary philosophy of how we should get together here. However, the condition of the planet is such that we need everybody. The leaders and such, they blew it," he says, "so what they're doing next is contacting the average human being on the planet with this kind of information. That's me. I am asking you, Dr. Mack," Credo exhorted me, "in the name of your sacred land, ask the Americans to stop arguing about this." Take the knowledge that the *mantindane* have given us, he urged, and pass it on to "the people who really matter, the guys who are polluting the sea. The reality of extraterrestrial intelligences should not be made the plaything of skeptics. This thing is too vital for the existence of the human race."

Some experiencers recognize that the radical actions that are needed to cease the destruction of life on the Earth requires that they, or we, first become filled with knowledge. He would not feel so lonely, Carlos says, if "more people were working for the preservation of life on Earth." He quotes Jacques Cousteau, whose television programs he has watched since childhood. "'Man protects what he loves,'" says Cousteau. "But I believe that in order to love," Carlos continues, "you have to know first. You have to have more information." Karin says that "the ones of us who are pregnant with this information are responsible somehow," for so many people have "a film over their eyes."

Sue was inspired by her experiences to educate herself about relevant subjects. She studied physics ("I couldn't do math. For me to even approach physics was really amazing"), ecology, philosophy, and religion, and she read about plants and anything that had to do with the environment and gardening. "I needed a broad idea of what the world was all about in order for me to help. I had to know what it meant to be a person of a different religion. I had to understand what it meant to be hungry. I had to understand what it meant to pollute the environment. Without that knowledge I would not be effective enough."

Many abductees use the word *awakening* to describe the process of change they are experiencing as a result of all the information that is coming to them. "The awakening must happen now," Karin says. "Time is running out." According to Carlos, his environmental education has been more an evolution of consciousness than "a curriculum that you study and master." Nona says that each of her experiences has "stretched" or "expanded" her. When she sees water now as it runs through her property in New Hampshire, "it's not just water running down the rocks. It's liquid energy." "[I] perceive and treat everything differently," she says. After the time in which she experienced being taken to a sacred site in the rain forest of Brazil, Nona felt especially strongly that she wanted to bring back to her home, and especially to her children, the feeling she had had there.

The expansion of consciousness that seems to grow out of their knowledge of the threat to the Earth may have the quality of a spiritual birth or rebirth. As she "downloads" more and more information, Karin feels as if she is "punching" herself "out of an egg. It's like having to be born." Nona's heightened awareness is bringing energies to her that are "out and beyond the physical, the material, what's surrounding us that we can perceive. It has an essence of spirit to it," she says.

Isabel also perceives that "neutralizing the pollution" of the Earth requires a "whole transition from physical into spiritual," a kind of global movement to "a higher consciousness." But she sees the death ("removal") of millions of people who give off so much negative, destructive energy as possibly necessary to "bring about the balance. They [the aliens] have tried to do it in more subtle ways in the past, but we're not getting the message." As a species, she concludes, "we have to prove to everyone else that we can handle the responsibility that we have been given."

Abductees may speak of their experiences as a "trigger" that released something latent within themselves, bringing about a shift in consciousness and an enhanced sense of responsibility in relation to the Earth. But they may become filled with despair for a time, especially if their identification with the destruction of the planet's life is particularly intense. Carlos's twelve-year-old son, Carlitos, said to us, "My father is always talking about that if we don't care for the Earth, we are all going to die." Carlos himself says that we have all the information that is needed, "but man is not conscious of the wonderful opportunity we have of being alive. We don't use it for the preservation of life."

Taking Action

Experiencers may feel pressed by their evolving knowledge and personal transformation to act in some way, but they are daunted by the enormity of the task. What can be done? they ask. All the information she has received is "really important," Nona says, but "what do you do with it? How am I supposed to tell the world that we're killing ourselves?" Karin protests. "Nobody is going to listen to me."

Yet some, certainly not all, abductees do find a way to participate directly, even fervently, in efforts to help protect the Earth's environment. This can occur as a result of their sense of urgency and from facing their fear and other distressing emotions directly. "I have to do something," Sue said. "I knew it on a very deep level. . . . I had a choice, but I didn't have a choice." It was through her identification with the Earth that she was eventually to become an intensely committed environmental teacher and activist.

The environmental activism of abductees ranges from speaking with spouses and children about their new knowledge and concerns for the Earth to becoming, like Sue and Carlos, major teachers at a community and even national or international level. Some experiencers choose to work for environmental causes and organizations. More rarely, like Jim Sparks, they may become involved in direct political action. Not infrequently they come to regard themselves as people with a mission. "I'm not the chosen one," Carlos told us. "I am a messenger."

In a "meeting" on the ship, the beings told Jim Sparks that they had made agreements with leaders of the Earth so that "steps would be taken to correct the environmental condition of your planet with our advice and technology," but that these had been broken. This was the reason why they were concentrating their energy on the "average" person like himself. He has been told,

> Your air, your water is contaminated. Your forests, jungles, trees, and plant life are dying. There are several breaks in your food chain. You have an overwhelming amount of nuclear and biological weapons [that have brought about] nuclear and biological contamination. Your planet is overpopulated. Warning: It is almost to the point of being too late, unless your people act. There are better ways of deriving your energy and food needs without causing your planet any damage. Those in power are aware of this and have the capability of putting these methods into worldwide use.

When Sparks asked the beings in the "meeting" why these methods were not being used, he said he was told that "those in power" view such measures as "a military and security threat." Only if they were granted complete amnesty for their crimes against nature, the beings told him, would "these leaders come forward with the truth," and "it is necessary that you do this in order to work together and survive." Sparks has done precisely that, including initiating an amnesty bill (which he calls the "National Security Amnesty Bill") that would exempt from prosecution any official who chose to disclose government information concerning the alien abduction phenomenon. In addition Sparks has given a great deal of his hard-earned money to Earth-sustaining causes, has produced, largely with his own money, an educational video related to these matters, and is working with various foundations and environmental groups on projects of Earth preservation and protection. Sparks's desire to have his book documenting his alien education published derives in large part from what he has been taught about the danger to the planet's ecology.

Carlos is especially devoted to teaching his children about the positive interaction of all creatures in nature. He told us, for example, "We have scorpions here," but he tells his children not to kill them. "Think of this," he says to them. "These animals were on the planet for millions of years before us. If someone is invading its territory, it is we. I know that they can kill me, so we take them down to the field and let them go." These teachings have had a powerful impact on Carlos's children. Carlitos, for example, is enthralled with wildlife programs on the Discovery Channel, reads Time/ Life books about the natural world, and has developed great skill in catching insects without hurting them. When I asked him how he had developed his respect for nature, he replied, "My father taught me that."

When Carlos is able to bring information to people about the Earth, it is through helping them to feel things and not simply by telling. He likens the process to learning to swim. "You could talk to somebody for five years about how to swim and how to paddle and all that, but the person wouldn't understand one bit about swimming until he actually did it." Despite his feeling of aloneness and the resistance he encounters to his message, Carlos continues to feel that he has "a wonderful opportunity to transmit my experience." When he can bring his experience to other people, it "makes me feel alive."

At the Düsseldorf conference, Carlos issued a statement to the attendees in which he wrote of his certainty that "one of the manifestations of life" elsewhere in the universe is "living peacefully among us and respecting our human integrity." His experiences, he said, had led him to realize "the wonders of the planet we live in, a world based on human interaction and cooperation between each particle, from the smallest to the most complex, which is our own home, the Earth. Unfortunately mankind, us, has endangered our planet's integrity. We are headed toward extinction" (Diaz 1995). Nevertheless, he told us a year and a half later, "We *can* save the planet. We *can* save the planet."

Although there are cultural differences, and the craft and beings in Carlos's encounters appear to be quite different, Nona's commitment to bring back knowledge from her encounters is quite like his. Whatever "gifts" she has received from the beings, she feels, she must give back to others, especially to "care for the children of the Earth." In particular she decided to share the magic of her vision with her husband, mother, brother, sister, children, and other relatives and friends in her community.

Nona's children's sensuous appreciation of the feeling of water and air seemed to increase as she was "able to give them a better sense" of the energy that surrounds us. Her youngest child, Nancy, speaks to her mother of an underground place to which her mother believes she has also been taken. The walls are of a smooth stone, and there are spiral patterns on the floor. This place can be entered by water that runs into it. "The water was just sparkling and alive, Mommy, like diamonds," Nancy said. Nona tries to bring that feeling to their own land. "That happens here," she tells Nancy. As a Brownie leader, she can draw out subtly the joy of her troop in the potential beauty of the natural world. Having become more of an observer herself, Nona has become capable of enabling others to be observant of their own experiences.

Her ecological commitment has affected Nona's nine-year-old daughter, Elizabeth. In the 1950s citizens had created a four-acre pond by shoring up a beaver dam on a two-thousand-acre state reserve. It had become a popular recreation area and had drawn moose, wild cats, and other wildlife to the area. But the dam was breaking down, the fish in the pond were dying, and upon the recommendation of engineers, who said the dam was unsafe, the state Fish and Wildlife Department was planning to drain the pond rather than to pay for repairing it. When Elizabeth heard about this plan, she was very upset and angry, and beneath a drawing of the pond surrounded by deer, fox, and raccoon, she wrote a letter to "Dear Mr. New Hampshire Person." In the letter she wrote, "Please don't drain Albert Pond. Many animals live there. Animals drink from the pond, owls, fox, deer, coyotes, heron, bear, moose, and raccoons. I live near the pond in a big light blue house."

Elizabeth gave the letter to her father to take to a meeting at which the townspeople would have a chance to discuss plans for Albert Pond with the director of operations of the Fish and Wildlife Department, Anthony Nigro. Nigro, a thoughtful, gentle man, read the letter at the meeting. Then he said that just this child's message had made him consider saving the pond, and he promised to look into this possibility. An article in the local paper covering these events concluded, "We hope that Mr. Nigro will tape Elizabeth's letter above his desk and look at it often as he considers such weighty matters as engineering surveys and the availability of state revenue" (January 1997).

At a follow-up meeting the next month, various possible plans for repairing the dam were considered. After this meeting an article in a major regional paper carried the headline *Portsmouth Girl Brings State To Its Knees* and showed a picture of a pleasantly smiling Anthony Nigro down on his left knee holding Elizabeth's right hand. The caption read, "Director of Operations for the New Hampshire Fish and Wildlife Department, Anthony Nigro, hopes that in the future Portsmouth third-grader, Elizabeth Skylar, will see eye-to-eye with him on the future of Albert Pond." The article concluded, "Especially touching was the way Mr. Nigro responded to the concerns of third-grader, Elizabeth Skylar, with a personal letter thanking her for her involvement with the issue." In November 1998 the state agreed to fund the final proposal for protecting the pond.

As with Nona and her children, Sue's urgency about the environment has paralleled her abduction experiences. It was as if someone kept telling her, "I have to do something." The range of her activities, which she only rarely relates publicly to her encounters, is remarkable. She designed an environmental awareness program for ten classes in three elementary schools in her home town, which included planting three hundred trees donated by a large timber company and a lecture by a forest ranger about ecological sustainability. In 1991 Sue became a local organizer for the Youth Environmental Sanity group, and she and her husband have donated a teacher resource library on nature, ecology, and the environment to their local library. She also works with the conservation trust in her town, taking students on nature walks.

In addition Sue has become an avid gardener and landscaper. She became president of her local earth gardeners club and landscaped the center of her town. Her "inner promptings" made her "know I had to feed the hungry," and she also worked in a food pantry in her town, opened a second one, and volunteered at a third in a large nearby city. "I know after this there will be something else that I will need to do." She has spoken at various elementary and high schools in her region and on several radio programs and has connected her work with Greenpeace. Sue's thirteenyear-old son, whom she believes has had UFO-related experiences, is also very interested in and concerned about the environment.

In Düsseldorf Carlos said that many people ask, "What do the UFOs have to do with ecology?" In this chapter I have attempted to address this question by setting out the rich store of information that has come to some of the experiencers with whom I have worked in the course of their encounters and their responses to it. Some abduction investigators argue that the images that abductees receive about the destruction of the Earth are presented to them, not to change their awareness and impel action, but rather to test their reactions or to deceive them about the beings' true, more sinister purposes. I suspect this way of thinking reflects more the way our minds can work than the agenda of the alien beings. For in the end it seems quite a stretch to see as a test what so accurately reflects our reality, as has been documented by the best scientific information about the ecological state of the planet.

It is also argued that if the aliens are so concerned with the Earth's fate, why do they not do something more directly to help its cause? The answer, I believe, has to do with issues of responsibility and how human beings grow. The alien abduction phenomenon may, in fact, be thought of as a kind of intervention, sometimes harsh, that may have the purpose of bringing about change in the ways of humankind. But when it comes to our responsibility for the fate of the Earth, the "method" seems to be to bring about psychospiritual growth or the expansion of awareness.

Perhaps this is the method of Source, through its alien emissaries, by which we are being invited, urged, but not forced, to fulfill our responsibility for the care of the Earth. The abduction encounters, whatever their ultimate source, affect profoundly the Earth consciousness of many if not all experiencers. As much as any aspect of this remarkable phenomenon, change occurs as a result of the opening and expanding of human consciousness. However painful the realizations may be, experiencers become exquisitely aware that they are connected to a great whole, a vast web of life, for whose preservation they, together with all of us, bear responsibility. If we fail in this responsibility, it will not, as Carlos says, be because we need to know more or because we did not realize the consequences of continuing on our present direction.

In the mid-1980s Budd Hopkins discovered that at the center of the UFO abduction phenomenon there appeared to be some sort of project to create hybrid beings by joining human and alien beings (Hopkins 1987). As we will see in the next chapter, I have come increasingly to see this hybrid "project" in the context of the growing ecological crisis that the human species has wrought upon the Earth. We turn now to a consideration of this "project" and its possible interpretations.

He talked of the "future of mankind," and of a new race that "will be able to reproduce, and they will know love and happiness like humans know, and they will know their soul and their consciousness like we don't know, and they will inhabit the planet and take care of it and make it a beautiful place." (from p. 132). Illustration by Karin.

Chapter 6

The Hybrid "Project"

Whatever race is dying out, unable to breed, [then] I don't mind being a part of the next one starting up.

Nona

[This] intelligence is saying, "Well, we mean to 'impregnate' in a deeper, metaphoric, sense and you don't get it, so we'll try to make this in some form that you can get."

Eva

The Hybrid "Project" in an Ecological Context

Since the publication of Budd Hopkins's pioneering *Intruders,* some investigators have come to see the creation of a race of human/alien hybrid offspring as an important, if not *the* central purpose or meaning of the abduction phenomenon (Hopkins 1987; Jacobs 1992 and 1998). Although I do not perceive the hybrid "project" as so literally biological as do these researchers, experiences related to some sort of human/alien sexual and reproductive connection are an important aspect of the phenomenon in many, though not all, cases in my work. I have gradually come to see the hybrid "project" in the larger context of the ecological crisis, as discussed in the last chapter.

Some abductees report that the hybrid "project" grows out of the fact that the beings made their own planet unlivable and destroyed their own capacity to breed. Now, they say, the aliens are replenishing their stock by mating with us. Jim Sparks, for example, says that the aliens need humans "for their long-term survival" and "to create worker beings for trade and commerce." He finds it remarkable that "aliens, with all their wondrous technology, still need a human mother to incubate." In addition some experiencers see the beings as using images of their own past ecological and biological devastation to confront human beings with what we are currently doing to the Earth and ourselves.

Some abductees report that the hybrid phenomenon is more directly related to the damage we are doing to ourselves and the Earth. "My husband is a physician," Sue says, and he sees that "women and men are becoming more infertile at an alarming rate." She relates this to the toxic pollution of the soil. "It's going to take centuries for us to truly get rid of it," she says, "unless we come up with some technology that can eliminate it." Sue also sees the reported taking and examination of ground samples (see Hopkins 1996, p. 254) and animal parts (Howe 1993) by the beings as related to the deterioration of the Earth's capacity to sustain life. Catherine believes the hybrids are being created "so that if humans did destroy the planet there would still be alternatives" (Mack 1995, chap. 7). Perhaps, she suggests, by crossbreeding with humans, "the aliens are trying to come up with a form that would be more physical but could still exist in the other realm."

Some experiencers, like Karin and Jim Sparks, perceive the hybrid "program" (Sparks's word) as related to the needs of *both* species. Jim has been shown a "little hybrid girl" that "could have possibly been a part of me." He believes that "if we fail to correct our seriously endangered environment," the "hybrids will be used to repopulate the Earth." The hybrid program is thus, he says, "a secret club" or "insurance program," a "backup plan." Perhaps the hybrids, Sparks suggests, being "a bit more intelligent" and "a bit less emotional than we are," will "have a bit more respect for the environment." Similarly, Nona sees the hybrid "project" as related to our potential for "wiping out the entire planet." At times she seems to accept the taking of her genetic material as a contribution to the preservation of both species.

The Reproductive Sequence and Its Actuality

Budd Hopkins first brought to our attention the fact that at the center of the alien abduction phenomenon was some sort of vast "project" or "program," seemingly initiated by the beings, to create a hybrid race that combines human and alien characteristics. Since Hopkins's discovery (1987) that reproductive activity might be a regular feature of the phenomenon, abduction investigators, including myself, have consistently replicated a number of Hopkins's findings (Jacobs 1992 and 1998; Bullard 1994b; Mack 1994). As we shall see, in considering the apparent reproductive and sexual dimensions of the human/alien connection, difficult ontological distinctions become of particular importance.

Although many of the details vary from experiencer to experiencer, the basic elements of the hybrid "project" that have been reported are as follows. Sperm is forcibly taken from males and eggs from females of childbearing age. Later the teenage girls or women experience that they are pregnant as a result of the reimplanting by the beings of a fertilized conception, which presumably contains an added alien component. Subsequently, during another visitation, the fetuses are taken from the human females. On the ships the abductees may see rows of incubators containing hybrid babies in early gestation. Later women experiencers—and less frequently, men—are brought together and urged to nurture one or more hybrid offspring, which they are told are theirs and which they usually recognize to be their own offspring.

Some of the most disturbing and poignant moments for the experiencers, and especially persuasive ones for investigators, occur when the experiencers recall or relive how it feels to be brought together with a creature toward whom they feel a strong maternal or paternal attachment but whom they may never see again. A number of experiencers, in the course of the investigation, may learn that they have an alien, hybrid, or even a human mate in the "other world" with whom they feel a strong bond, sometimes creating a moral dilemma for marriages of this Earth plane. (This subject will be discussed more fully in chapter 13.)

I am convinced that the reproductive narrative is powerfully real for the experiencers. To the best of my knowledge, after thousands of hours of investigation with scores of abductees, no Freudian or other individual psychodynamic explanation seems to account for its basic elements. In other words I have found nothing in the experiencers' histories, current personal lives, desires, needs, or conflicts, conscious or unconscious (as might occur, for example, in hysterical pregnancies where the underlying wish to be pregnant is obvious), that would explain this strange part of the story.

Whether hybrids are being created literally on the material plane of reality, or whether the phenomenon needs instead to be looked at some what differently—as, for example, an aspect of collective consciousness occurring largely in another reality—has important implications for our understanding of it. A literalist interpretation could understandably give rise to a threatening scenario involving an agenda of alien colonization of the Earth for selfish purposes (Jacobs 1998). An "interdimensional" view would be more complex and could include energetic, mythic, and metaphoric components with an emphasis on the understanding of human consciousness and spiritual evolution. My own investigations found evidence to support both views. I will present these data as objectively as I can and invite the reader to join me in trying to make sense of this compelling mystery.

For most, but not all, of the abductees with whom I have explored sexual and reproductive experiences, the encounters and images are so vividly present, so real and emotionally intense, that their language becomes quite literal. In Andrea's experience the aliens are "feverishly collecting the seeds of life," and "the hybrids are here to populate the Earth as an insurance policy." Andrea is the mother of two daughters from her twenty-year marriage. They "got me at my weakest point," she says—her motherliness. "They really know how to do it. It just feels real. I'm already a mother. I know what it feels like. It feels like I have a son." Nona believes she has many hybrid children on "these large ships that I've been on, but I don't know that for a fact." Jim Sparks sees the aliens as literally taking body materials from us. "They use us," he said. Credo Mutwa believes the *mantindane* are "mining" or "harvesting" us. "Perhaps we're just walking stock with a little bit of brains," Isabel suggested in a cynical moment.

For many abductees the reproductive experiences, including unmistakable symptoms of pregnancy and subsequent loss, are so vivid and real that they use the language of genetic biology and speak of DNA alteration and genetic harvesting, although no studies of which I am aware document actual genetic changes. Nor, for that matter, has research successfully documented the fact of sperm or egg harvesting, alien impregnation, or the existence of hybrids in the material world as we know it.

Obstetricians and gynecologists do sometimes find that their patients have pregnancy symptoms and positive pregnancy tests, then subsequently discover that there is no fetus and the symptoms have subsided. From the physician's perspective, this is a "missed" abortion; the fetal tissue was reabsorbed or passed without the patient's knowing it. In a few cases abduction researchers have even correlated such accounts with recovered abduction memories that occurred at the time that the fetus seems to have been lost (or taken). But to my knowledge no gynecologist has been able or willing to verify that the product of conception may have been taken by alien beings or even ended mysteriously. (For a careful discussion of the diagnostic questions involved in regard to diagnosing an "alien pregnancy" see Miller 1994, pp. 262–70.) Having, however, gone through over and over again with abductees the pain, trauma, and resentment associated with the apparent taking of sperm or eggs and the processes of impregnation and fetus removal, together with the sensitive discrimination of which some abductees are capable between "alien" and ordinary pregnancies, I have become persuaded that whether or not babies have literally been created, *something* of great power and intensity has occurred (see also Mack 1995).

Impregnation and Pregnancy

The concrete sparseness, consistency, and certainty of abductees' descriptions of their reproductive experiences, their clarity of recall about the impregnation and gestation cycle, and their conviction about its actuality, virtually rules out the possibility that fantasy alone can explain these accounts. It may start, Karin said, with "a needle thing that goes way in you" when they take her "seed." In another instance a fetus was "vibrationally planted." The being "turned my stomach into light, and so it became penetrable." The timing of this "needle thing" for her is odd, as it seems to occur "a week *after* a typical ovulation" (emphasis mine). Perhaps, she suggests, this is when "they do the implant."

Isabel has the impression that the beings "really need" to take her physical body to maintain her health as a breeder ("for tune-ups"). As part of this process, they give her a bitter liquid to drink and "put in" her what she calls a "vaccine." "I don't remember seeing any actual needles," she said, but afterward "I had a mark on me." The drink, she believes, is "just like a medicine" or "a supervitamin." "If I'm healthy, their babies will be healthier," she presumes. The beings need her physical body, she says, to hold the "funny-looking" babies or to try to have her breast-feed them. Within twenty-four hours of the experience in which she believes she was impregnated "my belly's bloated," and she has the sensation "of a mild pregnancy" that she distinguishes from "real pregnancies" that she has also had. In the alien pregnancy "the body shifts chemically. It's subtler. I don't get morning sickness like I do with a normal pregnancy." For three months Karin's periods are "not right, where I almost don't bleed." She has been shown, after about three months, how they "took it out when they opened the tummy with light."

"When they take you physically," Isabel has said, "that's when I wake up with bruises or my whole pelvic region hurting." When she is experiencing an alien pregnancy, she will "feel things in my womb, like little tummy tickles," but much earlier than with a normal pregnancy. "At five weeks the movement is like the way it would be if you were four or five months pregnant. I had three children, so I know what the fluttering feels like," she says. "My breasts got tender. I just got the whole nine yards, pregnancy symptoms." On one occasion she was so "absolutely positive" that she was pregnant that she took a pregnancy test, which was negative. Something like this process is familiar to Credo Mutwa. He says that the *mantindane* (his description of them is virtually identical to our gray aliens) "are sexually compatible with human beings and are capable of making terrestrial women pregnant."[1] Like American abductees, he was shown, in the place to which he reported being taken by the beings, "something that was swimming in a big bottle. . . . I could see this fetus moving like a little frog inside this liquid. I couldn't understand a thing, and this creature, sir, was trying to make me understand what I was seeing" (see also p. 211).

The Hybrids

The straightforward and highly detailed way abductees describe hybrids and their relationship to them is very convincing and leaves little doubt that these experiences, and the hybrids themselves, are *in some sense* real. But this does not mean that they are flesh-and-blood babies or children in a purely physical sense. Nona, for example, reported a memory of "these children" who came "walking off the ship" and "formed a semicircle in front of me. They looked very much like my daughter" Elizabeth (who is especially short), she said. "Their bodies were short for their heads. Their heads seemed oversized. They had very blue eyes. They had very thin, wispy hair. . . . I would say they were probably three and a half feet tall, but they all looked the same age." "You're our mother and we need you," they said. Nona felt conflicted and told them, "'I can't go. I have my family and I can't go.' I felt badly about saying no, but I couldn't just go. I couldn't leave."

Isabel has seen "funny-looking" children on the craft and also dreamed about "weird-looking babies." She describes these "creatures" as solid but lighter in weight or density than human children. Of one of them, she said, "Her face was mottled. It had dark and light patches. She had long limbs, and she wrapped her limbs around me, and I held her like this on my hip and her leg was in front. The other one was dangling." The "skin looked dry and scaly and flaky, like she needed lotion. She looked so lonely. I felt she was mine in a biological sense." A year later Isabel described a boy who "looked like he was made of marble toast." He had "two-tone skin," which looked "really rough, very thick." He was "very small" and had patchy hair and nails that looked almost like claws. Another baby had a "squarelike" head and big eyes. He was a "tan baby" and looked weak and even smaller. Isabel has dreams of being in a room, surrounded by all these strange children.

Isabel, like Nona, felt conflicted about holding and nurturing these babies. "I'd like to say I feel maternal instincts, but I don't. . . . At first it's almost repulsive, like I don't want to touch the babies. But then the babies are so sweet, so beautiful, their disposition is so sweet and curious." I asked how their bodies feel. "Very fragile," she replied, "like you had to hold her gently. She didn't feel solid. She was so light—so very light." Sometimes Isabel has "dreams" in which the babies are "wanting me to hold them and breast-feed them, but I don't have any milk." These dreams feel like real experiences. When she wakes up, her nipples are sore and she still has "that feeling of holding that child." She does not want to be helped to "remember everything. I don't want to remember what it's like to give birth to all these babies because, being a mother, I know I would constantly be worrying about them."

Sometimes experiencers in our sessions relive elements of the "reproductive cycle" with such precise detail and such powerful emotions that it is hard to believe that what they are reporting did not literally happen just as they describe it. Karin remembered a recent abduction experience in which a "live fetus" was extracted from her and put inside an "incubator." Crying out in pain, she recalled watching the beings take out of her a "little, little, bitty thing" that she estimated was less than two inches long. "God, it's ugly. It's so sad and so ugly. They're so small," she said. The head was "pink, kind of reddish." One of the beings took the thing in his hands. Then they took it through "kind of a U-shaped doorway" that was "off to the right, down the hallway."

This time the beings told Karin telepathically that they were going to show her where they took the conception. It was "time to learn it," she said, "like it's part of the science class." "Normally we don't have to move this quickly," she was told, "but because we have a live fetus, we need to get it into its incubator." A hybrid "nurse," who Karin estimated was about five feet tall and was known to her, led her along. Karin and the nurse followed three other beings. One of them had the "fetus" in its hand and led Karin to a "wedge-shaped" and "reddish, rust-colored" room to the left that was dark, "except for these things that are lit up. And there's the bubble sound I always hear. We always hear these bubbles. It's like a fishtank." They put the fetus into one of these tanks and attached "this thing over its head and it goes in its ears" because it cannot just "free float." This "thing" seemed somehow to connect the fetus to the tank. "They say it doesn't hurt," Karin said, "and you're thinking, 'God, it's so small.'" Karin said she saw lots of "other incubators all around in the room, and lots of other little hybrids" at "different stages." A foot-long creature was floating in a nearby incubator, "but his eyes are covered. That's weird. You could see where he had big black eyes, but they were covered with skin" or a "membrane. You could see the slit, like when a lizard closes its eyes."

Trauma

Needless to say, several aspects of the sexual/reproductive sequence can be intensely traumatic for the experiencers and fill them with resentment and sadness. They may become particularly troubled when they fear or believe that their children, especially teenage daughters, are being used in this process. In *Abduction* I wrote of the bitter humiliation for men of having their penises stimulated, ejaculation induced, and sperm taken against their wills. Credo Mutwa confided, "I don't know why the *mantindane* stole semen from me. Once a *mantindane* has dealt with you, you become afraid of making love to a woman. The moment your semen comes out, you recall that terrible day and something becomes rather flat in you at night, I assure you." For women the whole process of being used as a "breeder" can be hurtful, which is compounded by the sadness and loss associated with feeling they have offspring on the ship or in whatever place or realm the hybrids exist.

Karin is frustrated that the beings take her eggs and her fetuses. "You have these babies," she says, "and they just take them." In one of our sessions, her rage boiled over as she recalled an intrusive vaginal procedure. She was in the ob-gyn position, like "in the stirrups." "So there you are in this spaceship, and your legs are spread again. Then this needle thing, this thing I don't like, is inserted in my body, right through my uterus." Although there was "this gentleness about them," Karin said, "I don't want to do this right now." After such an intrusion, "my body's going to be screwed up again for the next three months." She "knows" she has a son, whom she calls Barien, "out there." "I've always been subconsciously traumatized by the loss of that child. . . . It was my child, and even at a really young age, it's within your womb, and your brain knows it. Deep inside, your soul knows it. . . . I've never wanted children since then, largely because I'm still subconsciously mourning the loss of that one."

Nona has been troubled by "the idea of taking eggs from my body. I had difficulty with that, and with the potential for being bred without knowing it. Sustaining their race, or whatever it is," is "okay with me," she said, but she feels anger and hurt that the beings do not "share that with me." She cannot allow herself to think about the pain associated with her "emotional attachment" to her hybrid offspring.

The general subject of relationship between experiencers and alien beings will be discussed in chapter 13. Here I will note only that about three years after I began this work, experiencers began increasingly to report to me instances of powerful, loving connection with the beings, especially in the context of the hybrid "project" (see, for example, Peter in *Abduction*, chap. 13). In some instances they tell of intense, intimate relationships with alien or human/alien beings whom they consider to be their mates in the other realm and with whom they may create and parent hybrids. This may bring with it jealousies and a potential feeling of betrayal on the part of a spouse on Earth, which provides a challenge for the couple to work out together.

Andrea, for example, has described to me with strong emotion and great detail her ecstatic, erotic relationship with a human/alien mate that she carries on "up there." She believes that a little boy and a little girl have come from this union. The boy in particular, she says, "wasn't made the way they make babies"—that is, by the elaborate artificial sequence described in this chapter, in *Abduction*, and by other investigators (Hopkins 1987; Jacobs 1992 and 1998). Together Andrea and this man, she believes, are the parents of this boy, as a result of their intimate connection. All of this is so real to her that she feels guilty that she may be betraying her husband, whom she loves. But this guilt is mitigated by the fact that the relationship with her space mate is not occurring on Earth, although Andrea believes he "is living here in human form at least some of the time."

Acceptance

Despite the pain and trauma associated with the hybrid "project," some abductees do not necessarily see themselves as victims and may come to accept their participation in it.

Nona acknowledges that the aliens are "intrusive by our standards," but "the sense I get from them is that they are not of a malicious nature toward us, that they have a purpose." The beings are "not here to harm; they're not here in an aggressive way. There's always been a sense of caring," she says, "and they need to be received that way." At first, Nona said, "I had difficulties with the idea of the taking of eggs from my body. . . . It's like taking my children. How can someone take my children? And yet I wouldn't be having more than five children." Nona and others have moved into a mode of understanding. "Our emotions and our sense of reality are so different from this that that in itself creates terror," she notes. "We're terrified of going crazy. We're terrified of hallucinations. We're terrified of nightmares. We're terrified of anything we don't understand." "I'm just so accepting of this at this point," Karin says. "I keep using the word *understanding* in my thoughts for them, and they understand that word. They know that I want to comprehend why."

The acceptance that Nona, Karin, and other experiencers may come to feel derives from their sense that they are part of a life-sustaining mission, and they attribute what is happening to a higher purpose. Karin believes she may have as many as seventeen hybrid babies: "Unbelievable! And I only know two of them." Yet she feels "better about the loss" because "I'm part of giving life." Nona has told me repeatedly that she feels "honored" to be part of what she believes may be the "reseeding" of civilization, saving the alien species and "human genetics" as well. "I honor them," she says. "I don't know everything they're doing," but "whatever race is dying out, unable to breed," then "I don't mind being a part of the next one starting up." "My ego rebels against this," Karin says, but "in my higher self-consciousness, I'm in complete agreement with the whole process. . . . It's creating life. It's just creation. It's what God does." Andrea says, "I think it's kind of God's plan too."

Problems of Health and Emotion Among the Hybrids

A consistent theme among the experiencers concerns the health or well-being of the hybrids. They may seem listless, almost like failure-to-thrive human infants and children. Sometimes the abductees learn from the beings of specific anatomical or physiological defects. Nona and others attribute them to the problems of cross-breeding between the two species.

Karin has observed that the hybrids that the gray beings are creating with humans have seemed sick, physically and emotionally, and appear to "get sicker the older they get. They feel really sad," she said, "and they don't understand the emotion as sad, but when I see them, they feel sad. Their bodies look sick. They look emaciated, kind of atrophied." Furthermore, the hybrids appear to lack emotion, which she believes for some reason they have "genetically altered" out of their species. According to Karin, the hybrids have not "got the feeling part" yet, which would apply to the aliens as well. They do not interpret sensation as "pleasure-pain" or "love as love"; they just interpret it as "vibration." They have been trying, she says, to "acquire both of those things"—viable bodies and emotionality—"by integrating with us."

Andrea noticed that the hybrid waste-elimination system had not been working. In one of our sessions, she saw a kind of "nursery" with "a whole bunch of babies in a row." But "they weren't making it; they weren't living" because their "kidneys were shutting down." (The aliens themselves, she believes, excrete waste through their skin.) Similarly Nona was told by one of the beings, "We are having problems with the palates of the children," and in one of her encounters one of her sisters, who is a nurse and had been a surgical assistant in many cleft palate operations, "looked in their [the hybrids'] mouths and explained to this being what the problem was." To Nona it was logical that if "something's humanly deformed, then it would make sense that they would have to ask, or want to ask a human" in order to "accommodate the crossbreeding."

Over the years the hybrid "project" appears to have changed. The principal change relates to the difficulty of combining such disparate species as human beings and gray beings, or whatever aliens are presumably crossbreeding with us. "The children that have been created," Nona says, "are a crossbreed of races or beings," and the task has been to create a "balance between us and them" so the hybrids can live in the Earth's environment. For example, she says, the aliens have had to learn about our bodies and how the human eye works. The "problems with the palate" have made her wonder if "maybe they're having digestive problems." Along the way, Andrea says, "they made mistakes," and some of the hybrids "didn't turn out so good." Later in this chapter I will discuss to what extent the changes reflect a literal change in what the abductions are "about"—Nona, for example, has said that she believes the aliens "have created enough hybrid children for their needs"—and to what extent they reflect an evolving expression of the developing consciousness of both the experiencers and those who are working with them.

Alien/Human Integration

In 1997 I began to hear of the creation of hybrids in which the human/alien integration had been more "successful" in producing beings with special qualities. Andrea has told me of a seven-year-old hybrid son of hers she calls Kiran, who is "different from the other babies in the incubator," which are "half-human and half-alien." Kiran, on the other hand, is "fully human and fully alien. . . . He's fully integrated." "I think it worked this time," she adds. There are others, she says, that are also different. "I think the combination of the two fully is new." She said that Kiran's father, with whom she feels bonded, "is incarnated from them" and is also human. "He exists on the Earth-plane dimension, and he's also part of their world." Andrea has nursed Kiran several times and loves him very much. "I see how beautiful he is" and "how I am committed to him." She feels "a sadness in me over the fact that [the other] little beings are not making it" whereas Kiran is "so different and healthy." Speaking like any proud mother, she says that Kiran "is going to live and be beautiful and be extremely gifted and have a sense of himself."

A number of experiencers have observed or been told that integrating our and the beings' emotionality has been particularly difficult. Nona has observed that we are an emotionally intense species with "deep-seated feelings" while, she says, "that doesn't exist for them." In order "to integrate the emotions back into it," Karin believes they have had to learn "what makes somebody experience a vibration as an emotion."

In a session in March 1997, Karin too recalled with intense feeling seeing hybrid children of hers in an encounter in which the emotional dimension appeared to be fully "integrated." The beings let her explore and "feel his little head and, in the back of his head, a little ear. It's very small, but you can feel a bump or something." Gasping with a mixture of awe, joy, and loss, she said, "The tall one tells me that these are mine, 'these are your children, and as you can see they are successfully integrated.'" He talked of the "future of mankind" and of a new race that "will be able to reproduce, and they will know love and happiness like humans know, and they will know their soul and their consciousness like we don't know, and they will inhabit the planet and take care of it and make it a beautiful place."

Preserving the Future

Abductees are repeatedly informed that the hybrid project is related to the perilous state of the Earth's ecology and is being conducted for the purpose of preserving both the human and alien species. Nona, for example, says that the hybrids are "being created" because "the potential for us to basically wipe out the human race is entirely possible. We may not survive and they may not survive, and it's very important to perfect this species"— she calls it "fine-tuning"—so they will "be able to live here on Earth within this environment." Because the hybrids have been raised in an artificial environment, there is "much that they're going to have to teach them for survival" on Earth.

Karin says, "The problem is, we don't realize that we're in an emergency state. . . . I get that more and more every day." "There's so much that's going to die," she says, sobbing. Christ, she laments, "was a metaphor; he was a piece of poetry from Source," and in killing him, "we killed ourselves." Now "we're doing the same thing, and the universe is watching us kill ourselves again." She relates the hybrid "project" directly to the fact that "we've written God completely out of our awareness. . . . Our dimension is going to be penetrated by theirs in a really effective way, so the hybrids are the preservation of the beauty in us, and it's the opportunity for the grays to have viable bodies. . . . To human beings it's going to be like God. They're going to know God again."

The aliens have communicated to Karin and others that they cannot reproduce, so the hybrid "project" will insure that something of humanity will endure "when mankind fully screws itself and its environment enough." The fully integrated hybrids, the beings have told Karin, "are your planet's future." Through them "a part of you will continue for all eternity, but the hybrids don't have any business here yet. They're to be exposed as little as possible to the Earth's environment as it is right now."

According to Andrea, the aliens "see more of the damage we're doing than we see" and are saddened by it. She also foresees advanced hybrids coming to Earth. "I think that they really do want to maybe live here, or have some part of them live here." She has been told that "in five years" Kiran "would come down here." She dismissed as a "misconception" the idea "that they want to take over the planet. They're not taking over anything. . . . They don't have it in their makeup, their heart makeup, the ability to overtake another species." I asked what she thought they were trying to do. "They want to merge with us," she replied. "They want to find a way to reach us and merge with us."

What Is Going On Here?

This is perhaps a good point to stop and ask ourselves what this is all about, to consider how we are to understand these accounts. In short, what is going on here?

A lot in this material could be used to support the idea that hybrid babies are being created materially and that they are now penetrating, or in the future will penetrate, our world on the physical plane in a kind of colonization process. Certainly for the abductees these events are, by and large, experienced as actual memories, events recalled with vivid detail and intense emotion appropriate to what is being noted. Experiencers believe they have living hybrid offspring "out there" and have terrible feelings of loss over the fact that they are kept separate from them, except when they are brought together as the aliens may arrange it. Particular problems with the hybrids' organ systems are noted. Largely consistent accounts are provided by otherwise sane people of the whole sexual/reproductive cycle. Abductees tell of pregnancylike symptoms, such as a swollen abdomens or breasts, or even sore genitalia, in association with the process. Some will report clearly identifiable small bodily lesions following their abduction experiences, which appear to be related to the bodily intrusions they have undergone. Even Credo Mutwa and, presumably, other African medicine men believe that the *mantindane* actually impregnate human females.

Isabel struggles with where to place the hybrids on the continuum of spirit and matter. Human beings, she says, are "spirit and matter at the same time, but we're so dense that we cannot comprehend the spirit in us right now." Both spirit and matter can "exist simultaneously." The aliens are also both, but "if I had to say, I would put them more in the spirit realm." The hybrids, however, "are more matter [than spirit]—because, well, going by my experience, they do need the physical touch and breast milk. They do need nourishment, and that's more physical than spirit."

But there are problems with an entirely literal physical interpretation. To begin with, despite liberal use of words like *genetic*, *DNA*, and *mitochondria*, there is no solid material evidence of which I am aware to support the notion that any of this, including the creation of the hybrids themselves, is occurring on the material plane to the extent that detectable or measurable changes are happening at the molecular level. At best what we have in the physical domain are small lesions (which skeptics say could be self-inflicted, but I have found no evidence for this) and bodily symptoms that might be manifestations of subtle forces, real energies originating on another plane of reality.

Isabel, who has incontrovertible pregnancylike symptoms in association with her experiences and does believe that in some way she is being used as a breeder, insists on calling the experiences "dreams," despite the fact that "the next morning I don't look back on it as a dream. To me it's a memory." But she does not "claim it's an experience, because if I don't have a physical proof that I can show to you and say, 'Well, here, here's a piece of her clothing,' or 'Here's a lock of her hair.' I don't want to say it's an experience, so I prefer to call it a dream."

Furthermore, abductees may experience a dimensional "otherness" in conjunction with these experiences. Karin observed incubators with hybrids at "different stages" and sizes, but in that place "everything feels weird dimensionally." In order for the hybrid "project" to succeed, she says, "our dimension" will have "to be penetrated by theirs." Andrea, as we have seen, struggles with the problem of the differing Earth/alien realms. Her hybrid son's father, she says, exists "on the Earth-plane dimension, and he's also part of their world." The entire process of human/hybrid adjustment and merging, whose problems and complexities are recounted by abductees in such detail, itself casts doubt for me upon the notion that the hybrids can be thought of in purely literal, material terms or that they will someday land here and populate the Earth. The fact that the "project" now seems to some abductees to have progressed, and that they perceive the human/alien integration as successful, does not necessarily argue for its literalness, as I will discuss in the conclusion to this chapter.

The powerful religious or spiritual element—for example, Karin's ecstatic association of the hybrid "project"'s evolution with a coming again of humanity to the knowledge of God—while not arguing against the physical aspect of the phenomenon, suggests to me that something more may be going on. Dave spoke to me of sperm being taken from him, but he said that the significance was as much spiritual as physical, representing the future of two universes "intertwining with each other." The purpose of this connection, he said, was to rebirth ourselves to the next plane, into a "whole different body form." "Our spirits," he has learned, "will not be recycled into this world, but we will actually rebirth ourselves into the next world," where we and the aliens' spirit will "come together as one" (see also pages 160–162). The abductees' repeated references to light, to vibrational and dimensional differences between humans and aliens or hybrids (see chapter 4) also argues to me strongly that none of this should be thought of entirely in literal terms, at least not on the Earth material plane.

Andrea's experience of human/alien mating, though ecstatically pleasurable, is "very different" from human mating. "I think it's done with vibration" rather than mainly genital stimulation. It is "more than just a localized orgasm, or even a full body," she says. "Your cells start to vibrate with the movement of the ship, and your cells start to vibrate with the universe, and it's wonderful. It's not like what we do here." Kiran, the presumed offspring of this union, is "very, very advanced" and looks human. But he is also "all bright light." Andrea seems to have been able to bring some of this higher vibrational energy to sex with her husband (see p. 275).

Karin has awakened to see "my pelvis glowing white." She feels that the aliens are on "a higher vibration than we are. . . . The aliens will be able to manifest themselves three-dimensionally, but it's very uncomfortable for them to do that. It's a lot of hard work. The hybrids will be able to do it easier." In June 1997 I asked her directly whether she felt her participation in the hybrid creation "project" was occurring in "our" reality or in "another vibratory dimension or another universe, or something like that." "I vote in the vibratory dimension," she replied. An alien pregnancy, she noted further, "never processes itself completely three-dimensionally." For Andrea and some other abductees, the merger of human and alien forms is not simply about physical reproduction. "It's about consciousness, a door that's going to open for some people who really want to change their consciousness level."

For several years Eva has attended the Barbara Brennan School of Healing (see *Abduction*, chapter 11). As a result of this training, she has become more sophisticated than most abductees about psychic energy in general and its role in her abduction-related experiences. The exploration of Eva's abduction experiences has occurred in conjunction with her desire to feel closer to God. Her recent educational experiences also seem related to her inclination to interpret her abduction experiences in less literal, physical terms. This tendency can be seen in her interpretation of an experience that occurred in August 1996, six months before she told me about it.

At about ten in the morning, Eva found herself getting tired and felt the need to take a nap. She lay down on her side and was almost asleep when she felt that "they were behind me." She said an electric blue light that looked like lightning "zapped" her back, going down from her spine and then up the front of her body. The sensation became "really hot and stinging" and so painful that "I just couldn't take it anymore, so I just kind of let it go and I went into unconsciousness."

After that "I woke up in another dimension" in a "park" with "green grass" and "swings," which Eva found very strange because there were no trees, people, or traffic and not even a visible sky. The energy around her, which until this moment had seemed formless, "turned into some kind of male, which looked quite human." Then "it said to me telepathically that I was going to seduce it" so that it could "impregnate me." In so doing, she said, "it was serving me. It had nothing to do with itself." Eva was "dumbstruck" and filled with "total disbelief." She thought, "'I know that that thing needs me to seduce it, or I need to seduce him or whatever," and I blank out for a second, and the next thing I'm aware of is rolling around with this male human form on the grass, rubbing myself against its legs, being aware of its penis, which is ivory colored and very limp looking, like a worm, like a big worm." I asked if the penis went inside her or emitted fluid. She answered no to both questions, but her recall ended as she was thinking, "This cannot be happening. It's like I had no control over my body, and at that point I blanked out." During all of this, Eva recalled, "the lower part of my body was doing something," but "there was no feeling in it." She does not believe the experiment ended there, but she was unable to recall more. After a dreamlike transition period, "I returned. I woke up. I came back."

Despite how experientially vivid and real this encounter was for Eva, she does not believe it occurred in ordinary physical reality. "Impregnation in that experience is very different from sex," she explained. "Some kind of seed from them was left in me," but "energetically, not physically. . . . I'm not going to be pregnant and have a baby now, a physical baby." For her the experience "was really not about sex at all. That's the way my mind interpreted it."

The initial formlessness of the energy that became embodied in the being that had contact with her seems clear to Eva. She recognizes that her perceptions are limited by language and her habits of thinking: "Here's an energy, a formless energy, and it's somehow sending this telepathic message that it's going to impregnate me." It "understood not only my disbelief at what was happening, but my confusion if this was true." For "how is some formless consciousness going to impregnate me, the fact being that I have a body? . . . In my mind creation *is* form. The only way my mind could understand," she observed, "was to put its own metaphors. The being or the energy adapted to my limitations and spoke my language. . . . It was trying to maybe meet me in my territory by putting on a human form, hoping that that would make me feel more comfortable and would subside the terror of that communion."

Encounters like this one are an important part of Eva's spiritual journey. They serve as "a bridge, a bridge of contact, a bridge of communication." Her experiences have enabled her to "reconnect with that place within myself where I don't necessarily have to be serious all the time, or structured, or confined, and [can] learn how to have fun." It is all about "becoming aware. It's about seeing, perceiving, feeling, experiencing more of who I truly am," about "being in the light" and "a part of God."

Five months later in her thesis, which she called *Communion*, Eva documented her "journey of self-discovery." She summarized her view of her sexual or reproductivelike encounters with the beings:

> I have also had several sexually oriented encounters with the Beings. During the process of writing this thesis, I came to understand that the sexual connotation of the experiences was only a metaphor used to enable me to understand certain intrinsic and subtle personal metamorphoses. In reality, the encounters were a collection of diverse communions, Godly and sacred encounters allowing me to touch, experience, and remember additional aspects of my-Self. In one encounter I learned that the impregnation process I experienced (which during the experience itself was full of human sexual behavior) served as a process for the elevation of my conscious awareness into an individuated Being who is on a path of Self-discovery back to God, learning and experiencing along the way wholeness, completion, nonattachment, and most of all, humility.[2]

In summary, that the human/alien sexual and reproductive process appears to result in the creation of a hybrid race that will someday come "down" to Earth is altogether real for the experiencers, who do not in other respects have aberrant ideas or suffer from some sort of emotional disturbance (McLeod forthcoming). But despite the intense conviction of most abductees that they are parents of beings who exist "out there," that they develop symptoms of pregnancy, that small, readily observable bodily lesions exist that seem to reflect intrusive procedures inflicted during abductions, and even that they feel injury to genitals and reproductive tissues or organs, the primary evidence we have to document this reality is the experience, consciousness, and reports of the abductees themselves. On the basis of this evidence, Temple University historian and abduction researcher David Jacobs has come to the ominous conclusion that hybrids or aliens will "integrate into human society and assume control" and that "the new order will be insect-like aliens, hybrids, abductees, and finally, nonabductees" (Jacobs 1998, pp. 251, 253).

But as we have seen, there are problems with this literalist, material interpretation. Most obvious is the absence of solid evidence of actual pregnancy, genetic changes, or the physical existence of the hybrids themselves. But that is only the beginning. Some abductees perceive this process as occurring in another realm or dimension with different space/time qualities and possessing what they often describe as a higher vibrational frequency. Sometimes they themselves notice that they are in a different state of consciousness, as if between sleeping and waking, and that the images and events around them seem "fuzzy." At least one experiencer, Eva, who is quite sophisticated in matters of energy and consciousness, interpreted an important sexual/impregnation encounter in metaphoric, consciousness-evolving, and even spiritual terms. The apparent problems for the hybrids of survival on Earth, which abductees consistently perceive, may in themselves reflect the ontological "otherness" of this whole "project." At the very least, the manifestation of such beings on the Earth plane would require elements of a physics and biology that are now unknown to us.

One may argue that it is mainly a matter of research, of collecting more or better evidence, to document the physical reality of all this, and that the main obstacle is that the aliens are so deceptive, subtle, or furtive. Surely we *should* try to obtain further physical documentation of this process. But it may not be simply a matter of gaining physical evidence. The fundamental difficulty may be more one of philosophy, consciousness, and method. The matter may be more mysterious than we appreciate, requiring different ways of knowing or thinking. For instance, the hybrid "project" itself might be thought of as a reflection not so much of biological procreation or colonization as an expression of an evolution of consciousness.

But in order to consider this, we would need to put aside or overcome the radical split between spirit and matter, or between the visible and invisible worlds, that has dominated both Judeo-Christian tradition and Western science. If we could allow the possibility of an interpenetration of consciousness and matter, or even that physical images, or the physical world itself, could be a manifestation of consciousness or spirit, then the apparent and sometimes real physicality of the human/alien sexual and reproductive process could be seen as the expression in concrete form of a change in human identity or connection in the universe.

This is not to say that the aliens or hybrids are not in some way real. Rather, I would argue that the process might be occurring largely in another realm, one with a different vibrational frequency, a kind of in-between domain—neither pure formless spirit nor dense matter—which, under certain circumstances, can penetrate our world and be perceived with such vividness as to bring intense experiential conviction and even create subtle physical signs on the bodies of abductees.

We saw in the last chapter that Jim Sparks, Andrea, Nona, Karin, and others see the hybrid "project" as a kind of evolutionary insurance program, the creation of a new breed that preserves the best of both species, a form of life that can survive in case we cause the Earth to no longer be able to support human life. But it is also possible that the hybrid "project" may itself be a kind of life-sustaining metaphor-made-real, a response of the creative intelligence to the very serious threat to the Earth's ecology that has become increasingly perilous to life itself. From this point of view, the fact that for some of the abductees with whom we have been working certain of the hybrids themselves seem to be evolving to more whole, viable, and self-aware beings—that is, that the project is becoming more "successful"— could reflect as much an evolution in the consciousness of the experiencers and their facilitators as a literal evolution of the beings themselves.

To say that the reproductive hybrid "project" might not be altogether literally physical does not in any way diminish its significance. But it may exist largely in a realm that can be known through experience and consciousness, a domain that may subtly penetrate or manifest in our physical world but is not primarily of it. If we think of the phenomenon this way, and not simply in terms of whether it is good or bad for the human species, we may see it as less threatening. We might then learn from it about our evolving relationship to the Earth and to the unseen intelligence or intelligences of our cosmos, and ultimately about our own emerging psychological and spiritual existence and identity.

The alien abduction phenomenon appears to evoke in experiencers a rich world of symbolic images that open them to the deepest levels of the human psyche, both individual and collective. They seem to know that this is important, even though initially they may not understand the meaning of these symbols. This provides further evidence for me that it is insufficient to think of the abduction phenomenon simply, or even primarily, as the intrusion of extraterrestrial beings into our world. I will turn now to a consideration of this dimension of the phenomenon.

Part Three

Sequoyah Trueblood (conducting pipe ceremony at tea school in Kamakura, Japan, September 2000) and Credo Mutwa (with cultural figurines in Kwa-Khaya Lendaba, "Home of the Story", South Africa, November 1994). Each of these men has had encounters with humanoid beings that have profoundly affected their consciousness.

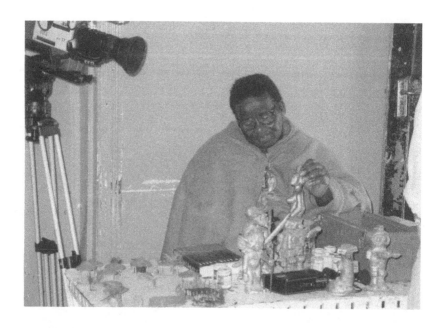

Chapter 7

Shamans, Symbols, And Archetypes

The phoenix seemed ominous and intimidating to Jim, and radiated a blinding light. *It represented power and glory. It was overwhelming. I was spellbound, filled with awe. My heart was racing, and I could hardly breathe.*

Jim Sparks
August 1996

Abduction Encounters and Shamanic Journeys

It is well known to abduction researchers that the humanoid beings reported may first present themselves to experiencers in the form of animals or in other disguises. But there has been little consideration of why this might be so or what deeper significance could underlie this observation. As I have looked into the question more systematically, I have discovered that abduction experiences lead many abductees into a rich and meaningful world of symbols and archetypes that take them far beyond the level of everyday psychological or material reality. This world or language is familiar to indigenous peoples, especially to shamans, native healers, or spiritual leaders, but is less well known to citizens of our mainstream culture unless, like Carol, they have made a special effort to study its forms and meanings. As we noted in chapter 5, abductees come quite literally to identify with native cultures and consciousness (recall, for example, Sue's comment that she came "ultimately" to Native American spirituality to understand the UFO abduction phenomenon), especially because of the close connection tha t people from these societies feel with the natural world in all its forms.

As always in trying to understand the abduction phenomenon, we face the mystery of its source. But when we consider the nature of the phenomenon, it should not surprise us that experiencers are drawn to archetypal symbols or shamanic themes and consciousness.[1] Like shamans in their preparatory training or practicing their art, they are brought by the experiences into nonordinary states of consciousness in which space and time lose their defining power and a world or worlds of nonhuman spirit beings becomes manifest. When experiencers relate to those dimensions, nature and being itself may become sacred, and as we have seen in chapter 5, a sense of reverence and caring for the Earth and its fate, akin to the experiences and perspective of traditional native peoples, may emerge. Further, the altered consciousness and traumatic ordeals that experiencers undergo seem in some ways like the harsh and ecstatic elements of the shamanic journey and its encounters with animal spirits and other levels of reality.

In sum, then, abductees are opened by their experiences to the deeper levels of the psyche and reality, of which their schooling in our culture has given them little knowledge. As experiencers' awareness of these dimensions grows, they may find themselves drawn increasingly to the nature-based consciousness of shamans and other indigenous peoples with whom they feel great empathy. As we will see more fully (in chapters 11 and 12), the process of psychospiritual opening that the abduction phenomenon provokes may bring experiencers to a still deeper level of consciousness where the oneness or interconnectedness of creation becomes a compelling reality and physical form seems hardly to exist at all (see the discussion of Bernardo Peixoto's experience in chapter 8).

As we saw in chapter 5, Nona has been powerfully drawn to shamanism. "I had never studied shamanism at all," she told me, but after several months of exploring her experiences, she realized that the intense bodily vibrations and altered consciousness that she had felt while they were occurring, and also relived during our sessions, was similar in many ways to the states of mind that shamans seem able to enter at will. The abduction experiences have brought her, as in a shaman's journey, to "a raising of our frequency." Nona has compared her experiences specifically to a shamanic initiation. "When you become a shaman," she said, the "initiation brings you to the edge to meet death." Similarly, she says, her encounters also take her "to the edge." As she is "taken out through the window, at that moment it is like meeting death."

More specifically, as we saw, Nona was "taken" in one of her experiences to what turned out to be a sacred place in the rain forest of the Amazon basin. Four months after exploring this experience with me, she met in Boston, as if by some fine design, Bernardo Peixoto, a Brazilian shaman who was becoming a leader in the struggle to mobilize the indigenous tribes of his country, the Brazilian government, and the peoples of the world in a determined effort to save what remains of the rain forest from further destruction (see chapters 5 and 8). She and Bernardo have become friends, "planetary partners" (her phrase) in this struggle, and he invited Nona to come to a huge gathering of indigenous leaders and tribespeople in Brazil that is an important part of this political process. She was also drawn to Carol, an experiencer and nurse, who has made a life study of shamanism.

Archetypal Symbols for Our Time

Several of Nona's encounters have involved tall, thin, dark-haired, and quite beautiful beings wearing a tunic whom she takes to be Egyptian. These beings are especially gentle, and one in particular is familiar to her. On one occasion, she recalled, this figure, who was quite solid ("not like a misty ghost"), lay down over her body yet was somehow outside of her aura, or human energetic field. He put his hands over her, and she was filled with a pure love that was "total" but not erotic. This being held up a golden ankh, telling her "this is the magic." Nona has learned since then that the ankh is an important Egyptian symbol of eternal life.

One night as Nona was anticipating her trip to Brazil, she stood outside with a group of friends and silently asked the stars what she might need for the journey. She does not know whether what happened that night was a dream or a waking vision, but it affected her profoundly. In the dream or vision, the other people saw what they took to be a cloud in the sky, but Nona said, "Watch," for she saw that it was not a cloud but a ship. As the craft came closer, she felt strong energy coming from it and began to rise. The people below gasped, and Nona noticed that whenever doubting or negative words were spoken, she would start to fall.

As Nona flew higher through the trees, her hands seemed to turn to pure light. The people below were running about anxiously, certain that she would fall. She told herself no, but the huge spaceship began to recede, and Nona started to float down. Then an "incredible white horse appeared," and she said, "I'll ride the horse." The people said, "No, there is no bridle or saddle, and you'll die." But she leaped on the horse and held on to its mane, which seemed to be made of cornsilk. Then she and the horse seemed to take off, leaping through the air.

Nona "woke up" then with the thought, "Jesus, all I need to do is ask, and I will be given anything I need to know. If I trust my true self, I can do what I need to do without reins." She felt that this confidence had come from the beings, whom, she said, were "the clearest messengers of Divine Source." She spoke then of how deeply moved she had been that Bernardo Peixoto chose her to attend the gathering in Brazil. It had been "scary," at first, "a sacred trust." Referring both to this opportunity and the dream/experience above, she said, "I'm amazed what happens when you open yourself." The spiritual power and symbolic significance of the soaring white horse seems virtually self-evident. For Nona as in many cultures, the white horse seems to stand for fertility and strength, life and light. In this case it transports her and affirms her potential creative power.[2]

Sue

When Sue and I met in 1994, I had not thought much about the connection between the abduction phenomenon and the initiatory journeys of shamans. But in reviewing the transcript of our meeting, I realize that it contains many of the basic points outlined above, which she seemed eager to convey to me. Sue was drawn by her experiences to read about native cultures and compared them specifically to "the journey of the shaman." For her the experiences were like power or "big" dreams, "dreams that are teaching" or "a vision quest," in which "you put yourself into an altered state."

Sue suggested that the intense light that so regularly accompanies abduction experiences might serve to induce the altered state, much as shamans use drugs, music, rhythms, drumbeats, or even lights for the same purpose. At first she looked upon her frightening experiences as a dangerous "personification of evil." But as in a native healer's vision quest, through her abduction experiences she chose to confront her most intense fears and "demons." She "kept getting tested," undergoing a "rite of passage," which she likened to a kind of "dark night of the soul," until she lost her fears. "That's what this is really all about," she said.

In the first abduction experience that came into her memory, nine years before we met, Sue recalls being awakened twice during the night, first by what seemed like a "tremendous crack of thunder and lightning in the house," and then by the sensation of a probe, something cold and round, passing up her nose, between her eyes, into her head, and then to one of her temples. Feeling a "tremendous pressure" in the center of her forehead, Sue spoke out, "What are they looking for now?" as if the experience were somehow familiar.

The next morning, when she tried to remember what had happened, Sue recalled the sensation of a hand going over her face and of becoming more calm. Then she saw herself going through a long winding tunnel, at the end of which was a soft yellow light. She saw what looked like a triangle with an eye in the center of it and "all these arms, from about the elbow up, reaching up to this triangle—all different color races, black, white, yellow, red, children's arms, adults' arms, and they were all reaching toward this eye in the center of the triangle. I felt extremely comfortable and very much at peace after this." The idea of human oneness or unity represented by the many-colored arms reaching toward this icon was obvious to her, but Sue was not aware at the time of the symbolism of divinity in Christianity and Freemasonry represented by an eye in a triangle pointing up, which is also on the back of a U.S. one-dollar bill.

Although she does not deny the possibility that her body may be taken during her experiences, Sue prefers to think of them as "our way out" of the present impasse rather than as abductions. "The human consciousness is doing this for us," she observes, "because it's telling us, or someone else is helping us. It's a gift, is what it really is, the beginning of our salvation." Whatever is behind the phenomenon, she thinks, "is using things that are going to shake us up most, to get our attention." In the case of our culture, she suggests, the forms are mechanical or technological. There are "universal symbols," she believes, "but each civilization has its own symbols, whatever is in the human consciousness at the time, whatever's most appropriate" or "most easily understood. A scientist working at his machines would probably be more willing to accept the idea of ETs manipulating us physically than an angel coming down trying to say, 'Look, you know, you've got to do something with your world.'" Perhaps, Sue speculates, "these beings and these craft fall into what would be an acceptable [that is, perceivable] phenomenon." In our case "it can't be gods" (as in ancient Greece) because "nobody believes in gods, so what would be the next best thing? Extraterrestrials manipulating us, doing scientific experiments. I think it's a possibility. These may be archetypes, modern-day archetypes."

Alien Encounters and Animal Spirits

Deer, raccoons, cats, panthers, owls, eagles, snakes, and spiders are among the animals that abductees have encountered in their experiences. Often their recollection that the eyes were somehow too prominent or large for the particular animal may give the first clue that another kind of being was represented in this particular form. In our first session, Carol remembered an owl that came down to her from the skies, but with further questioning we found out that the owl hovered close to her face, its wings did not seem to flap, and its "big dark eyes" took up "three quarters" of the head. "This is a mutant owl or something," she remarked dryly.

I asked Bernardo Peixoto whether there was a relationship between the gray alien beings (in his tribe they are called *ikuyas*) that abduction experiencers may initially encounter in animal form, and the power animals that connect the human and animal worlds among traditional peoples. "It is just exactly the same, John, there's no doubt about it," he replied. "When we ask them [the *ikuyas*] in some ceremony that they come and show themselves to us in the form of animals, they do, and some of them come always in the same form to us." For example, he said, "people that have the black panther as the power animal, always when they are doing the ceremonies they see a black panther. That's the same humanoid in the form of a panther." The beings seem to take a form that is familiar to human beings, Bernardo explained— perhaps the animal spirit with which the person is most connected.

He told of the *bacarorro*, a funeral ceremony among his people in which a dead warrior's body is burned and the ashes and crushed bones are sent to friends and relatives so that the warrior's spirit will continue among the living. He remembered a huge fire ceremony when an owl appeared to be perching at the top of a tree. The elders chanted, "*Ikuya! Ikuya! Ikuya!*" Bernardo asked them why they thought the creature was an ikuya and not an owl. They said that, because they were in a trance, they could see light and force around the owl, which told them it was a humanoid in disguise. Also when they shoot arrows at the *ikuyas* disguised as owls, the arrows seem to pass through without killing them.

But animals do not appear to abductees only to disguise alien beings. They may also carry a symbolic power that will become apparent only if the meaning of the manifestation is explored. In one of her experiences, Karin emerged into a black space that contained a huge tree with a great canopy of leaves. On the different branches of the tree, there were large nests with thick twigs and an eagle sitting quietly and peacefully in each one. Karin felt strongly that "I am being shown something." Our exploration of these images was incomplete, but the eagles seemed to represent her soaring higher self, while the nest and the tree related to her maternal, care-taking nature and the power of life itself.

I did not know that Will had ever thought much about totemic symbolism, power animals, or anything to do with Native American consciousness until one day PEER's executive director, Karen Wesolowski, and I were at a sacred place on the bank of the St. Lawrence River with him and a Mohawk Indian woman friend, Marlyn, who invited us to make an offering of tobacco to the river. After we did the ceremony, the sun broke through the clouds, and Marlyn said that this was a response to our offering. Afterward we spoke to each other of experiences, signs, or symbols that had appeared in the sky to one or another of us at certain dramatic moments. Marlyn remembered hearing that a cloud in the form of an eagle feather seemed to manifest in the sky at a significant moment during a Native American gathering in western Massachusetts.

When Marlyn told this story, Will remembered an incident several years earlier, when he was on his way to New Mexico. A friend had given him some tobacco and asked him to use it in a prayer offering. In Taos Will had offered the tobacco and been praying for two or three hours when a voice said to him, "Your name is Wounded Eagle." (Will, we may recall, lost his arm in a freak accident when he was fifteen.) This name was totally new to Karen and me, although Will and I had been meeting for two years. But Marlyn, without hesitation, told Will that his name was Wounded Eagle, and he would soar like an eagle but with one wing.

Although by virtue of having only one arm Will was particularly dependent on his friends and community, his transcendence of the limitations of his handicap, and his sharing of what he had learned through his abduction experiences, was indeed becoming a great gift to a widening circle of people. At the St. Lawrence River, Will was then able to share with us the details of the nearly fatal electrical accident that he had had as an adolescent, which had left him with one arm and a badly scarred hip. A meaningful conversation emerged among the four of us about individual woundedness and healing and its relationship to the wounds and healing that is needed by native peoples and the larger human community.

Spiders

Somewhat to my surprise, spiders appear not infrequently among the images of abductees. Spiders are associated with complex symbolism, representing variously the hub of the web of all creation, the sun and its rays, the Great Mother or moon goddess, the spinners of destiny, and the forces of birth and death. They are also perceived by many people as curiously loathsome and frightening. To Isabel spiders appear to be a disguise that alien beings can assume. She has had "dreams" of "big tan spiders with light brown spots" as big as her hand, "but they don't really look like spiders." There may be hundreds of them all over the room, and they have smooth gleaming bodies "like the shell on a lobster" with "big black angry-looking spider eyes" that cover "their whole face." The largest one has "a huge horn sticking out the side of his head like a scorpion tail."

Once a customer at the pub where Karin was working gave her a two-pound bag of chicken hearts—a gruesome prank that filled her with horror. Not knowing what to do with them, she put the hearts in the freezer, and that night when she went to bed, she felt strong vibrations. Her next conscious memory was of being in a room on a spaceship ("not the medical room") and "this spider was crawling up my arm. I hate spiders," she exclaimed, "and they [the beings] want me to let the spider be there, and I don't want the spider to be there." She screamed for the beings to take the spider off and make it go away, but they kept insisting that it had a right to be there and would not hurt her. "I have a horrible fear of spiders," she said. The battle of wills continued until the thought came to her that it was okay because "spiders were as much a part of God, of the universe, as I am."

Just as Karin was pondering whether the spider was a trick, an image—holographic, perhaps—was shown, as if to test her. "They opened up my chest and took out my heart." She protested violently that that does not happen.

"You don't take out somebody's heart." By this time Karin had done a good deal of self-educating about hearts, metaphors, symbols, and so on, and she suggested to us that this was all a metaphor, "an archetype for all that is love and all things that are life." She went on about the symbolic lesson and how all animals from chickens to cows have hearts. The lesson in "having me look at my heart," she said, was to show her that all animals have hearts and that by caging and killing them, we are robbing domestic animals of the "right to participate in the web [web symbolism again] of life." Native Americans, she said, used to pray over their food every time they hunted and thanked the Earth and each animal for the sustenance it gave—"for giving up its life so that it can be part of life in its afterlife, whatever that means." "Food is sacred. Food is God. Food is love," she said. The customer's act had been a kind of profane event invoking in Karin the true, sacred symbolism and meaning of the heart.

For Sequoyah a spider was an important teacher at a critical time in his life. In the summer of 1987 he was forty-seven and had just completed a year in various North Carolina prisons (see chapter 9), the last of his several incarcerations in federal and state correctional facilities for the possession, transfer, and sale of illegal drugs. Although he had done intense personal healing work, which included yoga, meditation, and psychotherapy, and had worked with native elders to establish a youth healing program on the North Carolina Cherokee reserve, Sequoyah felt "ready at any time to leave this planet and go back to the spirit world." There was a rock on a cliff where he liked to sit, hang his legs over the edge, and look down the valley. One day "I was just letting my mind open, and I saw this spiderweb next to me. I saw this spider working there, and all of a sudden the spider was teaching me, like 'see how intricate these relationships are. That's how the universe is. That's how it is on Mother Earth.'"

The spider seemed to say to him, "How many relationships do you think you destroyed by the way you walked from where the pavement is out through these woods to get to this point? When you leave here and go back, see what you can do to make your way back out without stepping on anything." The spider told Sequoyah he was not walking gently enough on the Earth and to wear moccasins instead of shoes, for the reason his people wore them long ago was so they would walk more respectfully on the Earth. After that Sequoyah began to wear moccasins ("I don't even own a regular pair of shoes anymore") and traditional native clothes, even at meetings at the White House and at a Harvard graduation.

Then the spider said, "Watch me. Watch me," and Sequoyah saw how gently it moved things around in its web, "teaching me about gentleness and the need for that." As he was watching the spider, all of a sudden out of his right eye he saw a shimmering violet light coming up toward him from below the cliff. He soon saw a being, "almost like an insect" with transparent wings, except that it had breasts. "I knew it was a woman, and it had hands and arms, and it just came up right in front of me, hovering right there." Sequoyah knew that this being had come to take him back to the spirit world, "and I knew that when she reached her hand out to me, and was getting ready to touch my leg, that if she did, I was going with her. So all of a sudden I just yelled out, 'No, I'm not ready to go yet,'" and when he did that, the being leaned over "as if to acknowledge that and went back down and disappeared." This experience seems to have initiated, on the part of this native leader, what is at the time of this writing (January 1999) one of the most intense and productive decades of human service that I have witnessed. (Sequoyah's work will be discussed further in chapter 9.)

Alien Forms and the Human Psyche

It is possible, as some experiencers believe, that the form in which humanoid beings appear may depend as much on their own level of consciousness as on the initiatives of the various species "out there" or on alien "agendas" that are independent of the minds of the experiencers. Reptilian beings might appear to those wrestling with dark inner forces; worker-bee-like grays could come to open the psyches of people who are not ready to accept their reality; luminous beings to enlightened folks; and so on. This does not mean, of course, that the experiencer invented, or even summoned, their own sort of alien. The difficulty with this idea, which might have some validity at a subtle level, is its implicit elitism. I even once heard an English UFO researcher declare in all seriousness that only blond Nordic beings—not the homely little grays—visited Great Britain, an absurdity that my own experience there has shown to be patently false.

But it is possible that each of us contains potentially within our being virtually all possible levels of consciousness. The form of a visitation may have something to do with the direction of consciousness of the individual at a particular time in that person's life-journey. Karin was convinced that an unpleasant and frightening encounter with ugly, scaly, lizardlike beings that she had not seen before occurred at a time when she was struggling with "reptilian" energies and feelings toward a rough crowd of construction workers at the pub where she worked—people whose level of awareness she was also trying to raise through sharing her experiences (see also Greg's story on pages 226–227). She drew this experience to her, Karin suggested, because she had been dealing with an angry, frustrated, and judgmental part of herself, and she saw a "resonation" connecting the energy of the people at the bar, "the reptilian things" in her encounter, and negative or rageful elements of her own psyche that she was trying to integrate.

Carol's experiences demonstrate well Bernardo's notion that the aliens assume at first a form or forms that are familiar or comprehensible within the individual's own perceptual background or framework. Although her strong propensities as a healer had drawn her into the nursing profession, Carol had always had a great interest in other cultures and studied anthropology in college. "I'm interested in the way other people relate to this world," she told Roberta Colasanti and me in our first session, and she said that "there are other perceptions on many levels" that are not part of the usual experience of people in our culture. Like indigenous people throughout the world, Carol has become aware of other physical dimensions of reality, which she distinguishes from our familiar material world. Her teenage daughter Cara, whom she describes as highly precocious, has the capacity to enter into an imaginal realm where she experiences herself as being in contact with shape-shifting animals. It is "just another world," she tells her when her mother asks about it.

By the time she came to see me, Carol had read and traveled widely among indigenous peoples and was quite knowledgeable about native beliefs and shamanic practices, which played a major part in her psychospiritual development. She now speaks publicly on these subjects and has a special understanding of the ways of knowing of native peoples, who rely much more on direct experience and the use of altered states of consciousness than do clinicians or scientists trained in the West within a largely materialist worldview.

Carol first consulted me when she came to realize that the troubling experiences she had had throughout her life seemed to conform to what I had written about and did not fit within the framework of her knowledge of ancestor worship, spirit visitation, shamanic journeying, and the like. For Carol, like a number of abductees, owls in particular seemed to play an important part in her personal development, perhaps because they provide a link between the middle world of everyday life and the darker underworld of the shamanic universes. Carol had come to see the owl as her "spirit animal," although her relationship to this creature had certain disquieting features. For one thing owl images would come to her, especially in dreams, in which the eyes were solid black and proportionally too large for the head.[3]

Carol distinguishes three types of dreams: ordinary dreams; "spirit" dreams, which contain the elements of her experiences in the native worlds; and a third, more disturbing kind of "dream." Spirit dreams may involve a spirit guide, and she will wake up comfortably from them in the morning, perhaps with a sense of awe or even shock, but no fear. The third type of dream is different. These dreams, Carol told us in our first meeting, are "extremely intense and realistic," and she will wake up from them terrified, "covered in sweat" and her "heart pounding." These terror dreams, Carol said, really happened, but "they didn't happen in this dimension."

Beginning at about age five, Carol had noticed that her perceptual ability had begun to change, but the first experience that she can recall in which the beings seemed to represent themselves to her occurred when she was about ten years old. Carol was raised as a devout Roman Catholic, but between the ages of ten and thirteen, Catholicism began to lose its meaning for her. Around this time she would wake up sometimes to see a radiant being dressed in a white robe. She had trouble separating this figure from the "cultural images of divine beings" that she was learning about, and she thought it was Jesus, "the guy with long dark hair and dark eyes you see in Catholic churches." Carol remembers that the being would come down the hallway and enter her room, stand next to the bed, and then sit next to her "and communicate without verbalizing." If the being had not had such big black eyes, she might still think it was Jesus. After these experiences she would be very frightened and would wake up her mother.

Carol and I devoted several sessions to examining a particularly vivid and disturbing terror "dream" that had occurred several months before we first met. In this "dream" an owl image played a prominent role. She was lying on a grassy mound or hillside, unable to move as she watched a small speck in the sky that seemed to be spiraling down toward her. She felt a wind, heard a high-pitched buzzing sound, and saw bright light around her. As the object seemed to come closer, it appeared to be an owl, and she felt a mixture of fear and awe. She turned her head and saw what looked to be a typical shaman, with a heavy fur robe and an antlered head-piece. Carol took this to be Cernunnos, an ancient Celtic deity, half animal and half person, that presides over the animals of the forest.

As the owl from the sky came closer, Carol realized that it seemed much too large for an owl—its black eyes were at least four inches across, and it had no other owllike features, such as feathers or a beak. Next she recalled feeling a heavy weight on her mouth and chest, as if a pillow were pressed down upon her, and she had difficulty breathing. Then the experience seemed to "escalate" quickly into a negative one, and she woke up panicked and wheezing, her heart pounding and sweat pouring off her body.

Carol and I went over the same ground in a relaxation exercise that enabled her to relive the experience more clearly. This time the light seemed to be blindingly bright and to have a pressure of its own. The grass was brown and dried, and the ground seemed rough and "very hard." The owl now seemed to be a source of light, grayish white, and without animation. As it spiraled closer, it clearly had no wings and was huge, many feet across. It was the "shaman," standing right to the side of her, that now seemed to have the dark eyes, and she began to cry as she realized that she had been mistaken in thinking it was Cernunnos or even a shaman at all. "He's phony!" she exclaimed bitterly. "He's not what I'm seeing. It's not him. He's not a shaman! He's not Celtic. He's not prehistoric, and I'm uncomfortable and I can't breathe!"

I said I was sorry and encouraged Carol to relax and breathe deeply, as she sobbed more intensely. "Something that was very important to me" and "wonderful" had been taken away. "It's like the facade disappears," she lamented. What seemed to frighten and disturb her most at this point was the seeming impersonality and loss of control. "It's like bringing your cat to the vet," she said—"that wild look that an animal has." She complained further about the apparent betrayal and deception that she felt had been imposed upon her. The "mesmerizing" or "awe-inspiring" scene was not really that way. The "owl" was not an animal at all, and she was no longer outside on a hill. Instead she felt panic in the presence of a familiar being who stood over her "watching and controlling."

The scene then became rather like an operating room in which Carol felt suspended or buoyed, as she was staring into bright light that prevented her from seeing much that was around or beyond her. The owl had given way to this O.R. place or structure. I asked Carol to tell me if she could recall anything further about the being. Mainly she remembered the eyes, which seemed like black "bulbous eggs—maybe that's what was giving me the image of an owl." Later we concluded that she had condensed the image of the being, who was the source of the owl-eyes, with the spiraling object in the sky, which seems to have had some of the characteristics of a UFO.

The experience left Carol badly shaken. She felt that her belief system had been "used" to manipulate her into accepting, and even liking, an otherwise traumatic experience. She observed that it had taken a long time for her to construct her belief system, and that it would be difficult to integrate this experience. Nevertheless, from reliving this incident, she had learned that although "I have experiences that I still feel are relevant to my belief system, *this is new.*"

Over the next few months, Carol struggled to reconcile this experience with her journey as a healer and teacher. Until the exploration of this encounter, she had felt a degree of certainty, even some sense of mastery and control, as she immersed herself ever more deeply in the world of shamanism and indigenous belief. "Before, when I would do a meditation to contact either ancestors or spirits, I was so secure, I was so comfortable, and so confident in that, and now . . ." Now she was faced with something that did not fit into the framework of her knowledge, inconsiderate entities that seemed to manifest according to their own rules rather than by the familiar, traditional methods of initiating contact. She continued to feel anger and a sense of betrayal that these beings, whoever they were, could manipulate, like sorcerers, her perceptions and her beliefs as a way of disguising from her their actual form. "They have an ability to change the way you look at things," she noted.

But gradually Carol came to realize that this was itself a lesson—that her analytic mind, with its "natural aversion" (her words) to experiences outside of her control, and her fear of the unknown, were "holding me back in continuing to explore different spiritual things." She continued to object to "the idea that someone would use your personal spiritual belief to deceive you," and she did not want her understanding to be "usurped by something else pretending to be a spiritual being." But she also came to accept that she was in communication with "something else that was a lot less voluntary." "I now believe in something that I wasn't so sure I believed in before; extraterrestrial if you want to use that term; alien if you want to use that term. There's another party here now."

Carol continued to debate whether this and related encounters were of divine origin—she seemed to want to reserve the word *spiritual* for experiences of a more positive or "higher" nature. "The very word *alien*," she observed, "tells you that it's outside of our world. Aliens don't fit into a spiritual part of our life." Furthermore, she argued, "you wouldn't try and counsel somebody who'd been abused and say it's a plan of God, that you were abused and you're going to learn from this." "But," she concluded, "I believe that any type of experience that is out of the realm of the ordinary does have a purpose." Whatever the purpose of these encounters, Carol concluded that to develop as a healer, "I had to encounter something that I wasn't comfortable with. It was the not knowing that frightened me." She even came to accept to a degree that the beings' use of her belief in shamanism and her faith in spirit guides helped to ease or "mask" what would otherwise have been more disturbing, traumatic experiences.

The "purpose" of these encounters remains for Carol a mystery, although she continued to think it was "important to find the right purpose, not just a purpose." She settled, at least in part, the question of whether such disturbing, intrusive, and even traumatic encounters could be "valid spiritual experiences" by separating in her belief structure the realms of matter and spirit. "They [the beings] may be from a different world," she said, "but they're just as much made of matter as we are." In a presentation at a conference a year and a half after the exploration of the experience reported above, Carol argued that the physical world itself might have many "different levels and dimensions." Abduction experiences, she suggested, might provide a "portal" to "another material realm that coincides with ours" while at the same time having a powerful physical and spiritual impact. Like the people of the Outer Hebrides in Scotland who have contact with seallike entities they call "silkies," greater spiritual heights, Carol suggests, can be reached through interaction with beings "on another material plane" (Williamson 1992).

Teaching Through Symbols

Abductees frequently report that they see or are shown strange writing in the ships, which they assume represents a symbology of some sort that they do not comprehend (Pazzaglini 1991 and 1994). Jim Sparks's case seems unusual in this regard, for his "alien boot camp" experiences have included a rather comprehensive curriculum taught by the aliens mainly through symbols, whose meaning they gradually made clear to him. The aliens, Sparks suggests, "use symbols to establish a common ground of communication." Before each abduction, he has noted, the aliens show him a symbol. Most often it has been an owl, projected into his visual field or consciousness like a hologram. When the owl appears, Sparks writes, it is time to "prepare for school or to learn."

In the ships lessons have been specifically devoted to teaching him the meaning of various complex symbols. He is guided to draw them by an electriclike energy that moves his finger together with the rest of his body. "Symbols," Sparks suggests, could be "a common ground tool for communicating a message between extraterrestrials and humans." Through his experiences he has learned that "certain symbols have the same meaning to us as to them, only it's a faster form of communication."

On one occasion Jim was sitting on an easy chair in his living room in the middle of the afternoon. He was exhausted and had a headache, which he attributed to being "pulled" by the beings the night before. All at once he felt as if his body were surrounded by static electricity, and then he sensed a foul, sulfurous smell like rotten eggs. As if out of nowhere, three marble-sized phosphorescent green balls of light hovered about five feet in front of him. They formed a triangle and floated down onto the top of his coffee table. In the center of the triangle (itself an important universal symbol of eternal life), an image of an owl appeared, and he was "frozen with fear." "*School!* Be prepared for school; that's the symbol for school," he blurted out loud. Then the owl disappeared.

Another time Jim had a strange experience, mediated by symbols, that seemed to be a kind of test of his character. It began when the beings "escorted" him from his car, through a cow pasture, and into a landed craft. Inside the craft he soon noticed a huge red ant crawling around in a circular space, which Jim estimated to be about eighteen inches in diameter. The words *experiment* and *kill* were communicated to him telepathically, and at the same time the word *kill* appeared on a screen on a wall next to a symbol that represented the meaning and power of killing. Then the beings communicated to him telepathically, "*Draw The Kill Symbol To Kill The Ant.*" As Jim protested, air pressure seemed to build up in the room, and his heart began to "race" so intensely, he became afraid he would have a heart attack.

Although Jim knew that drawing the symbol would cause the ant to be killed and thereby bring the end to his pain and discomfort, he refused to comply and shouted that they would never force him to kill anything. Then, while he was still experiencing intense pain and discomfort, a quite tall alien being approached him and "began to stare over the top right side of my head." The being seemed to radiate an intense strength, and "I could feel him probing through to the deepest fiber of my mind," as if he were searching for a weakness. Apparently an area of vulnerability was found, as the image appeared before Jim of his brother in a hospital room clutching his heart and apparently in the throes of dying. (This was not actually happening to his brother.) Jim then believed that by drawing the symbol for *kill*, he could prevent further harm to his brother. When he did so, the red ant instantly curled up into a ball and died, Jim's discomfort was relieved, the cruel image of his brother disappeared, and the alien backed away from him.

The experience left Jim feeling badly shaken and demoralized. He sat weeping and murmured, "Why did you do this to me?" In response he was told telepathically, "We Had To Be Sure." "To be sure of what?" Sparks asked. "That You Are Not A Killer, And You're Not." Then he blacked out, and when he regained consciousness, he found himself back in the car still paralyzed, sitting in the driver's seat with his head "slumped back" on the top of the seat and a sharp pain in the neck. His wife was "asleep" in the passenger seat (apparently "switched off") but woke up when he turned the key in the ignition to leave. Looking at the clock in the car, they realized that two hours had passed. The neck pain indicates that Jim could have been in the car with his head in an awkward position for a long period, perhaps the whole two hours, suggesting that his physical body might not have been taken anywhere.

One day Jim was sitting before a teaching machine in a ship when the light in the room dimmed. Several feet to his left he saw an intensely bright and astoundingly clear image of a steep, jagged cliff, on top of which a large, magnificent bird was perching. The bird seemed ominous and intimidating to him, radiating a blinding light, and he realized "it represented power and glory. It was overwhelming. I was spellbound, filled with awe. My heart was racing and I could hardly breathe." All activity "on board" stopped, and the aliens themselves seemed to stand transfixed with their eyes focused on the great bird, which opened its wings as if ready to fly. Then suddenly it was gone, and activity on the ship resumed as if nothing had happened.

Although the beings would not explain directly what he had just witnessed, somehow Jim learned that the great bird was a phoenix, which symbolized "the species of aliens from all parts of the galaxy and perhaps other dimensions." The phoenix, Jim wrote, is a symbol of great depth, "so deep, it is universal in nature." It represents, he has come to believe, the organized structure or intelligence, including in certain humans, that is "in the process of saving this dying planet from complete environmental destruction." The phoenix is indeed, as Jim has learned, an ancient universal spirit or symbol, carrying great power and meaning for many cultures. It stands, among other things, for destruction and perpetual renewal, for death and rebirth by fire, for gentleness (as it hurts nothing and feeds on no living thing), for gods related to the moon and the sun, for the transcendence of all duality. Finally, it comprises all the elements that make up the entire cosmos.

Symbols of Birth, Rebirth, Death, and Transcendence

In chapter 4, I described a number of instances in which abduction experiencers recalled that tunnels and cylinders of light appeared to contain the energy by which they were transported into the spacecraft. Passage through these tubular spaces also seemed like metaphors, archetypal representations of some sort of birth process. Dave, whom I first met in 1992, has been able to recall consciously a number of abduction experiences in which tubular structures clearly represented birthing canals through which the beings brought both him and themselves back and forth between one dimension or plane of reality and another. In some instances he remembers that these passages were rebirth experiences that followed his death in a prior life. At other times it seemed as if the beings were teaching about interdimensional journeying for the purpose of deepening his knowledge and perspective in this lifetime.[4]

Every night as a child, Dave had the sense that he was not alone and slept with a light on. Sometimes he would ask his parents if somebody had been in the house during the night, which naturally was confusing to them. On a particular night when he was eleven, he remembers going downstairs to check if there was anyone in the house. The next thing he recalls after going back to bed was that he was taken someplace by several beings, along with two other people, a little girl and an older man. He recalls that the beings, whom he could see at that point only as silhouettes, attached him to some sort of machine that took his "inner self" or "inner spirit" out of his body and brought him and the other two people through large transparent tubes, which he estimated to be about five feet in diameter, into "the next plane." Dave estimated that there were hundreds of these tubes, which appeared physically altogether real and were placed on top of one another.

In our session Dave likened passing through these tubes to a birth, especially as there was some sort of fluid inside of them. In the next plane there were no clouds, and they seemed to be surrounded by a kind of "moat" of water. A strong light shone around him, and the beings themselves now appeared luminous and fuller, with light coming into their bodies as if from a source beyond them. Light itself appeared to be the source of life for these beings. Dave described them as like "giants," with "crystal" bodies. They had something like a shield on their chests, and the rest of their bodies, as best he could see, appeared quite narrow. They looked "masculine" to Dave but had very feminine voices. They had big heads with large eyes through which streamed light of indescribably beautiful colors, "more brilliant than I could describe here on Earth." The beings, like himself, Dave observed, underwent a "rebirth" into another plane of reality when they passed through the tubes, changing into the crystalline forms.

The beings would not permit Dave to go further into the light, which seemed to be coming from a great "inner city" of some sort, because, they told him, he was going back to the Earth plane. But even if he were to die today, Dave believes, he would not be allowed to go to this plane of ultimate light, for the beings that go there are of a "higher intelligence." On the middle plane to which he was taken, the beings seemed to be dancing in some sort of "cosmic celebration," which reminded Dave of an Indian celebration he had seen in Boulder, Colorado, when he was eighteen years old. Dave has learned from the beings that they brought him to this plane to show him that there was "life beyond this life," for the Earth was becoming so "contaminated, it won't last" and "the salvation of man" depends on our knowledge of the existence of these other planes of reality into which we will eventually pass.

Dave and the other two people felt a warmth in this other plane, a sense of belonging there, and he did not want to come back to Earth. He described a place of overwhelming joy, without pain, filth, anger, or distrust, an awesome realm where nothing and no one was above another and existence itself was like light. The realization that this was only a demonstration, and that he could not actually fully experience the light, filled Dave with a sense of loss. But he has a strong sense that after death in prior lives, it is into this other plane that he has passed and that he will return to it again when this life is over. He feels certain that "we are transformed back and forth through those tubes" when we die and are reborn, and that the spirit is "transferred" into "a whole different body" when we are born again on the Earth plane.[5]

Dave recalls a smell like burning flesh when the beings attached him to the machine that separated the spirit from his body, which he connects with the fact that the next morning the top of his head was sore. He showed his scalp to his mother, who saw that the skin was indeed burned, and she wondered if he had scalded himself with boiling water or acid. She took him to a doctor, who was puzzled and said that apparently he "did something to it" and told him to call "if it gets worse." Dave showed me the red mark that he still has across the top of his head.

Experiences of this sort make little sense if approached primarily from a literal, material perspective, even though there may be minor corroborative physical evidence, like Dave's scalp burn. But at the same time such experiences may be profoundly meaningful and important, certainly for the experiencer and potentially for our evolving knowledge of reality. The report of this encounter of Dave's contains several examples of the paradoxical phenomenon I have called reified metaphor. On the one hand, the experience is vividly and undeniably real and concrete for him, while at the same time it is deeply metaphoric or archetypal, including representations of death, birth, rebirth, transcendence, and enlightenment.[6]

Experiences like this, as told by individuals like Dave who are of sound mind and are stable members of society, go a long way toward breaking down the rigid distinctions between matter and spirit, body and soul, that were fundamental pillars of my cultural and philosophical upbringing.

From Shamanic to Transtribal Consciousness

A number of shamans with whom I have spoken, from native cultures of North and South America, Africa, and Australia, know of, or have had encounters with, beings that have properties much like the gray aliens that visit abductees in the United States and other Western societies (see chapters 8, 9, and 10). Each culture has its own name for them. According to these shamans, beings of this sort have been around for thousands of years and seem to have a great interest in the fate of the Earth, functioning as its protectors or scavengers, depending on a particular shaman's experience or point of view. There seems to be some agreement among these leaders that humanoid beings are coming more frequently or insistently to the Earth now because, as Bernardo Peixoto says (see chapter 8), "We as human beings in this planet are destroying ourselves" and much of the Earth's life. Even his own people, he feels, "are not really Earth honoring. We love Mother Earth, but not that much." These beings, as in Bernardo's case, seem to have the power to affect the journey, role, and identity of an individual shaman.

Bernardo asked to work with me because he wished to confront the power and meaning of his connection with the *ikuyas* (his tribe's word for beings that resemble gray aliens) which he was having a great deal of difficulty integrating. According to Bernardo, they possess a different energy and a higher standard of knowledge than the ancestor spirits and other beings with which he is familiar and with whom he has felt a degree of mastery (Walsh 1990, p. 9). They bring to him a powerful "spirit force" that he cannot control, and recalling his contact with them makes his body vibrate with a great intensity. His encounters with these beings, especially one of overwhelming vividness that occurred about two years before we met, seem to give Bernardo frightening new powers. His connection with them has brought him so far beyond his previous understanding that he has come to believe "that all I have learned, all the suffering moments of being a shaman—it was useless."

The encounters, as we have seen in this chapter, open the consciousness of the experiencers to deeper levels of mind and reality, a world of images, spirits, and symbols familiar to shamans, to which they may feel themselves inexorably drawn. Even the form in which the beings themselves appear may have symbolic meaning for the abductees, possibly reflecting some currently relevant element of consciousness. Reptilian forms, for example, could be linked with aggressive elements, luminous beings with "higher" levels of consciousness or Self, and so on.

The humanoid beings themselves seem at times to communicate in a language of universal symbols that may be unfamiliar to the experiencer until, as in Jim Sparks's "alien boot camp," they are enabled to learn its meanings. The beings and their UFO-related "props" may seem almost to "possess" the experiencer, appearing to disguise themselves, as in Carol's encounter, through inhabiting the familiar images of the experiencer's knowledge base. This may not, as is suggested in her case, be simply a deception or betrayal. One might also consider that it may be a means that the beings, or the intelligence behind them, utilize to mute the traumatic impact of the intense energies and the shock of unfamiliar images, while at the same time opening the experiencers to the mysteries of the unknown by breaking down the boundaries of their familiar world.

The altered consciousness that abduction encounters bring about resembles in some ways the trance states of shamans, and like indigenous peoples, abductees are brought closer to a natural world that is alive with spirits of all kinds and is increasingly perceived as sacred. Animal images that abductees encounter may, as they do for some native peoples, serve to disguise humanoid beings, but they may also represent archetypal symbols of great power and meaning that can propel them on their transformative journeys. We have seen how a connection with spiders for Isabel, Karin, and Sequoyah, owls for Jim Sparks and Carol, eagles for Karin and Will, and Nona's leaping white horse all possessed deep personal and symbolic meaning that played varying parts in their shifts of consciousness.

Other archetypal symbols, such as the Egyptian ankh in Nona's case and the more universal phoenix in Jim's, represented the eternal love, life, and transcendence that accompanied their transformative processes. Tunnels and other tubular structures appear frequently in the experiences of abductees and represent interdimensional passages or vehicles of birth and rebirth. In Dave's case moisture-filled tubes seemed almost like actual birth canals, representing the means through which both human and humanoid beings undergo birth, death, and rebirth. Encounters with humanoid beings, which are called aliens in the West, may have other names among indigenous peoples and can bring some shamans to a level of consciousness that is transtribal, and even beyond form itself, if they are able to integrate the ego-shattering energies of these experiences.

It is interesting to me that for shamans like Bernardo Peixoto and Credo Mutwa, the humanoid beings, though familiar and considered to be emissaries of some sort from the spirit world, are sharply distinguished from other spirits, like those of power animals or ancestors. While we in the West would emphasize that, if indeed these entities come from the spirit world, they seem to be unique in their capacity to manifest in or "cross over" into our physical world, this is not what the shamans emphasize. For them this crossover is not so important, as they are already able to perceive other entities from the unseen realms in the physical world. Rather, these beings are distinguished by the fact that they are not manageable through the spiritual skills that shamans have learned; by the intense, sometimes overwhelming, energies that the humanoid beings possess and transmit to the experiencer; by the transtribal universalism that they represent; and finally by the direct linkage they seem to have to a divine intelligence that exists beyond symbolism and form itself.

When I visited Brazil in 1994 to study the abduction phenomenon with my associate Dominique Callimanopulos, we were told repeatedly that Brazilians in general, who were somewhat more familiar with the abduction phenomenon than we were in America (at least at that time), also distinguished the alien beings or "ETs" from other kinds of spirits or ancestor beings. The ETs seemed to be more "prestigious" than the other entities, representing "progress" and the future, while the other beings were associated with "more backward-seeming tenets and traditions of the past" (Callimanopulos 1994). We were also told that mediums, when they worked with people afflicted by encounters with ETs in contrast to other spirits or entities, needed many other people to help them in the healing process because of the intensity of the energies involved. As Dominique wrote in her notes at the time, "While popular Afro-Brazilian religions like Candomble and Umbanda prepare the ground, to some extent, for the appearance of extra-dimensional beings, ETs are still viewed as quite distinct and possessing their own very unique level of energy."

In my view the further exploration of the symbolic and archetypal elements that appear regularly in narratives of abduction experiences, and the manifestations of encounters with humanoid beings among shamans and other indigenous peoples, may help us gain a deeper understanding of the phenomenon, whatever its source may be.

Perspectives of Indigenous People

Shortly after the publication of *Abduction*, I began to be contacted by medicine men and other native leaders in the United States who were familiar in their own societies with what I had been finding out about the alien abduction phenomenon. They had sensed my relative isolation and the controversy that the book had stirred. Their purpose in contacting me was to share knowledge and offer support and in certain instances to gain assistance in understanding disturbing aspects of their own encounters. I have been deeply grateful not only for their welcome support and corroboration of my findings but also for the new insights and perspectives that have grown out of my meetings with these special people.

When I asked them why the familiarity of indigenous peoples with these matters was not known in the UFO or academic communities, I was told that the subject is sacred and also that it is difficult enough to be a member of an Indian minority in our culture without being tagged with the opprobrium associated with belief in actual visitations of creatures from outer space. Bernardo Peixoto thought that other anthropologists had not asked him about the association of animal spirits with humanoid beings because they did not know enough about the matter.

Beginning in June 1996 at a conference in the Lakota Sioux region of South Dakota, native peoples have been bringing to the white community some of their knowledge about the role of the "star people" in the origins of their cultures and current lives. This effort has been controversial and risky for them, as there is fear that the information will be misunderstood or misused. But it appears that at least some Native Americans think the potential benefits of this information for bridging the gulfs between red and white "brothers" may outweigh the dangers.

It has been my impression that contact with extraterrestrial or interdimensional beings (native peoples seem to distinguish these from ancestor and other spirits) is frequent among shamans and other indigenous leaders, as if such contacts were part of their training or initiation. Sequoyah Trueblood told me that all of the more than a hundred medicine men and women and chiefs with whom he has talked have had such encounters. I have been encouraging PEER to take on a more systematic study of the forms, frequency, and significance of "ET" contact among native Americans, with the thought that it might yield insights into our own culture and identity.

☆ ☆ ☆

In the next chapters I will tell the stories of three native medicine men whom I have come to know. Each has played an important role as a teacher, both to whites and in his own culture. Two, Bernardo Peixoto and Sequoyah Trueblood, have mixed indigenous and white parentage. All three have had some Roman Catholic upbringing. Sequoyah and Credo were baptized. Each of these men has had encounters with humanoid beings that have profoundly affected their consciousness and identity. But among the three there are also important differences in the nature of their contact and perception of the beings, and in the impact and meaning of the experiences for their lives.

Chapter 8

Bernardo Peixoto

··

When you come from nowhere and everywhere, there is no space and
time. It's like we are trying to adapt ourselves to a new level.

Bernardo Peixoto
May 10, 1998

Background and Upbringing: Bridging Two Worlds

··

B ernardo Peixoto is a shaman and anthropologist of native Brazilian
and Portuguese parents. He works at the Smithsonian Institution
in Washington, teaching individuals and offering classes about
South American native culture, especially about plants with healing powers.
Among his students was Chelsea Clinton, who was particularly interested
in this subject. Bernardo was fifty years old when I met him in 1996. About
two years before we met, he had an encounter, which I will describe shortly,
that dramatically changed his sense of himself and his life's purpose.

Bernardo and I were brought together in November 1996 by Nona
and Carol, who had made a trip to Boston to attend a Whole Life Expo
conference. They were drawn to the seminars and lectures Bernardo was
giving, and when they heard him speak and talked with him, they thought
we ought to meet. Peixoto is a bridging figure, bringing the knowledge of his
people to the North American white culture, while trying to help protect
and develop Brazilian indigenous societies that are being wiped out by the
destruction of their native lands.

Bernardo was born into the Uru-ê Wau-Wau, a small tribe in the state
of Pará in northern Brazil, near the Venezuelan border. Because his tribe
was so small, he was taken to the Ipixuma people, a much larger and more
powerful tribe, to learn their ways and legends as well. Uru-ê Wau-Wau

means, literally, "people from the stars," and their legend tells that "a long time ago" (there is no written language and time is not measured with numbers) a *huskerah*, something from the sky that makes no sound and was not a bird, landed in the Amazon basin, and *makuras*, small glowing beings with large eyes who came from the sky, taught the Uru-ê Wau-Wau how to plant seeds and grow corn.

According to Bernardo, representations of these vehicles and their occupants or *atojars*—which also means "entities that come from the sky" or "people with so much knowledge that they cannot be from Earth"—are engraved on cave walls. To his people, Bernardo says, such beings represent the Great Spirit taking a physical form, because that is the only way they have to understand such matters. The legend continues that after the creation of his peoples, the Great Spirit told the beings from the sky, "Your mission's finished here. I need you somewhere else," and they went away. Bernardo's people, rather like Christians expecting the Second Coming of Jesus, are waiting for the star people to return.[1]

Bernardo's mother was an Uru-ê Wau-Wau, and his father was a Portuguese Catholic. His mother took him to the tribal elders, and they told her that because of his skills, Bernardo must become a shaman. They taught him what a medicine man needed to know and understand, especially about sacred plants, or herbs with healing powers. In Peixoto's tribe shamans deal only with light or healing forces, in contrast to witch doctors, who may do ceremonies that harm people. (In Credo Mutwa's culture, *shaman* or medicine man and *witch doctor* seem to be the same thing, or at least functions of the same individual.) Among the initiation requirements for an Uru-ê Wau-Wau shaman was to lie on a carpet spread with honey that was covered by thousands of big army ants. Needless to say, the ants bit Bernardo unmercifully, bringing tears to his eyes and causing swelling all over, including the testicles and penis. The idea was to establish whether the initiate could endure any amount of pain.

Bernardo's mother was doubly honored. It was a great blessing for her to have carried a son in her womb who would become a shaman, and she thanked the Great Spirit for this privilege. But it was also considered an honor for her to be the mother of a child that was half-white, as it was thought that someday white people would come to respect the native people and their traditions.

Peixoto's father was a Portuguese tradesman who had a store about half a mile from the Uru-ê Wau-Wau tribal village. He participated in the village life but was also familiar with the world outside. When she was dying, his mother said to Bernardo, "You have to learn the white man's ways," for that was the only way "to protect our brothers and sisters," a task to which he has devoted his life. After his mother's death, Bernardo's father sent him to the Catholic Church to be a priest as well as a shaman. He attended a Catholic school for five years, then told his father that he was not fit to be a priest, would like to be a "normal man," and wanted to be an anthropologist. His father agreed, and Bernardo studied at Belém de Pará University, where he obtained his Ph.D. degree.

In Brazil salaries for anthropologists are small, but Peixoto was fortunate to have learned two languages of Brazil and Peru, Tupi and Quechua, and the dialects of many Brazilian tribes, which enabled him to work as an interpreter between indigenous tribes and the government. This was made somewhat easier by the fact that many dialects are variants of Tupi, which is a kind of main language. Working for the government was very difficult for Bernardo, because he would find himself having to get native people to agree verbally to government deals which contained promises that were never kept.

Bernardo had to watch as native peoples were illegally removed from their sacred homelands to make way for businessmen prospecting for oil and other raw materials, while the trees, ancestral homes—everything of value—was destroyed. Many people died before they could return to lands where nothing of theirs was left. Peixoto's life is devoted to reversing these wrongs, especially through the political empowerment of indigenous peoples. In 1990 he came to the United States, where his extensive knowledge of Brazilian and indigenous cultures enabled him to obtain a teaching job at the Smithsonian Institution in Washington, from which he is in a stronger position to understand what is required for him to fulfill his mission.

Bernardo, UFOs, and the Ikuyas

Among his people, Bernardo has told me, the invisible can become visible, and beings residing in the spirit realm can take physical form—indeed, they must do so to be perceived by humans. It is only through beings that manifest in this way that the Great Spirit can be perceived and understood. As he was growing up, Bernardo heard from the tribal elders about little people, *curipiras*, who came from another realm. Among these little people were the *ikuyas*, spirits who take human form in order to be seen. The word *ikuya* is so sacred, Bernardo said, that it could only be spoken in the presence of someone highly trusted.

As Bernardo describes them, *ikuyas* seem very much like the "grays" that are encountered by abduction experiencers in Western societies. But Bernardo distinguishes the *ikuyas* from grays. Like Credo, he sees the grays as troublemakers, less evolved than the *ikuyas*. The grays are the ones who have intercourse with women and create hybrids, and encounters with them can be very traumatic. But the grays too, Bernardo believes, can evolve into beings of light. As we saw on page 148, *ikuyas* can appear disguised in animal form.

I invited Bernardo to take part in PEER's Star Wisdom conference in May 1998, which was to bring together Western scientists, indigenous medicine men, abduction researchers, and experiencers. At dinner the evening before the two-day conference was to begin, Bernardo and I were sitting at a table with several American experiencers. He said very little, but I noticed that he seemed quite agitated. He readily acknowledged later that he was undergoing so much turmoil that his body was shaking, for being with other experiencers evoked the memory of an encounter and the fear of the unknown connected with that incident. When I was lecturing at the conference about the abduction phenomenon, I appeared to Bernardo to be "surrounded by lights, and I knew 'they' were there," he told me. Bernardo stayed at my home during the conference and for two days afterward. He asked if we could have some time together, and the day after the conference ended, we had what turned out to be a five-hour meeting.

Bernardo's purpose in requesting the meeting was to share a powerful encounter that had occurred in Brazil about three years before, and to consider its implications, especially for his role as a shaman. The meeting took place in my office. Bernardo told me that at our last meeting, six months before, he had "tried to really skip" this experience, but he told himself, "Bernie, there is something here that is missing." In the ensuing months he had had dreams in which he imagined speaking to me and chided himself for not having done so sooner. "I am coming here to report," Bernardo said, but "I am only allowed to tell this to people that I love and trust, and you know I love and trust you." He had promised the elders he would tell his encounter story "to the right person," even if this meant the return of a headache from which he had been suffering. Despite this determination Bernardo exhibited considerable anxiety, resistance, and even mild suspiciousness of my motives as we explored his experiences.

In his part of northern Brazil, Bernardo said, stories of sightings of unidentified flying objects are common. Sometimes they are silent, or they may be accompanied by a high-pitched humming or buzzing sound. Shamans have reported talking with entities that come from the sky, and strange women are said to have taken people to places to show them where special herbs grow. Bernardo himself has seen great blue balls of light, moving slowly or very rapidly, close to the water or "swirling over the tops of trees." They may give off so much light, he says, that young girls are embarrassed to bathe naked there at night lest they be seen. The local people, he says, believe these lights are spirits of the rain forest. There is a place, Bernardo says, near the junction of the Río Negro (Black River) and the Amazon River, where no vegetation grows, and such balls of light are said to emerge from a deep black hole in the ground. (For discussion of Nona's association with this place, see pages 104–105 and 144–145.)

As Bernardo began to tell me of his own powerful encounter with what he calls "the humanoids," he became so tense that he reached out to hold my hand for a brief moment in order "to be connected." Several beings, "not as tall as you are," but with especially long arms and wearing luminous shiny suits, appeared on the other side of the Irunduba River. The beings appeared to have a kind of aura or capsule of pure light around them that separated them from the surrounding environment. Nevertheless, they looked quite solid and seemed to move in slow motion, which frightened Bernardo. They were grayish in color, with triangular-shaped faces and pointed chins, "like a dragon lizard." They had "big, big, big eyes" that were black and slanted, and they seemed to be able to see in the dark. He could not make out noses or mouths, but he believed they had at least small ones. Although the faces were "weird," they did not seem "aggressive."

One of the creatures seemed to be a "researcher," a second he called "the engineer," and a third one's purpose seemed to be to make the connection with him. "He was the one that can send the message. He stretched his arm toward me, and I felt that force coming from him." As he did so, Bernardo, still half-asleep, felt compelled to paddle across the river to the beings, then follow them into the middle of the jungle, bring

ing with him a camera, as if he were going on a normal hunting or sight-
seeing trip.

Bernardo asked the beings where they came from, and they told him,
"We come from nowhere," which made him feel very uncomfortable. For
the only way that beings could come from nowhere would be "because they
are everywhere." With this thought Bernardo had the sense of "millions of
molecules being disintegrated in myself," as he "could see clearly we are from
nowhere." The question also bothered him considerably, because according
to tribal mythology his people are descended from humanoid beings that
came from the stars. But beings descended from entities that are nowhere
and everywhere is an altogether different matter.

The *ikuyas*, Bernardo is discovering, are direct messengers of the
Great Spirit, from whom we are all descended, sent to us because we "are
not capable of facing that huge energy" directly. They visit us as humanoid
beings because "the great spirits know that the only way for us to understand things is through forms." Each culture, he said, has intermediaries and
messengers between it and the divine energies. Speaking of coming from the
stars, Bernardo now realized, might be largely metaphoric. The implications
of this idea were staggering for him. "I am more confused now," he told me.
"I have so many doors to open, and I don't know what's the next door to
open. . . . Nowhere. It's like . . . how can we explain nothing? There's no way
to explain nothing."[2]

After Bernardo followed the beings into the jungle, many hours
seemed to pass, and he found himself in the forest lost, tired, and soaked
from rain, which had begun to fall during this time. He could not tell
where exactly he was or where he had been, but somehow he made his
way back to the river, paddled across it, and returned to his shack at about
eleven p.m.

After this experience Bernardo went to the tribal elders, who were not
surprised. "Sometimes we talk to them and call such beings *ikuyas*," they
said. They had always known about the *ikuyas*, for they had been taking
care of the people for thousands of years. The elders took Bernardo to a
sacred cave. It was dark, but they burned wood so he could see engravings,
hundreds or thousands of years old, that looked like representations of
the *ikuyas*. "They come in different forms," Bernardo was told, "like those
balls of shining blue light hovering over the rain forest." His wife, who is
Peruvian, was also not surprised, for such entities had been seen to come

and go in the highlands of Peru. I had the sense that Bernardo had had other encounters with the "humanoids" that he was not ready to tell me. Yet he did say, "I don't know if they come tomorrow, or tonight, or in a couple of months, but as soon as they come, I have to contact you and tell you."

Between Two Worldviews: Becoming Whole

Bernardo has had a good deal of difficulty reconciling his indigenous shaman and white Ph.D. selves. "I don't see any intercommunication between them," he remarked during our long meeting. This conflict was evoked powerfully by his encounter with the *ikuyas* and was brought into sharper focus by our exploration of it. As a shaman Bernardo felt relatively secure and competent in a world of healing tasks and embodied spirits whose characteristics were familiar to him within the indigenous communities in which he had lived and worked. His extensive studies of the dialects and cultures of these peoples supported his role as a medicine man. The creation story of descent from humanlike star people was well established in his tribe and part of a familiar mythology involving concrete entities with known forms.

But this encounter with the *ikuyas* disrupted Bernardo's worldview, frightened him, and brought him to the edge of the unknown. My task, it seemed, was to help him understand the implications of this encounter and to reconcile the disparate parts of himself. In one sense his indigenous world could be more accepting of his encounters with humanoid beings. "With my people back in the jungle, I had no struggle," Bernardo said, for they interact every day with entities that are unseen, at least to nonindigenous people. But his white relatives mocked him when he spoke of these beings. A sister-in-law, for example, called him "my alien brother-in-law." "I don't want people laughing at me," Bernardo said. Even for him in his "different role as a white man," the experience he had had was "abnormal." "Sometimes I think I am going crazy," he told me.

The experience by the river raised difficult, complex questions for Bernardo. In a world of concrete places, images, and forms, it is natural to think of descent from beings who come from the stars. But how would he explain to his people the idea of entities that exist nowhere and everywhere? Indeed, if these beings came from nowhere and were everywhere, then perhaps *all* of us were descended from them. Furthermore, as

Bernardo realized, it would be difficult to understand and teach about beings who seemed to exist in a realm or realms without the properties of distance or time, whose existence and powers seemed to go "far beyond" even what he had learned of physics. Also, his encounter(s) seemed to give him healing and intuitive powers that frightened him, for he had not learned them in his training and experience as a shaman. Even the energies he felt in his body that he related to the encounter(s) were intense and disturbing. "I feel myself" to be "a tiny little vessel holding more energy" than it can, he told me.

In order to enable Bernardo to address the sense of division within himself and to integrate his encounter with the *ikuyas*, we did a relaxation exercise in which he entered a mild trance state. In that state Bernardo found himself transported to the rain forest of his native land and was with his deceased mother and other native people. He was torn in his heart between the two worlds in which he lived, and he felt the conflict painfully in his body, for it is in the body, he said, that "the soul dwells." In the nonordinary state, Bernardo felt himself to be "pure essence" or soul, and death did not exist. Like the *ikuyas*, he could transport himself "nowhere and everywhere." Although such a world was not part of his daily existence in white societies, the realm he entered in the trance state seemed to him to be "true reality."

After we did this work, Bernardo said that he felt "more comfortable with myself, like I have released a bunch of pressure that was going through my body." Most importantly he seemed to be better able to balance the indigenous and white parts of himself, "to integrate the extraordinary experience [the encounter with the *ikuyas*] with my daily life," and to "adapt myself to a new reality." In sharing with me in the way that he had, Bernardo felt "I am opening my heart for the first time." But he remained somewhat afraid, "facing the unknown." He felt "like a little-boy toddler that doesn't know how really to walk," as he began to accept living in a world where there were things "far beyond my comprehension," including encounters with beings from nowhere and everywhere from whom, he suspected, we are all in some fundamental sense descended.

Protecting the Rain Forest and Its People: Spreading the Prophecy

Bernardo's primary purpose, furthered by his encounter(s), has been to protect his people and their lands. "The people are dying, wiped out," he said. They are being devastated by the destruction of "Pachamama" or Mother Earth, as a result of industrialization, cattle farming, and ecotourism. Fires lit by farmers seeking to clear the land for cattle burn out of control, for the land is already parched from the cutting down of the forests. Animals are killed wantonly. Bernardo has seen hundreds of dead alligators floating upside down, killed by Japanese, American, and German tourists in boats, using rifles with telescopic lenses. They shoot any kind of animal, including birds, and then take pictures of themselves with what they have killed. But as a bridging figure between native peoples and the white community, Bernardo recognizes that he has an educational and political role that extends beyond the indigenous communities. He seeks to stop the devastation by increasing awareness of our essential connection with the earth and sky and by mobilizing concern for the Brazilian rain forest and its life nationally and internationally.

To further this purpose, Bernardo has organized a giant ingathering of tribal leaders and members, to be attended also by selected whites, which is to be held in northern Brazil. The purpose of the meeting is to unify native Brazilian peoples, increase awareness on the part of both Indians and whites of the ecological peril the region faces, and to mobilize political will and power to change course. The conference has been twice postponed because of flooding that made access to the site too difficult. This flooding is itself the result of poorly conceived land use that has made the ground incapable of holding large amounts of water.

Bernardo faces an acute dilemma, for the process of political empowerment of native peoples, which may be essential for their survival, will itself create contacts with the outside world that undermines their cultures. This conflict may apply even to the sharing of knowledge among native peoples, as the following story illustrates.

In 1997 Bernardo was asked to consult for the Krenacroro, a remote tribe living in peace upriver from his own, in a place that could be reached only by arduous traversing of canals. These people, unlike Bernardo's own, seemed unfamiliar with star people or flying saucers. A woman from this tribe came to his shack—a journey requiring three days—carrying small gifts and spoke to him urgently: "We know your people come from the stars. Can you come tomorrow to our village?" Many Krenacroro people had experienced things that frightened them. For several days and nights, they had seen objects that seemed to come from the sky, including balls of light with different colors, a huge *penebialpa* (the Krenacroro word for "something that is there but unknown"), and strange people by the river that appeared to float over the surface of the river grass.

Bernardo felt conflicted about what to do. He wanted to go, and it would have been rude not to. But the Krenacroro lived in an area so unspoiled that they had not seen TV, read a newspaper, or been in touch with white people. The woman who contacted him did not know a single word of Portuguese. But it was a rare opportunity for him to build a bridge between Brazilian tribes of the Amazon, and the people were frightened and clearly needed help. At the same time, however, he feared that this initial opening might lead to exposure to the media, to ecotourism, and to other forces of the outside world that might eventually destroy the integrity of the Krenacroro culture and exploit it.

Bernardo decided to make the journey. An American wanted to go with him, take pictures, and write a story. But Bernardo told him that "they don't want white people there" and chose to go alone. The journey required crossing the territory of the Yanomami people, known for their fierceness. But he arrived safely, and when he reached the Krenacroro, he counted eighty-three people, ranging in age from five or six to quite elderly, all of whom told more or less the same stories. "'Your people are coming,'" they said, for they had heard the legends of the Uru-ê Wau-Wau, who considered themselves to be descended from the stars. They thought the balls of light were *Apus*, forest spirits or deities. One man took Bernardo by canoe to the place by the river where he had seen a shiny *penebialpa* many, many times the size of his shack, which seemed to have many fireflies of tremendous force at its bottom. The object would seem to come closer, then fade away and disappear without a sound. The man was frightened and covered his head with leaves. He had been unable to sleep for three days, he said.

A woman and a child told Bernardo that they had seen a man who did not talk, with huge eyes like a "big, big owl" and skin color different from their own. Despite their fear the tribespeople had felt love coming from the strange beings. As Bernardo spoke with the people about what he knew from his own knowledge and experience, the Krenacroro seemed to understand and became less frightened. "They felt so good. Everything is okay.

They are in peace. Nothing is wrong." But Peixoto remained concerned that the contact might begin a process that would harm them. Gilberto Macuxi, another native leader who knew of Bernardo's journey, was bothered about it. "Now there's another man that knows, and pretty soon, who knows?"

Bernardo's encounter(s) with the *ikuyas* have played an important part in the expansion of his awareness and his sense of the scope of his responsibilities. The *ikuyas* are closer to the Great Spirit than we are—"messengers," he says—and their nonlocal nature relates directly to his broader definition of his purpose. As in the case of Yahweh in the Bible, he says, the energy of the Great Spirit is "too much for us to take," so messengers, like angels, are sent to help us understand. The *ikuyas* are coming now "because they are conscious that we as human beings in this planet are destroying ourselves, and they love us and wouldn't see this happening." The *ikuyas* come and go, appearing in forms that are familiar to us, he continues, and they "attach" to certain people. "But they don't want to impose on us," he suggests. The *ikuyas* and other *apus* are on another level and bring knowledge and understanding, he says, especially of our connection to each other and to the Earth and of the fact that "we are just one part of a big, big whole."

Bernardo believes that the *ikuyas* are coming at this time because we are at the end of the sixth *pachacuti* (five-hundred-year intervals of prophecy, in which a number of indigenous peoples in South America believe) and are beginning the seventh. The *ikuyas* are "the messengers in this planet to spread this prophecy" and are showing themselves more frequently and with greater intensity, he says. The time we are entering is one in which obstacles to change will fall away, and space and time will seem not to exist. It is a time "when the condor and the eagle are going to fly together." The condor is of the South and is seen at the top of the Andes. It is a bird of prey and eats carrion, cleans up, and is very "environmental." The eagle is from the North, an aggressive killer, and until now it has forced itself upon the South. The condor represents the knowledge of the South, and the eagle the power of the North; the time has come for them to cooperate and learn from each other.[3]

Bernardo perceives that we in the West are becoming more open to gaining knowledge from "the other world." Barriers between people will be broken, he says, "so there's no difference between an indigenous man and a doctor here in Washington, D.C." It is important, he says, for people who have had interdimensional encounters to share them with other experiencers, for it is painful to be alone with them. When he talked with people who could understand his experiences and discovered he was not alone in his fear and knowledge, he felt much better. "Who wants to talk about these issues? It's not easy." He feels certain that the further we get away from the "great, great power," the more the *ikuyas* will be present.

All his life, Bernardo told me, has been spent learning the dialects of the various Brazilian tribal cultures. But the experience with the *ikuyas* has brought him to the realization that "we are just one," there is no separation, and "when you come from nowhere and are everywhere, there is no distance" and "no space and time." "It's like we are trying to adapt ourselves to a new level," he observed. This "new level" might be thought of as "transtribal" (my term). Shamans like Bernardo Peixoto, changed in part through their encounters with humanoid beings, are moving into a wider leadership role in which they are able to forge connections between the traditional knowledge of indigenous peoples and the challenges facing the dominant Western worldview. Bernardo once asked the *ikuyas* why they have such big eyes. "To see more than you can see," one of them replied. "We need to learn to see as the *ikuyas* do," Bernardo now says.

Chapter 9
Sequoyah Trueblood

....

Our youth are experiencing tremendous hurt. They feel abandoned,
unloved, and cast-off from their families and communities. Since
they can no longer trust adults, since they can no longer get their
questions answered, they turn to drugs and alcohol in a misguided
attempt to ease the pain and obtain some comfort in their lives.

Sequoyah Trueblood,
letter to Judge Michael Vigil
on behalf of a Navajo teenager
February 3, 1999

"Another Face of Spirit"

....

Sequoyah Trueblood was fifty-six when we met in May 1997. With
his long white hair, craggy features, erect stance, and simple, fine,
colorful native clothes, he looks the part of a distinguished native
elder. Sequoyah and I were brought together by a mutual friend who was
studying Native American spirituality. She told me that he had a lot to say
about "ETs," and Sequoyah, who had taught and taken graduate courses at
Harvard, was glad there was someone in Cambridge interested in helping
people to understand such matters.

Sequoyah's mission is to help people, red and white, transcend pain
and suffering and discover "who we really are in spirit." Pain and suffering, he believes, have come about because human beings decided they
could run the universe better than the Great Spirit and turned "their
backs on the original instructions of the Creator." He lives and works as a

teacher and a bridging figure for the peoples of Turtle Island (North America), between "the people of the straight line" (Western whites) and "the people of the circle" (Native Americans). He says he was instructed by spirit to help me, and he wrote in a proposal for a book he plans to write, "Native peoples who are aware of our true relationship are happy that John Mack is bringing this face of Spirit called 'extra-terrestrial' to the people, and we want to support him."[1]

Sequoyah is an enrolled member by blood of the Choctaw nation and is also part Cherokee and Chickasaw. The bear is his main totem, he says, for the bear is big and powerful but can teach us about gentleness too. He can also heal himself from terrible wounds that would be mortal for the rest of us. Sequoyah's spirit name is Awh-Awh Naw Sui, meaning "brings light." The name is associated with the raven, which in some native legends is thought to bring light out of the darkness to Turtle Island. Sequoyah's mother is German-English, and although his father is Native American, he turned away from those teachings at a young age. Like Bernardo Peixoto, Sequoyah had a Catholic upbringing, and he was even baptized in the Church and given the name Stephen, so that he grew up as Steve Trueblood. Like Bernardo's people, the Cherokee and Lakota/Dakota believe that they are descended from star people, specifically from the "seven sisters" constellation or Pleiades. "Extraterrestrial" landings and interactions are commonly spoken of by native peoples, Sequoyah told me.

Sequoyah has led a remarkable, inspiring life. As a child and youth, he was brutalized physically, mentally, sexually, and spiritually. As a U. S. Army officer in Vietnam, he became addicted to amphetamines and used heroin, and he later served prison terms for possession and transfer of illicit drugs. I hope that when he tells his own story, Sequoyah will write about criminal government activity related to trade in illicit drugs in Southeast Asia.

On several occasions, Sequoyah believes, his life has been saved, seemingly miraculously, by protective beings that seemed always to be there when he needed them. As we shall see, he connects these entities to beings that were involved in an important journey to another reality. "So-called extraterrestrials," Sequoyah says, are but "another face of spirit, just as are we sacred two-leggeds."[2] "I define *spirit* as the mind of God in motion here on Mother Earth," he says. "Spirit can manifest any form it wants to, and the star people are spirit made visible too just like we are. These [our] bodies are just the way that the spirit has chosen to do it here on Earth."*

It was not until quite late in his life that Sequoyah became knowledgeable about native ways and ceremonies. Native ceremonies and rituals play an important part now in his efforts "to help our Brothers and Sisters recognize the true nature of our existence here on Mother Earth."[3] Friends, colleagues, and I have been with him in healing circles and sacred pipe ceremonies. We always know when Sequoyah is in our home, for the house smells wonderfully of burning sage. Despite his age and the physical pain and stress of having his body pierced, Sequoyah has participated several times in recent years in the sundance, the most powerful and important of all native ceremonies, which was outlawed in the United States until the 1970s.

A Traumatic Childhood

Indians, Sequoyah says, were considered less than human in the 1930s and 1940s, when Sequoyah's mother married one, and his grandparents, who lived on a farm in Oklahoma, were intensely disapproving of the union. Sequoyah's mother was sixteen and his father seventeen when Sequoyah was born on a small farm near Stroud, Oklahoma, on December 15, 1940. Sequoyah tells that as his mother was going into prebirth contractions, she heard a barn owl hoot four times. She experienced intense fear and walked barefoot across the fields in a blinding blizzard to the home of a friend, where he was born.

His parents drank heavily and fought even before he was born, and Sequoyah believes that "in my mother's womb I was experiencing everything my mother experienced." They all went to live for a time on the grandparents' farm. He can recall clearly how he would hide in a gully outside the farmhouse to avoid the violence that would erupt among the adults, and how his German grandmother would put a pillow over his head and sit on him to stop his crying. When he was two and a half, she

---

* Similarly, His Holiness the Dalai Lama, in a meeting with a small group in 1992, remarked that the aliens too were "sentient beings" in the universe, though apparently troubled by what is happening on the Earth (personal communication, April 15).

succeeded in running his father off the farm, and Sequoyah was told that he was killed in an automobile accident.

Through much of his childhood, Sequoyah experienced physical and sexual abuse at the hands of his maternal grandmother and his alcoholic parents, as well as in Catholic schools. It was in childhood, Sequoyah wrote on a fellowship application to Harvard, that "I learned about rejection, abandonment and loneliness." His childhood experiences left him with a fear and distrust of women, which stayed with him for many years. He can still hear sometimes the words he heard daily and the shame he felt when he was told that he was a lazy stupid Indian and would never amount to anything. But in the summers he would live in a tent with his brother and paternal grandmother, who taught him the use of medicinal plants.

When he was fourteen, he met an uncle there who ran a gas station, and he told Sequoyah that his father was still alive and that his Indian name was the same as his father's—Sequoyah, which is also the name of the great Cherokee Indian leader who created the first system of writing for a Native American language (Mankiller and Wallis 1993, pp. 81–83). He did not use this name until he was in his forties, partly because he thought it sounded like a girl's name. As of 1997, Sequoyah's father, himself a healer, was retired on an Indian reservation near Ponca City, Oklahoma. He was divorced from Sequoyah's mother and remarried several times. In November 1998 Sequoyah visited his father, still healthy in his mid-seventies, for the first time in fourteen years.

The adjustment to the new school was difficult for Sequoyah, and he skipped classes often to be by himself in the woods. He would look at the skyand feel comforted, as he had as a young child, in order to escape his fears and to feel more secure. When he was fourteen years old and a sophomore in high school, he saw a pleasant-looking man on a trail who said to him, "Don't worry, Steve Trueblood, you're being taken care of." Then the man disappeared, but this experience has "traveled with me vividly through my life."[4]

One time when Sequoyah was still a teenager, he went duck hunting with a man and two women. They spent the night in a small duck blind supported by fifty-gallon barrels on a frozen lake. As he watched the sun coming up, the structure flipped over and he was trapped underwater, while the man and one of the women managed somehow to make it safely to shore. Sequoyah remembers that at first he panicked, but then "a soft gentle feeling came over me," and a voice told him that it would be all right, that it was possible to "go beyond this thing called death" and that he would have "all kinds of extraordinary experiences that would go against the normal grain of thought." He also saw that he would get married, go to war, confront atrocities, join with his native relatives, and be always around other beings that he might not be able to recognize. When he "popped up out" of the water, he saw the second woman, who could not swim, sitting on top of one of the fifty-gallon barrels crying. She told him that he was underwater for ten minutes, and she had been certain he was dead. But he did not even feel cold and was able to push the barrel and the woman to where the others could pull them to shore by a rope.

When Sequoyah was seventeen, he got his girlfriend, Patricia, pregnant, and with the help of a priest, they eloped to Texas and were married to avoid the wrath of her father, who threatened to kill him. He and Patricia were to have four children in all, born in 1958, 1961, 1964, and 1967. In 1958, before he was eighteen, Sequoyah joined the army to escape the pain with which Oklahoma had become so indelibly associated.

A Green Beret

Sequoyah's twenty-three years in the army contain in themselves a larger-than-life story of great military, political, and psychological significance, which I am hopeful he will soon tell in detail himself. (Some of it is documented in Perry 1986.) In what follows here, I will sketch in only those facts that are essential for appreciating Sequoyah's spiritual journey and transpersonal encounters.

In the army Sequoyah's high intelligence, language skills, and effectiveness with people soon became apparent, and his outstanding performance in college-level courses (perfect grades in some of them) resulted in his being selected for various leadership assignments. He was assigned to an elite Green Beret unit and in 1967 he was promoted to captain and sent to Okinawa with his wife and four children, where he served as executive officer of the Special Action Force Asia in a Green Beret combat center, training multicultural reconnaissance teams for "insertion" into countries in Southeast Asia. It was at this time that Sequoyah began using amphetamines to help overcome the long hard hours of training. Although the military officially denies that such drugs were used other than for legitimate medical purposes, they were apparently freely dispensed to enhance effectiveness, especially to enable the men to stay awake for several days at a time. As one Special Forces combat expert put it, "You had to stay awake. You had to stay alert. What else were you to do?" (Perry 1986, p. 11). Naturally many, like Sequoyah, soon became addicted.

Vietnam, Addiction, and Arrest

In the years that followed Sequoyah was assigned to many secret dangerous reconnaissance missions, which were approved at the highest level. Many of the men for whom he was responsible were killed, and he witnessed atrocities committed by U.S. forces against enemy soldiers and Vietnamese civilians.

Several times in Vietnam, Sequoyah survived, again seemingly miraculously, in situations where it seemed almost certain he would be killed. Sometimes he seemed to be spared while his comrades were slaughtered around him. Once he and another officer were surrounded in a clearing by twenty-five or thirty North Vietnamese Sappers (their equivalent of the Green Berets). But as they reached for their guns, the Sappers were frozen in place. Their hands went up, and they never touched their weapons, so that the two Americans were able to walk out of the clearing. In each of these incidents, Sequoyah says, a translucent being, with the shape of a human body, said he would be protected. He was becoming acquainted with death, the being said, for there were things he had to experience so he could understand life. This was as real to Sequoyah "as the two of us being here together."

As the months passed in Vietnam, Sequoyah began to think increasingly for himself and came to realize that he was witnessing or causing the death of "my brothers over a philosophy that was not mine and that I did not agree with."[5] Late one evening during a planning session, his Green Beret camp was attacked by North Vietnamese soldiers. As two of the soldiers were overrunning his position, Sequoyah fired at them. He could see in slow motion the bullets coming out of his gun, entering and flattening the heads of the two soldiers, who fell dead at his feet. With the help of an interpreter, he went through their wallets "and found exactly what I had in my wallet," pictures of loved ones and letters from them praying for the men's safety.

For Sequoyah this experience was devastating. He broke into uncontrolled sobbing, and hours passed before he knew where he was. He was brought out of his trance state by a luminous being standing near him, "and I could hear the words 'you're being taken care of; you'll be all right.'" After this, although he was involved in many intense combat actions, he never fired a weapon again and sometimes entered fire fights without a weapon, knowing he would not die and that "I was being watched over and taken care of."

Another part of Sequoyah's Vietnam experience involved his exposure to U.S. government trafficking in illegal drugs. Sequoyah, confirms Mark Perry, "was privy to some of this country's still kept military secrets." His lawyer at that time in Kansas City, where he was in jail, later said, "I think Steve knows a lot more than people think he should" (Perry 1986, pp. 10–13). In addition to all of these stresses, Sequoyah says he was shot down in one airplane and twice in helicopters. During the months in Vietnam he was becoming increasingly addicted to government supplied "super amphetamines," opium, and alcohol. "The drugs were essential if you wanted to stay alive," he told Perry. By the time he returned to the United States in January 1970, Sequoyah was severely addicted to amphetamines and opium and had had at least three psychotic episodes in Vietnam, treated with huge doses of thorazine (an antipsychotic medication).

Sequoyah joined his family in Maryland, but he felt "like an explosion getting ready to happen." For nine years between returning to the United States and his arrest, conviction, and sentencing for twenty-two months in the federal penitentiary in Leavenworth, Kansas, for possession, sale, and transfer of cocaine and marijuana, Sequoyah continued to function well, sometimes in highly technical and top-secret assignments in Maryland, Texas, North Carolina, and Korea. He even received further commendations from the U.S. Army and the Korean government (Perry 1986, p. 11). But his condition was deteriorating, and he attributes his survival and ability to finish his jobs during this period to the protection of luminous beings that were watching over him. Although he believes he was set up and falsely accused of being an international drug dealer (details of the "sting" are provided in Perry 1986, pp. 11–12), in the end Sequoyah welcomed his imprisonment as an answer to his prayers, for "all I was was a junkie," and now "I could finally get the drugs out of my life."

A Journey to Another World

The only "full-fledged" abduction experience that Sequoyah recalls occurred in July 1970, shortly after he returned to the United States from Vietnam. It might be argued that his encounter experience is somehow related to his drug addiction. But this experience, although in some respects not typical of the "classical" harsh abduction accounts, was consistent with his relationship to the spirit world in times when he was not suffering from his addiction problem. Furthermore, he says he was not taking drugs or alcohol at that particular time. Sequoyah's abduction experience must be seen in the context of his view of the UFO and abduction phenomenon itself, which I will summarize here from what he has said in many conversations. His view is quite different from that of most researchers in our culture.

Unlike some native people I have met with, Sequoyah does not distinguish the beings who he says took him into a spacecraft from the guardian spirits that have guided and protected him all his life. The use of the word *extraterrestrial* by whites, Sequoyah believes, is just another expression of our separation from spirit. There are many other planets, stars, and universes, populated, he believes, by a virtually infinite number of beings. Such beings are always among us and become visible in humanoid form so they can interact with us and bring us back to Source (see chapter 12). The form in which spirit chooses to manifest on any given occasion—as human, humanoid, or animal creature, for example—is itself a sacred mystery.

According to Sequoyah, we are all in a sense extraterrestrial, for star beings took part in the creation of the human species and have always been our teachers. Because of the perilous state of the planet, they are showing themselves more and more now to those who will acknowledge their presence and share their teachings. The general population, especially the educated elite in Western societies, is not ready to accept fully the presence of these beings and hear their messages. "Your study of psychiatry," he said to me, and my work with abduction experiencers, is helping to prepare people

for the understanding and acceptance "of what we call UFOs and extraterrestrials" and the messages that they are bringing us. Spacecraft are a very
rudimentary sort of travel. Sequoyah says the time will come when such
vehicles will not be necessary and we will be able to "travel anywhere as spirits." The so-called aliens have already mastered a way to materialize instantly
from millions of light-years away, Sequoyah says.

On July 4, 1970, Sequoyah was sitting by the swimming pool of his
townhouse in Laurel, Maryland. He was watching his children swimming
and his wife was sitting next to him when, without knowing why, he got
up, went into the house, changed his clothes, packed a small bag, got in his
car, and drove to the Washington/Baltimore airport. He took a plane to
Oklahoma City, where he called a friend, who drove him to another friend's
house in Norman. He felt a little strange at the time and asked to lie down
on a bed to rest. The man took him to a bedroom, where he lay down and
began to breathe deeply to relax. Then he saw a kind of vortex of swirling
lights "like a rainbow," into which he was sucked. I asked him if anyone
observed him to be unexpectedly missing from the house in Norman, but
he does not recall that he asked or that anyone said anything. He has not
had further contact with this friend.

Sequoyah then found himself standing in a beautiful garden surrounded
by hedges. He was now wide awake, "no different than me sitting right
here with you now." In front of him was a silvery saucer-shaped craft and a
shimmering small silver-looking being standing on steps that were coming
down from the bottom of the craft. The being looked grayish and had a
large bald head with large eyes, and Sequoyah sensed it was "androgynous,"
neither male nor female. The being communicated telepathically that it was
from "another place" and had been sent to take him there because "they"
wanted to talk with him. Sequoyah felt calm and relaxed, "as though I had
had these experiences before (I now know that I had) and that it was no
different from going to see the neighbor next door." He agreed to go, and
walked up the steps with the being into the craft.

Once inside the craft, Sequoyah heard no sound, but through a small
round window he saw the moon, the sun, and "millions of stars" instantly
go by. Then they were hovering over a beautiful white city in what he felt
was another planet in another realm or universe. "As a North American
Indian, our legends and oral histories are replete with such occurrences,"
he later wrote.[6] Getting down to the ground occurred in an instant and

seemed like "dematerialization and then rematerialization," Sequoyah recalled.

The people in this city appeared to be male and female, wore white robes, and were fair skinned, with "hair that was glowing like the color of sunlight." The androgynous being took Sequoyah down a street lined with beautiful white buildings not more than three stories in height to a clearing in the woods that seemed like a park. There were a number of people there, and a male said to him that if he would "pay attention," he could see that the people there were living in harmony without war or disease. The energy seemed different than on Earth, and there was no sense of time. Sequoyah was told that the beings had done something to him to enable him to be there and breathe. The people said that they did not need food, for the air they breathed was converted into whatever was needed to sustain life.

Sequoyah was told by one of the men, a kind of leader figure, that he had been brought to this place to be shown the potential of the human race on Earth, and that he would be reintroduced to his native heritage and "be involved in teaching, first the native people and then our brothers and sisters of other races, about the great peace and love that fills all creation. All the events of my life were preparing me for this task." He was also told that a lot of the experiences of his life were to help him overcome fear, and that he would have to endure many more difficult experiences before he would have the awareness and strength "to consummate this service to humanity."[7] The beings told him that they had been with him as a child and in Vietnam, that he had been "guided through the hallways of death," and as he had heard so often in the war, that he was being watched and protected.

Sequoyah saw that some sort of marriage, or what they called a "joining" ceremony, was going on, with men and women by a table with flowers all around. The reason marriages did not work on Earth, he was told, was that there was too much effort to control and manipulate, but that here people just decided to spend their time together. Sequoyah was asked for his blessings. He felt totally immersed in this blissful place and was told by the leader that he could stay for awhile if he wished.[8] At that moment he became panicky as he realized what he would have to leave behind—family, car, home, possessions. "I almost went into a psychosis, for this was my first lesson in realizing how attached I was to the material world." "This is one of the big problems on Mother Earth," they told him.

"You're only here temporarily. These bodies of yours are just tools that you've been given to learn with," and attachment to them was the source of pain and hurt.

As soon as Sequoyah said he wanted to return, he was again in the craft and saw the stars, sun, and moon go by until he was back in the garden with the androgynous being outside the spacecraft. He was told that they would come back for him later. Then he went again through the vortex, and "clunk," he was back on the bed in the friend's house, feeling well and rejuvenated.

This experience affected Sequoyah's perception of everything that happened to him afterward, even though he reverted "back into my human emotional state again." He began to doubt the reality of what had happened, especially as nothing quite like it occurred again. Soon after this experience, he told a psychiatrist about it. The psychiatrist told him he was hallucinating, for "it just wasn't possible from his point of view." Sequoyah told me that he has had hallucinatory experiences related to drugs, but they were different, more fragmented, and obviously related to toxicity or withdrawal. "I knew when I was hallucinating. I am clear that this experience was real and distinct from hallucinations or other drug reactions."[9]

Prison, Rehabilitation, and Transformation

The decade of Sequoyah's life that began in 1979 with his incarceration resembles a kind of prison novel bathed in the light of spiritual transcendence. His rehabilitation and transformational course are inseparable from his prison experience. In his story we find the worst and the best of humanity—horror and ecstasy, degradation and transformation.

A bare outline of the sequence of events from 1979 to his final release from prison in 1987 is as follows. In June 1981, when he was released from Leavenworth, he stated that he was drug and alcohol free. At the same time that he was set free from federal prison, he was dismissed from active duty "under less-than-honorable conditions." He lived then for four years in Kansas City, Kansas, mostly in a Hindu community. In 1985 he was arrested by the police in Kansas City, Missouri, probably through another setup. He had fled to Missouri to escape from North Carolina bounty hunters, who were dispatched by the governor of that state to bring him back to serve the forty-one-year sentence that was still on the books. Sequoyah then spent a year in solitary confinement in a Kansas City, Missouri, jail (which is where he was in 1986 when Mark Perry interviewed him), while the various authorities tried to decide what to do with him.

Sequoyah agreed to be extradited to North Carolina, since it seemed to be the only way he could avoid spending the rest of his life in that jail. He was imprisoned again in the Central Prison in Raleigh, North Carolina. He spent all together eighteen months in various facilities of the North Carolina penal system, including four months in a chaotic mental unit because someone noticed the diagnosis of post-traumatic stress syndrome in his record, until finally in 1987 a warden in Asheville, in cooperation with Cherokee tribesmen, released him to start youth healing programs on the Cherokee reservation. Even after his release, Sequoyah still often thought he was ready to "leave the planet." We may recall (chapter 7) his encounter with the spider and the angellike spirit being that beckoned him to his death, and his determination "not yet."

Sequoyah's ultimate verdict is that all of his trials, even four months of cleaning foul latrines in a North Carolina prison, have been gifts for which he is thankful to the Creator, learning experiences that have enabled him to transmute pain and suffering in order to serve others. "Every day the invisible ones, extraterrestrials, spirit (all the same) taught me and showed me how to be peaceful and loving in any situation, how to be thankful for all that has happened to me and to be thankful for all that was to come."

Sequoyah had met Native Americans in Leavenworth, and his return to the teaching of his people began with them. Even while he was in prison, he managed to attend many native healing circles. While still in Kansas, he was brought by a Sac Fox tribesman to a spiritual gathering in White Cloud, in the northwestern corner of the state. He was told that this was a site where materializations from the spirit world took place and spacecraft sometimes landed. His education in native ways continued throughout this decade, especially among the Cherokees in North Carolina. He made friends with a Cherokee inmate sleeping next to him who had also been in Vietnam. This man's uncle was Andy Ocumma, a medicine man, who started taking Sequoyah out on pass and talked to him about "extraterrestrials and beings from other planets." Sequoyah soon met, worked, and eventually lived with the Cherokee in western North

Carolina. Ocumma and another medicine man, Walker Calhoun, became his primary mentors, and they and others taught him about the medicine wheel, healing circle, sweat lodge, other native ceremonies, and much more. He went on vision quests and learned of his connection with the eagle, bear, raven, and other animal spirits.

During his prison years, Sequoyah came to know and participate in both Western and Eastern forms of therapy and spiritual practice. These included individual and group psychotherapy, hypnotherapy, AA (Alcoholics Anonymous), NA (Narcotics Anonymous), past life therapy, various martial arts, hatha yoga, and zazen meditation. He was even ordained in 1982 as a minister in the American Fellowship Church, which certified him to conduct marriage ceremonies in Kansas. It was in the Hindu community that he came to realize that "I am an eternally spiritual being," and that our bodies are "just a temporary arrangement of form."

Sequoyah found his year in solitary confinement (1985–86) to be "one of the most productive years of my life," and he "became happy in there." Soon after he got to this jail, he was lying on his bed when "all of a sudden" a light being came to him and said, "This is exactly the place you're supposed to be right now. You're going to be in this jail cell for a while." Sequoyah likened this to being a Tibetan monk in a cave, and as he sat in the cell it seemed as if someone were talking to him and filling him with teachings about love, peace, and how change comes about. He meditated and did yoga every day and decided he would become a vegetarian. His jailers refused, so he went on a fast and was prepared to die. But a doctor was called and talked the jailers into giving Sequoyah vegetarian meals.

It was in this decade that Sequoyah began his life of extraordinary service. He assisted in developing a school for autistic children and handicapped people in Kansas City, helped found the Institute for Psychic Studies there, and was chosen by veterans to represent their claims before government boards and courts. Toward the end of his prison time in North Carolina, he worked with the warden as a paralegal. Unknown to the warden, Sequoyah also used the typewriter that was available to him to type up inmates' reports on beatings and sodomization by their guards. He sent these to an attorney he knew in Winston-Salem. "They got a whole lot of stuff straightened up in there after that happened," he told me.

In addition to the work with the Cherokees mentioned above, Sequoyah developed a parenting program for them and an outdoor experiential intervention program in the area of drug and alcohol abuse. Eventually because of Sequoyah's work among them, the Cherokees brought in people from twenty-two tribes, including Seminoles from the south and Mohawks from the north, and he began to learn the teachings of these peoples. He takes pride in having become schooled in many cultural traditions.

A Decade of Service

Since 1981, Sequoyah has written, "I have been immersed in the teachings of the Original Instructions [see page 294]. I have been guided and trained by the most respected Elders on this continent."[10] But it was only after becoming free of the North Carolina prison system in 1987 that he has been able to devote himself fully to a life of service, one that in my experience has hardly any parallel. For Sequoyah the contacts with his guardian spirits, including the one discrete abduction journey he has shared with me, are so much an integral part of his everyday life that their role in his personal development cannot be separated from all the other transformative influences of which he has spoken. His life is essentially a journey of the spirit, and the ETs, as he calls his visitors, are just one "face of spirit."

Sequoyah has become a kind of ceaseless, ever-moving Johnny Apple-seed of human healing and change, traveling all over North America and other continents, "going from community to community" in the pursuit of his mission. Time on the Earth is running out, he believes, and "if we don't start changing a little faster, we're not going to have a place to live here much longer." Male energy, male aggression, is out of control, he says, and we must learn to "respect and honor the woman for her life-bringing," and the gentle energy of the woman "which moderates male aggression."

Sequoyah's "good works" in native and white communities need to be seen in the context of his personal philosophy or worldview, which derives from his ongoing life experiences. His universe is dominated by spirit, and the forms of the material world are transient. "Don't think we're going to have these physical bodies like this forever. They're just here as tools of learning," he told one colleague.[11] He quotes Crow's Foot, another elder, who said, "Life is like the flash of a firefly in the night, like the breath of a buffalo on a cold winter day."[12]

Sequoyah lives in a world of myth and symbol, filled with visible and invisible beings from many realms, which are among the forms that spirit can take. The beings around us may help, but they "will not interfere with our free will." Our responsibility remains with us, Sequoyah says, including for our thoughts, which are like "laser beams that can be directed in ways that can alter anything."[13] Once when he was asked during a meeting if he was speaking metaphorically or literally when he talked of teachings coming from "extraterrestrials," he replied, "Well, it's the same thing. One of the things that they're teaching us is that 'hey, you guys are pretty arrogant here,' thinking you're in this universe, this Creation, all by yourself. These beings that are visiting here are with me and they're helping me out with what I'm doing."

For Sequoyah everything comes from the Creator, from that one Source. "Spirit knows how to run the universe better than me," he says. "The flame of love—that's the Creator burning within us." He is constantly giving thanks and asking for God's help. The only "insurance that is ever going to work is a pure relationship with the Creator." To Sequoyah this means letting go of control and taking an attitude of defenselessness and vulnerability. As we open ourselves, we can become aligned with Spirit and discover that "there's no such thing as death; there's only transformation going on." Even disease is the result of being out of harmony or balance in relation to the Creator. But the Creator needs us too; we learn, grow, and evolve together.

For Sequoyah most human destructiveness, individual and collective, is the result of unresolved pain and suffering, "which tracks our minds like a magnet and keeps us from accessing who we really are in spirit." According to native history, Sequoyah says, pain and suffering "entered human consciousness when first man and first woman turned their back on the original teachings of the Creator."[14] The way to "transcend" pain and suffering is to "investigate" it by facing it directly and communicating anger and other negative feelings openly in settings that are supportive of healing, which is what Sequoyah tries to do in most of his work. Native people can help Western whites with this job, because "for five hundred years" they have been becoming "pain experts and investigating everything about pain. We've transformed ourselves, and we're rising above it."

Legend and prophecy, learned through the oral histories of native peoples, are important for Sequoyah's understanding of the contemporary human dilemma and his mission. Prophecies, he believes, are reminders, based on present realities. They are not literal predictions of what will happen. Native oral histories foretold that another people, another culture, would come to Turtle Island, "and as the two cultures interacted great turmoil and discontent would be upon the people and the land." But this confrontation was necessary and would "ignite the fire of truth as both cultures would learn, grow and evolve spiritually to a higher place in consciousness."[15]

Especially relevant to our current crisis is the Hopi legend of the red and white brothers born into the same family. It was the Creator's plan that the white brother (the people of the straight line or linear thinking) would go to the other side of the Earth to learn "all of those things about the operation of the material world." Then he would come back to Turtle Island so that the red brother (the people of the circle or nonlinear thinking) would be able to have the same opportunities as the white brother, and "find out we weren't nearly as strong as we thought we were." "We could look into the mirror of the people of the straight line, and the people of the straight line could look into the mirror of the people of the circle." According to this legend, "If these two races would come together, there would be lots of turmoil, conflict, and destruction, but through our interaction we would rise above that and come to this higher spiritual place together."

Sequoyah himself is a bridge—between the red and white brothers, but also, like Bernardo and Credo, between the unseen world of spirit and the manifest world of matter. "This is my path today," he wrote in his autobiographical summary, "to share the teachings of the Pipe with all people, and part of that is to help people recognize that many planets in many universes are inhabited and that these beings have always been here on Earth, and especially Turtle Island, guiding our medicine people and medicine societies in respectful ways of living."[16]

For Sequoyah the ceremonies he conducts with individuals, families, and communities are an essential part of his mission of healing and the promotion of spiritual development. Until the 1970s some of them, like the sun-dance, were outlawed by the U. S. government. As a medicine man, Sequoyah carries with him wherever he goes his "spiritual bundle," which contains sage, tobacco, the sacred pipe, and other things he needs. Ceremonies like the healing circles, the sacred pipe, sweat lodges, and the sundance create and sustain the bonds of community, cleanse the spirit, and give people the opportunity to open their hearts and "share the depths of who we are." In addition, they provide an opportunity to give thanks to the Creator, to summon the divine presence into the circle, and to enable the participants to connect with it. By his estimate between 1992 and 1996, Sequoyah worked with twenty thousand people in healing ceremonies.

Whenever possible, Sequoyah brings children into the center of the healing or other tribal circle so that they can grow spiritually and teach adults about trust, innocence, open-mindedness, and unconditional love. Increasingly he has been taking some of the ceremonies outside of native communities. When he did healing circles with prisoners in a maximum security prison in Canada, the warden was surprised to see that the men became calmer than he had ever seen them, which Sequoyah attributed to the presence of love that they did not ordinarily feel.

The most powerful of the Native American ceremonies is the sun-dance. Through this sacred and ancient rite, the participants seem to transcend ordinary reality or physical states and gain through prayer "a portal to the spirit world." Until recently nonnatives were not allowed to be present. The principal purpose of the ceremony is to free the community of pain and suffering. It culminates in a four-day period of intense dancing in which the participants, men and women, dance without food or water, sometimes in searing summer heat. At the end the men who are deemed spiritually qualified have their chests or backs pierced by a piece of wood and continue to dance hanging from the sacred sundance tree. At the end of the dance, when the wood breaks through their flesh, they break free.

In August 1997 the American Indian Movement conducted a great sundance in Pipestone, Minnesota, where Orvil Lookinghorse holds the most honored sacred pipe, made of a kind of reddish stone—pipestone—found only in that region. It was, according to legend, given to the people by White Buffalo Calf Woman, an important deity of the native traditions. Indians from all over North America attended this sundance, which lasted more than a week and was accompanied by a youth healing and other ceremonies. Sequoyah, who had first sundanced in 1993, was one of the dancers who was pierced in this ceremony. He invited several friends to be there and described to us how the pain transformed into a kind of spiritual ecstasy as he broke free in the culmination of the dance. For him personally, Sequoyah has written, "The Sundance has proven to me the power of prayer; the Sundance has made me aware that I am a child of the Creator, that I am eternal spirit, that I am God's mind in motion, that I am the spiritual representative of all who have gone before me, that I am Spirit made visible."[17]

Sequoyah seems indefatigable in the pursuit of his mission of healing and transformation, serving people of all backgrounds. He seems literally to have traveled all over the world. In 1994 he was invited with a group of native elders to present the prophecies from the oral histories of seven different cultures at the United Nations in New York. In that same year, he was asked to be a coordinator of a Native Council on Sustainability as part of a White House effort to develop a sustainable environmental policy. His work has been especially focused on youth healing, nationally and internationally.[18] Young people, he believes, can lead us out of this "long winter into the springtime."

Sequoyah serves on the International Council of Elders without Borders and the Native American Sports Council, which has a seat on the U.S. Olympic Committee. He also serves on or is an adviser to several boards committed to preservation of life on Earth. Sequoyah's journey is always supported by his relationship to the Creator and the beings, visible and invisible, through which the Creator manifests. In his book proposal in 1997, he wrote, "From 1992 until today my path has led me through many remote villages from the Southwest desert to inside the Arctic Circle of the Yukon, to the native people of Siberia and Mongolia, and to a closer relationship with those beings referred to as extraterrestrial. They are just as much my family as my parents, my friends and my children."[19]

Chapter 10
Vusumazulu Credo Mutwa

··

*The silence lasted only a few moments. Then all around me there was
a blue smoke which obscured the landscape. I could no longer see the
trees so well. I could no longer hear the birds. I could no longer feel the
heat of the sun. I was suddenly in a place made of iron. It was sort of
round, like a tank, a water tank lying on its side.*

Credo Mutwa
November 24, 1994

"A Living Treasure"

··

Vusumazulu Credo Mutwa is perhaps the best-known African
sangoma or medicine man outside of his native South Africa. Like
Bernardo Peixoto and Sequoyah Trueblood, he is a bridging figure, bringing the knowledge of his culture to the West. Like them Credo
was raised as a Christian, but as a young man he renounced Christianity
and grew to become a *sanusi*, an "uplifter of his people" (Larsen 1994, p.
23). *Vusumazulu*, a name given to him during his initiation as a *sangoma*,
means "awakener of the Zulus," and Credo is indeed the spiritual leader of
the *sanusis* and *sangomas* of South Africa, while often resented by blacks
who have not remained true to their traditional cultures. He is also known
honorifically as Baba Mutwa among his followers. *Mutwa* means "little
bushman," and *Credo* ("I believe") was the name given to him by his Christian
father. Stephen Larsen has accurately compared him to what the Japanese
call "a living treasure" (Larsen 1996).

Credo's understanding of African spirituality and culture is astounding, and he knows that contained within this great body of knowledge are truths that can benefit humankind in our time of crisis. His vision is to use these teachings to transcend ethnonational separatism and human violence against nature, while keeping alive in Africa the ancient culture of his own people. As I write this (October 1998), Credo is seventy-seven and in failing health. He continues to work but likens his task to "an ant trying to bite a hole in Mount Everest. The ant is too small and the mountain is too big." In this chapter I will tell principally those aspects of his story that relate to his encounters with humanoid beings and their importance for his life and work.[1]

As we saw in chapter 5, Credo's view of the *mantindane* (the Zulu word for the creatures that resemble closely what are called "gray aliens" in the West) is quite different from that of Peixoto or Trueblood. To him they are parasitic, instill superstition, sow discord, and may even cause disease. But at the same time he sees the *mantindane* and other extraterrestrial beings as givers of knowledge to humankind, especially of the "real meaning" of things. He credits them with his own wide knowledge of art, language, medicine, science and engineering, subjects that he seemed to learn without commensurate study. Such beings, Credo believes, have influenced human culture from its beginnings (Larsen 1996, p.147), and should not be considered foreign. "Some of them," he said to me, "are not aliens at all, sir, but they are part of this Earth. They belong here.... We and the *mantindane* are one and the same stupid race. Far from these creatures being aliens, they are our future descendants. I am sure of this."

We have seen how deeply concerned Credo is for the fate of the Earth and the danger to its life that we now confront (chapter 5). The Earth, he says, is a "womb world" in which new forms of life can develop. "The Earth is unique, sir. There is no other Earth." Credo's sense of urgency is palpable when you are with him. He fears that his teachings, including about extraterrestrial beings and the knowledge they bring us, will be ignored, and he bursts forth with anger and frustration over human shortsightedness. "I just get furious," he exclaimed a few minutes after we first met, "because the people from the stars are trying to give us knowledge, but we are too stupid." The story of UFOs and their occupants, he says, is a "subject so huge, so incredible, and it is a subject that needs to be told by very deeply thinking people." If we would realize that we are not alone, we would treat the Earth with respect, Credo believes, and would "open channels of communication with these intelligences. The human race must accept that it is not alone on the planet; otherwise it will perish."

I knew very little about Credo Mutwa when I arrived in Johannesburg on November 18, 1994. The main purpose of the trip to Africa for Dominique Callimanopulos (my research associate) and me was to investigate the Ariel School incident in Zimbabwe. The stop in South Africa was something of an afterthought—we did not want to come so far without spending at least a few days there. But immediately upon arrival at the airport, we were taken by a member of the local UFO group to a television station, where I was to take part in a South African news magazine program, *Agenda*, which was about the Ariel School incident, UFOs, aliens, abductions, and the like.

Credo was also on the program, broadcasting from a local affiliate in Mhabatu, near his village in Mafeking, in the "Home Territories" northwest of Johannesburg. He seemed altogether familiar with these matters, said that they had been known by Africans for thousands of years, and exhibited for the cameras statues he had made of different sorts of extraterrestrial creatures, some of whom looked like the gray aliens familiar to us in the West. After Credo heard what I had to say about my work with Americans and Europeans who had had encounters with humanoid beings, he asked to see me.

The next morning we drove the four hours to Credo's *kraal* (small village), picking up Gary Sinclair, a "white shaman" and close friend of Credo's, along the way to act as a kind of guide or go-between. Credo told us that I was the first person from the West to come to Africa to investigate the UFO abduction phenomenon among native people, and he seemed eager to tell us everything he could. A year later he said to me, "Dr. Mack, you came to our country breaking new ground. There are [UFO] associations here in South Africa which say they are dedicated to looking into this thing, but they don't talk to us black people. It is as if we don't exist. It will be difficult. It will sometimes be painful, but the voice of the black people on this and other important subjects has got to be heard."

We arrived in Credo's village early in the afternoon. In the yard were his great sculptures of various sorts of creatures and large paintings depicting the life and legends of his people plus medicine wheels, sacred stones, and petroglyph designs. In Bradford Keeney's words, he had "created a place where his soul speaks directly in the outer world" (Keeney 1994, p. 114). Inside Credo's hut were several of his followers and friends.

Despite the simplicity of the surroundings, Credo seemed a noble, even regal figure with his colorful robes and heavy metal adornments of the *sangoma*, which seemed as if they ought to weigh him down. Even Credo's "bones"— the shells, animal bones, and pieces of ivory that he, like other shamans, uses for divination and healing—appeared larger than those of other medicine men we met.

Africans, Credo explained, are ordinarily reluctant to speak with someone they do not know, especially a white person ("you don't know how they're going to react"), about such intimate matters. "An African," he said, "will go about a subject in a roundabout way while he builds up trust between you and himself." He was troubled, he said, about how rushed our first meeting was, although he found some of it "very interesting." It was hard to talk about such "shameful and traumatic" matters when "we didn't have time to be acquainted. We didn't have time so that I could feel your spirit."*

When we first met and began to talk, I felt the complexity and ambiguity of Credo's situation. Here was a person of great stature among his people, in front of several of them, sharing with outsiders disturbing experiences about which he felt a good deal of shame. It was clear that he had carried within himself for more than thirty-five years traumatic events that were still highly charged for him emotionally. It seemed as if my arrival provided not only a chance for him to present his story so that it would be told and, hopefully, believed in my country. It was also a kind of therapeutic opportunity, a chance to unburden himself of matters that he had had to keep secret. "There are things that you must not discuss even within your own tribal culture, except with people of your own class," he

---

* Through Gary (who had brought me to see Credo when we first met him) I also met and interviewed in 1995 another Zulu medicine man, Claude Inyanga, who told me about various beings known to African lore and experience but did not speak of the *mantindane*. When Gary played for Claude the audiotape of the regression I did with Gary (see pp. 246–247), Claude laughed and said "we know the grays and keep them in the periphery of our vision. We all know of them. I have met many healers who acknowledge they exist and are negative" (letter to the author, May 20, 1999). Claude has had much less contact with Westerners, and it is Gary's view that his reluctance to speak with me about the *mantindane* had to do with the fact that this was our first meeting, and we had not had enough time together for him to speak of such matters.

explained. Furthermore, if you were to speak of "strange dolls that walked and staggered about as if they were powered by batteries, your children would think that you are nuts."

Credo's attitude toward me, as we began our first meeting, was a mixture of deference and gentle irony, as he interspersed the discussion with quite a few "sirs" and "doctors." When I asked him four years later if there was anything he had told me along the way that he would prefer I not tell, he replied that to place restrictions of any sort upon me would be "like a cat urinating inside the temple of knowledge."

The end of apartheid has not been kind to Credo. His village in Mafeking came under the jurisdiction of the park department, and he was forced to leave after various forms of harassment, which included several attempts on his life. "We are like pariahs to these people, who hate African culture," he remarked. He believes too that black magic has been used to terrorize him and that precious sacred objects have been stolen from him. His bitterness has deepened, as the people who run the nature reserves seem to him more interested in the animals that attract tourists than in people. "They don't realize that to conserve animals, you must preserve African culture." Credo's special value is no more appreciated by blacks attempting to reap the benefits of modern society than it was by racist whites, and he has felt himself the object of hatred by both groups who, he believes, see him as an obstacle to progress. The new South Africa, he fears, is in greater danger than the old one, while the old evils persist.

In the years that I have known him, Credo has been forced to move several times and has had to depend on the generosity of his friends just to live. Through it all he has struggled to preserve the archives and artifacts of his culture that he has collected over a lifetime. In 1998 his symptoms of diabetes became aggravated, he suffered from a worsening of his asthma, and he was partially paralyzed by a small stroke. Yet there are hopeful signs. In June 1997 a sixty-acre piece of land was bought for Credo by the generosity of friends in the Magliesburg Mountains, a sacred place of healing powers where humankind is said to have evolved (Tintinger 1997). Here the village that he has dreamed of is being formed, which can become a center for the preservation of African culture and artifacts. A "house of mysteries" may be built there as well. Perhaps the spiritual awakening that is beginning around the world, together with an increasing appreciation in the West of the vital importance of indigenous cultures for our own survival, may make the fulfillment of Credo's vision more likely.

Credo's Life

Credo was born in the South African province of Natal on July 21, 1921. His father was a Roman Catholic catechism instructor during Credo's childhood and converted to Christian Science when Credo was fourteen. His mother was the daughter of Ziko Shezi, a Zulu shaman and warrior. According to Credo, this grandfather was a great healer and played an important part in his training to become a medicine man. Credo grew up loving the bush. "I love the mystery of going through the bush with my half-blind eyes, just feeling the trees around me. It's a magical experience," he said to us. Like Sequoyah, Credo was baptized as a Catholic. He was educated in a mission school, advanced rapidly, and completed the standard six, equivalent to ninth grade in the United States. He learned a great deal about Western civilization and ways in this school.

Credo's parents were not married, and he recalls being shunned as "a bastard, a thing born out of marriage." But he was not lonely as a child, for there were always "little people" around, "strange companions who used to tell me things that had to do with schoolwork," and sometimes, even though he says he had no books to learn from, he found that he knew more than the teachers. These beings were friendly ("not like these monsters," the *mantindane*). "Some were blue. All African children used to see such things," he said. As we have seen in chapter 5, Credo believes that these beings also imparted a great deal of other knowledge to him. When I asked him to describe how this learning came to him, he replied, "All of a sudden you feel . . . and then it's there. Your mouth speaks without your brain controlling it."

Educated in white people's ways, when Credo speaks of extraterrestrial beings and related matters, he feels "caught between, on the one hand, Western thought, including the Christian religion, and African thought, which accepts these things without question." When he was fifteen, he witnessed the last Zulu rainmaking ceremony, a magnificent spectacle that took place on the top of a mountain. He memorized every detail, and as an adult he has remembered this event many times. As a young man of twenty-two, Credo developed a feverish condition that caused such pain and debilitation that he almost died (Larsen 1996, pp. 2–4).

This illness was accompanied by nightmares and visions that seemed to "swallow" him, "body and soul." Neither his father's readings from the works of Mary Baker Eddy, which regarded such sickness as an illusion to

be fought against, nor the medical treatments he received, helped. He began
to recover when a loving Zulu aunt, who regarded his condition as a kind
of spiritual crisis, used traditional African methods to treat his condition.
It turned out that this crisis was the beginning of Credo's initiation and
training as a *sangoma*, and as he recovered his remarkable powers as a healer
began to be revealed (Larsen 1996, pp. 8–13).

"When you are an ordinary *sangoma*," Credo told us, "you are guided by
what are called your ancestral spirits. But when you reach a certain level, you
become guided by creatures that you accept as your ancestral spirits but that
are really not your ancestral spirits." Some of these entities that masquerade
as ancestral spirits, he says, are "parasites from other dimensions" that
victimize, manipulate, and control *sangomas* and can even "bring us to violent
deaths." As it is for Sequoyah, the pipe is important for Credo's conduct of
native ceremonies: "The pipe is the Earth; the smoke connects us with the
spirit world" (Keeney 1994, p. 115).

Credo's life has been filled with strife, and he has been the victim of
violence many times. He says he was raped more than once as a young man
and has been attacked by mobs during political riots. In 1960 his fiancée
was killed when South African police fired on a crowd. Interestingly (at least
for a psychiatrist) he has become an "expert" in dissociation. When Credo
was stabbed during the Soweto riots, "I could feel the knives going into my
body. The thing that always helps me happened then. I split into two, and so
I escaped the pain." He looked down and could see "the bloodied mess that
looked like me." (As we will see on page 213, the *mantindane* played a role in
his recovery from one stabbing.) Once, he says, a Christian fundamentalist
came close to stabbing him, calling him venomous, a Satanist, and an enemy
of God.

The only time he really felt fear, Credo said, was when a mob was
preparing to burn him alive by pouring gasoline on him. Africans believe
that if you are burned to death, your soul is destroyed as well as your body,
and that the soul will "go into the darkness" so that the person can never
be reincarnated. Credo told Bradford Keeney that after being stoned by
a mob in Soweto, he had been pronounced clinically dead. He saw then
the tunnel, and the great place of light that has now become familiar in
accounts of near-death experiences (Moody 1975; Ring 1980 and 1984;
Greyson and Flynn 1984). For Credo this was the Great Spirit showing
him its face.

Worldview

Perhaps not surprisingly in these late years of his life Credo has become an embittered man with a dark view of humankind and its future. He is admittedly "sick and tired" of "feeding and leading people who hate you," and just wants to be "an ordinary black man." He believes that a great intelligence, "something which covers several galaxies," created the Earth, but he regards this intelligence as material or "machinelike" rather than as God, which means a "superhuman being." According to African legend, it is this intelligence that has sent to Africa alone more than eight kinds of entities "to warn the people what to do and what not to do." But we know nothing really, Credo believes, about God, the galaxy we are a part of, the world we live in, or even ourselves. Reincarnation, he says, is the most important "pillar of our religion," and accordingly the *mantindane* may follow you not only in this lifetime but in many others as well.

Love is a wonderful thing, Credo says, but it is shallow, fragile, easily shattered, and not permanent in the human heart: "Love may move certain things fast, but selfishness moves them even faster." Indeed, as he said to me, "You know as a person of science that selfishness is the greatest driving force in human existence." Credo cites instances where people have abandoned their loved ones to save themselves. Why, he asks, do people "become estranged in the sunset of their lives?" In this respect his view of the motivation of the *mantindane* is the same as of humans. "They are obsessed with self-preservation," and that is why "they preserve us, not out of love." The beings, like ourselves, Credo believes, are driven by a hunger for power. "This wish to play God over lesser beings is with us and with them. Throughout the cosmos vice is the same."

UFOs and Star People in Africa

According to African lore, Credo says, "star people" have come from the heavens in "magic sky boats" for thousands of years, but this is not widely known because UFO groups do not speak to black people. The black man, he complains, is ignored and despised, "ostracized from sitting in important fields of science." Even the great Zulu warrior king Shaka was "kidnapped" by the *mantindane*. Ask the Pygmies, the Bushmen of the Kalahari, the

Ovahimba of Namibia, or the tribespeople of Zaire, he urges. All will tell, he says, of the growing presence among us of what we in the West call alien beings.

Like observers in the United States and other Western countries, Credo speaks of spheres, bright blue bands of light, and unusual disk-shaped objects seen over Johannesburg and Mafeking. In 1995, he told us, a black farmer in Lesotho came across a disk-like object that had "fallen out of the sky" and was emitting "tiny little balls of lightning all around its circumference." Credo links the *mantindane* to the *wandinja*, the sky gods of the Australian aboriginals, which are depicted in cave drawings with startlingly large black eyes, and to ancient Sumerians, whose drawings showed bald heads and faces with unusually large eyes, small chins, and rudimentary noses. He also relates them to other nonearthly creatures and events like Sasquatch sightings, animal mutilations resembling those documented in Western accounts (Howe 1993), and the mysterious, intricate "crop circles" seen in fields, especially in southern England. Credo himself has made many drawings and paintings of variously shaped spacecraft, most of which look familiar to anyone who has studied this subject carefully.

According to Credo, his people regard the stars, "those little things up there," with fear and awe. To them a star is even more important than the sun or the moon, for it is from the stars, their forefathers have taught, that important knowledge, wisdom, and enlightenment come. The people of Botswana, for example, call a star *naledi*, which means "light of the spirit," and have carved in wood, painted on rocks, or even scratched on metal "the so-called UFOs," the "magical vehicles" in which the *mantindane* and the star gods of the various tribes traveled. Unlike the Lakota Sioux, who believe they come from the Pleiades (see page 180), or the Dogon of central Africa, who tell of intelligent beings that have come to the Earth from the star Sirius (Larsen 1996, p. 130, and Temple 1976), the people of southern Africa are less explicit about from which star the UFOs come.

Credo believes that extraterrestrial beings have covertly influenced and "manipulated" all human cultures and civilizations profoundly for hundreds if not thousands of years, operating in the shadows. Warriors like the Masai go into battle wearing codpieces to protect their genitals from the *mantindane* who might otherwise drain their semen, and women wear certain ornaments to protect themselves from being sexually molested by them. From the art and oral traditions of various African tribes and from his own experiences, Credo has concluded that some of these creatures, especially the *mantindane*, "share the Earth with us. They need us. They use us. They harvest things from us," but he is not altogether sure why.

According to Credo, the *mantindane* have caused wars and other terrible cruelties and have "manufactured" diseases to destroy human beings or to test our resistance to various bacterial strains. But they have also had a positive influence and done helpful things. They taught the Zulus how to drill through stone and the Egyptians to cut the great stone with which they made their pyramids. When smallpox threatened to wipe out the Zulu tribes, "the star people told our people what to do to protect themselves," and during a terrible famine, when crops were failing and hundreds were dying, a race of *mantindane*-like creatures, only taller, came out of the sky and taught women how to grind and cook the poisonous cassava root to render it edible and palatable to human beings.

Although Credo is frustrated that people in the West do not accept the reality of these beings and that they interfere with human destiny, he is quite astute about the reasons for this resistance. "Human beings are subconsciously aware of the danger that we are all in," he told us, but "many of them are refusing to accept this truth." "You will find many cultures afraid of talking to you about such things," he said toward the end of our first meeting. "Why? Look, sir, a creature that can go through walls, a creature that can come up from my bed and close to me and smile at me; a creature that can play with my genitals even though I have every door locked; a creature, furthermore, that can leave visible scratches on my body to prove to me that it has been there . . ." (his sentence trails off).

"Let me tell you, Dr. Mack," Credo said in our next meeting, "that very often when you see these things, especially if you are an educated and Christian person, your mind rejects what you see. Your mind refuses to accept what you see. Your mind will not recognize what you see. I've seen it happen to thousands of black people and white people." Nevertheless, Credo insisted, "People should stop obscuring the facts. These are real beings. They should be communicated with."

There are many legends and stories in Africa, Credo told us, concerning UFOs and various creatures that come with them from the stars. "For the people of Africa," he told Stephen Larsen, "the skies are full of life, yes, even the origin of life can be attributed to the stars" (Larsen 1996, p. 122). Before they knew of airplanes, he said, African tribespeople called

UFOs "swings," as the nearest thing they knew to something a human being could fly in was a swing suspended from the branch of a tree. People's lives, Credo said, have been "changed by entities that were not of this world."

Credo told us of the appearance and habits of about eight or ten sorts of creatures thought to come from the stars. These creatures, he has said, watch over us with curiosity, "actually regulating human progress for some reason known only to themselves" (Larsen 1996, p. 147). "All over South Africa," he said, "you find stories of these extraterrestrial visitors" (Larsen, p. 148). The creatures, each of which he named, included tall blond beings that were knowledge givers; hairy creatures ("the *puhwana*") that give children scratches that never become septic; an entity with a very large head, unnaturally pink skin, and a long male organ; and creatures that wore a helmet and armor to protect them in this world. In "olden days," Credo told us, his people accepted these creatures and did not regard them as outside "the miracle of this Earth." Credo recalls that his mother used to urinate into a clay chamberpot and wash her children's scratches from the *puhwana* with her urine to exorcise the spirit of this creature.

The most feared, and apparently the most important for Africans, are the *mantindane*, or "sky monkeys," which, as we have seen (chapter 6), are thought to be able to impregnate women. Credo told Stephen Larsen that women throughout Africa over several centuries have told of being "fertilized by strange creatures from somewhere" (Larsen 1996, p. 152). The *mantindane*, he says, inflict pain, "torture us like the African secret police," and smell hideously. The last thing Credo told us in our first meeting was that when he drew a picture of a *mantindane* for his mother, she cried and corrected the drawing slightly, for she had seen such a creature herself in 1918!

Nevertheless, the *mantindane*, Credo told us with some irony, are thought of by some Africans as gods who honor people by taking "things" from them "to places that we don't know." When people are captured by the *mantindane*, he said, it is thought to be because they have done something wrong, and the gods want to take out the evil spirits in a very painful way. Injuries from these encounters, according to Credo, are called "god injuries." Yet in his angry moments of recollection, he rejects this notion. "Gods," he declares, "wouldn't stick things into people and injure and traumatize them. Gods do not need the organs of innocent women to put unknown fetuses inside them."

Credo's Own Experiences

Credo himself has had many sightings of UFOs and says that over Mafeking they are seen every month by hundreds of people. He scoffs at the American air force's stories of weather balloons. "A weather balloon doesn't have portholes that are visible through a powerful pair of binoculars," he said to us. Except for the childhood companions who helped him with his schoolwork (see page 202), Credo's encounters with the occupants of such craft have been largely unpleasant if not traumatic. He holds extraterrestrial beings responsible for ruining his love affairs, spoiling his marriages, and damaging his penis. At the same time, as we have seen, they are sources of vital knowledge, have given him powerful skills, and provide important warnings to the human species, which he urgently believes we should heed.

One creature, which he calls the "string skirt sister" because it wears a skirt made of strings, has been with him since he was a baby. In the Catholic world in which he was brought up, such beings were either angels or demons, "so I naturally believed that this creature was my guardian angel." This being, he told us, has reddish skin, intense eyebrows, and unnaturally widened eyes and speaks through a hole in its throat. Sometimes it wears a fish-shaped helmet with a crest on it. This same being also haunted his aunt Mina, who said to Credo, "This is no devil," and told him that hundreds of *sangomas* and healers in Zululand were "bothered and controlled by this creature."

Typically, Credo said, when a *sangoma* has terrible dreams and becomes "sick with the healer's illness," the string skirt sister will lead the sufferer underground, where he will see "all kinds of amazing and fearful things." She has also given him knowledge, most of which has been useless to him, but it includes the capacity to foretell the future accurately. It is this being, Credo said with some bitterness, that caused him to end his dreams of being a schoolteacher and to concentrate on preserving his people's culture. "I didn't *want* to build villages in various parts of Africa, but she tells me to do that." If he does not obey her, he said, "she screams and cries night after night after night." This being is "more me than I am me," Credo declared.

In *Song of the Stars* Credo describes an important UFO encounter that occurred when he was about thirty (Larsen 1996, pp. 134–5). He was called to a large village in Botswana where a "falling star" had been seen.

The trees and brush had been burned, as if by a fire, and Credo and others who came with him saw a round object the size of a large truck floating in the air. It lit up the surrounding trees, which had been scorched by the fire. Two creatures, jumping and running rather like children and wearing dark garments, got into the craft, and it "just took off and disappeared." (This description is similar to the one given to us by the children at the Ariel School.) The creatures left behind some "white rubbish" that crumbled "like bone turning into ash." According to African tradition, Credo said, such material should not be touched because it can cause burning and blistering of the hands, hair to fall out, and even eventual death.

The most important encounter with humanoid beings that Credo has experienced occurred in 1958, when he was still learning to be a *sangoma*. He has summarized this event in *Song of the Stars* (Larsen 1996, pp. 141, 142). He talked about the incident to me in great detail and with an intense combination of emotions, which included shame, anger, and a kind of awe. He was also clearly eager that I tell of such things back in my home, but as he told the story once again, he felt dirty and ashamed. The incident occurred in the sacred Inyangani Mountains in Rhodesia (now Zimbabwe), where he was working with a traditional healer, a Mrs. Zamoya, digging for special herbs that are used to treat backache.

Here is how Credo began his account:

> Now it was an ordinary day, sir. I loved being alone in the bush. I loved the smell of the animals, the smell of the trees, the sound of the birds, and I was just digging away, when all of a sudden I was aware of this strange silence that had fallen around. The silence lasted only a few moments, then all around me there was a blue smoke that obscured the landscape. I could no longer see the trees so well. I could no longer hear the birds. I could no longer feel the heat of the sun. One minute I was standing there looking stupid and feeling even stupider when I was suddenly in a place, a place made of iron. It was sort of round, like a tank, a water tank lying on its side.

Credo found he had no clothes on, and his body now was on a table that seemed to fit his contours. Several times he spoke to us of a horrible smell, variously described as "like an electrical smell mixed with a chemical of some kind," a "stink of copper," and "rotten fish." He was terrified, was "urinating like nobody's business," and struggled to get off the table. But except for slight movement of his eyes, he was completely paralyzed. Credo's asthmatic condition made it especially difficult to breathe.

Around him were six or more small doll-like beings, about three feet tall, with huge black eyes ("like nothing on Earth"). (See chapter 13 for Credo's detailed descriptions of the beings' eyes.) They had very small jaws, and their faces were like white clay with a pinkish tinge. The skin of their bodies seemed to be shiny, as if covered with oil, or "the texture and feel of a little reptile." For noses the beings had only small nostril holes, and the mouths were like a razor cut with no lips. They had no hair or ears and two, three, or four long, very thin, fingers that appeared to Credo to have one more joint than a human's. They were all wearing a seamless "grayish-silver, shiny, crackly uniform" and a round cap that, he said, made them look like Japanese soldiers in the Second World War. The beings "staggered about as if they were powered by batteries" or "like chickens with broken legs." The place was illuminated with a strange light that did not seem to Credo to be electrical.

A slightly bigger creature with a wrinkled face and wearing a kind of brown overall, whom Credo sensed was a female, seemed to be in charge and stood very close to his head. She had no breasts and only the slightest swell of hips, and the others seemed to be afraid of her. There was a blue curtain around him, but the creatures seemed to be able to walk right through it as they approached. Credo tried to scream, but the "brown lady" put her hand over his mouth and patted it. Her thoughts "were somewhere else. It was as if I didn't exist." None of the beings said anything to him. One of them stabbed some sort of pipe into his thigh, and something was stuck in his nose that seemed to cause a kind of explosion in his head. Credo compared the pain and fear to rape experiences he had undergone, but this, he said, was much worse. Normally, he said, he is able to dissociate when he is so frightened, to split his consciousness from his body. "But on that table that thing never happened. It seems there was a big witchcraft on me, a terrible witchcraft."

As Credo was lying on the table in pain, a quite human-looking white woman who was wearing no clothes came up to him. But her limbs were too short for her body, her skin seemed polished, and "she looked more like a doll than these creatures looked like dolls." This creature looked and felt to him "utterly unnatural." She touched his face and aroused him with her hand. Then she climbed over him "like a crazy Zulu girl." But it was not, Credo said, like making love to a real woman, for then "you feel the beat of her veins and arteries. You feel the warmth of her. You feel the heat and the smell. But this creature had none of these things. It was as cold as if you were making love to a dead body, sir, as cold as if you were making love to a machine." Her large eyes did not blink, and she felt as if she had no bones. The most frightening part of all was that the creature seemed to attach something to his penis that caused him to ejaculate "too much."

After this the female being went away, and Credo did not see her again. While he was still in intense pain, "these creatures pushed me off the table." "It was like pulling a goat," he said. His penis "was burning as if I had put it in scalding water." Then one of the beings showed him something strange that "even now, doctor, still is haunting my dreams," and "I shall remember [it] to the day I die." A big round bottle without a neck and filled with a pinkish liquid was suspended somehow from a wall, and inside of it was a creature, swimming like a frog, that Credo felt certain was an unborn human baby. He recalled that he had also seen other human beings being "tortured by other *mantindane*, exactly as I was."

In the next moment, Credo found himself once again in the bush, and "through a great dullness of the brain," he gradually became aware of things that were wrong. His trousers and shirt were torn, and his mining boots (with heavy nails "good for kicking crocodiles if a crocodile catches you by the neck") were gone. His body was covered with gray dust, and he smelled "awful, like in that stinking place." Credo followed a track that led to a village, and when he finally made contact, he asked for Mrs. Zamoya. He was shocked when he was told that he had been missing for three days. He continued to feel pain in his thigh, nose, and "man thing," lost strength, and fell down. He was then taken to Mrs. Zamoya's place and bathed from head to toe. She told him that he had been "caught by the God of the mountains." Credo said that tiny droplets of blood were oozing from pores in his skin, which was quite itchy. He showed me a nearly half-inch scoop mark in his thigh, which he attributed to this experience. (For similar scars, see Hopkins 1987, photos 7–9, between pp. 170 and 171.)

Credo stayed in the village for several days to recover and was bathed every day. Villagers found his boots in the bush, but curiously they were still laced, "as if somebody or something had pulled me out of my boots without unlacing them." He felt deathly ill, and in a state that he describes as "very close to madness," he was taken by Mrs. Zamoya to her "Solace Mission" in western Rhodesia, where it took him several months to recover. Most horrifying of all to him, skin started to peel off his penis, which developed sores and became "an ugly pink." Traces of this condition remained, which Credo says is why his first wife left him.

Mrs. Zamoya took Credo to speak with several other people who had had similar experiences and injuries. In Francistown an old man told him that what had happened to him was very common in that region, but that one should talk about it only to others who had had a similar "God injury." Credo was asked if he had done anything wrong or broken any taboos that might account for his misfortune. But he had never stolen from anyone, lied to his mother, or done anything he could recall that might make the gods angry. Another explanation offered for his illness was that he might have eaten the sacred flesh of a sky monkey, which was said to cause violent symptoms. But Credo said that he knew of people who had never eaten "*mantindane* flesh" but had had "more horrific experiences" than his own. In the end he is left without any convincing explanation for his encounters with the *mantindane*.

Credo told us of one other important encounter he had with the *mantindane*. It occurred after the Soweto riots in 1976. A mob attacked him (concerning his dissociative way of coping with this assault, see page 204) because of a newspaper article falsely alleging that he had said that the army should be brought in to kill schoolchildren. He was stabbed many times and was severely injured. Credo was taken by friends to a farm in Natal province to recover and also to avoid professional killers, who, he says, were sent to look for him in his home or the hospital "to really finish me off."

At night when Credo was beginning to recover from these terrible injuries, he smelled the same horrible smell as he had during the 1958 incident. Although the door to his hut was locked, he saw a single *mantindane* standing by his bed, "the same little bloody bastard [still female] in the brown suit." Something in the creature's eyes—dry, unmoving, with a "viscous emptiness"—made her look very old, and she had a smell "of hundreds of years." She moved "like floating on water" or "like a ballerina, very slowly." She looked down on him, not saying anything, and "again I was asleep by witchcraft. Again I could not move."

Then the being touched the plaster cast that was on Credo's hand, took the blanket off his body, "and started looking at my man thing again." He wanted to shout angrily, "You're wasting your time, you little bitch," but his lips were numb. Then suddenly, in what seemed to Credo like a cruel, brutal action, the creature ripped the bandage off his badly wounded right hand, causing blood to come from it. She seemed frightened in a human sort of way, as if she were afraid of contacting the blood directly. Then she went right through the mud wall of the hut, taking with her the bandage, which, Credo says, was found, still bloody and full of medicine, some distance from the hut.

The people who assaulted him, Credo told us, had wanted to cut off two of his fingers so that as an artist he would not be able to paint again. He had been given emergency treatment by a Dr. Goldberg in Soweto, who told him that he had almost lost the hand and was concerned that the wound might kill him of "blood poisoning." But after the *mantindane* ripped off the bandage, the hand healed in two days, and he never had to put it on again. Credo and his wife found this very strange, for "we had not expected this thing. I was utterly amazed."

Interpreting Credo's Experiences

In summary, although he continues to feel rage, shame, and the residua of his traumatization by the *mantindane*, Credo's attitude toward them remains ambivalent and contradictory. "Once a *mantindane* has dealt with you," he says, "you become afraid of making love to a woman. The moment your semen comes out, you recall that terrible day, and something becomes rather flat in you at night. These beings scar you for the rest of your life. You're not able to relate properly to ordinary human beings after they have had a session with you." Yet not without some sympathy, he observes that "these creatures are moved by a desperate need." White people in South Africa call these beings "aliens," Credo said. "We don't call them that. They are part of us, part of our lives." "These beings are not cold," he concluded in our first meeting, "it's only that they've got feelings that we don't even imagine."

Credo's dark interpretation of the *mantindane*, however valid, seems to relate to his worldview, which has become more negative even in the short time I have known him, as his sicknesses and persecutions have increased under black rule. "These creatures want sick, impotent, debilitated, asthmatic, diabetic things like me to change the course of human history," he says bitterly.

Furthermore, as we have seen, Credo attributes to humanoid beings vital knowledge and skills that he possesses, the healing of near-fatal wounds, and essential warnings about the threat to the Earth from environmental destruction. The *mantindane* are "solvers of great problems," he concedes, "in whatever bloody world they live in." Their technology may be "several million years ahead of us." He urges Americans to stop arguing about whether these phenomena are real (see page 104) and enjoins us all to "swim against the tide of anger and the waves of ignorance" and bring the knowledge of Africa back to white people in the West. "Why aren't scientists testing these things," he asks, "instead of saying it's all nonsense? Instead of saying that [abduction experiencers] are all mad?"

Credo, like other indigenous people with whom I have discussed these matters, does not sharply distinguish material or literal reality from mythic truths. This has made it particularly difficult for me to sort out what he may have actually experienced and what is part of African legend. His 1958 abduction experience, for example, has many elements that are familiar to us from American studies. But when he speaks of Africans becoming poisoned by eating the flesh of the *mantindane*, or the "string shirt sister" who takes people underground, we are on unfamiliar ground. Certain ideas of his, like the dominant role of the *mantindane* and other extraterrestrial or star beings in human cultural history, seem related to tribal myth and legend.

At a personal level, Credo is a superb storyteller, and his accounts may contain exaggerations and hyperbole. In addition Credo's familiarity with Western culture and ufology, and perhaps his wish, consciously or unconsciously, to provide me with information that he would know I would appreciate, may have led him to include elements from this knowledge in his account. In trying to differentiate his actually remembered experiences from these possible embellishments or distortions, I have tended to rely on the powerful emotions of shame, embarrassment, and anger that seemed altogether authentic, appropriate to what he was telling me, and similar to what experiencers in Western societies have demonstrated.

When I asked Credo why he thought there had been such resistance in the West to acknowledging the existence of these beings, he replied, "Dr. Mack, I'm going to be very brutal in answering this question. The entire Western civilization is based upon a blatant lie, the lie that we human beings are the cocks of the walk in this world, the lie that we human beings are the highest evolved forms in this world, that we are alone and that beyond us there is nothing." He spoke too of the dictatorial religious falsehood that there can be no other godlike beings but *the* God of the Bible. Like Sequoyah, he experiences a cosmos that contains "many, many great beings, some of which we don't even remotely dream about." Credo speculated that if we were to announce to the world that "the aliens are here," people would look behind governmental facades of power and challenge "the corruption, the governmental lies," and the "rotten industrial systems."

In spite of his negative view of the dangerous nature and intent of the *mantindane*, Credo says that he would "gladly welcome a *mantindane* government over us. In fact, I personally believe it would be the best thing that ever happened to the human race." Such a government would "really bring us to our senses. That government would show us what real oppression is." For the human race, he continued, is "shamefully disunited, and not capable of bringing our collective energy to bear upon the serious problems that we face." If we had a "common enemy, a common source of fear," he suggests, then we would unite. All the things that divide us would "fall away under a common danger."

Bernardo, Sequoyah, and Credo: Differences and Similarities

My work with Bernardo, Sequoyah, Credo, and other indigenous people has been especially helpful in enabling me to see that the abduction phenomenon is not simply an American or Western story. Although there are obvious differences, especially in the way various cultures interpret the experiences, some of the features of these shamans' encounters are familiar to students of the abduction phenomenon in the West. Credo's abduction in particular contains most of the familiar or "classic" traumatic, intrusive, and sexual elements.

There are obvious differences in the experiences of these three men. Credo's most fully reported abduction, for example, was nasty and hurtful, while Sequoyah's, for the most part, was enlightening and inspiring, directed by the spirit guides who have always been with him. These differences are consistent with the contrasting worldviews of the two men— Sequoyah accepting all experience as welcome teachings of the creator;

Credo more bitter about his fate, the beings' purposes, and the works of God.

But there are also important features that the experiences of the three men have in common. Each has encountered beings that resemble, more or less, the gray aliens known to us in the United States and in other Western countries. None of them has a basic ontological problem with the encounters—they are consistent with their respective worldviews. For in their cultures the universe is governed by unseen forces and filled with beings that are, most of the time, invisible, but that can, as in the case of the *mantindane* and ikuyas, take material form. As Sequoyah said, the "extraterrestrials" are just "another face of spirit."

All three of these men have had a Christian as well as a Native upbringing; each is playing an important role in building bridges that connect indigenous and white cultures; and the encounters have had a part in their education and transformation. Each is a teacher in both worlds.

The encounters have deeply affected each of them, although in different ways. Bernardo was shaken to learn of beings who may be related to the beginnings of his people but whose place of origin cannot be located in space and time. For Sequoyah the encounters showed him the paradisiacal possibilities of human life in the cosmos, for which, at the time of his experience, he felt unready. Credo has been physically and emotionally wounded by his encounters but attributes knowledge and healing power to the *mantindane*.

The most important lesson for me and for our society, I think, lies in the fact that these men corroborate the reality of the abduction phenomenon. They make clear that it is not simply the product of the Western imagination or our interest in aerospace technology, and that elements of the phenomenon may be universal—that is, not entirely culture-dependent. Bernardo, Sequoyah, and Credo are all eager to tell me their stories, partly so that they may understand and integrate their own experiences, but also that I may bring this knowledge to my culture, which is so skeptical of anything that cannot be proven in material terms. Credo in particular is eager for me to bring the *mantindane*'s warnings about the perilous state of the Earth to my society. He wants the subject studied and urges scientists and others to stop arguing about whether this phenomenon—which, he says, is so well known in Africa—is or is not real. Time is too short for that, he believes.

These shamans see the pain and suffering of their crises, initiations, and other life experiences as essential dimensions of learning and growth. Western society, however, tends to see pain and suffering mainly as obstacles to be removed on the way to well-being. I have found the shamanic perspective helpful in working with abductees in our culture. As artist and student of shamanism Andrea Pritchard wrote to me, "This difference is one reason why the abductees feel more comfortable in the presence of a shaman than in the presence of most therapists. In shamanism everyone's path is unique" (personal communication, January 14, 1999).

Part Four

Chapter 11
Trauma And Transformation

When you're afraid here, your adrenaline is pumped up. You become
very sharp, very clear. You hear very well . . . it's like you become this
super person in the few minutes that you're at that point. . . . It's a
spiritual terror. It opens you up totally. Your whole song changes. You
become receptive. It's almost like you're a doorway and it opens up.

Isabel
March, 1997

Physical Trauma and Ontological Shock

Investigators of the alien abduction phenomenon understandably place a great deal of emphasis on its traumatic aspects. Invasive or intrusive procedures, together with apparent bodily symptoms and signs such as nosebleeds, waking with blood in the ear, vaginal or penile pain, cuts and other lesions, and possible small implants seem to combine to form a syndrome that resembles rape or other familiar physical traumata (Herman 1997). Although these elements are often found in abduction cases, I do not believe that they can be discussed apart from the experiencer's response to the encounters or their and our interpretation of their nature and significance. Furthermore, after working intensively with these individuals for more than nine years, it has become apparent to me that the fear and pain related to the physical dimensions, however real, is not a central aspect of the phenomenon or even the most important part of the trauma. Rather, the world or mind-shattering impact of the experiences, bringing about a state of what I have called "ontological shock," seems to come closer to the core of its power.

In this chapter I will examine the features of the abduction experiences that seem to distinguish them from more familiar physical and emotional traumata. I will try to show how and why these disturbing elements seem to carry with them the possibility of profound personal transformation and spiritual growth.

I do not mean to underemphasize the intensity of the terror that abductees experience when they recall that they have been rendered help-less and paralyzed by strange beings, taken to an unfamiliar place against their wills ("without permission"), and subjected to a variety of invasive procedures, conducted—or so it would appear at first—without considera-tion of their feelings. The intensity of the vibratory energy to which they appear to be subjected (see chapter 4) may itself seem nearly overwhelm-ing, not to mention the probing of the body by odd instruments and the sometimes painful manipulation of the genital organs. The terror and rage associated with these violations and loss of control is more or less familiar to anyone who has worked in depth with this population.

The apparent deception by the aliens, and what the abductees may see as the manipulation of their minds so that the beings can more easily fulfill their own agendas, can add to the fear and loathing that the experiencers often express. When one adds to this the isolation that abductees feel because, at least until recently, they could not share their stories without fear of ridicule, social ostracism, or even incarceration, the fact that they cannot predict when the experiences may recur, and their helplessness to protect loved ones from abduction encounters, it is not surprising that they undergo a high level of distress that is in many ways not unlike what occurs in any sort of human trauma.

Nevertheless, although abductees may have trouble finding just the right words to express this dimension of their encounters, they seem to agree that beyond the physical trauma, it is the impact of the experiences on their psyches and worldviews that is most profoundly disturbing. As they explore what they have undergone, experiencers speak of the mind-and belief-shattering power of what has happened, which leaves them challenging everything they had grown up to believe about themselves and reality itself. As Abby put it after a long session in which she had confronted what was for her the inescapable fact of one of her encounters, it was completely "life shattering" (*shattering* or *shattered* are the words most consistently used to describe the impact of the experiences on the sense of reality). Greg's experiences destroyed the "imprisoning and limited" structure of his egoistic beliefs—the idea, for example, that "humans are the most evolved thing in the universe."

Abductees seem to be drawn inevitably to the language of soul and spirit to express the numinous and totalistic nature of their experiences. Whitley Strieber told me that his first encounters were "terror absolute" and an "annihilating catastrophe of spirit." He spoke of "this enormity of soul that's connected with those eyes. It seems to be just obliterating when you connect." For Greg his encounters were "a rape of your consciousness and your soul," a violation "coming without your permission." Carol said that "the invasive, intrusive part, the physical part—that doesn't bother me as much as the spiritual part." As we have seen on pages 153–157, she objected particularly "to the use of your own personal beliefs to mask something that they are doing," and she likens this to "mind rape."

Some abductees feel that certain beings seem to want to take their souls from them. Greg told me that the terror of his encounters with certain reptilian beings was so intense that he feared being separated from his soul. "If I were separated from my soul," he said, "I would not have any sense of being. I think all my consciousness would go. I would cease to exist. That would be the worst thing anyone could do to me." Similarly, Karin, in our first meeting, spoke of the terror of being separated from her body. "The most traumatic part, so far, of my experience," she said, was "the ripping away from reality." She described "the sensation of being pulled from my chest," of "being ripped out of myself—I cannot describe to you the scream, my own scream, being ripped away out of my body."

Isabel experienced something similar. She recalled vividly waking up once in the middle of the night to find "one of the creatures right next to my bed, and another one bending over me trying to bring up as much fear in me" as possible. "I knew instinctively that whatever that thing was that was next to me wanted to enter me. It was just waiting to enter me." She felt certain that what these beings were after is "the human soul." Perhaps, she speculated, this is because "they don't possess a soul." But "they can't just take our souls," she said, "because they cannot come into this world physically. But they can fool you into handing it over."

As Isabel spoke further about her fear that the beings might take over her soul, it became clear that in her mind the soul was intimately linked with the body. "The real me, my spirit or my soul, was inside my body and held everything valuable to me, my loved ones, everything. But as long as I remained in my body, they couldn't just come into it. So it was almost like trying to scare me out of my body." "At one time these beings were physical like us," she said, and so their ultimate desire was to possess a body again. The soul, as she spoke of it, seemed to be a kind of doorway to the body, for "if you hand over your soul, that leaves your body totally empty," and through that vessel (body) the beings can enter this world.

For many experiencers the terror they undergo is linked ultimately to the shattering of their beliefs about the nature of reality. Greg came to realize, even as a child, that no matter what he might believe, "no matter how good I am," those beliefs would offer him no protection from energies that might "crush" him. The result of these experiences, he said, was to "make the world, the universe, the self, bigger." Carol too felt that the beings "intentionally rearrange your belief patterns." For Bernardo a dramatic encounter shattered some of his beliefs as a shaman and opened his consciousness to an experience of the infinite (see chapter 8).

But it is Jim Sparks who has captured for me most clearly the way in which an experiencer's terror is connected with the shattering of a worldview. "I admit the first five, six years [of his awareness of the experiences] was a culture shock to me, a traumatic culture shock of what the world or the universe, at least in my perception, is about, which is nothing like I would have imagined." After "getting over the trauma, it was all about getting over the confusion as to who I am in the universe and all the other things that go with it." It was "an absolute shock," he said, until he came to realize that "it's man who puts a limit on what God did and didn't create, and what He does outside this planet. So who's to say what God has done out there? That doesn't mean this goes against God. It just means that God has created more than you have knowledge of until now."

In the end, as we shall examine in more detail later, abductees may come to terms with the ontological shock brought about by their experiences. Greg has come to see the shattering of the psyche as part of a process of trying to make sense of something utterly unknown. Psychological "rape," he says, can be a kind of "translation" or "misinterpretation" of experiences that run so counter to accepted reality. "The pain and shattering of the psyche," he says, may occur because "the numinous is coming closer." Isabel says simply that "dealing with these aliens shatter[s] all those fake beliefs and shows you that there's more."

Even Carol could come to terms with the trauma of her contacts, at least in part, by comparing them to the way we treat animals and by finding comfort in the idea that she was in some way contributing to life (see chapter 6). "I don't like what they're doing," she said, but "in some ways I probably benefit from it. I don't think that they are intrinsically bad. People ask, 'Why does God let them do this?' Why does God let us experiment on monkeys? . . . I've taken a small child to the doctor when they didn't understand what was happening to them, and when they had to be injected with something or examined. The terror of my children when I have to drag them to the doctor—does that make the doctor bad?"

Confronting the Fear

Although abduction experiences can be intensely traumatic, at least initially, many abductees are not likely to think of themselves as victims if they are given the opportunity to face the fears and come to terms with the power and meaning of what they feel has happened to them. As Whitley Strieber told me, "acknowledging the fear is what gives you freedom." Further, as abductees are enabled to engage their experiences at the deepest level, and to struggle with the terror, pain, and sense of mystery that they evoke, a transformational process of great emotional and spiritual power can take place.*

During one of her experiences, Sue demanded of one of the beings that he turn and look at her. After he did, she was then able to say to herself, "I've seen your face and I'm not afraid of you anymore." Karin has been "terrified by something so profound and so beyond my ability to describe or relate to," but she has chosen to "interact with this experience and learn from it." After working with us for two years, she said, "I'm willing to walk through terror, to go through moments of not knowing, to find out what the ultimate knowing is. What I can do is be true to that sense of my own self, and my own information, and if at the end of my life I find out that I've got thirty percent of the information right and seventy percent wrong, then so be it."

---

* Philosopher Michael Washburn makes a similar point. As the ego lets go of the resistance to its awareness of a deeper reality, what he calls "the Power of the Ground," something that was experienced as "an injurious invasion by an alien force" begins to be experienced as a "rejuvenating infusion of spiritual power" (Washburn, 1995, p. 210).

Isabel's experiences "pushed me to the point where I was scared shitless." "The aliens," she said, "take you right to the limit and then push you over." For her it was the beings who made her face her greatest fears, after which "they just fell apart, and you kind of don't fear too much after that." "Extreme emotion opens up spiritual doorways," she observed. Without intense terror she does not believe that she could have gotten "to the point where your song is actually going to change." Isabel distinguishes both the intensity and quality of the terror that has accompanied her encounters from the fear that is caused by other human beings. If you knew, for example, "that a human is holding you," or "if someone kidnapped you, you'd be afraid on a whole different level. You're familiar with this. The intensity is not the same. . . . It changes you. When you're afraid here [in the encounters], your adrenaline is pumped up. You become very sharp, very clear. You hear very well. . . . It's like you become this super person in the few minutes that you're at that point. . . . It's a spiritual terror. It opens you up totally." Several years after she began to confront her fear, Julie observed that "everything that they've pushed me toward has been toward overcoming a major fear, and once I got past it, it seemed like it was nothing." "The thing that fries us," Nona said, "is the resistance. We have to not resist. We have to allow, to open up. It's a matter of breaking down the things that are built up for us to stay safe in the world."

Greg's struggles with his terror, and the beings that seemed to give rise to them, have taken on epic proportions, cast as a battle of darkness and light. "I have a fascination with the darkness," he said, "but I think the fascination with the darkness is just to see the light in it all." As he speaks of his struggles with the beings, it seems at times as if he, like the biblical Jacob, has been wrestling with the demons of his own nature and for the survival of his manhood. In his early teens, he remembers seeing "little people" that were altogether real to him walking in and out of his room through the walls. He remembers that he would scream out in his fear, but he succeeded only in frightening his father, who threatened to beat him to get him to be quiet.

As an adult, Greg struggled for many years with reptilian-appearing beings who came in spaceships. These beings terrified him, yet he felt drawn to them, possibly because they represented "the darkest, most ugly part of myself. I want to embrace it and ultimately heal it. I don't want to push it away because when I push it away, I push away a part of myself and I can't be whole. I want to say, 'Stop. You can't do this to me,' out of self respect. I want to come to a place where I'm not afraid." These struggles seemed to Greg to constitute a kind of "parallel life."

Greg felt certain that the reptilian beings were out to destroy him, seemingly out of a motive of revenge. They would do this by invading his soul and "sucking the life energy out of me, out of my soul." It was "unbelievably terrifying." Yet he resisted these beings intensely, for he felt certain that his life had a purpose and that he must "deal with this darkness" and not "suffer at the expense of it." But through this struggle Greg discovered that "the light is much stronger," and the battle was actually empowering and even "enlightening." He felt "a compassion for their pain" and did not want "to lose a total connection with them. I think I want in some way to participate in their getting in touch with their souls, to heal their pain." By saying to these beings, "'You may not do this to me,'" Greg found that he was himself, though vulnerable, "powerful and very loving and very strong." In the end, he said, it was consciousness itself that he loved most, and he saw in it "the luminous underneath the darkness." Of the reptilians he said that, although "I don't love what they do to me, I do care for them."

Opening the Heart: The Power of Love

As abductees are enabled to confront their fears, they discover that the character of their experiences often changes, and they may undergo profound personal growth. At the core of the transformational process is an expansion of their loving capacities, which paradoxically includes the emergence of a profound emotional connection between the experiencers and the beings themselves, even, as we saw in Greg's case, beings of the darkest sort.

As he overcame his terror, Whitley Strieber felt "a very deep heart opening," and "an incredible, powerful love for people" emerged. When he was with a group of people, he would experience directly "the richness and the immense integrity of this search that they are all engaged in." Similarly, Greg felt he had moved into "another paradigm where you grow through real love and real understanding." But despite his full engagement in his struggles with the reptilian beings, he questioned whether such pain was essential for growth.

But it is Isabel who has expressed most clearly the power of love to counter the dark or frightening aspects of the alien beings, including those of the reptilian sort. When the beings seem to threaten her, she sends out to them "as much love as I can, waves of love." One time she felt that a reptilian being was sending her images of her second son being mangled or buried alive (her first son had been killed the year before in an automobile accident). She responded by imagining a protective light around the boy's body. A reptilian image came to her with other horrible images of herself and other family members being killed. It seemed that as she sent positive love energy toward these angry beings, she could hear them shrieking and saw them running, then backing off through the wall. Then she saw beings that were gray and reptilian, followed by one of the blue beings she calls the "blue baldies." She sent a "last burst of love energy, calling on Jesus and feeling good inside toward" this being. It seemed to make "a weird sound" and went down as if it were in pain, "like the Wizard of Oz being stripped."

After this encounter Isabel was no longer afraid of the beings. Every time she felt their presence, she would say, "'Hey, if you want all the love you can take, come on,'" which "has given me back such a power." Love, she concluded, is the real power, "the most powerful thing in the whole universe. I think it's what everything is made of. I think it's what started everything." The further we get from that love, she suggests, the "more control" the beings have over us, the more "alien" they remain. "I look at love," she says, "as like an umbilical cord that connects my soul to the main, major Source where all this love comes from." The Source is "like my Father, or my parent. It's where I came from. It's what I am.... The soul eventually goes back to love, because soul came from love."

Trauma and Growth

However traumatic the abduction experiences may be, at least initially, virtually all the experiencers with whom I have worked find in them a spiritual power or the potential for personal transformation. Although I do not believe that I lead or otherwise try to influence the people who seek me out, I cannot deny that this group is self-selected and may at some level of consciousness associate me with at least an openness to a spiritual point of view. Furthermore, whether this spiritual element, which has been noted by other investigators (Lewels 1997; Downing 1993), derives simply from a kind of stretching of the psychic sinews that can occur with any sort of trauma and recovery process, or is a more specific dimension of this phenomenon, is one of the more hotly debated questions in this field. What seems clear is that the human support available to the experiencer, the degree of acceptance by people close to them, and the availability of a facilitator to "hold" the powerful energies associated with the encounters are all important in determining how the experiences are integrated—that is, whether they will lead to personal growth or result in a stuck "victim" position, or even cause emotional scarring.

Sometimes the issue becomes confused with the question of whether the aliens themselves are spiritual.[1] They may or may not be—who is and who is not a spiritual being is one of the more troublesome and perhaps pointless questions that confront explorers of matters like these, since it is we who determine what to call "spiritual." More important is whether the abduction *process* brings about genuine growth, or might even be "intended" or "designed" to do so by whatever intelligence is at its source. Greg, for example, distinguishes between the trauma itself and the spiritual growth that may *derive* from his experiences. He has said that "many alien events are a raping of your consciousness, and I don't think God manipulates us that way or would rape us that way." A higher intelligence, he insists, "would find another way to do it.... It's not a spiritual experience. A spiritual experience is uplifting.... It can, however, get some people into spirituality." But some of the examples that follow suggest to me that these are not, in fact, traumas like other traumata— rather, the transformative element appears to be intrinsic to the phenomenon rather than a secondary reaction that is part of the recovery process.

Isabel, for example, says, "I always knew that what I was dealing with was on a spiritual level." The experiences of everyday life in this society, she observes, are more traumatic than her encounters. "I feel like the alien encounters have helped," she told me. "In an odd way they've helped me to survive." "How so?" I asked. "Because they taught me a lot of lessons," she replied. "First of all that this isn't all there is to life. This is like nothing in the whole scheme of things. It keeps me from focusing too much on my little problems. ... Before some of my more frightening experiences I was what you would call stagnant. I was growing dust. I was getting cobwebs on me—spiritually we're talking here." The idea that life is limited to just "physical or material things" is "much more traumatic," she noted, and "takes a real bad toll on people emotionally, mentally," so that "they end up in the nut farm or taking all kinds of heinous drugs." In contrast to Greg, Isabel believes that her fearful experiences were more effective in "prompting" her to grow and that she would have resisted "something beautiful" or a gentler way.

Karin is convinced that the "ripping from reality" and "from ego" has made her "a completely different person, growing from a new place instead of growing from the place I was, growing from a place of altruism and love, instead of a place of self-defiance and anger." As her "awareness deepens and awakens" in that "new place," Karin has been able to share her experiences with a widening circle of sometimes skeptical people and has become a powerful spokesperson for the transformative power of the abduction encounters. "This experience has completely softened me," she says.

Similarly, Carol, Nona, and Abby, each of whom experienced one degree or another of pain and distress in relation to their experiences, testify to their transformative powers. For Carol the experiences have been "mind-altering," bringing to her "better perception ability, better reception ability. It is a gift. It is a completion." For Nona her experiences "allow the expansion of your spirit, of your soul . . . to the cosmos. You realize that you aren't limited to being a human being here on Earth."

The morning after a long relaxation session, in which she reexperienced the intense energies in her body related to a vivid encounter six years earlier (see pages 81–84), Abby said that she felt "like I have had a religious experience. I've been shaking all morning," she noted, which came from her extreme sensitivity to "energy in the air. I was tasting the air this morning." She felt that she had been "taken to a different level of understanding" by the session, and she wanted to "work on this level to expand humanity's awareness" of how we have "shut down" and "blocked ourselves" from "potentials that are greater than any we have ever perceived." Like many experiencers Abby observed that in "ancient cultures" and among "aboriginal peoples and the native peoples, this isn't abnormal." "Transcendent is definitely the word," she concluded, "*transcending* what you've grown to know as your existence, realizing that your existence is a hundredfold [sic] and this [ordinary reality] is the very bottom of it, energy-wise, the bottom step."

Earlier in this chapter, we saw that confronting and moving through fear and getting in touch with deep energies of love are important ways that experiencers overcome the traumatic dimension of their encounters.

"How do we know," Isabel asked, "that these ... whoever they are, aren't using extreme emotions to help us grow?" Carol compared the "alien encounters" to aspects of Christian mysticism. Fear and pain, she noted, are common to both and are sometimes used by monks "to transcend into a different, an altered state. Monks used to flagellate themselves. Celtic druids used to lock people in a cave for forty-eight hours until they were sensory deprived." Perhaps, Carol suggested, "the fear that we encounter may be literally a physiological necessity for us at that time to transcend."

A Different Kind of Trauma: Shattering Dimensional Boundaries

But there is another element that may contribute to, if not account for, the consistent capacity of abduction experiences to bring about a transformation of consciousness or, in Abby's words, the opportunity to transcend the material level of reality. The altered states and intense emotions that are an intrinsic aspect of the experience appear, with some consistency, to bring about a shattering of boundaries between this domain and the plane of reality where the alien beings seem to exist. That plane, as we have seen, appears to be on a higher vibrational level, and whatever or whomever these beings may be, they seem to have the capacity to break the barriers that separate our reality and theirs. They can then penetrate our world, while, at the same time, raising the vibratory frequency of the experiencers' energies so as to enable them to enter the level of consciousness or dimension of reality in which the beings "reside." (I use quotation marks since Bernard Peixoto and other experiencers have learned that the beings exist nonlocally, "nowhere and everywhere," as he was told.)

Karin has experienced this breaking of the barrier between the beings' dimension (what she calls "the fourth dimension") and ours quite vividly. "Vibrationally it just feels different," she says. "It's like somebody removed the layer that's right here, so now I don't have the safety of this three-dimensional world. It's like somebody flipped a switch and the wall goes away." (We can recall that Rusty likened this phenomenon to actors passing through a scrim in a theater to reveal another scene within the play. See page 59.) Karin says that she starts to "feel presence in the house," sometimes for several hours, before she has gone to bed. At this point "the fourth dimension has already entered the house," and "the barrier is already broken." "They can see me," because "they've integrated the third dimension in with them," but "I can't see them until I get in that altered state of consciousness. The easiest way to get into that altered state is just to go to sleep," she says.

Once this interdimensional penetration has occurred, Karin says, the beings seem to "exist simultaneously" in both dimensions. This used to agitate her quite intensely. Once she would see the beings on her bed, for example, she would struggle and be surprised to see "that they are stronger than you think that they might be, and probably some of it has to do with just vibrating." At these times she would relate her distress to her inability to break out of the energy field that appeared to be holding her. But after she moved through her fear, Karin has observed that the collapse of barriers between dimensions allows her to be "very aware of your soul. You're very aware of your higher consciousness, that thing inside of you that's you."

For Greg the opening to other dimensions or realities brought about by his encounters reconnected him to the natural state of his childhood. As a little boy, he recalled, "I had unbelievable openness" to nature and "the other realms. To me to go to bed at night was one of the most exciting things because I'd be free. I lived on a farm, and it was such a richness—all the animals—everything was living to me. Everything was alive. I just passed in and out of the dimensions. I would go to bed, and I would meet other people, and things would happen, and they were just as real to me. In fact, some had a more feeling quality than my other life." Over time, he says, the constrictions of his upbringing caused "a tremendous amount of pain, so I just withdrew and put up the structures that we all put up in our life and held sacred those things by hiding them."

Despite the intense distress associated with some of their encounters, abductees often speak of having in some way chosen to participate in this process. "We really do create our reality," Greg says. "We can heal and change the things where we allow pain to come in, and we can have a different reality." "When you are presented with an experience," Isabel says, "you make a choice at that point, whether you are aware of it or not, whether you're going to cause that to destroy you or to uplift you in some way. . . . I think even though we might never be able to admit this, all those really frightening experiences that happen to me—I drew them to me." Karin would agree, but does not know "whether it's a presoul agreement or a 'this life' agreement." We have seen how Nona, Julie, Andrea, and other experiencers feel that they have chosen to participate in the hybrid "project." "I have a sense that I have to do this," Nona says. "Even though I don't want to go through it again, it's important."

It has been difficult for me to understand just what abductees mean when they say they have chosen these disturbing experiences or drawn them to themselves. I have considered the possibility that they are somehow rationalizing in order to believe that they have control, when in fact they are quite helpless, or as in the "Stockholm syndrome" associated with hijackings, they might be identifying with their captors in order to feel less threatened. Perhaps the aliens have manipulated their minds in order to deceive them into complying with their agendas. But I have since come to a different view. My sense is that when abductees accept the pain and trauma, it is because at some level they are aware that they are participating in an as-yet-unfathomable process that involves not only their own growth and transformation but an awakening of consciousness for humankind more generally. It is as if their individual psyches were intersecting with an evolving cosmic consciousness with which they intuitively feel some sort of harmony or agreement.

Any trauma may carry with it the possibility of personal transformation and growth. But the alien abduction experiences seem different to me because of their specific capacity to shatter the boundaries of the psyche and to open consciousness to a wider sense of existence and connection in the universe. Nona has expressed well the transformational power of the destruction of identity that has accompanied the awareness of her experiences, which she likens to a shamanic initiation (see chapter 7). "Being lifted up with the fingers and being taken out through my window—that takes you to that edge, almost like meeting death would.... It's a matter of letting go. It's like the boundaries are gone after that happens," and "the same thing happens over and over again." Eventually she let go of her fear of dying and felt a powerful sense of freedom.

For some abductees this boundary-shattering or ego death leaves them with a sense that they are ensouled, even eternal, beings whose existence will survive the death of the body.[2] "I feel that on some level," Isabel says, "there's this huge, bigger part of me that's overseeing all these other little existences that I've chosen to live." She likens this "part" to a kind of game master, a true or eternal self that cannot be killed yet knows that life itself is "still just a game." "I won't die! I won't die!" Nona exclaims. Her sense of "wholeness" is "forever, eternal, separate from the body. Our physical body is our vehicle here and now, and that's fine, that's great, and we need it for doing what we're doing."

Through her experiences and elements of her everyday life as well, Karin has undergone "the loss of everything we know." For her much of the transformational power of the encounters derives from the altered consciousness that she experiences in the other ("fourth") dimension. In that domain everything exists as if in a kind of "spherical" way. In that realm she finds her truer, "Karin" self, in contrast to her three-dimensional existence as "Deborah." "I'm having a three-dimensional experience now," but in this "higher consciousness, Karin, the alien soul, knows no boundaries." In that consciousness her soul "is not bound by time or space" and is "alive and well."

Beyond the Darkness

Once abductees have moved through the boundary-shattering trauma that occurs when they permit themselves to relive their experiences, they may undergo a kind of rebirth that seems to connect them to a wondrous sense of luminosity. Abby expressed a feeling of awe as she recalled the changes she had felt in her body when it seemed to move through matter. It felt to her as if she had been brought in direct touch with a force that had the power to remove disease and "bring back the purity of cellular and molecular structures." Greg, throughout his struggles with the darkness of his nature, had felt protected by love. "There are dark shadows and light shadows," he said, for the shadow too "is one face of the soul." "We go through the dark shadow of ourselves" in order to "get to the luminous part." "You think you could just step into Divinity and let it hold you," he says, but for him "there is a lot of terror" even in "our incredible luminosity." We shall examine this phenomenon in greater detail in the next chapter.

In April 1997 Karin told a large audience that her experiences had enabled her to "look at the deepest, darkest parts of myself," and in so doing "helped me find the infinite love of the 'all that is one' that lives inside of me. I will never again be what I was. Yet there is not a word for how I feel about what I have become. Surely it must be what giving birth is like. There is so much pain because the beauty is so great."[3]

Chapter 12

Returning To Source

I traveled beyond conscious reality as I knew it, while retrieving details of my memories. During that journey I experienced an ineffable moment of total merging. I don't know how else to describe having all your senses experience what should be an impossibility. It is as if I were given a glimpse of my/our potential.

Abby
November 10, 1997

When you are in the presence of that Source connection, there is nothing like it. There is nothing you can conceive of that isn't understood. There is nothing that can't be done. It is a love that cannot be contained, and you know then why I get so angry that I have to be back here.

Will
August 15, 1997

Messengers from the Source

Virtually all religious and spiritual traditions in societies around the world and through time have in common knowledge of a supreme or ultimate creative principle or intelligence which is variously called the Divine, the Source (or just Source), the One, Home (especially favored by abduction experiencers), the Great Spirit, the ground of being, or God. The members of particular societies may experience a variety of relationships with this principle, ranging from a disturbing sense of estrangement or fear to a powerful feeling of spiritual presence or intimate oneness and harmony. The secular modern, or post-modern, Western culture in which I was raised and have lived is perhaps unique in the degree to which many of its members have become separated from any sense of the actuality of a divine presence or higher power in nature (Smith 1992). Some even deny the existence of any such principle, placing man at the peak of the cosmic intelligence hierarchy (Zimmerman 1998, p. 3).

I am not skilled in the disciplines necessary to argue effectively for or against the reality of a divine presence immanent in nature. My sense is that the kinds of evidence that people find relevant to such questions are more likely subjective or experiential than objective or empirical. What has, however, become clear to me in the nearly ten years that I have been wrestling with the mystery of the alien abduction phenomenon is the fact that the deeper power and meaning of the encounters cannot be understood without consideration of their transformative power and spiritual significance. "There aren't just little gray guys with big eyes," Karin says. "Ultimately it's about knowing God."

We seem to be experiencing now in the United States, and more or less throughout Western culture, a kind of spiritual renaissance. It reflects a deep hunger for something missing in the lives of many people, a sense, however vague, that there are other realms from which they feel cut off, and a growing realization that many of the catastrophic events of this century now ending have derived from radical secularism and spiritual emptiness. It seems clear that people in the West are increasingly seeking more direct contact with a higher power, which would usually be called God were it not for the anthropocentric connotation and other baggage that has become attached to this word.

Many of the phenomena documented in this chapter may sound familiar to students of the history of religious traditions. The longing for connection with Source or the ground of being; the anguish of separation from the Divine; the process of breaking down the barriers to connection or reconnection with Source; the cycles of the soul's incarnation or reincarnation—are all familiar aspects of spiritual transformation. There is an extensive literature on these various topics, and those interested in exploring them further might consult the sources suggested in the notes to this chapter.[1] What seems to be unique about the abduction phenomenon, as documented throughout this book, is its reality-shocking content, its energetic intensity, and its potentially rapid transformative power. This may enable individuals who, generally speaking, have not undertaken a path of spiritual practice to connect or reconnect with Source dramatically and quickly when they confront and work through the mind-shattering terror that often, at least initially, is produced by the encounters.

Some of the approaches to a higher power are initiated by individuals themselves. These include traditional forms of religious worship, such as prayer, meditation, and devotional service; twelve-step programs for the treatment of addictions; yoga, Holotropic Breathwork, and controlled out-of-body experiences (Buhlman 1996; Monroe 1971 and 1996); thoughtful use of psychedelic agents; vision quests and other activities associated with native and Eastern spiritual practices and rituals. But some transformational agents seem to come as if from outside, hardly expected or desired by the person himself, except in the broad sense discussed in the previous chapter. These include near-death and other spontaneous out-of-body experiences, traumatic losses, serious illnesses or other personal tragedies that propel spiritual growth, spontaneous religious epiphanies or "born again" experiences, and of course encounters with strange humanoid beings.

In this chapter I will try to show how the alien abduction phenomenon can potentially be one of the most powerful agents of spiritual growth, personal transformation, and expanded awareness that is now affecting people on this planet.[2] As Karin puts it, abduction experiences are the "fast track" for personal change (see also Whitley Strieber's remarks on page 18). "You want to know what it's like to be in Source?" she once exclaimed. "You want to know what it's like to be connected to the universe? You want to know about that fifth-dimensional part of yourself [she means a kind of fine vibratory resonance] that's in every other human being, and you want to know what it feels like to be talking to that and be communicating with that and be in communion with that? Here it is, honey. Let's go. And that's what I've been doing for the past two and a half years, being in that space, working through that stuff, and learning how to communicate in ways that we don't have a language for here."

In earlier chapters we have seen how the light, energy, and vibratory intensity of the abduction experiences, the traumatic shattering of the abductees' worldviews, and the shocking visions of the threat to the planet's life to which they have been exposed have combined to open their awareness to an expanded view of reality. Here we will explore more deeply the expanded sense of consciousness and the spiritual power and meaning of the encounters for the abductees' lives and for their view of themselves in a rapidly and radically transforming world.

In order to appreciate this dimension of the phenomenon, it is necessary, I have found, to bear with the experiencers the fear, pain, and nearly overwhelming vibratory energies associated with the abduction experiences, and to put aside as much as possible conventional worldviews and ontological preconceptions. If a facilitator is unable to do so, the experiencer may become stuck in a place of resentment and victimization from which personal growth is difficult or impossible.

Sue expresses this challenge clearly: "I think what this phenomenon is doing, the abduction scenario," is to press "really nasty buttons. It makes you feel like a victim. At the moment you have no control. You can't do anything, so what do you do? Do you lie back and take it? Do you withdraw, or do you fight? Well, I'll tell you, if you get up and fight and get beyond that victimization feeling, change happens. It's unbelievable what happens. It has been for me, and I know it can be for everybody else. But what most people are not doing is getting beyond that feeling of being a victim."

The alien beings are usually perceived by experiencers, not as spirits or godly creatures, but as emissaries or messengers from the creative principle, which they most often seem to call "Source." For Karin the beings function as "the go-between. It's the translator" or a "kind of interpreter," bridging the gulf that has developed between humans and "the One." "For us to get the message from the Divine Source, it has to come through something that's already connected," she suggests. Other experiencers note that the beings seem to have a connection with spirit or Source that we do not have or have lost.

Sometimes abductees perceive, or are told by the beings, that their (the beings') true nature is a kind of energy form, but that they have to become embodied to play this intermediary role between humans and Source. "There's an advantage that I think these beings have," Carol says, for "they are able to fathom more about the universe and all beings' relationships in it. There's such an unbelievable comfort that I can get from communicating with these beings," she notes, for "by helping me feel something that I can't see, touch, smell, taste, they help me feel closer to that Universal Source." "I don't think technologically advanced aliens come all across the universe just to look up your ass," Greg observed caustically. "I think this whole phenomenon is about the desire of humanity to touch the numinous and the numinous coming closer."

According to Karin, "The messengers of the Source are the grays, and they are in touch with the Source, even closer than we are, so they're that middle connection ground" and will "assist us with the transition on Earth." "The blond ones, the tall blond ones, are still closer to Source," she says, as do many other experiencers. They are the "spiritual supervisors," or "Source incarnate, and can teach us things about how Source in its true form, its true energy form, exists." Another time she said, "These blond guys to me are the spiritual leaders that kind of watch over the grays that interact with us." "The Creator," she says, has "messengers of all sorts that are calling us to continue our evolution."

"We're Not from Here:" The Pain of Separation

As I explore their encounters more deeply, especially their experiences of Source, abductees sometimes express the conviction that the Earth is not their true Home, which is in another realm outside of space and time. Even the spaceship may feel like Home or a part of Home. "The ship is my Home," Karin says. "I miss my Home. I miss all the things I know that are familiar, like the walls that curve around. I'm familiar with the lighting." She has a kind of spirit guide or head alien she knows well in the ship, whom she calls Fresca. When she experiences being taken up, "he's immediately there. It's like being in ER or something. There's this team of people there, and the first thing that happens is, a connection's made telepathically: 'Welcome back, you're here, you're loved and with the One.' That's what they call themselves, the One."

Experiencers may have quite clear notions of Home, or what it is like to be in the presence of Source or God, as if it were a totally familiar place. "The Source," Catherine says, is "not bounded by any particular dimension or universe or place, as we would see it, or time as we know it. It's the energy that surrounds everything. . . . It's the energy that makes things do whatever it is that they do, what gives things life, what gives the energy its energy. It's got a knowing to it." Gary speaks of knowing in language that echoes Old Testament fears of Yahweh. The encounters "awaken ancient Source," he says. "There is all-knowing in the craft," knowledge so powerful that if we were "aware of our full potential," or if we were to face "what we are," the "trauma" would be so enormous that the body would "disintegrate." Karin experienced the power and beauty of the Source energy in relation to the hybrid babies (see chapter 6). "It's pure energy," she says, "and seeing those little ones and all the love that came out of the experience with them was so beautiful."

Will, speaking of Home or "Divinity," says, "The love there is incredible. There is a depth that just doesn't exist here. They [most human beings] are not ready for it here." When I asked him to speak further "about the depth," he began to cry and said, "If you can, try to imagine the deepest, most beautiful color that you've ever seen. It would be like the next moment knowing that you were going to be blind for the rest of your life. There's a depth to the connectedness and to the feeling nature. It's as if at one level we are one, and yet the sense of individuality that has taken control in this world still exists." In the summer of 1997, Will spoke about his experiences to an audience consisting mainly of therapists. "When you are in the presence of that Source connection, there is nothing like it," he said. "There is nothing you can conceive of that isn't understood. There is nothing that can't be done. It is a love that cannot be contained, and you know then why I get so angry that I have to be here."

The pain of separation or disconnection from Home or Source that is suggested in Will's words is felt by many experiencers. I have seen Will himself weep on several occasions when he expressed his longing to be reunited with God but had to face the fact of his commitment to life on this plane. On several occasions in his life—most strikingly, when he brought upon himself as a fifteen-year-old boy the severe burns that cost him his left arm, an event he sometimes refers to as "the execution"—Will has more or less consciously toyed with the notion of killing himself in order to return to his "Home" or be reunited with God.

From this perspective Will's relationship with the beings is ambivalent, to say the least. On the one hand, they seem to bring him close to Source, with all the poignancy of the attendant separation. At the same time, as in the incident of near-fatal electrocution in the tree, the beings appear to protect him and bring him back from the edge of death. Just before he grabbed the wire that completed the circuit that sent intense electrical current through the left side of his body, Will remembered being able to "see forever," which expressed both his view from the tall tree and a feeling of closeness to the beings and Home. In the next moments, Will remembers thinking, as if from both his own and the beings' point of view, "This little shit is going to do this as often as he can, bring it right to the brink," and "the little shit knows that we're not going to let him die, that we're not done yet."

As he spoke further of the moments surrounding the "execution," Will seemed to relive his life-and-death struggle, and the experiences surrounding the electrocution in the tree appeared to merge with memories of other encounters with the beings. "As much as I want to be them, I can't be them," he lamented. "When I'm in their presence, and I'm around them, and I'm close to them, and I feel like I'm being used by them, I'm okay. They're going to make me go back, John, and I remember it now, the smells, the body, the tearing of the membranes." "There is something I can't reconcile yet," he continued. "I don't want to have to forget this closeness. . . . When they look at me, there's total understanding in the eyes. . . . The problem occurs not even that day but later on in the hospital. . . . I'm going to just want to freak out. . . . They, they're going to put me back."

Going back to the moment in the tree just after he grabbed the charged wire, Will poured out a jumble of thoughts with a confusion of pronouns that seem to reflect a fluidity in his identity between himself and the beings:

> We're going to let the body drop now, and I'm going to be with this for a while. I accomplished what I wanted. I got in, and I'm going to hang with them for a while. I'm going to be with the One, and it's beyond intoxicating, because the bulk of my ordinary systems are bulked down or tuned out, so we're going to let the body drop, and I'm gone for a little while. You really don't need to see this. You're going to go away, but you'll come back and check in. We're going to give you this information. It's not so much to get you up to speed, but you're also going to have to forget it for a while. But you're going to have to access it again, as you are. I don't know how to say it. . . . This isn't really necessary. I really didn't have to do it, I, Billy [Will's name for his flesh-and-blood, less spiritual self].

Though Will's torment is extreme, most abductees also have trouble reconciling the sense that they are different from other people and do not belong here with their earthly existence and commitments. Isabel sometimes feels unbearable loneliness and that "I'm some weird species." "I've never felt a part of everyone else," she told me in one of our first meetings. "When I'm with them, I feel at Home. I feel a part of them. I feel more a part of them than I do here, even though I went through a lot of terror with them, and it's been very confusing."

Karin speaks again and again of her painful separation from the other realm:

> It's really hard to feel so much love, and so much connection to those children, and to all of the people there, and be so separate from all of it down here, and be so different, because I feel like this fish flopping around on the pier with no air.... I can't express that in this life . . . I have this part of me that knows the universe, that knows the Creator, and I need to connect it to somebody, and I can't. . . . Right now we [experiencers] can't integrate the two. . . . This new species [this was after a powerful encounter involving hybrid babies] is going to be able to do it.... I'm angry that I'm separated from the ship. I'm angry that I'm separated from that consciousness, and for the most part I'm separated from anything here on Earth.

The reconnection with God has been the purpose of Eva's life, and her experiences have been an intimate part of this process. "I have searched to quench a thirst I could not name," she wrote in her graduate school thesis. "I experienced a longing I did not know how to express, and I wept for my broken heart."[3] In the language of religious ecstasy related to her study of Kabbalistic texts, Eva wrote of "committing the rest of my days to do Your work, to unveil Your light in the darkness, to re-member [sic] and reclaim orphaned parts of our Selves back into wholeness and oneness, to Be a bridge between Heaven and Earth, a communion of spirit and matter."

Some abductees note the relationship between sexuality and the spiritual union they are seeking. They are not, of course, alone in perceiving this connection, but for them there may be an additional understanding. "Physical soul communion" can occur when two people have sex, Karin has remarked, and for many people "that's the closest we literally get to feeling God." "But it's not the flesh with the flesh," she suggests, it is the separate energies "becoming one energy," and "in communion with another energy we stop feeling so alone. We recognize that we're connected to something," and "for a brief moment" one may know "what Source resonating in your body feels like." But this, she says, does not gratify "the soul thing inside of us." "I don't need to have sex with somebody to feel that I'm in union in this spherical timeless, spaceless space. I know that I am part of Source. I am aware of my connection. But other people don't feel their connection, or they feel it only in very brief moments. One of the ways we get in connection all the time is in a sexual experience."

Separation from God's Point of View: The Cosmic Game

At times experiencers may perceive the dilemma of duality and the pain of separation as if from Source's viewpoint. Karin speaks as if she knows the anguish of separation as God might feel it. She identifies with "all the pain of all the people in our world, the pain of separation from our Home, the pain of separation from not having children, and just the thought of separation from the One, and then the Universe's pain that it feels for our experiences." When she is "out in the universe in that altered place and those other realities" and is awakened by experiencing Source within her, it is then that Karin feels, especially from the blond beings, their hurt "for all the lost souls that aren't going to get it. It's just horrible," Karin continues. "It's God being so sad about what's going on. It's like I can feel the weeping of the womb, of the earth. . . . I have to feel this pain." From the anguish of their separation from Source, it has occurred to some experiencers that perhaps the pain caused by this duality might have to do with our concreteness, the density of our physical embodiment. Julie likens embodiment to being in a lead-lined room.

Karin and other experiencers may come to see all of perceived reality as an expression of God consciousness in which human beings participate. Karin, Isabel, Will, Greg and others relate their abduction experiences to a kind of cosmic game in which a lonely Creator learns of Itself though a splitting of consciousness—"an explosion into the multiplicity of Self," Greg says. Out of the primordial potential, God spawns beings who separate from Him and then choose to reconnect. But in the case of humankind, the experiment went awry, as many of us have lost connection with the creative principle altogether. The alien beings seem to play a part in reconnecting the experiencers to the Creator or Source. Psychiatrist Stanislav Grof, from his own researches with nonordinary states of consciousness, has come to a similar view of the process of cosmic evolution (Grof 1998).

It is Catherine whose abduction experiences led her to the most elaborate understanding of the relationship between human embodiment and separation from Source. In January 1993, in a relaxation session in which she moved readily into an altered state of consciousness, she brought forth a kind of parable of human/alien/Source incarnation or reincarnation. Once a "very, very long time" ago, she said, in a sort of "training center" that was "not a place like we have places here," something like a project developed wherein some beings (potential humans) would, after a kind of council or debriefing, choose to come to the Earth and become embodied (really more densely embodied, since beings in the Source realm were, Catherine insisted, "embodied somewhat"), while other ones (the aliens) would "check up on the ones who were embodied, keep track of what they were doing, problems, changes that needed to be made." The purpose of this project or experiment was to increase knowledge of our awareness and connection to Source and in a sense Source's knowledge of Itself.

After the "debriefing," those beings who would become human "go to another place—it's not an easy thing to move between realms—where there is a machine or device that enables us to make a temporary hole or tunnel [a tunnel again] between realms," that is, between "this physical plane" and a kind of primordial or sourceful dimension from which such differentiation can evolve. "There are other physical planes," she remarked, "but this just happens to be the one we went to." After passing through what seemed like just a few feet in the tunnel, Catherine and the other beings who were headed for embodiment emerged "in this [Earth] realm." When I asked her to describe the tunnel itself, Catherine said, "We do have some physical matter there [in the Source dimension]," although with "slightly different physical laws." The "tunnel is an actual physical tunnel, like maybe three feet long, and on the other end, I can see stars and blackness and Earth." But the transition the Earth-bound beings make is a kind of "projection of consciousness," for "we don't have to physically move down to Earth."

The decision as to "where we want to be born" appears to be based on what a particular soul in its evolution needs to "work on" or, in Catherine's case, "what will make it easiest for me to reestablish the energy connection." The decision to take human form, she says, was "made before," but it was "my option as to what circumstances I want to be surrounded by." In this instance Catherine chose "a very hard life" that would "force me to look for other answers." Her memory was of entering a woman's body at the moment of conception in what appeared to be India thousands of years ago. Because of the extreme poverty of this family's situation, Catherine thought she would be "less distracted by physical things" and might be forced to "look for other meanings" and thus be able to make an "energy connection" with Source.

Catherine then seemed to remember in vivid detail the experience of pregnancy ("this warmth, this liquid") and the crushing, squeezing sensation of her birth, this time as a baby boy. "This seems like a hell of a way to start an embodiment," she remarked. Equally vivid memories followed of feeling "very cold all over" after she was out of the womb, being hit, crying, and then being shown to her mother, who had dark hair and olive skin, after which the umbilical cord was cut with a curved blade of some sort. What struck her most was "how physical everything is. Everything's so solid." Catherine, as this baby boy, could "feel everything" and "hear and smell things," taste what he was fed, and make "somewhat of a connection" with the mother. But the energy Catherine had been surrounded with before was not there, and she felt terribly isolated. "I don't know if I can survive a whole lifetime of this," she wondered, but "It's too late now. I can't really get out of it."

It did not take the Indian baby boy more than perhaps a few months to lose his "knowledge of who I really am" and "of the Source." But this is all "planned," she said, for the alien beings, who keep track of this process, "know that you're going to lose the knowledge of the Source." The purpose of the project was to "force us through the isolation to make different connections with the Energy" and become "disengaged once again from the physical." "If you keep the knowledge of the Source, that kind of defeats the purpose of the experiment, which continues over many lifetimes.[4] The spaceships and the alien beings have been around for thousands of years," she said, but "have been interpreted differently." The embodied form in which human beings see them "is the form that they have to take to come here, to check up on us." After the relaxation exercise was over, Catherine and I reviewed this session. She was struck by the vividness and coherence of the details and "overwhelmed by the physicality of it." (Other material from this session is contained in chapters 3 and 6.)

Reconnecting and Remembering

As experiencers explore their encounter history, they may discover that they have had an intimate relationship from the beginning of their lives with beings of some kind or with Source itself. As a child, when Andrea would play outside with her brothers and sisters or be alone in nature, she would feel "deeply connected with everything around there." As the experiencers grow up, they are likely to lose awareness of this connection. After we had worked with him for about two years, Will realized that his relationship with the beings was lifelong. In the session in which he related in detail the "execution" (see pages 239–243), the beings had run by him "the full movie" of his connection with them, "which is something I'm kind of in denial of." As a child he "envisioned a little red devil, which was the earliest way that I could conceive it." The message from them was "'We are going to be with you from the get go'" and "'Every time you've gone through the fire of something, it's been okay.'"

"The soul gets placed with a body" or "shell," Karin said in her first meeting with us, and "decides, yes, I'm going to be a part of this," but "what happens through the birth process is that the soul loses its consciousness of itself." As she explored her encounters over the next year, she realized that she had been "seeking to know God since I was young" and had been aware since she was eight years old that "I am a spiritual being." The role of the aliens—one of whom she described as "insect looking" with segmented arms, a thin neck, sticklike legs, and "this huge head with these huge eyes"— seemed to be to enable her to become aware that "we are not alone" and to "find the consciousness" of Source once again.

Before the one regression that we did together, Gary told us of a vision that occurred while he was being held as a two-year-old in his mother's arms. As he looked around in childlike wonderment, his attention was drawn to a high church steeple that was back-lit by a golden object that "rose higher and higher until it was above the steeple."* A voice that "appeared like God was talking to him" and said, "I have something for you to do." Gary had remained convinced all his life that "the Creator, the

---

* After he read his passage in the manuscript, Gary wrote to me, "I would like to emphasize that there was no fear in the light. A feeling of perfect peace accompanied by colleagues. I felt equal and connected" (letter to the author, May 20, 1999).

Source of everything," had talked to him, and by the time he was fifteen he had "made a decision to do what I'd been asked to do."

In the relaxed state, the energies Gary was experiencing were so intense that he had trouble speaking coherently. He immediately recalled from perhaps age five a humanoid being without hair and a head too large for its body. I encouraged him to go back to age two, when he was with his mother. Now, referring to himself in the second person, he recalled a "golden disk" and said, "You're sitting in a craft with a being. There's possibly others behind." As the session continued, he experienced a profound feeling of trust and a sense of "presence." He seemed to move into a deeper state of consciousness, a state of awe, where "there is only knowing," and those of us present, himself and the beings, were all a "circle of colleagues" with "one intention, one complete agreement," and "complete trust." "The human mind is separate and restricted," he said, but in this place there is no time, death, separation or fear, only mutual understanding.

Gary then struggled to put together "the boy and where my being is in the ship." The ship, he realized, was not as our minds ordinarily understand this, but of light. "The little boy is seeing our vehicle. We are in the vehicle, and he is connected. It is like we become One. We agree to be together." Gary attributed his mission as a healer who "awaken[s] ancient Source in other humans" to this early experience "of all-knowing in the craft" and "relating between craft and child." In this somewhat ecstatic state, he realized that since earliest childhood he had never really forgotten his relationship to the Divine and had always felt protected. He spoke of an awareness of destiny, of the powerful energies that surged through him during the session, and of his need for colleagues to help him fulfill his purpose. "Source," he realized during the session, was "far beyond what man has put up as gods." The human body "can't take the full vibration." "More shamans" need to come together, he remarked, to "lift the consciousness of their people."

As abductees explore their encounters, they may discover that finding a way to reconnect with Source, to "return to the One," has, as it was for mystics of an earlier time, been a central project of their lives. "I just want to go Home, and I know that they will get me there as soon as I acknowledge that every opportunity, every circumstance in my life is exactly that," Will told the audience in 1997. We have seen how his determination to rush the transformation process by destroying his body nearly cost him his life when he was fifteen. In April 1998 he told us poignantly that on that day "I tried to make a call [Home], and that's not my place." The understanding he had at fifteen "did not prepare me for the grief that I feel in my humanness for what I have done. I was getting a little ahead of myself. I was getting pretty arrogant."

We will consider now the role of the abduction experiences and the alien beings in bringing about this reconnection with the supreme principle. In my view this process is at the heart of the abduction phenomenon. It begins with choosing and remembering. Eva wrote in her thesis, "Transcendence occurs when one chooses unity over duality." Karin told us, "Each soul, each consciousness has to choose for itself that it wants to awaken, that it's ready. When you make a conscious decision to sacrifice, to love, to be scared, to walk into all of those places, boom, something starts happening." Each person who "is opening themselves up is doing it at the pace that's comfortable for them." She, however, is "doing it at this unbelievable speed. It's like I'm just devouring it," for "I have this one lifetime and I have a ton of stuff to do."

As we saw in the previous chapter, the reconnection to Source that many abductees speak about seems to depend on a breaking down of barriers or layers of the mind, confronting pain, terror, annihilation, death, and above all the surrender of control to the energy or spirit of the universe. "Without that process," Eva says, "being embodied and being with the mental mind that a human has," it would not have been "possible to get where I am now." Whatever the "aliens'" ultimate "purpose" or "intention" (I use quotation marks to recognize that such designations and concepts reflect the way our minds work), the abduction encounters seem to provide a virtually unparalleled opportunity to bring about the transcendence that so many abductees seek, and in the process they may lose the fear of death.

"It's like somebody takes the inside of my skull and all the crap that keeps me from being open," Karin once said. "They peel off the layers, and that's when the lessons start happening." "I'm not going to be annihilated by my own pain," she said two weeks later. "Maybe I'm being incredibly naïve, but I completely trust the universe." And two weeks after that, she declared, "Pain is almost synonymous with lesson." "It's not about making sense," Eva says, "I'm talking from a level where there's just pure existence" and "no barriers." As another abductee confronted her fears, "blockages melted like snow in the summer sun," she said. (This woman's case has not been discussed elsewhere in this book.)

Sequoyah Trueblood said to a group of my colleagues in 1997:

We've got all these abduction cases that our brother here, John, is working on. When some of these people are taken by extraterrestrials, what they've shown is that "hey, we don't have control. . . . I do have this fear here." . . . So when we do have these abduction experiences, it puts us in a situation where we get to experience that fear, and we have a chance to transmute it, to let go of it at that time. The only way we can do it, though, is through prayer and giving ourselves back to that Source that we came from, acknowledging that Source first. . . . So when people come back reporting, "Well, I didn't have any control there," it's true. We don't, and what we're being shown in those cases is that everything in this universe is an example of unconditional love.

Isabel regards her abduction experiences as "a school to help you remember what you already know," which is that "we are all part of God, but living in this backward structure, and through centuries and centuries of doing this stupid backward way, we have forgotten the original way, how creation was supposed to be. I don't know why these beings are helping us to remember, but I'm glad they are." "What's important," she continues, "is creating life and remembering who you are. The spiritual part, this remembering, is the main objective" of the abduction experiences. "I had to go through all the terror. I had to go through letting go of everything, having everything shattered in my life. All of that was just a preparation for where spiritually I'm ready to start remembering everything. . . . If I had chosen to remain at the terror stage, I could be in that stage for ten years."

"There is an intention" in all this, Isabel believes. "They started grabbing us, and the end result is we started remembering our powers. . . . The remembrance program, the awakening program, whatever it is, I think they have actual steps. You know, it's not random." Even dying to her means freedom, discovering other "facets" of herself, which she likens to the many facets of a diamond, "other Isabels that are living other lives, other experiences in other dimensions."

In the Presence of the Love

In the early fall of 1997, Karin had an experience that seemed to bring her directly into the presence of Source. It began when a blue light came into her room, and the next thing she remembered was seeing an orange light at the bottom of a ship, into which she was brought quickly. Once in the ship, she found herself inside of what appeared to be a small metal ball with a piece of metal that came up around her head. Next to her was a tall blond being who appeared to be wearing an odd monklike robe. She recognized this being as her tutor, mentor, teacher, and guide—all words that she used—and it was he who had put her inside the ball, "'for transport to the light,'" he explained. In front of her face, Karin saw a deep brown red color, and the being told her to stand up and "watch the light."

Karin began to cry as she saw "the light coming from a distance" in the form of a huge ball. As she relived the rapid approach of this light, she screamed in what seemed to be a mixture of fear, release, and awe. "I'm being baptized in this light," which is "going to take me," she cried, "a wash of light, and it's all knowledge. It's Home. It's Essence." Her words at this point became somewhat incoherent, filled with metaphor, as she tried to convey what was for her a kind of ecstatic spiritual epiphany. What follows is a sample. (Ellipses indicate her asides [like "this is weird" or "I can't describe this to you")], which seem less necessary for capturing the quality and meaning of the experience.)

> There are moments of time that are like breaths in the wind, and each of these moments is a life. . . . There's a soul that comes to greet it, and the soul has no form, yet it has a hand. . . . This is communion. This is gestation. This is Myself that I'm meeting [crying again]. . . . This is a mirror to my soul. . . . I'm standing in this white yellow light, and Presence is in front of me. As I am touching this white yellow Presence, it forms a hand out of just the yellow light. . . . I'm standing in the presence of the One, who is Myself. . . . This is about being at peace with my mission. . . . It's very difficult to talk because communication is happening nonverbally.

The robed being was at "a very different energetic level than any of the other beings I've been around," Karin explained. "He resonated very deeply, very wisely, and I couldn't see his face." He took her to a another place, where she remembered standing in a kind of odd spread-out position. A powerful force of light and vibration seemed to explode and rip through her like "the force of water coming out of a dam. Water doesn't even describe it." As this force tore through her, she felt as if she would be knocked over backward, and she sensed that she was becoming smaller and smaller. She was taken through a tunnel and found herself "in Presence," where there were no walls or rooms but "just light, like being in the core." In this moment she felt "there is nothing more than this."

The ripping sensation continued in the tunnel, Karin explained, and it seemed as if some sort of adhesive that bound her to her body was torn through by the energy or resonation she experienced. What made this particularly difficult, beyond the discomfort that she felt, was that she was given an opportunity to stay in that "place," stay out of her body, and not complete her earthly mission. It felt like a cruel choice, but she chose to come back. "It's weird to come back into my body," she said. "They have a room on the ship that's for this, maybe like a temple. I went from being expansive and formless in shape to a pinpoint dot, and then I'm standing there in my body, and my body has not changed position." After this experience she found that her intuitive empathy for others seemed to increase. As she reflected on this experience, Karin wondered, "How can I be meeting myself? But it is me. . . . You feel that there is One there and at the same time an infinite number."

When Karin is with her mentor/guide, "he speaks to the One inside of me that is One of us, that is One of them" and "resonates with my soul vibration." He tells her that on the plane of his existence, they do not experience "the ecstasy of love that you do, but we experience something that resonates of Home and safety." "Your love is very unsafe," he tells her, for "it is given and taken in passionate moments that do not have any consistency, so it comes in explosive bursts and leaves in draining pain." (Sharon remarked similarly that the alien beings seemed to know "love without all the stickiness that we have.") The communications carried a specific personal meaning for Karin, as it occurred when she was working through the pain of a recent broken love relationship. She experiences the love that comes from Source as "a resonance inside my body." It is unconditional and cannot be killed. "I'm always in this love," she says, and no matter how much pain she is in, "that makes me know I can't commit suicide."

Growing and Expanding: Metaphors of Birth

Abductees seem always to live in the paradox of their human individuality and separateness from Source while at the same time experiencing a sense of wholeness or oneness in an unfathomable reality. "When I experience the beings—whatever you want to call them, the angels, guides, spirits," Eva says, there is "the perspective of being separate from them, an object-subject, object-relationship thing going on." But at the same time, "there is a very close connection" and "a feeling of wholeness" and completion. "There is no separation between me and the space. I become part of the space. I merge into the space."

When abductees are so able, either through their own efforts or with the help of a facilitator who can be with them through the extreme emotions and intense energies that accompany their passage to connection or reconnection with the creative Source, they go through an awakening at every level of their being. They may feel that they have gone through a profound transformation. These changes are sometimes corroborated by relatives and friends.

Nona feels that her experiences have brought about a great sense of openness, "a total awareness," that enables her to communicate with other people "on an energy-emotional-physical-spiritual level that changes your entire relationship immediately with everybody." Sue's experiences, she feels certain, have "changed the way I think. I am more tolerant. I don't judge people, as I know I did, any longer." Andrea experiences this awareness on what feels like a cellular level. The cells "speak to you. They're like little universes. They're asleep, and we wake them up. We have so much more ability in our body than we know," she believes. "Each cell has a memory, and each memory can tell us how to move energy and become more connected to each other."

Abductees often say they are expanding, growing, evolving, or becoming whole. Karin speaks of her experiences as "not only life-preserving but life-growing. Everything that you get is about moving forward, moving forward, moving forward, expanding, expanding, expanding, expanding. You open and you open and you open. This is the awakening, this is the flower, unfolding. This is what the becoming is." Concomitantly experiencers know that their capacity for love, compassion, caring, and service to others has grown. With the opening of her consciousness, Andrea says, comes "unconditional love, acceptance," and a sense of responsibility for "taking care of everything," especially children.

According to Isabel, at least some of the beings seem to find our evolutionary struggles quite funny. "These creatures have an incredible sense of humor," she notes. "We think this is all so serious. This isn't serious to them. I think they would joke about it, like, 'Well, it was about time. We thought you'd never wake up.'" During one of her abductions to what seemed like a strange planet, she met a being that at first she did not recognize. She says that he laughed, "and at that moment I recognized him. He thought it was funny that I didn't know it was him all along," and "that we had known each other for thousands of years. I didn't think it was funny at all. It's a big deal for us, because we have fooled ourselves into thinking that this [the reality of life on earth] is it."

As we saw in chapter 7, the process of becoming or expanding consciousness is often expressed in the language of birth, as in Julie's idea of interdimensional "delivery," Catherine's vivid recounting of actually being born at the beginning of a previous life, Dave's passage through "birthing canals" from one level of reality to another, and the prominence of tubes, cylinders, tunnels, and so on as symbols of passageways from one place or domain to another.

Karin speaks of how consciousness itself appears to "birth its way into the understanding that it's not separated." She likens the process of returning to Source to "being born again." "There is literally another birth that you go through that is the awareness and the awakening to 'this is my existence.'" "The Creator, the creation, universe, wants us to create life, to move forward. All of this is a birthing experience," she says, while decrying the choice of death through suicide made by the followers of Marshall Applegate. Karin compares her rebirth to emerging from a chrysalis. Karin, Isabel, and others think of us as developing, seeking, and healing *with* God. Using the imagery of disease and health, Karin suggests that we are a part of God that is "infected." The abduction phenomenon is "surgery. That's what it is. This isn't about annihilation. This is about birth and about growth and about healing."

Awakening of Consciousness: Individual and Collective

Many abductees report that their experiences have awakened in them powerful psychic gifts, such as unusual intuitive capacities, healing abilities, and clairvoyance. Carol, for example, speaks of developing "extreme perceptive abilities." Isabel believes that these powers are already present in us but that, especially in our culture, we have shut down and lost touch with them. "This is something that basic people have been experiencing for so long," she said to me. "But it's almost like you guys at the top are just beginning to learn about it." It seems to her as if "the more educated you get in a way, the more your spirituality closes off." "My father," she said gently, "used to call such people educated fools."

Isabel's perceptions have become so sensitive that when she hears water running or the wind blowing, it can sound like "a whole bunch of voices singing at the same time, really beautiful music." She feels that she can actually hear other people's thoughts, but she has not "fine-tuned" this capacity because "you could really intrude on someone that way." She reports that she was also able to visualize—accurately, as it turned out—the location of an ID card that a friend of her daughter had misplaced. Her possession of these abilities has convinced her "that we are all connected" and of the energetic power of thoughts. I have not written much of these matters in this book, except in passing. This is one of the areas that does lend itself to objective study and verification, but research has yet to be undertaken.

Abductees frequently feel that the process of transformation that is so powerful and immediate for them personally is part of, or even heralds, a collective shift in human consciousness and behavior. Carol feels that the abduction phenomenon has to do with "an evolution of consciousness for all of us." I asked her if she meant for those who go through the experiences. "No, for everyone," she replied. She even implied that abductees have a responsibility to go through and accept their encounters for the sake of others. "Everyone who's experienced it has to go through it and recognize it and accept it because it affects and will affect everybody here," she told us. Even Jim Sparks expressed the hope that the abductees' experiences would somehow help humanity to "grow in this galactic neighborhood and become more of an aware part of it." Andrea, like Carol, foresees "a big shift in consciousness that's coming. Everyone's drawn to self-awareness," she notes, "but you have to be out of your denial in order to help yourself, in order to do the grounding work."

The sense of connection with other peoples on the planet may be so acute that it becomes disturbing. Isabel has tried to meditate only once, she told me, but her consciousness was so porous that "I connected with all these different people all over the Earth." She heard the voices or otherwise felt connected with people from Australia, South America, Alaska, and other countries. All the voices, male and female, seemed to be talking at once, telling her "we're all brethren." "Oh my God, what's going on here?" she asked herself, and was so upset that she never meditated again. Furthermore, when she reads the myths of other cultures, she finds that they all seem familiar to her. "This stuff is taken as mythology," she protested, but "that's not mythology. It's what's happening." This openness extends to nature in general. "I seem to be in tune with animals and trees and the water and even the air," she observed.

Beyond the general notion of a shift of consciousness, abductees, as we have seen, can be more specifically preoccupied with what the future holds, often having experienced visions of what is to come (see chapter 5). "I guess I want to know why I've dedicated so many lifetimes to this," Isabel says. Not surprisingly there is very little agreement among experiencers about how the future will turn out, and some inconsistency on the part of individuals, although the impact of what they have encountered in their travels can be quite intense. Isabel, for example, was shown in a dream that the Earth in its present form would be gone in a few years, and she asserted that this was the way it will be. But a few weeks later she told me that her notion of the future had changed, and she no longer believed it was predetermined or "set." Instead, she now thought it was "pretty pliable, gel like," and "you can just about mold it into anything." The important thing was that people like herself, who had learned the ability to travel into the future, might have the ability to change it, "so that's a pretty heavy responsibility." The abduction experiences, she felt, are a way of educating people "about spirituality" and "about other realities," to prepare them for the future.

Over and above the big shift that is to come, Andrea puts her faith and trust in God, but then she is a bit unsure as to whether He is creating the shift or "we're all going to create" it. In the end she seems "okay" with the idea that "it's all an amazing adventure," and that "God and the Universe don't necessarily know either." But then she wonders how "we're going to hold on as a race with our limited brain capacity." Greg is more optimistic. "I think we're turning the bend," he says. "We're going to evolve not just with a better physical body or a bigger brain. We're going to evolve physically, emotionally, psychically, and spiritually. I think it's happening here on Earth." He attributes his positive outlook to his conviction that "we're incredibly loving here on this planet." All in all, Julie says, the abduction phenomenon is part of "a spiritual emergence" that is "easing humanity up the ladder a little."

Discovering Who We Are

The abduction experiences affect profoundly the experiencers' sense of who or what they are as beings in the cosmos. Their transformation, which they attribute directly to their encounters with the infinite or the creative Source, is often expressed in the ecstatic language generally associated with mysticism or other experiences of transcendence. Speaking at a board meeting of our Center, Karin told the group that her spiritual transformation had occurred because she had come "face to face with the infinite," before which she had humbled herself. The encounters had made her "one with the Earth and whole," she said. She had come to feel that she too was an infinite being, "connected to all that is." Sometimes abductees' spiritual epiphanies are associated with a singular experience; more often encounters over time bring about these dramatic shifts of consciousness and identity. Out of these experiences they often come to feel an aching oneness with nature in all its beauty and pain.

At PEER's Star Wisdom conference in May 1998, which brought experiencers and abduction researchers together with indigenous shamans and Western scientists, Sequoyah performed a sacred pipe ceremony "given to us by native elders and also so-called extraterrestrials," during which he told the audience, "We are eternal spirit," and counseled us to be "in this world but not of this world." This viewpoint, so widespread among indigenous peoples, is more unusual in Western societies. It is one that abductees frequently come to share.

While sitting in a coffee shop, one day, it occurred to Julie that she herself was "an eternal body of light" and that this life was unimportant compared to what is unseen, that all is timeless and endless, and "I'm eternal and here forever, although not in this form." During one of Nona's encounters, she had an out-of-body experience, which she felt the beings engineered for the specific purpose of showing her that she, and we, are beings of spirit and of "glowing light" or "light force."

Abductees learn not to separate spirit from the physical body, as is so common in Western religious traditions. Eva called her "impregnation" experience (discussed on pages 136–138) "an experience of the spiritual-ization of matter." It was, she said, "about being fully in the body, being fully grounded, fully being present and aware of the body, the physical body, and feeling ecstasy and feeling spirit." This sense of oneness of body and spirit led Eva to the writings in the esoteric Jewish Kabbala that have to do with the spiritualization of matter.

Five months after her dramatic session in which she experienced intense and ecstatic vibratory sensations in her body (see pages 81–84), Abby recalled "feeling heightened and open" during the regression. "I traveled beyond conscious reality as I knew it," she wrote, "while retrieving details of my memories. During that journey I experienced an ineffable moment of total merging. I don't know how else to describe having all your senses experience what should be an impossibility. It is as if I was given a glimpse of my/our potential."

When they no longer deny their experiences and confront them hon-estly, abductees tend to lose their fear of death. "There is no death," Isabel said after an experience in which she felt she made contact with her son, who had been killed in an automobile accident a year before. Physical death "is just a transition. You change from one thing to another, from one form into another, but there is no end and there is no beginning. It just is." Similarly Karin has come to believe that "death is nothing more than the death-of-the-flesh thing. It's of the shell.... To me death is an irrelevant term, because there is no death. It's just the body terminates itself."

Reconciling Different Realms: Sharing and Teaching

As they become aware of their encounter experiences and open to the dif-ferent consciousness that develops when they do, experiencers may find it increasingly difficult to integrate their "alien" existence and life on the Earth plane. They may feel so identified with the beings that when they are "resonating" in the consciousness of the other realm, they sometimes feel that they *are* aliens or have a dual human/alien identity. "I'm a gray in my soul," Karin says. Whereas they may have had a vague sense all their lives that they were not from here, now they feel pain and anger that they spend most of their time separated from the beings and God or Source. They may even have different names for themselves in the two planes. Karin's original first name was Deborah (see page 50), which came to stand for her three-dimensional or Earth-bound existence, while Karin was her truer, soul name. Similarly Will called himself Billy when referring to himself in his Earth body.

At a practical level, experiencers may find it difficult to adjust to the harshness of everyday life in this culture, or this "vibrational plane," as they sometimes call it. They may find it hard to stay in routine jobs in the commercial marketplace and tend to gravitate toward jobs in the healing or human service sectors. Marriages can become strained, especially if the spouse is not an abductee and cannot share the shifts in consciousness. Eva says that when she is fully in "the space" of her experiences, "it really doesn't matter what happens with my marriage." But when she "drops into the physical level, or the human perspective, I go, '*Aaaaah!* [screaming] How am I going to survive? How am I going to make ends meet, and what will happen to my kids?' I need to be in all spaces because just going to the higher levels is a form of escape." (There will be further discussion of such conflicts in chapter 13.)

Experiencers frequently feel a strong urge to teach or share with other people what they have learned during their journeys, and they may even feel that they have been told to do this directly by the beings. "They told me to be a teacher," Andrea says. But this effort can be conflict-laden and perilous for them. They know that, at least until recently perhaps, this whole phenomenon was greeted with a mixture of scorn, doubt, and ridicule by the media and much of the general public. Rarely if ever does a TV or radio broadcast or newspaper article present the issue accurately or knowledgeably. Programs usually stress the sensational, bizarre, or arcane aspects or, in the name of balance, give air time to uninformed debunkers, usually misnamed "skeptics," who speak from an ideological bias, putting their viewpoints forth as a scientific perspective.

Experiencers may feel all right themselves about appearing in public but be concerned that their spouses or other loved ones will suffer embarrassment. Abductees who have appeared in the media have been threatened in their jobs, if not fired, or been compromised professionally in other ways. Nevertheless, they usually feel a responsibility to share their experiences and knowledge, and an increasing number are speaking at conferences or appearing in the media and seem to be having an effect in legitimizing the subject and awakening people to the significance of the abduction phenomenon.

Karin, for example, calls her responsibility for talking about her experiences, and what she has learned from them, "full discipleship to Source." In addition to speaking effectively and movingly in public presentations, experiencers are finding that they can sometimes talk about their experiences with friends, relatives, and colleagues in the workplace who they sense would be interested. Karin has worked in a restaurant pub and found increasingly that customers want to talk with her about her experiences and what they mean. "People want this," she said. "I find that they are like really dry sponges. They are so much seeking this information, I mean really want it."

Karin was able to establish so much trust and interest at her work that the owners invited us to present an "Alien Night at The Thirsty Scholar." The place was packed, and we were able to penetrate the somewhat drunken din to tell our story to about 150 customers. Karin has observed that when she talks about herself and can "be myself," people "find themselves in you." Isabel, who is less comfortable with sharing her experiences, said something similar: "I bond with someone to give something of me to them, so they can understand where I'm coming from, so they can eventually share what I'm sharing. . . . After a while they start to change too."

I have been working with two Jewish experiencers who are finding ways to revive a sense of the sacred and breathe new life into this ancient tradition. Eva has been studying the sacred mystical texts of the Kabbala and practicing Kabbalistic healing, which as she explains in her thesis uses the sacred energies of the teachings, together with prayer, song, and meditation, to "sacredly lead" clients to a greater understanding of Self. Another woman, whose experiences have not been shared elsewhere in this book, has been studying Jewish tradition with a rabbi, who also uses the Kabbala as a vehicle for developing contemporary Judaism. At first she did not tell him of her experiences, but they have brought about in her a deep understanding of the vital core of her religion. The rabbi tells her that he is now learning from her and that she is bringing new light to the original "container" of Jewish orthodoxy. Together they are going back to the original power of their shared religious source. Perhaps a fuller appreciation of the spiritual power of the abduction encounters will bring new vitality to other religious traditions as well.

In the last few years, I have been increasingly impressed with the fact that as abductees experience a reconnection with Source, something profound occurs in the relationship between the experiencers and the beings themselves. In a sense this transformation of the human/alien relationships, or the ways that they are experienced, may be a direct outgrowth, or even the most essential expression, of the spiritual opening that the experiencers have undergone. It is possible that the capacity to form more profound or transcendent relationships, not only with alien beings but at all levels, might be the direction in which the phenomenon ultimately leads. Perhaps it is through relationships that we experience our connection with Source, and it is in relationship with oneself and others that, in the end, we live our lives and discover their purpose, meaning, and greatest satisfactions.

Chapter 13

Relationships:
Contact Through The Eyes

*Wonders happen if we can succeed in passing through the harshest
danger; but only in a bright and purely granted achievement can we
realize the wonder.*

*To work with Things in the indescribable relationship is not too hard
for us; the pattern grows more intricate and subtle, and being swept
along is not enough.*

*Take your practiced powers and stretch them out until they span the
chasm between two contradictions. . . . For the god wants to know
himself in you.*

Rainer Maria Rilke

Overcoming Fear

Human life is lived in relationships—to one another and to other
creatures, to the Earth and to God, or to a higher power or to
whatever creative intelligence we may experience as residing
in nature and the cosmos. Although the human/alien relationship as
described by the people I work with has particular qualities that seem
to distinguish it from other relationships, it follows in some respects the
qualities that appear to govern all relationships. These include the vari-
ability of closeness and distance, of comfort and fear; opportunities for

misunderstanding that grow out of difference and egocentrism (certainly on the human side); and finally an arena for growth, self-knowledge, and evolution to another level of purpose and consciousness. Indeed, the intense but highly specific, consistently reported, terrible, awkward, or sometimes poignant qualities that characterize the human/alien relationships contribute greatly to my conviction that the phenomenon itself is in some way real, not simply the product of the imagination or subjective experience of the abductee.

As I will try to show in this chapter, once the fears associated with this strange connection are confronted and transcended, relationships between human beings and the "others" can reach emotional, sensual, and spiritual intensities and depths that exceed anything with which I am familiar in human relationships. It is as if the connection partakes directly of what we might imagine to be a joining with qualities of God Itself. Much of the power of the relationship occurs through contact with the beings' extraordinary eyes, which will be discussed in detail in the last part of this chapter. I am increasingly persuaded that a deeper understanding of the nature and power of the human/alien connection will lead us closer to knowing the mystery and source of the phenomenon itself. The fact that entities seem to be reaching each other at all across what appears to be an almost unsurpassable energetic and dimensional gulf seems to me to be a creative miracle of considerable proportions.

I have come gradually to the view that it is the fundamental foreignness of these "strange beings," our almost total inability to understand in human terms what they are up to, that more than anything else brings about the terror that the abductees and the rest of us experience in relation to them. Trying to understand the abduction phenomenon has brought home to me how much, as human beings, we perceive everything around us from the standpoint of our own values and ways of thinking. "We look at everything as good and bad," Isabel says. "We look at things and think, 'Oh my God, how horrible!' But that's because we're looking at it through these eyes. We're not looking at the whole picture." Similarly, abductees often perceive the beings as simply cold and indifferent. As Credo Mutwa suggests, "These beings are not cold. It's only that they've got feelings that we don't even imagine."

It seems also, at times, that it is the beings' fear of us that causes them to use paralysis and the other means of controlling our violence that abductees experience as so disturbing. As Andrea came to realize, "The problem with us is that we're aggressive. We have anger, but we haven't learned how to transform it. We're in our lower selves a lot." Similarly, as we saw in the previous chapter, the aliens perceive our passionate and contingent way of loving, even when it is heart centered, as "unsafe" or "sticky," while their love, in Karin's words, "resonates of Home and safety."

In Chapter 11 we saw how the intrusive medical/surgicallike "procedures" (even *that* is an interpretation) may be experienced as a terrible violation. Greg spoke of a "lack of caring" and the rapelike nature of his experiences. For Will it was not knowing "when they're going to make the connection" that enraged him and felt so violating. Among the children in Zimbabwe whom I interviewed in 1994, the reactions to the dramatic encounter ranged from a kind of nervous fascination and attraction to great terror, depending upon how uneasy the child was with the mysterious nature of what occurred. One child called the beings "evil" purely on the basis of their otherness, even though nothing untoward had occurred (also Kay Leigh's experience, see page 281).

It appears sometimes to be the strangeness and our lack of power and control, more than any real harm or physical pain that may have occurred, that at least initially gives the human/alien relationship such an adversarial or traumatic cast. As has so often happened in human history, something that seems to threaten us from outside, or challenges a worldview, tends to be perceived as demonic, which of course has provided the television and film industries with almost limitless commercial opportunities. Sue's religious background led her to consider that perhaps her initial fear was of "demon possession." She was helped to reject this notion when a voice said to her, as she was waking up one morning, "You are like children of the universe, and fear is used as a manipulative tool." This experience and many other "little things" led her to "change the way I think."

When abductees face the terror and unknown quality of the abduction experiences directly, the disturbing nature tends to give way to something altogether different, and their relationship with the beings changes, sometimes dramatically. They overcome their fears in several ways. They may simply acknowledge the fear directly and accept what is happening to them, sometimes with the help of a facilitator. Some, as we have seen (chapter 6), come to believe they are part of a life-creating or transformative process. Julie confronted her terror and uncertainty directly, without, at least at first, much support. She told me, six years after we began to work together, that she had come to feel part of a "vanguard." "I'm on point," she said, "and I'm going to forge ahead with this stuff—two steps forward, and then I'll take a step back." Others demand—sometimes angrily, as in Catherine's case (Mack 1995, chap. 7), and may be granted—a more reciprocal relationship.

As we saw in chapter 11, Isabel confronted the threat that the beings presented by "throwing positive energy" or "waves of love at them." This seemed to jolt even an angry reptilian creature, and it changed its image from reptilian to a typical, bald-headed, bluish "regular gray" and then to a human-looking figure. Karin found that her encounters on the ships enabled her to send out with dramatic effect healing love energies to people in pain around her in the pub restaurant where she worked.

An Ancient Relationship:
Teachers, Healers, and Guardians

Once the abductees have overcome their fear, at least to some degree, they may come to an awareness that the relationship with the beings is an ancient one. When she allowed herself to look closely at the face and body of a familiar being, Karin thought to herself, "I have known this one forever." The *mantindane*, Credo told us, will "follow you," not only in this life "but through all lifetimes." Similarly, Isabel feels that "I was with them before I was here . . . I always was working with them, and I'm just becoming aware of it now. I've had a relationship with them for thousands of years—not just thousands of years, thousands of lifetimes. I think that a lot of the information that I tap into when I fall asleep is just information that I already know on that other level."

Abductees report that the relationship with the beings in this lifetime changes as they grow from childhood into adolescence and adulthood. As children, they may assign them names from the entertainment culture of childhood, like Muppet figures, clowns, spacemen, midgets, and the like. Adults tend to recall the childhood relationship as pleasant and fun and the beings as friendly playmates, although many children have been observed by their parents to be afraid of the beings at night. Later, as we have seen, the relationship takes on more serious, sometimes disturbing, reproductive, informational, and transformational, directions. Andrea remembers that when she was little, "they were teaching me these energy games, and it was absolutely wonderful, and then something happened. Our relationship changed." Similarly, Carol said that "whatever visited me as a child is probably the most wonderful relationship I've ever had." Sometimes, as in Joseph's case, the experiencer may recall being paired as a child with an alien or hybrid being who will later become a mate or partner.

The difficulty of knowing the actual quality of the childhood relationship with the beings may be compounded by a particular child's need to maintain the feeling of trust no matter what seems to be occurring. Will recalled in a relaxation session a disturbing experience from when he was six years old. He felt blind trust of a tall, "milky white" leader figure whom he called "the One Who Knows," a being for him with quite godlike qualities. Nevertheless, this figure seemed on one occasion to turn him over to the little ones he called "workers" or "drones" ("I would have squashed them. I still resent them"), who had "no receptor within them" and with whom communication seemed impossible. Will recalled feeling frightened and abandoned as a "wiggly" filament he called an "implant" was threaded into his penis while he lay on a table paralyzed. "They're leaving something in me so I know I'll never be alone again," he remarked.

Although he recalled the experience as an emotionally scarring one, Will refused to blame or resent the leader figure. He could say that this being told him that "it was going to be all right" and that this was "a lie," since "kids are supposed to be safe," but he stopped short of saying he felt betrayed. Will wondered if perhaps his trust in the connection was being "tested" by the temporary separation from the tall white being, and he became angry and upset with me when I suggested he might have felt resentment toward this figure. After all, Will protested, the connection was reestablished after the traumatic procedure, and he even seemed to blame the six-year-old's rage for whatever threat to the relationship had occurred.

"No matter what the frustration, the anger, the fear, nothing is worth jeopardizing or losing that connection," Will proclaimed. He accepted what had happened to him during this incident, as he had ended up back in the presence of the One Who Knows. "Would I do it again? Yes. Did I do it again? Yes. Do I trust him? Yes." For "he's the one I am connected with. He's the one that understands everything about me, and there is an understanding that surpasses anything I can explain right now. There is this incredible need in me," Will explained. "I want to be one with them, with him, with it."

After they overcome their fear, the experiencers may come to realize that the beings have played a teaching, mentoring, guiding, or guardian role for them in this and other lifetimes. We even once called them gods, Isabel believes, but our estrangement from them has led us to call them "aliens." Through time, she says, "some of them have been like our leaders and have tried to teach us how to love each other and about peace." She feels as if "I'm in a partnership with them. They give me the feeling of powerfulness. They teach me things spiritually. They teach me how to protect myself."

Experiencers often report that the examinationlike procedures they have undergone represent some sort of health-monitoring and -maintenance program on the part of the aliens. Whether this is for our benefit, or to keep our organs healthy so that the beings might use them for their own purposes later, as some experiencers have suggested (see chapter 6), is one of the questions that seem to depend, in part, upon how we choose to interpret the phenomenon. Be that as it may, Isabel says that she trusts her principal alien teacher with her life and "with my kids' lives." Sometimes there is a female being with him. "She sings to me. She touches my face sometimes, and I feel their presence all the time."

Isabel attributes her excellent health and apparent immunity to colds and other illnesses to the alien health-monitoring program. As "a loving parent would talk to a child," the beings warn her about smoking and other dangers to her health. They even instruct her about what to eat or not eat and where to go, whom to meet with or avoid, and where to find things she has lost. They also teach her how to "scan" people, and how to use the "energy field around me to protect myself against negative energies of other people trying to drain energy from me."

A Deeper Connection

As experiencers become more fully accepting of the beings' presence in their lives, they come to appreciate a deeper affinity and identification with them. Karin calls this a "symbiosis." Abductees discover that humans and the beings have common roots, but, as we saw in the last chapter, we have lost contact with that Source. "I do believe we all came from the same place," Isabel says, "and at one time we were, like brother and sister, all related." One of the beings' jobs appears to be to help us remember where we came from and who we are, to bring back to us "memory of Source" so that we may "start listening to our own spirits. Our spirits tell us everything we need to know. But we don't recognize our own voices anymore. We don't recognize the voice of the Source anymore."

When abductees are enabled to move beyond their fears and self-protective defensive attitudes, a consistent and quite moving empathy for the beings may develop. This can start as an appreciation for what the creatures appear to lack and may progress to a loving bond of remarkable proportions. Sue told us that as she overcame her fears of the beings, she made a conscious decision to reach out and interact with them. "Whatever this phenomenon is," she said, "you have to be part of it. It can't progress unless you allow it to progress." Although the beings have "tremendous psychic ability, tremendous healing ability," Andrea said, and fell silent. Then she continued, "They've lost their home inside themselves. . . . they've evolved to something that's not quite right, that has something lacking. Their heart centers are not as open as they should be. They have a feeling level that they've bred out." They have become "just too practical."

Along similar lines, Isabel has noted that the beings seem to be love deprived, and seek "our love and our experience. I think they envy us," especially our capacity for physical intimacy. She suggests that perhaps by creating "half-and-half babies," they might be able to "get enough human qualities." Somehow the hybrids at least might be able to get enough nurturing, even vicariously, from the human mothers. "They are like starving children who are trying to break in with the other kids, the other babies who are being breast-fed." Isabel wonders if the beings might "remember what this felt like," but paradoxically, when it comes to physical love and sensual experience, it seems to her they have moved farther away from the creative center than humans and "have to go through us to connect to the Source." Eleven-year-old Lisel in Zimbabwe had the strong impression that the being she saw needed love (see p. 283). (see p. 283)

Karin has also developed great empathy for the beings and notices "a huge sense of desperation about them." They appear to feel as if they are "running out of time and want something that they can't get fast enough." When she is with them, she feels "a sense of longing for something we have, and they don't have it. . . . They covet . . . there's a reaching out." Karin recalled a vision in which she saw her hand reaching out, and another hand reaching toward hers, rather like the hand reaching toward God in Michelangelo's painting in the Sistine Chapel in the Vatican. "When my hand comes out, there's a connection, like they want the connection as much as we do." The beings also seem curious about parental and sexual love. "They want to know how love processes itself in the body," Karin said. Several years ago I had a case where the beings were reported to stage sexual intercourse between humans on the ship and to watch intently, sometimes to the embarrassment of the participating couple. In the last few years, the human/alien relationship, at least among the people with whom I have been working, seems to have moved in a somewhat different direction.

From all of this turmoil, confusion, and misunderstanding, powerful, sometimes transcendent connections form between human beings and the alien visitors that appear to grow out of mutual need. For the abductees the relationships seem to serve a desire for self-knowledge and for a less ego-centered kind of cosmic love that takes them beyond their bodies to a sense of oneness with the creative Source. As we shall see, the depth of knowledge and understanding reflected in the beings' great eyes is an important aspect of this connection. For the beings the contact seems to fulfill a hunger for nurturance and eroticism, lost or never before known, even for the experience of physicality itself. The actuality and power of the relationship can be so intense that it seems to override ontological considerations, such as "where" all this is taking place.

On occasion the relationship may have a touching, even comic quality. Karin told us of an experience she had one night when she had gone to bed sensing with some distress that she "was going to have company in my room." She recalls that she "tumbled" out of her body, and as she did so, she virtually fell "on top of a little gray guy in his natural out-of-body state." The being appeared to have no suit, and when it looked like it was startled, Karin sent out the message, "Please don't run away." Then in a "soft gesture" the being raised its head up to her and "nuzzled on my neck," which felt like "little hamsters running around the back of my neck, a nice childhood warm connection." She felt this gesture to be very loving and supportive. "The being gave. I didn't take. I didn't ask," she remarked.

Carol took great pains to describe to me precisely the quality of feeling she experienced as she relived an encounter with a being to whom she had felt close through much of her life. She feels the relationship is complete and that she will not see this entity again, because she does not believe it exists anymore, "in its realm or in mine." "There is no way I can describe this," Carol said, but the contact had left her with a change in her "percep-tive ability." It was as if "I could give you part of me that you would be able to keep with you, that would become a part of you." "It's a memory of a friend," she continued, "a very good feeling, a relational connection that has comfort. If you took somebody who is dying, and you held them in your arms and comforted them, if you took a baby that was crying, and you have it in your arms and you comforted it, *that* connection. It has a lifelong quality about it." It was in part because of this connection, she believes, that Carol has not been afraid of death, even as a child.

On several occasions experiencers have described intensely erotic experiences with the beings, which can also seem a bit comical when they are described. One night Isabel went to bed feeling particularly sexually frustrated and had trouble sleeping. "In the middle of the night, I woke up, and, I swear to God, someone was having sex with me, and I thought it was Ben," her boyfriend, and she thought, "This is great, Ben is having sex with me, this is good. But then I became conscious that there's someone lying next to me." Ben, she saw, was asleep. "So who am I having sex with?" she wondered. After "that initial shock," she felt "really good."

Comparing the experience to having sex with a man, Isabel said she felt the penetration and thrusting—"I felt sex"—but "there was this intense feeling all through me, and then peacefulness, and I felt loved. It was different than sex with a human being, physical sex. It was more—I know this is going to sound dumb—but it's like having spiritual sex. It wasn't just on the outside. It was more internal. I remember feeling that whoever did this cared enough about me that they felt the state I was in, that I felt distressed, and that they came and helped me. I didn't feel like, 'Oh my God, who did this without my permission!' I just felt, 'Thank you.'"

"There is a lot of ego involved in sex with a human being," Isabel continued. "You're thinking a lot of thoughts while you're having sex," such as "if this doesn't finish off really good, we're both going to feel funny later or whatever. There's just so much involved. It's too technical. So with these beings there was none of this 'okay, we have to have a certain amount of foreplay, we have to do this and that.' It was just like a connection, a spiritual connection. This person looked at how I felt I was ailing in some way, and was offering that bond out of love, not out of 'what am I going to get back from you.' . . . It was just pure warmth. It was just love, and it felt like the person caused my spirit and body to bring forth. It was an awakening within me. . . . It was like they were allowing my spirit to awaken, and to feel the love from them." Isabel knew and trusted this being, and that she had been given a great gift. Afterward she felt "greater" than anything else that could ever happen, a "peacefulness that comes from just knowing."

Alien Mates:
Parenting on the Other Side

As they become more aware of their connection with the beings, some experiencers may come to the realization that they have an alien mate on "the other side." This relationship may or may not involve some sort of spawning and parenting of hybrid offspring. It inevitably causes conflict for experiencers who are in committed marriages. Because of their strangeness, these accounts sometimes seem absurd, especially in the retelling.

Whitley Strieber spoke with me of experiences similar to Isabel's. "The sexual part of my relationship [with the beings] has been very complex and very rich and very difficult at times because I'm a married man. I've taken marriage vows, which I believe in. To an extent this aspect of it has been thrust on me, and it's not something I've been able to control. If it had been under my control, I would have felt very guilty." There is a specific alien female with whom he feels mated. "It's like having a second wife with whom I have a secret relationship." "There was never a seduction," he said. "I would wake up in a state of sexual excitement, in mid-intercourse. . . . The physical dynamic is different in the sense that the sensation of intercourse moves through your whole body, and you become totally devoted to it for longer than I do in normal intercourse." In normal coitus, he said, orgasm can be "a very colorful moment, but in this the power of the moment starts at the beginning and extends through the whole thing, and at the end I black out." It feels to him "as if a level of sexuality I'm normally not involved with is engaged. It's very, very powerful."

Strieber has fully informed his wife of this connection, and they have decided that "what we have together, human love, is fine for us, and so we're very happy with our love. This other experience is not one I could live with with the degree of comfort I have with my relationship with Anne. If that happened every night, I think I'd blow a gasket." Although he does not recall ever having had the experience of sperm being removed by the "doctorlike little aliens," Strieber has seen a hybrid child in the ship whose appearance makes him think that it might be the offspring of his union with the alien mate.

Whatever may be the creative intelligence or principle behind the hybrid "project," it has "discovered" that the biomechanical mode of baby-making does not work out very well (see chapter 6). In addition to the frequently reported listlessness of these children, they also sometimes appear to have deformities. Joseph was shocked and saddened during one of his encounters to see a room on a ship that was filled with deformed offspring. One hybrid, for example, had an arm that looked almost human, while the other arm appeared "alien"; another had an alien face on one side and a more human one on the other.

At the same time, the aliens have communicated to Joseph that they are concerned about genetic deformities on our planet and the increasing rate of sterility in the human race that has resulted from nuclear explosions, radiation, pollution, and other causes. Thus the reproductive "exchange program," at least from the alien perspective, has a certain urgency. "They are concerned," Joseph says, "about how quickly our race is going to disappear," for Earth changes are leading to our not being able to reproduce at all. Because of the way we have lived on this planet, he has been taught, we have "altered the divine creative process that was started here." "It doesn't feel like they're so concerned about themselves," Joseph remarks, in contrast to statements by Jim Sparks and others that aliens are driven by their own self-focused agendas.

What has been missing, the beings seem to have discovered, are the elements of parenting that the human dimension of the hybrids requires. "It's like the sperm and the eggs are not enough," Joseph says. "There needs to be some kind of desire or, I want to say, the emotion of wanting to 'produce'" a baby. To correct this deficiency, human beings are being paired with an alien mate with whom they seem to be encouraged to form an emotional, erotic, and spiritual connection. "It is clear," he says, "that what has been successful is that when this bond is created from infancy or from childhood up, the chance of successful hybrid children is so much better." As we have seen, this bond can be extremely powerful. It also seems to have purposes and meaning that go beyond a literal reproductive agenda.

With considerable conflict and resistance, Joseph came to accept that he had an alien mate "on the other side." Like Strieber, he has struggled with "the core issues" of abandonment, betrayal, and trust in relation to his wife. In our last regression, he recalled that among the children on the ship he was brought to play with, there was one with whom he had been paired from the beginning. "I was always close to one little kid," he recalled, "and the whole time it was meant that I would then eventually breed with her." As sometimes seems to happen on the ships, Joseph was shown images of his and his partner's development over time. As he saw himself changing from childhood through adolescence and young adulthood to contemporary manhood, so this female being seemed to mature from a young, small female alien with wisps of stringy hair to a taller, more full-bodied, sexually attractive creature with whom Joseph felt deeply connected. Although this being seemed quite human in some ways, she still had overly large eyes (though not as large as the pure aliens' eyes), a flat nose, and virtually no lips.

With a good deal of internal resistance, Joseph was able to share with me the details of one of his sexual encounters with his hybrid partner. The "idea" that he had "made love with an alien and enjoyed it" was extremely difficult for him to accept. As he first described what he recalled, it seemed to Joseph as if he were himself an alien and were watching what was happening from outside. As the episode progressed, the being seemed more and more "humanoid" and less alien, but hybrid qualities persisted. He described her as soft and gentle, with a broad forehead and whitish, light hair. The eyes, he said, were "almost Oriental-looking, not huge like the eyes of aliens," with "a whisper of eyebrows." He recalled walking with her down a hall, then up a small ramp into a square area with walls of smoky black glass, which he called her "bedroom" or "suite," a "place of sanctuary."

The lovemaking began on some sort of chair with Joseph squeezing his partner with his legs while they embraced each other. Then in the room they made love on a rather uncomfortable hard slab that served as a bed. Joseph and the being were both naked, and she laid her body across his chest. She was thin and bony, and her skin felt cooler than his—"I don't want to say clammy"—and he could not tell if she had nipples. She did not seem to do anything to stimulate him, but he remembers that they rolled over and he mounted her, with no sense that he had an erection, but with a sensation of genital contact. "It feels so good. Her skin is so white, angel white. She was so gentle with me," he said.

Strangely, there was "a deadness in the eyes." Nevertheless, Joseph wanted to make love with this being so much that he was "afraid that I

PASSPORT TO THE COSMOS ■ 273

love something more than I love my life here on Earth. I'm connected to some other woman in another world, and she's not alien, not to me. It doesn't feel like sex. It feels like this wonderful bonding, lovemaking. She's responding to wherever I'm at. The problem is that I'm married. I live here. I'm human. I'm in love with my wife." As the experience was ending, Joseph had a feeling of revulsion, and then the being stopped responding. He had an image of himself coming, and then "waking up and snapping out of it."

In our next session, Joseph seemed able to speak more easily about his pairing with his female partner, who had come to seem more grown-up and full-bodied, darker and obviously attractive to him, although still an alien hybrid. He realized now that they had come together repeatedly to have sexual relations in this special room, and that he felt a deep connection with her. He realized that he had been paired with and *taught* to love a desirable female, and that he, like many other couples he observed on the ship, had been brought together to be parents for their hybrid children.

It was now clear to Joseph that "when this bond is created from infancy or childhood up, the chance of successful hybrid children is so much better." The beings, he said, had "created" many families for this purpose, and that his role had progressed from giving sperm, to mating with an alien female, then to parenting hybrid children. He asserted that he had been a willing participant in this process, which he considered his life purpose, so much so that he had chosen not to produce children on Earth. "It's like I have a wife and a family and kids over there, and when the time comes, John, that's where my real family is."

Beyond the apparent evolutionary service of his parenting function, Joseph's relationship with the female hybrid seemed to have another, transformational, purpose. "It has to do with the transfer of knowledge, with the transfer of energy, with the transfer of power. Something is going to shift. People are going to change," he says. When he is with his alien partner, it seems to Joseph as if each of them is giving an essential life element to the other. During the lovemaking he feels it is "almost like I'm giving her life," as if he were an "older man and she the younger woman. I was teaching her." He, in turn, is meant to bring back to Earth "extraterrestrial energy and feeling and whatever they embody. It's a two-way street. I'm teaching them, and they're teaching me." The relationship has brought to Joseph the conviction that "I'm connected to something greater. It's like going from the idea of a state to the idea of the United Nations."

I first saw Andrea four years after these meetings with Joseph. We may recall (see page 135) that she believes that she is the parent of a beautiful boy she calls Kiran who is the issue of her mating with a man in another dimension. This human/alien union is, like Joseph and his mate's, sexually and emotionally very powerful. It plays a critical role for Andrea in "knowing who I am." The relationship is different from Joseph and his mate's insofar as the boy and his father both appear to Andrea to be fully integrated, that is, fully human *and* fully alien. In addition, she has been told that this being resides on Earth as well as in the craft, and she told us that the aliens have encouraged her to find him here so that they can parent Kiran in this plane. Andrea, like Joseph and other abductees, feels herself to have an alien as well as human identity, especially when she is in the environment of the craft. Some elements in this story are so bizarre, from the standpoint of our space/time reality, that they bring into question the material literalness of these experiences, however powerful or meaningful they may be.

Although she recalled playing with her "extraterrestrial" lover as a child, before we began our work Andrea had little conscious memory of being with him at other times. Several months after we started meeting, she was able to speak in detail about one of her intimate encounters with the human/alien man. It had occurred over a year before, on the ship, and she was "completely" in the form of an alien woman with "droopy," perhaps "sticky" skin that is looser than human skin and "breathes out stuff through it." She described her body as "skinny," and although her limbs might appear bony, Andrea does not believe that she had bones. "If they're bones," she said, "they're more like cartilage."

Andrea felt certain that in her alien form she had fingers and toes, but only four fingers, which seemed longer than humans'. Her head was large, with no hair, "really little" ears, a mouth like a slit, and a flat nose. The eyes were huge, and she noted that the space between them seemed a little bit bigger than ours. "I think I have breasts," she said, but she was not sure whether there were nipples. Her chest "sticks out a little bit, and there's power in here." When I asked if there were genitals, she replied, "It's, it's smaller. Everything's smaller. I have like ovaries and things. I think I do. I'm getting confused."

After the leader alien ("the guy with the big eyes") had left, Andrea feels she was "set up" to have sex with her mate, who, she believed, had been her partner in several lifetimes. At first she could not see his face.

This time he was naked and in human form, with a "very nice brown body" and skin that was somewhat darker than hers. When he first got close to her, he was "grossed out" and terrified, and she could not figure out why she did not change to human form or he did not change to alien form. "I could read his thought, 'They want me to have sex with *her*? Oh my God! I gotta get out of here,' and then 'I know who you are, but I still don't want to have sex with you.'" Nevertheless, as she moved closer to him, he moved closer to her.

After the man relaxed, they held each other standing up, and some sort of "very subtle" vibration began all over their bodies. Then he had an erection, "and his body moved into mine," Andrea said. But it was not like regular intercourse, she explained. "It was better, and I'm remembering how much we cared for each other," and that it "lasted a lot longer." Although pleasurable sensations may have begun in the genital area, they spread throughout her body. No back-and-forth bodily movement, as in regular intercourse, occurred, as the vibration brought about a feeling of merging. It seemed to Andrea as if "you expand everything, and it goes into the universe, like enlightenment.... His heart came into my heart, and I loved it," she said. The whole experience "opened up very much my heart."

Andrea told me that for the past two years her body had been vibrating every night, and that she had sometimes brought such intense energy to her lovemaking with her husband that it "blew us both away." It was, she thought, not a normal way of having sex or an orgasm: "It was a total kaboom, like expansion." She felt certain that the vibratory aspect of such experiences had resulted in making her body healthier.

Despite this dramatic change in her sexual experiences with her husband, whom she truly loves, Andrea remained very much concerned that her involvement in the other world could, as in Joseph's case, create a major problem for her marriage. "The big guy with the big eyes looked right at me and told me I have free choice." Yet she felt torn. "I feel like there's two of me. One is very, very committed to this mission, whatever it is, and the other one is sitting here wondering 'what am I doing, what am I doing, what am I doing,' and 'if it isn't real, it's screwing up my life.'" When Andrea tried to tell her husband that she had had a sexual encounter in relation to her experiences, he made a joke of it, and she sensed he felt threatened. He did not seem to want to hear more about it, or any other aspect of her experiences, and would change the subject when she tried to talk about them. She decided therefore to keep this "other life" largely to herself and did not, for example, tell him that she had a son "on the other side." But at the same time, she was determined to continue to discover more about her encounters, as "it's so much a part of who I am" and "there's bigger plan here."

In the next session, Andrea relived with a great deal of fear an experience of flying out of a ship with another woman with dark hair, whom she later called a nurse. Some sort of cord seemed to link her to a blue light that came down from the ship. "When you're in the blue light," she noted, "you don't experience any weather. You're warm and completely fine." On the ship she seemed to have been in alien form but was surprised to find that she changed to human form as she flew out of it. The whole thing startled her intensely, and she cried out, "Oh my God, I can't believe this is happening. I'm flipping out. I'm flying out of the ship. Oh my God!" The purpose of this journey down from the ship, she was told, was to have her find her mate from the ship so they could parent Kiran together on the Earth. "I have a dual life," she said, and "I think they want it to come together."

In the blue light, Andrea could see the Earth and then a road coming up to meet her. She does not recall the moment of impact but found herself on a beach of what she took to be one of the Hawaiian islands, the same one that she had envisioned exploding (see page 100). She then set off with the other woman to find her lover, the father of their beautiful hybrid child, in order to tell him that he had a son and "you have to do something here." This seemed to be, as Roberta Colasanti remarked, the first case of hunting down an extraterrestrial "deadbeat dad." As she spoke about this, Andrea remarked several times a bit resentfully that she felt she was part of some sort of "experiment."

Andrea realized that identifying her lover might be rather difficult, as she had never really seen his face clearly. Somehow she found the house where the man supposedly lived, but she was overcome with fear, both at the time and as she recalled the incident in our session. She remembers that she stepped onto the porch of the house and that the terror intensified, despite the fact that the nurse was there to encourage her. Then Andrea knocked on the door. Someone was standing in the doorway, but her fear was so great that she could not recall whom she saw. She found herself warning this person about the danger to Hawaii, but she would not look at him and chose not to tell him about her son, even though the leader figure with the big eyes had wanted her to talk about raising him. "I don't want to go any further with this. I don't want to see this," Andrea protested, attributing her hesitancy to the possibility that the man "might say no" or that an encounter with him on Earth, real or imagined, might pose a further threat to her marriage. Andrea said she felt vulnerable and "did not want to rock the boat for everybody."

Other Realms and Other Lovers

Three months later, in a relaxation session, Andrea found herself taken by a ship through time to a city in an ancient desert civilization she identified as Mesopotamia or possibly Egypt. It was difficult for her to explain, for although she was an "ancient person," in this older culture the events were "happening now." Andrea was with her lover once again, but she was in another body with darker skin, while the man's skin was even darker than before. "He knows me, and I know him on a very deep level. He has beautiful dark eyes, and we work together," she recalled. Arriving in this place was like a "welcome home," Andrea said, for these were "my people." In this society people loved their bodies, and she felt "much more present with my body, much more fully embodied." Life in this society was "delicious and free," people had many close friends and were more deeply connected than in our culture. Andrea remembered sitting on a step talking happily with five other people.

Andrea said that "back then" she knew about how the Earth would be "right now" and what she would be bringing from that time into our present-day reality. In particular, she would bring the capacity for healing with her hands, for in her state of expanded consciousness, she knew how to heal people through the higher vibration of her touch. Once again Andrea found herself inhibited by fears that her intense relationship with her lover in the other realm or time would "disrupt" her Earth life. "I have this commitment to two people. I don't know how I can do that. I hate that struggle," Andrea complained.

Andrea spoke then of how the beings, one of whom seemed to have his face close to hers, had been a bridge between ancient Mesopotamia and our Earth world here and now. "They've been a bridge for a long, long time," she said. "They are part of our seed," and "they're helping us remember who we are, just to feel, to experience the connection between us and the Earth. Back in those days, they were with us, part of us, living with us, in alignment with us, and then they left. They actually are us, a piece of us, but are more highly evolved in the sense of vibration. So what you're doing, and what I'm doing," Andrea continued, is "connecting the threads, to remember that we're all one, and they want to more deeply connect the threads by meshing the two genetic materials, us and the beings'. That's why I have a son, so I can mesh the material." Credo Mutwa, who has a far-from-charitable view of the alien beings (see chapters 7 and 10), has a similar view of our identity with them, which, he says, is why they are sexually compatible with human beings and can make terrestrial women pregnant.

When human sexual union with alien beings has been reported to me, it has most often been with apparent hybrid forms of the "grays," or integrated humans/aliens that appear, as in Andrea's case, like human beings. Nona told me of an intimate encounter in her bedroom with a gentle Egyptian-appearing being, apparently of the same sort that showed her the ankh and the beautiful gardens on the ships. She had been saying a sacred mantra she had learned from a Peruvian friend a couple of times a day for about a week when one night she awoke to find a dark-haired Egyptian being by her bed while her husband continued to sleep next to her. She was lying on her back, and he put his hands lightly over the outside of her body, "almost like a healing." The being was quite solid and wore a tight tunic that came below his waist. The figure was very familiar to Nona, for he had come to her before and said, "Nona, we need you," and shown her gardens on the ship. She felt a pure love, unlike anything she had ever experienced in her life, and hardly wanted to breathe or move lest she take him "by surprise" and he would be scared away.

The experience, Nona said, was not so much erotic as "what I would imagine as knowing complete love within my being." By her estimate the contact continued for another five minutes. It seemed to her that this very powerful experience was a kind of next step in her understanding, and that she could consciously draw this being to her. "I understood more of what was being done in terms of what we need to understand about ourselves," of learning to feel total love. In somewhat the same way that Andrea felt she was bringing past knowledge into present reality, Nona felt that encounters like this one represented a commitment from another time. In that earlier period, as represented by the Egyptian figure, Nona had had experiences that she could bring forward and work with "at this time when it is needed."

The Eyes

The power of the connection with the alien beings seems to occur most often through looking into their eyes. Because this contact can be such an overwhelming experience, evoking overwhelming emotions, abductees will often avoid such contact or suppress the memory of its intensity. The large eyes of the beings are consistently reported to be by far the most prominent feature of their faces, and an important locus of connection. It is as if the eyes were an opening to the infinite. When they actually do make contact, the eye-to-eye connection may seem the most compelling dimension of the human/alien bond. In this section I will report how the beings' eyes are described, the range of experiences that abductees report when they look into them, and where this aspect of the phenomenon seems to lead.

The image of the gray aliens' eyes has become a kind of commercial icon in this culture. These eyes are usually described by experiencers—before and since the media depictions—as large and black, oblong or almond-shaped, slanted or "wrap-around," and without pupils. But there are other, less familiar features that abductees sometimes notice about them. The eyes are perceived as intelligent and at least initially as frightening or intimidating. Often experiencers see some sort of membrane that may cover a portion of the eyes. Usually, but not always, experiencers do not see the eyes close or blink. I have heard on several occasions the idea that what is seen is not the eye itself but a kind of goggle, a lens, or even a mask that covers the surface of the actual eye, possibly to protect it from certain kinds of light.

Nona described the two eyes of a being that seemed only six inches from hers. They seemed huge, about five inches wide and three inches tall, very dark and so glossy she could see her reflection in them, yet also somehow transparent. She thought that perhaps the beings are sensitive to ultraviolet light and that what appears shiny and so dark is really a lens to protect the eye underneath.

Celeste wrote to us of waking up to see one of the beings standing near her bed. She yelled for help as she saw eyes that "shone like the black opals that I have been thinking about, and reflected rainbows of colors in their convex shape." Credo Mutwa's descriptions are equally dramatic. "The eyes were like nothing on Earth," he told us. They looked like "plastic bottles, very black plastic," and they did not blink or close. He compared them to "a type of windscreen that was used in Africa not so long ago for cars, so all the windows were jet black and you couldn't see the people inside the cars." The children in Zimbabwe were also impressed by the eyes of the beings. "I saw this person," Emma said, "and it had big eyes. That's all I saw about it—the big eyes and a black body. . . . He was just staring at me. The eyes didn't have any pupils or color."

Even when the beings they perceive are not the typical small grays, experiencers still tend to stress the prominence, large size, or odd features of the eyes. Blond "Nordic"-appearing beings may be seen as having slitted cats' eyes, and mantislike entities may have eyes like some insects. Greg told us of tall reptilian creatures with "unbelievable eyes, but not the kind of eyes that the little guys have. These eyes have detail, all the beauty of a cat's eyes. The pupils are oval, with the long axis up and down, not round like humans.'"

The emotional impact of contact with the beings' large eyes is vastly greater than might be expected from any description of their unusual nature. Experiencers often have the feeling that they are being stared at, sometimes with the beings' faces close up to theirs. This in itself can be quite disturbing, especially if they feel pulled toward the figure or that the being seems to want him or her to look into its eyes. During one of her experiences, Andrea told us, three beings were standing over her, "and one of them really put his eyes into my eyes. It's like his eyes are in my eyes." Greg said of one of the reptilian beings that it seemed to be "looking at us with wonder."

Despite their fear, experiencers may feel themselves inexorably drawn to make contact with the beings' eyes. Lisel, an eleven-year-old girl at the Ariel School, felt afraid when it seemed that one of the beings was staring at her and other children, for "I've never seen such a person before." Emma, another eleven-year-old girl at the school, saw a being at what she estimated to be a distance of three or four yards. She felt a mixture of fear and excitement. "His eyes looked at me as if, 'Oh, I want you,' like, 'I want you to come with me.'" "Did you go with him?" I asked. "Only my eyes went with him—and my feeling," she replied. The tug to go with the being was strong, but accompanied by the feeling, "I shouldn't go."

Andrea told us that in one of her experiences the beings' eyes them-selves—rarely reported, I believe—seemed to contribute to the energy that transported her to a ship. On one occasion she saw three beings on her porch and thought they seemed restless, "like, 'Let's go.' They just

look into my eyes, and I'm numb. Now they're saying, 'Are you ready?' And I'm saying, 'Yeah, I'm ready. I'm all set.'" On another occasion she felt that one of the beings "just wants me to look into his eyes and stop the baloney"— that is, her avoidance. She did so, and then "he's got them [locked her in the eye connection] now," and "he's lifting me off the bed." Andrea felt dizzy as she recalled "floating off" her bed. (Olivia, a nineyear-old girl at the Ariel School, also said it made her dizzy when she looked into a being's eyes.) I asked Andrea what started her floating. "His eyes . . . I think so. I don't know what got me up. I think it's the light. His eyes are on my eyes. I'll tell you, he doesn't want to lose my eye contact at all."

Much of the fear that the aliens' eyes seems to inspire comes from the fact that they are so apparently different or unfamiliar. Emma thought the being with its big black eyes "was scary because it was so strange." When I asked Kay Leigh, age nine, another child at the Ariel School, what made the beings so scary, she said, "The eyes looked evil." I asked her what she meant by evil. "It looked evil because it was just staring at me." These eyes, at least in one experience that Andrea reported, are so acute, they seem as if they can see things that human eyes cannot. "Some guy was looking at my body really closely. . . . His eyes are right down on my skin, and he says that there's living things on me." "Bacteria," she guessed.

The contact with the beings' eyes can be so intense that the experiencer may feel utterly taken over by the encounter. In one of her first recalled experiences, Sue found that she could not help looking into a being's eyes. "The more I looked into his eyes, the more all I could see was his eyes. Suddenly I had the most horrible feeling of terror, and of having to get out of there. I felt like I was falling. I was falling and falling into his eyes." Andrea described a similar feeling. On one occasion a being with "big black Oriental eyes" stared at her from about a foot away. He was "looking right at my eyes, and I'm not looking. I'm looking away. I don't want to look. It looks like they'll just absorb me into their body or something. It looks like they're going to suck me right in, and as soon as I look, my body starts vibrating." Another time she said, "They look very, very deep, and you get absorbed into them, completely absorbed into them." Six months after this she spoke of this feeling as engulfing so that "I sort of lose a little bit of stability, and then you have to recenter."

Abductees sometimes have to go beyond everyday language to capture the overwhelming nature of the contact with the beings' eyes. Whitley

Strieber called his first experiences of this "terror absolute, annihilating catastrophe of spirit. It seems to be just obliterating when you connect." "These eyes," Credo told us, "if you look into them, you don't see detail like the beautiful eyes of a human being. You just see this eternity, this emptiness, this void of a creature whose thoughts are so completely unimaginable that there is no expression." For Celeste, "These eyes are radiant, illuminating and fully embracing. Just as you peel back layers of memory and experience with words that twist into the mind with surgical precision, the eyes strip you to the bare soul" (letter to the author, February 10, 1999).

As we have seen (in chapter 5), the aliens' eyes sometimes seem to contain or be linked to a vast store of information that is communicated directly to the experiencers. "While the thing was looking at me," Emma said, her "conscience" told her that we are doing harm to the Earth (see page 97). They also seem to be able to look into the depths of a person and to know immediately their most intimate selves. At the same time, the eyes may provide a kind of inescapable mirroring of truth for the experiencer.

Isabel has felt at times as if she were looking into the eyes of a predator when she sees the "midnight blue" alien eyes. As she looked more deeply into the eyes, she felt embarrassed and foolish. "They know your emotions. They know what you're thinking. You get the feeling they know a lot more about you than you know about yourself." The beings seem to her to be accepting, although at times they appear to be a little impatient, "as if they have to remind us every time, 'Oh come on! You know us. Why are you acting this way?'"

The eyes reflect back "so much truth of what you're missing," Andrea observes. "It is you seeing that which you have kept so deeply hidden and are afraid of, especially our fear of loving ourselves, our fear of being seen, our fear of letting them see us, our fear of seeing them, our fear of accepting. It is a cataclysm of the deepest proportions." (Compare her remark with Strieber's "annihilating catastrophe of spirit.") "That's why there's no pupil," Andrea suggests, for "it would stop the reflection" and "all the different projections that are made onto" the eyes.

When experiencers are able to move beyond their fears and accept the reality of the existence of the alien beings and their own relationship to them, the connection through the eyes may take on comforting, even poignant dimensions. Will came to find the eyes extremely soothing, and

he, like many experiencers, sensed the longing in them. "This eye is not looking at me to frighten me," Nona remembered after one of her encounters, in which at first she could see only one of the eyes clearly. There was a feeling of sadness. "It just gave me a sense of wanting to cry, and a sense of knowing, familiar, almost like an animal, like a bird would look at you, a tipping of the head." The eye contact was direct and would not go away, like "when you have a baby, and the baby can't speak to you, but you communicate when you contact the eyes. . . . It's like just a personal communication to me. There's a recognition, or communication of some feelings. . . . That's why I'm not terrified. I know I'm not going to be hurt. . . . It's just what you emanate. . . . It's like they get it, and you get it, the recognition, the sending of the love, the sending of the feelings, of light, of happiness. . . . The eyes are a great communicator, and they can send that information through the eyes."

Lisel, even though she felt a good deal of fear, also felt the sadness in a being's eyes. "They just looked horrible and sad," she said. Despite her fear she "felt sorry for him because I had a feeling they had no love or caring." Perhaps "in space there is no love and down here there is," she suggested, and "they need love and they're trying to copy us."

Some abductees have the feeling that they can see from the perspective of the aliens' eyes (Mack 1995, chap. 14). This experience not only can overcome the sense of separation but may obliterate the distinction of identity between the abductee and the "alien" beings. "The eyes of this [being] are so deep," Will told us, it is like they can "get behind me, so that wherever I think I am, I'm never not connected." "Sometimes when I close my eyes, I see the inside of those black eyes," Karin said. "I know what it looks like from the inside to look out of those big black eyes." At those times she feels especially the separation from Home and looks at the night sky with great longing. Andrea spoke of the beings' eyes "beating" into hers. They showed her the Earth as if through their eyes. It seemed as if the Earth was "in my eyes."

From this eye connection, Andrea came to the feeling during one of our sessions that "there is no difference in the essence of any being. Right now he's looking at me with his eyes. There's absolutely no difference in our core," she asserts, and whether we choose to experience this reality depends on "how deep the longing is" and how strong "the fire is that kindles it." The sense of oneness Andrea feels with the beings extends to the Earth itself. "Isn't it funny that we feel so separate from the Earth. It's all one big heartbeat, and when we decide, that's when it will shift, when we make a decision that we've had enough."

In the end, as we saw earlier in this chapter, beyond all the trauma and fear, a profound love of extraordinary power and depth may develop between the experiencers and the alien beings. Andrea feels unequivocally that "they're deeply in love with us." It is above all the power of feeling communicated through the beings' eyes to which experiencers respond most intensely.

In June 1991, about a year after we began our work together, Julie told me of an encounter with her familiar "doctor" that had occurred when she was eighteen. Her account in a relaxation session captures the compelling quality of the eye connection. She recalled lying on a table, and the doctor was standing over her. Julie described his forehead as protruding and "knotted," and his head as having no hair or detectable ears. The tiny mouth seemed to her to be smiling. "He's really kind of handsome in a strange way," she said. "He's got great big eyes and he's smiling," all black without pupils, "enormous almond eyes, and they're really pretty because the light's shining in them." Julie remembered what the connection felt like.

"It was like being engulfed and just being treasured and protected, and I think that if you were to see him, you would think he was godlike," Julie told us. I asked how much of his appeal came from the eyes. "Almost all of it," she replied. "I'm looking at the eyes," she continued, and "it just sucks you in. It's like a giant fix. Like you'd do anything to get it. It's—it's communication. It's everything." I asked her to say more about what the "giant fix" was like. She answered, "It just makes you feel loved, and it makes you feel very important, and it makes you feel like everything's worthwhile, and you're helping, and you're good, and it's everything. And it's so warm. It's like being in a warm place."

This experience, Julie said, affected her whole body. "It's more powerful than anything I've ever experienced." I asked her to compare this contact with the strongest earthly love or sexual experience. Was it more powerful than that? "Oh, fifty times, easily," she replied. "It's so important. I think once you get something like that, you have to have it. It really is like encountering something omnipotent, even though I know mentally he's not a god. . . . It almost feels like a father figure, just somebody who'll take care of you."

Anticipating Freudian interpretation here, I asked her about her father and if she were "father deprived." "He's neat," she said—a pretty good caretaker, though. My dad's not really a sharing open type, but you always knew he was there. Everybody can say they didn't quite get enough, I think. He's more than making up for it now." I asked her what could be said to someone who might interpret this psychologically, or as a transfer of feelings from me as "the doctor" to the figure in the ship. "I had this me   y before I met you," she responded. "It actually happened. This is not something that I think happened. This is real."

Seven years after this meeting with Julie, Celeste recovered on her own, from her day-long period of missing time overseas, a memory not unlike Julie's, though she expressed it in more dramatic language. These words, she told us later, seemed to flow effortlessly and instantly from her heart. Rereading them drew her powerfully back into the experience.

> Please imagine that you are looking into eyes that are convex and huge, and they shine with brilliant flashes of color through an opalescent dark exterior that flows with movement in some lyrical, magnetic way that captivates your eyes and transfixes them, penetrating into your being. When [they reach] so deeply into the core of your being, the eyes evoke feelings and emotions and communicate thoughts of supremely intense love, like a powerful and seductive sedative. Your mind is so open to the power of the experience that you cannot draw away. The energy intoxicates you with an abundance of love, and it mesmerizes you with kaleidoscopic colors that dance into your soul (letter to author, June 9, 1998).

In summary, I am doubtful that the human/alien relationships are occurring simply in our material world. Some of the narratives—like Andrea's flight to Hawaii, for example—are just too preposterous from the standpoint of this physical reality. Nevertheless, a great number of these connections possess psychological and emotional qualities as complex and powerful, if not more so, than any earthly relationship with which I am familiar. Indeed, at times they have a truly cosmic quality. It seems as if the achievement of these connections across dimensional barriers has required the overcoming of such great energetic hurdles that their fulfillment seems to possess a depth and intensity greater than what occurs in most, if not all, relationships in this material plane.

To think of all this as a kind of divine play of consciousness requires, of course, a definition of that much-maligned word. Here I mean simply an exquisite expression by the creative intelligence, which functions as a kind of cosmic puppet-master or shape-shifter, bringing into being new possibilities of relationship(s). These relationships, when they move beyond the fear and resistance naturally associated with anything so apparently unfamiliar or strange, seem in their essence to be of such emotional, erotic, and/or spiritual power that they bring human beings closer to Source, God, Home, or whatever we may call the infinite creative principle or place. The division the human mind has made, at least in the Judeo-Christian world, between Eros and spirit is radically transcended in these connections. The experiencers may, as Julie suggests, truly be "on point" for the rest of us in shattering the barriers we have so scrupulously erected between matter and spirit, between ourselves and the Godhead or ground of being (Huxley 1970), awakening us to a truer and more transcendent identity.

The beings' awesome eyes appear to contain huge treasures of knowledge and love and draw the abductees into their seemingly limitless depths. If eyes are a window for the soul, in the alien abduction phenomenon this time-worn maxim becomes a kind of ultimate metaphor. For when they look into these eyes, the experiencers sometimes discover their deepest and truest selves. They may discover also in these dark pools that they are one with the beings and with all of life. As one of the beings looked at her, Andrea felt in that moment that "they are us, and there is no difference in the essence of any being."

As we have seen in this chapter, the human/alien relationship seems to have extraordinary creative power both for the experiencers and for the alien beings. In Andrea's words "it's so deep and mysterious and all about creation." Other abductees have the same experience once they overcome the fear that accompanies the invasive elements and the shattering of their reality. For those of us who are not experiencers, the meaning of the connection might be as significant as it is for them if we did not tend in our culture to diminish the importance of experiences—in this case, human/alien relationships—that do not conform to our notions of reality, or whose actuality cannot be verified materially. Yet curiously these experiences seem in the end to possess great transformative possibilities, whatever their ontological status may prove to be. Indeed, ontological distinctions themselves seem to pale in importance in the face of matters of such transcendent power.

Conclusion

The Emerging Picture

*We all know more than we allow ourselves to know because of a
certain cowardice in face of the inexpressible, and fear of accepting its
effect on us as guide to the nature of its reality.*

Laurens van der Post
A Mantis Carol, 1975

Memory is for me a sacred force.

Poet Geoffrey Hill
November 18, 1998

What Sort of Reality Is This?

To a large extent, the debate surrounding UFOs has focused on
the question of whether they are real in a strictly material sense
and if their existence can be proven by the methods of traditional science. Similarly, with regard to abductions, interest has centered on
whether people are being taken bodily through the sky into spaceships by
alien beings. These may be intriguing questions. But after nearly ten years
of work with abductees, I have come to the view that these are not the most
significant questions posed by the alien abduction phenomenon. Rather, the
most important truths for our culture may lie in the extraordinary nature
and power of the abductees' experiences, the opening that these experiences
provide to other deeper dimensions of reality, and what they may mean for
our culture and the human future.

Efforts to pin down physical evidence for the existence of UFOs and
the material aspect of abductions will and probably should continue, if for

no other reason than the fact that they corroborate the actuality of the phenomena. But I am increasingly convinced that the subtle and elusive nature of the abduction phenomenon is such that its secrets will be denied to those using a purely empirical approach, who try to keep observer and observed, subject and object, totally separate. I am also concerned that if too much attention is brought to studying the physical manifestations alone, the potentially profound significance of this subject may not be realized.

The alien abduction phenomenon is one among a number of manifestations—including near-death experiences, intricate crop formations, apparitions of many kinds, unexplained powers of healing (Dossey 1993b; Cooperstein 1996), and parapsychology (Jahn and Dunne 1987; Radin 1997)—that are forcing us to appreciate that cosmic realities exist beyond the three-dimensional universe that has bounded our earthly existence. There seem to be as many names for these domains as there are methods of approaching them: the "implicate order," the "invisible world," "other dimensions," and "transpersonal" or "daimonic reality" are a few of them. Philosophers like Michael Zimmerman (Travis 1998) and Michael Grosso (2004) posit a "third zone" of reality that is neither purely internal nor external but lies beyond, including or subsuming the familiar dualism of inner and outer worlds. Whatever words we may use to describe this realm or realms, it appears ever more likely that we exist in a multidimensional cosmos or multiverse, within which space and time appear to be constructs of the mind that order or simplify the chaos of energy and vibration in which we are immersed.

In addition to the methods of hypothesis-building, experimentation, and replication that have formed the basis of the physical sciences, penetrating this multidimensional universe or multiverse seems to require the full range of powers that human consciousness may possess, including intuition, contemplation, or what one of the experiencers has called "the heart's mind." The cosmos that is revealed by this opening of consciousness, far from being an empty place of dead matter and energy, appears to be filled with beings, creatures, spirits, intelligences, gods—the names vary according to the apparent worldview of the observer or function and behavior of the entity at hand—that have through the millennia been intimately involved with human existence. In some instances, it would appear, certain of these entities may even cross over the divide that we created in order to keep unseen realities and mysteries apart, ideologically speaking, from the material world.

The idea that we live in a multidimensional universe populated by beings or life-forms that are less densely embodied than we are, or perhaps not embodied at all, is not new to Eastern religious traditions or to most of the indigenous peoples of the world. But it is not a cosmos that is familiar or accepted as existing by the scientific culture of Western society, which has, perhaps once necessarily, constructed a universe in which the material or psychological, the seen and unseen realms, have been kept largely separate so that the physical world might be understood and mastered in its own right (Tarnas 1991). The difficulty is that this almost exclusive concentration on the material world, whose extreme manifestation is unbridled consumerism, has resulted in the virtual atrophy of the capacity to perceive or experience the exquisite and awesome beauty, magnificence, and transcendent power of these other dimensions. I think that this is what is meant by the loss of a sense of the sacred, of a connection with the spaces or places of higher value, a separation from the Divine.

When Sigmund Freud set forth his notion that whatever human beings repressed or denied would tend to return in another form, some-times with a vengeance, he had in mind drives, feelings, and memories. Being a product himself of the extreme intellectual secularism of late-nineteenth-century Europe, he clearly was not thinking that the unseen or sacred domains of reality denied by his and our culture might eventually clamor once again for recognition. But he was perhaps identifying an aspect of a larger reigning principle in nature, namely a tendency toward balance or harmony, a kind of homeostatic corrective principle that manifests when extremes of imbalance occur.

Against the backdrop of this emerging cosmology, we may ask: What kind of a business is this alien abduction phenomenon? First and foremost it appears to belong to that class of phenomena that do not respect the epistemological and ontological walls that we have erected between the unseen realms of the cosmos and ourselves. The aliens, whatever or whomever they may be, cross this barrier with ease and apparent insouciance. The abduction phenomenon is not the only one that does this. As I have noted, crop formations, near-death experiences, some forms of healing at a distance, telepathic communication, and the mind-affecting-matter experiments of parapsychology are a few of the other activities of nature that do not seem to respect this barrier. But the abduction story appears to be especially well suited for breaking down these walls by virtue of its democratic ubiquity, the energetic intensity that seems to accompany it, and its capacity, through its vivid aerospace and biotechnical elements, to "speak our language," that is, the "language" of science and technology.

Those of us who study such phenomena confront a curious circularity that acts as a kind of resistance to appreciating their power and significance. On the one hand, someone who holds to a worldview that keeps radically separate the manifest and the unseen, the subject and object worlds, cannot see or admit the possibility that abduction encounters may be real in more than a purely subjective sense. On the other hand, it has become increasingly clear to me that the phenomenon itself represents a kind of return of the repressed that is "designed" (I use quotation marks to warn against attributing purpose to the creative principle, a kind of linear thinking that is sometimes characteristic of the human mind) to break down this separation. But paradigmatic shifts may occur slowly, and energy will most likely continue to be expended upon fitting the alien abduction phenomenon into familiar categories or, failing that, upon dismissing it altogether.

We still know very little about the forces that act together to bring about a fundamental change in worldview. But it seems clear that for particular individuals such a shift can occur only when some new information or experience, utterly incompatible with previously held beliefs, reaches them beyond the intellect so powerfully that the inadequacy of the worldview that they have hitherto used to explain or contend with reality becomes viscerally and intellectually inescapable. This is what has happened to the abductees who turn to look at their experiences. It is what happened to me in the course of experiencing and studying their stories. It is what is happening to increasing numbers of people who are being exposed to this phenomenon, especially when they meet or hear abduction experiencers tell what they feel quite certain happened to them.

The Abduction Phenomenon in the Human Story

I cannot offer proof of the material reality of the abduction phenomenon. Instead, I think its principal elements and place in human history can best be pulled together as a story that is coherent, even if it contains elements that may not be consistent with the worldview in which I and others of my culture were raised. Within the structure of a story or parable, I can travel more comfortably between the literal and the symbolic, between metaphoric and material reality, between certainty and uncertainty, and between the manifest and the unseen worlds.

In saying this, I do not mean to imply that it does not matter whether abduction experiencers are referring to an actual event in the physical world; are describing subtler matters that may not be literally true in a material sense; or are even (whether they know it or not) speaking metaphorically. Where these distinctions seem important, I do try to make them. But I must confess that the more deeply I have explored this phenomenon over the past decade, the less certain I have become about when the abductees are speaking of something that happened to them literally in this material reality and when they are communicating in metaphoric language events they experienced as utterly real in a physical sense but that happened to their subtle, astral, or energetic bodies, which may be the actual locus of the sense of self (see chapter 4). Although these differentiations may be of theoretical importance for philosophy and science, they do not seem to matter much to the abductees unless I engage them intellectually in a discussion of such questions.

The abduction story moves more in the direction of mystery and the unknown than toward certainty and conviction, although some of the material has come up so consistently, and with such narrative clarity and emotional power for the abductees, that it is doubtful to me that other investigators would not discover the same things were they to expose themselves to this information. Finally, I cannot avoid the fact that not much sense can be made of any of this material without positing an ultimate or overarching creative principle or intelligence in the cosmos that is doing its work through this and related phenomena that break into our material reality from unseen realms. Once we can acknowledge at least the existence of such an intelligence—which the upbringing of my childhood and youth largely denied—many of the pieces of the alien abduction phenomenon seem to fall into place. Without it the whole phenomenon seems at worst malevolent and at best absurd.

The story would go something like this. It all starts with the ultimate creative principle, which abductees call variously God, Source, Home or the One. (Greg calls it "God-Goddess-All that is.") From some primal beginning—which, according to one or another cosmology, was the work of the

God force, a mysterious creation of all out of nothing, or a cosmic explosion (Big Bang) from which all matter/energy emerged out of a tiny omnipotential seed (Guth 1997, p. 14)—everything we now know of as this universe came almost instantaneously into being. Perhaps, as physicist Alan Guth suggests, there may be an infinite number of such universes. Be all that as it may, afterward a sequence of evolutionary events occurred, including the creation of the planet Earth and the emergence of biological life and the human species.

Human beings, having been formed originally by the God force, retained some experience of a relationship to it. But then something else happened. We developed a consciousness, a self-awareness, different from other species in that we came to know our own mortality, that our time on this Earth was limited, and that this body at least would die. For most peoples on the planet, the sorrow associated with this inescapable fact was mitigated, at least to some degree, by the sense of a persisting connection with the Source, the potential ecstasy and fulfillment of that relationship, and the conviction that there was something—a spirit, soul, psyche, or consciousness—that was eternal and would survive the body, returning to God after its death.

Sometime during the second millennium after the birth of Christ, human beings in the West (analogous processes seem to have occurred in other parts of the world) went to work to solve the problem of the body's survival and possibly to achieve immortality in a physical rather than a spiritual sense, which had never seemed altogether certain or satisfactory to many people. Through the development of powers of observation and reason, we developed modern science, medicine, and technology, through which we have sought with considerable success to struggle with the problem of mortality, to reduce some forms of suffering, and to prolong life. The part of ourselves that is devoted to this project of survival, called initially by Freud the "ego," grew in its power and importance until most human endeavors have seemed at times to be devoted to its (the ego's) preservation.

Until perhaps the middle of the eighteenth century, people in the West—as well as the indigenous peoples of the Earth, who have never lost their connection with the Creator—experienced their advancing understanding of the material world in the context of a cosmos that was ensouled, in which God continued to inhere (Barrett 1976). But sometime in that century—perhaps in part because the methods of empirical science were also applied to studying the creative principle itself, and by these methods It could not be proven to exist—many people in Western society became in large part "secular." They lost their sense of connection with the Divine, the sacred realms, the Source, God, the Creator—or whatever other name is or was used to describe an ultimate creative principle. The universe came to consist largely of dead matter, energy, and space, and our pleasures, for the most part, became restricted to earthly emotional connections and material satisfactions.

This approach to the nature of our mortality has led to some big problems. One of our great scientific areas of success, the prolongation of physical life, has led to a staggering growth in the human population, to the point where we have become one of, if not the largest, biomass on the planet. At the same time, we have created increasingly efficient methods for taking precious, nonrenewable materials from the Earth. As a result we have begun to exceed our energy resources, and by expelling into the air, land, and water the poisonous by-products of our consumption that we have not found a way to get rid of safely, we are killing off many of the planet's life-forms.

Meanwhile, our successes in the material domain have led to improved standards of living and understandable expectations for a better life among many of the Earth's peoples, thus requiring the consumption of ever more physical goods per person and putting still more pressure on the Earth's fragile environment. This increasingly short supply of food and other precious materials has exacerbated tensions between human groups, given rise to simplistic ideologies for solving economic and political problems (communism, capitalism, fascism, and so on), and threatens to bring about the virtual extinction of life as we know it through the use of weapons of mass destruction.

Humankind is now caught in a vicious spiral. The loss of our relationship to nature and the Creator instills in us a great longing whose roots are not understood (Huxley 1972; Tarnas 1991; Almaas 1987, 1989). So we turn to one or another form of addiction and to the increased consumption of material goods to fill the hole within us that this spiritual bankruptcy has brought about. In collaboration with consumers, governments and corporations cooperate to stimulate our material hungers further through marketing strategies, while promoting policies of increasing economic growth to meet these artificially induced needs. It is not surprising that astute environmental and economic analysts predict that the Earth's capacity to sustain human life will soon collapse if no fundamental change occurs (Meadows 1993; Hawken 1994; Daly 1997; Henderson 1997).

Forgetting the Original Instructions of the Creator

As I have discussed in this book, many indigenous people, led by shamans like Bernardo Peixoto, Sequoyah Trueblood, and Credo Mutwa, have not followed this cycle of destruction and have retained their connection with the creative Source. Often I have heard native medicine people and spiritual leaders say that we have "lost the original instructions of the Creator." Dhyani Ywahoo, a medicine woman who retains her connection with Cherokee traditions, expressed it to me this way: "Our original instructions are that different groups, different people, through their mindfulness, their spiritual activities, and how they care for each other in the environment, actually maintain the balance of the whole organism, which is the planet. And those who are more awake in their awareness recognize the relationship with the solar system and the universe. So when we say 'original instructions,' we say all this is encoded in the blood" (Ywahoo, personal communication, August 1994). According to Sequoyah, "People from other planets," the "invisible beings" who were living here before we were, are now trying to help us heal the Earth, for the male energy has gotten out of balance with the female or goddess energy, and we have turned our backs "on the original teachings of the Creator."

Some contemporary theologians like Thomas Berry have come to understand the endless harm that has been created by the separation of matter and spirit that has been contained in much Christian teaching. For this Earth, Berry has observed, is the highest or finest creation of God of which we are aware (Berry 1990). Similarly, Credo Mutwa tells us that according to African lore, the Earth is a "womb-world," one of the very few planets in the entire cosmos that is capable of creating and sustaining life. It is indeed a jewel in the cosmic crown, and our increasing destruction of its life appears to be a crime of cosmic proportions.

The Human/Earth Problem from a Cosmic Perspective

Up to this point, we are pretty much on familiar ground. But now the story moves in a direction that is strongly at odds with the worldview in which I—and, I suspect, most of my readers—were brought up. I would not even have considered what follows, had not the experiencers with whom I have worked for nearly a decade provided me with this material so consistently and clearly. Evidently what we have been doing to the Earth has not gone "unnoticed" at a higher, cosmic, or cosmic/regional level. Some sort of odd intervention seems to be occurring here. We are not, apparently, being permitted to continue on our destructive ways without some kind of "feedback" (Schlemmer 1993).[1]

What *sort* of feedback is occurring? Well, to begin with, no united planetary environmental balancing team has been sent in to stop us, for it seems to be God's way to leave us a lot of rope. The highest intelligence appears to respect our free will and does not try to block us directly. (How could that be done anyway?) But this does not mean no intervention is occurring. I look at what the abductees have told me and then try to put myself in the Creator's place. How might it look? Two of the kinds of entities that have been brought into being—aliens and humans—appear to be in difficulty. Each has needs that the other can fulfill, although their agendas, while intersecting, are rather different in some respects.

When it comes to the aliens, there are several types with differing properties. The little gray ones with the big eyes are reliable for what is needed here, although their methods can sometimes be thoughtless and rather crude. They are especially good at shape-shifting, disguising themselves as animal forms when this is useful. The grays have been interacting with human beings and affecting their cultures and identities, usually without their knowledge, for thousands of years. They are especially "useful" now. Other beings are more luminous or transcendent. Some, like the reptilian ones, really play rough. These can fulfill a more limited role, depending on the level of consciousness of the particular human beings that are chosen or have volunteered for this project.

The aliens seem to have lost their bodies, or at least have become less densely embodied than the human beings. Some abductees are informed that something went wrong biologically for the aliens as a result of an overstepping or technological hubris of the kind we are engaged in now on this planet, and like the angels, they long to have a body. We have countless examples of the aliens' fascination with our dense physicality, sensuality, sexuality, parental love, and the like, and their apparent desire to form a union with us both for their own purposes—to enjoy, for example, the pleasures of dense embodiment—and to produce a hybrid human/alien race. Although the aliens are not themselves gods—their behavior is sometimes anything but godlike—abductees consistently report that the beings seem closer to the Godhead than we are, acting as messengers, guardian spirits, or angels, intermediaries between us and the Divine Source.

The humans, on the other hand, have the capacity for deep and intense caring, nurturance, and physical and emotional love, but they have lost the connection with their Source and seem to be treating God's finest creation, the Earth (Berry 1990), as a piece of private property belonging to them only. This cannot be allowed to continue. By the human/alien union, a hybrid race can be created—in what realm we do not know—that maintains the biological identity and continuity of both species, should the human race succeed in its project of destroying itself and much of the other life on the Earth. Energetically speaking, this has been a tough job of adjustment, since the aliens vibrate at a considerably higher level than the humans. Lately the human/hybrid integration seems to be going better (see chapter 6). The aliens' superior communications technology can also be used to try to get across to this stiff-necked people what they are doing to their beautiful planet and see if that will make a difference. The alien beings can also help to raise human consciousness and bring this species back into connection with the creative principle.

Shattering a Worldview: Awakening

For environmental education something more is needed. Spawning a lot of hybrids cannot go very far toward preserving the Earth's life if human beings remain devoted to their own egoic pursuits, if their psyches do not change. This is a very big challenge. The materialist juggernaut is loose and gaining momentum, and the only thing that can stop it is a radical change in consciousness. The human ego, especially in Western cultures, bolstered by great powers of intellectual rationalization and denial, is highly resistant to change.

This brings us to perhaps the most critical and controversial aspect of the abduction phenomenon. Many, perhaps the majority, of the experiencers find their encounters to be highly traumatic, at least until they have confronted and integrated their power and meaning. But this type of trauma has some unusual characteristics. In addition to the familiar terror and helplessness that all traumatic events have in common, the abduction experiences have two other important elements.

First, the experiences seem to be created, as if by design, to shatter (the word virtually all abductees use) the previously held idea of reality (which usually had no place for such entities) and topple the experiencer from the sense of being a member of a uniquely intelligent life-form at the peak of the Great Chain of Being. In the face of forces beyond their control, abductees are confronted with their helplessness and with the existence of intelligent beings possessing technologies and other powers far in advance of our own.

Second, as they remember or relive their experiences, abductees often realize that they have encountered intense vibratory energies, still held in the body, that have also profoundly affected their consciousness. It is difficult sometimes for them to put this change into words, but they speak of it as an "awakening," or a moving to a higher level, as a direct result of the vibrations themselves. Andrea, for example, tried to explain to us that as a result of her encounters, all of the cells of her body seemed to be vibrating differently. It felt to her as if changes had occurred deep inside her "core," which seemed to transcend blocks in her awareness. "It is so much about choice and intent, and getting really conscious," Greg wrote to me (letter to author March 20, 1999).

Now we seem to be coming closer to the heart of the matter. For this awakening, the heightened awareness that grows out of the ego-shattering impact of the encounters, carries with it quite consistently certain interrelated psychospiritual changes, especially if the experiencers are enabled to work through the traumatic dimension of what they feel certain has happened to them.

First, they have access to what in Western societies is called nonordinary states of consciousness, similar to the symbolic worlds of the shamans of indigenous cultures. They become aware of the great archetypes of the collective unconscious, of birth, death, and rebirth, which helps them to experience their connectedness to other beings and to the Creator or Source.

Second, as a result of this deepening and expanding of their psychological and spiritual powers (abductees will often also speak of and manifest particular psychic abilities), together with the experienced shift of their bodily vibrations, they may undergo a profound connection or reconnection with the Divine, God, Source, or whatever they may call the ultimate creative principle in the cosmos. They may become, as Karin spoke of it, "disciples to Source."

Third, they experience a heart-opening, a sense of loving connection with all living beings and creation itself, which can at times take on mystical proportions. Abductees may find God or love in the perception of *light* that is a regular part of their experiences, which they see as the source of all of creation. Karin spoke of "light with a small 'l'" and "light with a capital 'L,'" which is "literally the presence of God within everything." Sharon saw or felt "love that was coming off the light" in her bedroom. "The love was overwhelming," she exclaimed. This is consistent with the findings of Norman Don and Gilda Moura, who observed that Brazilian abduction experiencers could enter voluntarily into states of hyperarousal revealed by their brain waves to be comparable only to the states of ecstasy or *samadhi* of advanced meditators or yogis (Don and Moura 1997).

Fourth, abductees experience a renewed sense of the sacred and a reverence for nature. Some, like Carlos Diaz, see divine light, like an aura, surrounding each living thing. Like Carlos, they may become aware of the interconnected web of life and be viscerally, sometimes unbearably, pained by the destruction of the Earth's living forms, committing themselves to their preservation. "I've learned to go back to the natural flow of things," Isabel says, "and everything just connects the way it's supposed to be."

But a good deal more happens to the abductees during their journeys. Some develop a deep and enduring relationship with a particular alien being, usually described as more powerful than any earthly relationship, and they may speak convincingly of having an alien mate and of parenting in another dimension. The connection with the gray aliens' great black eyes may seem to draw abductees into seemingly limitless or infinite depths, where knowledge and relationship occur on a soul level.

The fundamental changes that abductees make in their lives as they come to grasp the power and meaning of their experiences has been important in convincing me of the truth and significance of their stories, whatever their ontological status may be. Many give up mainstream jobs, often for less well-paying ones in the healing or other human service professions, and become active in Earth-preserving projects. The change in their worldviews and core beliefs is lasting and continues to evolve. They usually feel compelled to share what they have learned as a result of confronting their experiences. But they may debate whether to expose themselves and their families to the criticism and attacks that, at least until quite recently, they have had to face when they would go public with their stories. When one or more experiencers have shared a lectern with me at conferences or symposia, the effect on heretofore skeptical members of an audience has often been quite stunning. Other investigators have had the same experience.

But there is a painful side to the spiritual awakening that abduction experiencers undergo. Although they may feel that they have a special responsibility or mission as teachers or Earth stewards, their deepening connection with Source or Home brings with it for them a feeling that they do not belong here. They may even feel they have an alien identity or soul and that the spaceships themselves are part of Home. The negativity or toxicity, material and spiritual, that they experience in their environment, especially in urban centers, may become literally unbearable. Not infrequently, experiencers become estranged from close family members unless these individuals can grow with them. When they confront their longing to "return" to Home or God, they may literally sob with the pain and grief of their separation.

The abduction phenomenon seems to be one of a number of intrusions into our reality from other realms that are contributing to the gradual (at least so far) spiritual rebirth taking place in Western culture. It seems to have something to do with the human future. Each of the principal elements of the phenomenon—the traumatic intrusions; the reality-shattering encounters; the energetic intensity; the apocalyptic ecological confrontations; the reconnection with Source; and the forging of new relationships across a dimensional divide—contributes to the *daishigyo*, the great ego death, that is marking the end of the materialist business-as-usual paradigm that has lost its compatibility with life in the world as we now know it.

Remembering

Just what will take its place is not clear. Abductees, like Native Americans, emphasize the need to remember: remember where we came from (Karin);

remember the original purpose of this planet (Will); remember that we are all part of God (Isabel); remember who we are (Andrea); remember the original instructions of the Creator (Sequoyah). New knowledge, new mastery, another way, cannot, as Plato taught, happen unless we recollect what we knew at birth but forgot. To go forward, it is essential to remember our spiritual origins and goals. For Western cultures this means to reconnect with the wisdom traditions of our early history (Metzner 1994, 1997; Smith 1992).[2]

Abductees and those, like myself, who work with them are often drawn to Native American spiritual leaders, for they appear to have a deep and enduring familiarity with the entities we call aliens and the role they have played in enabling them to maintain their own connection with the Creator. Their encounters with the aliens bring abductees closer to the Divine Source or God, but for some native leaders like Sequoyah, the Creator has already been considered first in every moment. We must allow ourselves to be vulnerable again, like children, he teaches, and shed the arrogant notion that we can "do it all ourselves."

In the end, the abduction phenomenon seems to me to be a part of the shift in consciousness that is collapsing duality and enabling us to see that we are connected beyond the Earth at a cosmic level.[3] No common enemy will unite us, but the realization of a common Source might. Our notions of the Divine, like everything else, seem to grow along with the evolution of our consciousness. We no longer expect an Old Testament God/bully that will part the seas and bring us where we need to go. Nor is it likely that a messiah/savior will lead us into the Divine Light. For that light, we are learning from phenomena like the one in this book, and from near-death and other out-of-body experiences, is an eternal part of ourselves and the essence of all creation. The creative principle is within us, not without— thus it cannot befall us. As Bernardo Peixoto discovered in a shattering realization, it is nowhere and everywhere.

We cannot nostalgically turn back the clock to a time before industrialization, materialism, the building of instruments of mass destruction, consumerism, and the Internet. They are not the enemy, although as eleven-year-old Emma wisely said, "We mustn't get too technologed [sic]." The god for this time, we seem to be learning from abductees and others, is more of a partner than anything else, working through and with us. Now that is really scary, for it places choice utterly within us. From this perspective the alien abduction phenomenon is largely an opportunity or a gift, a kind of catalyst for the evolution of consciousness in the direction of an emerging sense of responsibility for our own and the planet's future.

In April 1997, in a plea to a large audience in New York City, Karin spoke passionately of the possibilities she saw in this choice:

> Perhaps it is that we have found ourselves at a fork in the road, and we are once again faced with making a choice. Couldn't we this time, finally, make the right one? Couldn't we simply reach out and embrace this experience and all that it brings with it, including the terror as well as the questions, truth and beauty? Because don't you think in doing so, we would at last learn about who and what we are? And isn't it possible that we just might learn what it is exactly that is the nature of the connection to the Creator as well as the universe? Please, can't we this once choose the path that will finally set us free? Free to love, laugh and cry? Because after all, it is our ultimate destiny to live in the joy of being alive. (meeting of Friends of the Institute of Noetic Sciences, April 29, 1997)

Notes

CHAPTER 1

1. Some shamans can make these distinctions. Shaman Alberto Villoldo identifies four levels of "greater reality":

1. physical or literal reality
2. psychological, symbolic reality
3. magical, mythical reality
4. energetic or "spiritual" reality (statement prepared December 28, 1996 for Richmond Mayo Smith by Wellesley College mathematics professor Patrick Morton).

However, even if levels of reality are theoretically valid, if a person's way of knowing is primarily experiential, it can be difficult to distinguish these four domains.

2. When Edgar Mitchell read a review copy of chapter 4, he wrote back that aspects of the abduction phenomenon might not be so far from what physicists are able to model. Here are some excerpts from his e-mail letter: "An experiencer's description of energy, light, vibration, etc., is not metaphoric but likely a real and accurate perception. Most physicists know absolutely nothing about modeling internal perceptions. I am convinced a large part of our problem with these anomalous events is that our perceptual machinery is too limited to be able to perceive many of them. Our perceptual machinery is shaped both by the physics of our local environment and our experiences. Most of the experiences your subjects describe have now been or can be in principle modeled in modern scientific terms, that is, being picked up on light beams and teleporting through walls."

Upon receiving this e-mail from Edgar Mitchell, our own webmaster at PEER, Will Bueché, was reminded that he had asked Whitley Strieber via the Internet why there so often seemed to be perceptual discrepancies during abduction experiences. Strieber, rather in the same vein as Mitchell's comments above, had replied, "The perceptual problems are significant and complex. I think that the fundamental indeterminacy of all perception (the quantum perception problem) makes it extremely difficult for us to correctly observe things for which our brains lack any reference point at all. This is probably why alien figures are so difficult to see. If the people on the other side understand this problem and can exploit its consequences, that may explain things like their seeming ability to appear and disappear at will. It may be that this is more like hiding in plain sight than some kind of magical process."

3. Anthropologist Ralph Metzner wrote on my manuscript, "They *are* helping us fix things by expanding our awareness, which is the source of the disaster" (July 31, 1998).

CHAPTER 2

1. In the fall of 1998, Harvard physics professor Paul Horowitz expanded the program by installing equipment at the Oak Ridge Observatory in Harvard, Massachusetts, to scan the heavens for laser light signals (Caballero and Langer 1998, pp. 1, 10).

2. The McLeod study employed the following established psychometric instruments: BORRTI (Bell Object Relations and Reality Testing Inventory), SNAP (Schedule for Nonadaptive and Adaptive Personality), TAS (Tellegen Absorption Scale), DES (Dissociative Experiences Scale), MSC-PTSD (Mississippi Scale for Civilian Post-Traumatic Stress Disorder), ICMI (Inventory of Childhood Memories and Imaginings), CIS (Creative Imagination Scale), GSS (Goodjjonsson Suggestibility Scale), and SCL-90-R (Symptom Check List 90-Revised), among others. Several papers analyzing details of these findings are being prepared for publication.

3. Colleagues have made the argument that by screening out cases of gross mental illness we are skewing the sample. I do not believe this is a valid criticism because our purpose is not psychiatric in the sense of diagnosing and treating a mental condition. Rather, we are interested in determining whether or not there are a substantial number of cases where a psychiatric disorder cannot explain the phenomenon. If this should prove to be so, then it would be highly unlikely that the abduction phenomenon, to any significant degree, can be explained on the basis of psychopathology.

4. Roberta Colasanti and John E. Mack, *Comparative Narratives of Reports of Multiply Witnessed Anomalous Experiences Commonly Called "Alien Abduction": A Pilot Study*. (Cambridge, MA: Program for Extraordinary Experience Research, 1996).

5. The question of false memory, with or without hypnosis, as applied to the abduction phenomenon, is discussed in Appendix A of the paperback edition of *Abduction* (Mack 1995).

6. I would prefer thinking of the "total self" as the instrument of knowing, for as Whitehead noted (1933, p. 180), there seem to be "non-sensuous" organs or modes of perception.

7. Healer and clairvoyant Rosalyn Bruyere remarked to Karen Wesolowski, "There has never been a group of people in religious ecstasy who did not think the world was coming to an end. Their world is coming to an end. Not *the* world, *their* world. The world as they knew it will fall apart. Because the old world isn't going to be here anymore, and everything you thought to be true is going to turn out not to be true" (Interview August 17, 1998).

CHAPTER 3

1. At a lecture at Wellesley College in June 1998, mathematician Patrick Morton spoke of "living outside of time" as an essential aspect of the creative process.

When we commit ourselves to being creative in answer to a real need, we are helped by divine agencies, which are simultaneously a larger part of ourselves. Put another way, each of us lives inside and outside of time, and in creativity the part of us living outside of time pours itself through the part of us living inside of time. Plato called this greater being our daimon, the guiding principle of our lives, which seems to exist prior to the living out of our lives.

2. See also Kaku's *Visions* for a somewhat speculative discussion of wormholes, time travel, and black holes. The enormous energies required for travel via wormholes can be calculated but are beyond anything we know on this planet (Kaku 1997, pp. 339–45).

3. The relationship between the physicists' notion of wormholes, or interdimensional bridges, and the out-of-body experiences or astral travel that abductees describe needs further study (Buhlman 1996).

4. After writing this, I read that philosopher Michael Zimmerman's study of the abduction phenomenon led him to posit a third "soul realm," an "intermediary dimension between the spirit and material realms." (Travis 1998, p. 21)

CHAPTER 4

1. Will's wife, Marjorie, told us that she too saw these lights on a vessel that appeared unexpectedly in the fog and did not respond to their foghorn. She did not want to deal with the idea that this was something mysterious that she could not explain, and she suggested perhaps it was a cruise ship, although the configuration of the lights did not look to her quite right for this. When we asked Will if it could have been a cruise ship, he rejected this idea because the vessel had no red and green running lights, fore and aft, and no layers of lights like the portholes of an ocean liner. There was no response to the foghorn or to their effort to contact the craft by radio. Furthermore, the vessel seemed to come straight toward them, as if sideways, and appeared to have a kind of square depth. Finally, a strong beam of light shone upon their boat, which was unlike any light that a ship would possess.

2. University of Illinois researcher Norman Don, Ph.D., also emphasized these relationships to me in a December 5, 1998 communication.

3. In remarks prepared for the Multidisciplinary Study Group Conference on Anomalous Experiences, Rudolf Schild noted that this phenomenon is now called "quintessence." Heretofore the known laws of physics predicted that the universe was slowing down, not expanding at an accelerating rate. Perhaps, he suggests, this mysterious pressure is caused by other universes in our vast "multi-verse" that are interacting with ours. This and other uncertainties in quantum theory itself lead Schild to ask whether we may be discovering "the workings of some higher intelligence or purpose within the multi-verse, guiding events in our 4-D universe in ways we don't yet understand" (Schild, interview with author, March 18, 1999).

4. Although abductees may speak of the physical sense of vibration, and the intensity of feeling they experience suggests that energies have been "stored" somehow in their bodies, this may not be the best way of thinking about what is occurring. It is possible that the experience began with some sort of information that was contained in the energies that they encountered during the experience. Perhaps this information, with all of its meaning and power, is revived when the experience is recalled or relived. Both Karin and Dave actually spoke at the Multidisciplinary Study Group of information seeming somehow to be contained in the light that they perceived at the beginning of their experiences.

CHAPTER 5

1. Remarks at Board Meeting, Center for Psychology and Social Change, June 11, 1998, at which board members and invitees were asked to respond to a draft of this chapter.

2. Celeste expressed her sadness for the Earth's pain in a poem she sent to Roberta Colasanti:

> *I weep for the earth.*
> *With all of her glorious beauty, she cannot survive.*
> *Our destructive ways have escalated.*
> *She struggles and she continues to support life.*
> *God's great earth is dying.*
> *We humans are all clinging with fragility to life-support.*
> *There are no possibilities to avoid the certain fate of the earth.*
> *Delicate and fragile life.*
> *Challenged to live.*
> *Suckling at the breast of a dying Mother.*
> *Quietly, I weep*
> *. . . for the children of the earth.*
> *And their cherished Mother. (Letter, February 18, 1999).*

3. When I spoke of Carlos' experience with anthropologist Charles Laughlin at the Study Conference he called my attention to the work of Fritz A. Popp (Popp et al. 1984; Ho et al. 1994) on bioelectrodynamics and bioluminescence. In a follow-up letter Dr. Laughlin wrote, "Basically they are showing that cells participate in producing a sea of nonthermal light and they use this light for intra- and intercellular communication— that light is fundamental to life and the organizational properties of living systems. We do not see the light with our unaided eyes because the frequencies produce interference patterns that cancel out the visible spectrum" (letter to the author, April 12, 1999).

CHAPTER 6

1. Yet it is still not certain whether this should be regarded as altogether literal. Sequoyah (chapter 9), for example, has remarked that "spirit can impregnate a woman any way that spirit wants to."

2. Eva's unpublished thesis, *Communion*, January 22, 1997, p. 3.

CHAPTER 7

1. The term *archetype*, as I am using it in this chapter, derives from Carl Jung's idea of symbols that link the inner world of the human psyche with the patterns inherent in the universe. Although archetypes may be internal, universal structures, the nature of their expression for human beings varies with the evolution of culture and shifts in the collective unconscious.

2. In Celtic mythology a white horse can be a messenger from the gods, while in ancient Greece it could depict the passage from one plane of reality to another. In the mythologies of Japan, China, and India, a white horse can symbolize the goddess of mercy or the Great Mother. This is not inappropriate when one considers that Nona has five Earth children and believes she has many others "in space." Nona is a kind of Earth Mother figure in her community and has been given the mission by the beings to "take care of the children." Joseph Campbell tells a story of how white horses were seen as the helping spirits of an old Eskimo shaman (Campbell 1983, p. 171), which is interesting in the light of Nona's imminent role as an assistant to Bernard Peixoto.

3. Interestingly, owls, like the alien beings with their large black eyes, are associated with seeing, especially in the nighttime (Ralph Metzner, personal communication, July 31, 1998).

4. Ralph Metzner reminded me that in shamanic journeys, passages occur through tunnels, and the traveler will then emerge in another world.

5. The experience of traveling through tubes after prior deaths to a plane inhabited by light beings has been researched for ten years with dozens of clients by therapist Michael Newton, Ph.D. (Newton 1994, especially pp. 17–25).

6. Metzner suggests that the emphasis could be placed instead on reality with "metaphoric overtones or associations." He quotes Goethe's remark that all phenomena are metaphorical (personal communication, July 31, 1998).

CHAPTER 8

1. Interestingly, in some legends of the Amazon basin, beings that come from the sky seem to be connected with freshwater mammalian dolphins, which are found in the river near its mouth. When a girl from the rain forest becomes pregnant and swears that she did not have intercourse

with a man, the pregnancy may be attributed to a dolphin. But Bernardo has also heard that these dolphins are thought actually to be beings from the sky that took this form in order to inseminate virgins and then return to space. When a "baby from the stars" is born of such a union, it is said to have skin like a dolphin and will not survive long on Earth.

Nona was startled when she heard this story, for she recalled an experience in which beings took her to what appeared to be an inlet from the ocean in South America, where beautiful dolphins came upstream to be with her. The beings told her that she must wear the symbol of a dolphin over her heart. From that time Nona has worn a dolphin pin on her chest. She has been shown children on the spaceships that were hers but were also related to dolphins. Dolphins, Nona believes, are inseparably involved with the abduction phenomenon and also with her coming to meet Bernardo, whose tribal name is Ipupiara, which means "dolphin."

2. Actually, modern physicists and astronomers have begun to report discoveries that do give evidence that "nothing" is, in a sense, the source of everything. MIT Nobel Prize–winning physicist Dr. Alan Guth writes, "the question of the origin of matter in the universe is no longer thought to be beyond the range of science. After two thousand years of scientific research, it now seems likely that . . . everything *can* be created from nothing" (Guth 1997, pp. 2, 15). Cosmologist Brian Swimme says, "Careful investigation by quantum physicists of . . . what we modern peoples refer to as 'emptiness,' 'pure space,' or 'the vacuum' . . . reveals the strange emergence of elementary particles. . . . The usual process is for particles to erupt in pairs that will quickly interact and annihilate each other. . . . Such creative and destructive activity takes place everywhere and at all times throughout the universe . . . even between the synapses of the neurons in the brain. . . . The ground of the universe then . . . is not inert. It seethes with creativity, so much so that physicists refer to the universe's ground state as 'space-time foam'" (Swimme 1996, pp. 92–93, 101). Such observations by modern science echo the teachings of ancient Hindu and Buddhist masters that the world as we know it emerges from an Absolute Void or from soul emptiness and nothingness.

3. This symbolism was also mentioned to me by John Perkins (conversation with author November 9, 1997), who has lived for many years among Amazon rain forest tribes and other indigenous cultures. He has written about what he learned in *Shapeshifting* (1997), *Psychonavigation* (1990), and *The World Is as You Dream It* (1994).

CHAPTER 9

1. Sequoyah Trueblood, Autobiographical Summary, 1997a, pp. 21–22.
2. Ibid., p. 21.
3. Ibid., p. 21.
4. Ibid., p. 4.
5. Ibid., p. 8.
6. Ibid., p.12.
7. Ibid., p.13.
8. In Dostoevsky's story "Dream of a Ridiculous Man," the protagonist experiences an extraterrestrial journey that sounds similar to Sequoyah's:

> The eyes of these happy people sparkled limpid and lustrous. Their faces radiated intelligence and a kind of consciousness which had attained to the condition of serenity, but these faces were blithe and a childlike gaiety echoed in their words and voices. Ah, at the first sight of their faces, I immediately comprehended everything, everything! It was an earth as yet undefiled by the Fall. It was inhabited by sinless people, who lived in that paradise in which, according to the tradition of all mankind, our sinful ancestors had lived—with this difference, that the entire earth here was one and the same paradise. These people, smiling gladly, crowded around me, showering me with affection; they took me to their homes and each of them sought to set me at ease. (Dostoevsky 1995).

I am indebted to Christopher Lydon, for bringing this story to my attention.
9. Trueblood, Autobiographical Summary, 1997a, p.14.
10. Sequoyah Trueblood, 1997b. *Native Spirituality: Pathway to Peace.* Senior Fellowship Research Description, Harvard University Center for the Study of World Religions, p. 4.
11. Sequoyah Trueblood, Conversation with Peggy Huddleston, June 14, 1998, p. 9.
12. It is striking to me how similar these words are in feeling to the last four lines of the Buddhist Diamond Sutra:

> *So you should see all of the fleeting world*
> *A star at dawn, a bubble in the stream*
> *A flash of lightning, a summer cloud*
> *A flickering lamp, a phantom and a dream*
> *(Price and Mou-Lam, 1969).*

Price, A. F., and Mou-Lam, Wong 1969. *The Diamond Sutra and the Sutra of Hui Neng.* Boulder: Shambhala.

13. Trueblood, Conversation with Huddleston, p. 9.

14. Sequoyah Trueblood, "Healing Our Youth: A Proposal for a Youth Healing and Development Council," 1996, pp. 21–22.

15. Trueblood, *Native Spirituality,* pp. 1-2.

16. Trueblood, Autobiographical Summary, 1997a, pp. 20–21.

17. Sequoyah Trueblood, Senior Fellowship Application, Harvard University Center for the Study of World Religions, 1996, p.8.

18. In 1993 he received a call to come to New Brunswick, Canada, where eighty-two Micmac teenagers had signed a suicide pact. By the time he arrived, seven had already taken their lives. His healing work was focused upon reconnecting these young people with their cultural traditions and finding models for them among the native elders. Since 1993 there has been only one suicide—a boy who was known to be at especially high risk and did not receive the attention he needed. Sequoyah has also worked among youth with problems of drug and alcohol abuse and has helped to develop a Youth Ambassadors program.

19. Trueblood, Autobiographical Summary, 1997a, p. 19.

CHAPTER 10

1. There is much more to be learned about Credo Mutwa and his teachings from his own writings: *Let Not My Country Die* (Pretoria, South Africa: United Publishers International, 1986); *Indaba My Children: African Tribal History, Customs and Religious Beliefs* (New York: Grove Press, 1999); and *Africa is My Witness* (Johannesburg, South Africa: Blue Crane Books, 1966). Essays about him include Larsen, "The Making of a Zulu Sangoma," and Keeney, "Credo Mutwa," in *Shaking Out the Spirits* (Barrytown, NY: Station Hill Press, 1994), pp. 111–121. Larsen's book, *Song of the Stars: The Lore of a Zulu Shaman* (Barrytown, NY: Barrytown Ltd., 1996) contains the story of Credo's life together with extensive tales of African mythology and wisdom told in Credo's own words.

CHAPTER 11

1. Says Whitley Strieber,

I do not differentiate between physical and spiritual worlds. "The spiritual" is simply a matter of seeing better. But there is no break between the spiritual and the physical. This is why I see the exposure of implants as a spiritual act—the act of a spiritual rebel, really. To me, the placing of an object in the body is the placing of the object in the soul. And so I am deeply concerned with the meaning of these objects, because they must necessarily affect the whole self, from the trembling mortality to the highest serene edge.

(1998 letter of Whitley Strieber to Michael and Ian Baldwin, in response to Ian's reading of the manuscript of Strieber's book *Confirmation*.)

2. The experience of ego death and opening to the sense that we are ensouled beings whose existence will in some way survive the death of the physical body occurs in near-death experiences (Atwater 1988: Ring 1998), the use of mind-altering substances (Grof 1985), religious epiphanies (James 1902), and devoted spiritual practices, including meditation, prayer and yoga (see also Newton 1994).

3. Remarks at conference of the Friends of the Institute of Noetic Sciences (FIONS), New York City, April 1997.

CHAPTER 12

1. The following works report on nonabductees having experienced themes discussed in this chapter:

The intense feeling of returning "Home": After-death experiencers are documented by Moody 1975; Morse 1990; Greyson & Flynn 1984; and Ring 1980.

The pain of feeling separated from one's ultimate Source: Dawson 1994; and Shucman 1976. Both authors, moreover, regard this pain as the unconscious root of susceptibility to many kinds of disease.

The soul's chosen incarnation into human infancy and life cycle: Many authors write about incarnation as a received theory, but Michael Newton reports the recollections of prelife incarnation journeys by individual interviewees. See Newton 1994, chaps. 12–15.

Breaking down emotional layers and surrendering to the universal energy, then connecting to it and growing: Washburn 1995, chaps. 7 and 8.

Increase in psychic abilities; perceptual sensitivity; identification with the rest of the planet and concern for its future; sense of mission; need to change occupation: all these frequently occur after the near-death experience (Atwater 1988; Morse 1992; Ring and Valarino 1998).

Reinvigorating institutional religion with experience of direct communion with Source: Fowler (1981) identifies this as part of the sixth (and final) stage in an individual's spiritual development.

2. I have the impression—and it is only an impression, for the question would need more formal study—that the spiritual directions of the experiencers bear little relationship to their religious background. In a few cases, however, experiencers have seemed to breathe new life into an established religious tradition, whether or not it was originally their own, rediscovering its authentic spiritual power. In his book *Stages of Faith*, James Fowler gives other examples of institutionalized religious forms being reinvigorated by the experience of direct communication with Source (Fowler 1981).

3. Eva's, *Communion*, graduate thesis, 1997.

4. In Eastern philosophy such cycles of birth, death, and rebirth, associated with suffering, are spoken of as *samsara*.

CONCLUSION

1. Something close to this idea was expressed to me by Theodore Roszak: "I think that the planet communicates with us empathetically and alters our culture to meet its needs. I take intelligence to be a transhuman planetary loop of a highly complex and subtle kind" (letter to the author, June 28, 1998).

2. Also stated by philosopher Michael Zimmerman to the board of directors of the Center for Psychology and Social Change, Cambridge, MA, December 4, 1998.

3. Psychologist Ken Ring, who has studied both the near-death and alien abduction phenomena, has come to a similar conclusion. (1992)

Bibliography

Almaas, A. H. 1987. *Diamond Heart, Book I: Elements of the Real in Man.* Berkeley, CA: Diamond Books.

———. 1989. *Diamond Heart, Book II: The Freedom to Be.* Berkeley, CA: Diamond Books.

Atwater, Phyllis M. H. 1988. *Coming Back to Life: The After-Effects of the Near-Death Experience.* New York: Ballantine Books.

———. 1998. *Three Very Different Types of Subjective Light.* Privately published, Charlottesville, VA.

Barrett, William. 1976. *Irrational Man: A Study in Existential Philosophy.* New York: Doubleday.

Berry, Thomas. 1990. *The Dream of the Earth.* San Francisco: Sierra Club Books.

Bhajan, Yogi, and Khalsa, Gurucharan. 1998. *Mind: Its Projections and Multiple Facets.* Espandla, NM: Kundalini Research Institute.

Black Elk, Wallace, and Lyon, William S. 1991. *Black Elk: The Sacred Ways of a Lakota.* New York: HarperCollins.

Brennan, Barbara Ann. 1987. *Hands of Light.* New York: Bantam.

———. 1993. *Light Emerging.* New York: Bantam.

Brenneis, C. Brooks. 1997. *Recovered Memories of Trauma: Transferring the Present to the Past.* Madison, CT: International Universities Press.

Bridges: Magazine of the International Society for the Study of Subtle Energies and Energy Medicine (1989–1998).

Bruyere, Rosalyn. 1994. *Wheels of Light.* New York: Fireside and Schuster.

Bryan, Ronald. 2000. "What Can Elementary Particles Tell Us About the World in Which We Live?" *Journal of Scientific Exploration, vol. 14, no.2, pp. 257-274.*

Bryant, Darrol, ed. *Huston Smith: Essays on World Religions.* New York: Paragon House.

Buddhist Door, 1997. Vol. 2, no. 7 (July). Vancouver, Canada: Tung Lin Kok Yuen Society.

Buhlman, William. 1996. *Adventures Beyond the Body.* New York: HarperCollins.

Bullard, Thomas E. 1994a. "The Well-Ordered Abduction: Pattern or Mirage?" In Pritchard, ed., *Alien Discussions*, pp. 81–82.

———. 1994b. "The Influence of Investigators on UFO Reports." In Pritchard, ed., *Alien Discussions*, pp. 571–619.

Caballero, Maria Christina, and Lenger, John. 1998. "Researchers Searching for Light from E.T." *Harvard University Gazette*, vol. XCIV, no. 11. (December 3), pp. 1, 10.

Callimanopulos, Dominique. 1994. "Notes from Brazil." Cambridge, MA: PEER (Program for Extraordinary Experience Research).

———. 1995. "Exploring African and Other Abductions." *Centerpiece*, no. 5 (Spring-Summer), 10–11. Cambridge, MA: Center for Psychology and Social Change.

Campbell, Joseph. 1983. *The Way of the Animal Powers*. Vol. 1. San Francisco: Harper & Row, 1983.

———. 1991. *The Masks of God*. Vol. 2, *Oriental Mythology*. New York: Penguin Arkana.

Carpenter, John S. 1991. "Double Abduction Case: Correlation of Hypnosis Data." *Journal of UFO Studies*. New series, no. 3, pp. 91–114.

Collinge, William. 1998. *Subtle Energy*. New York: Warner Books.

Cooperstein, M. Allen. 1996. "Consciousness and Cognition in Alternative Healers." *Subtle Energies and Energy Medicine*, vol. 7, no. 3, pp. 185–237.

Daly, Herman. 1997. *Beyond Growth*. Boston: Beacon Press.

Dawson, Michael. 1994. *Healing the Cause*. Findhorn, Scotland: Findhorn Press.

Dennett, Preston. 1996. *UFO Healings*. Mill Spring, NC: Wild Flower Press.

Diaz, Carlos. 1995. Typed remarks for presentation at an international conference in Dusseldorf, Germany, October 29, 1995.

Don, Norman S., and Moura, Gilda. 1997. "Topographic Brain Mapping of UFO Experiencers." *Journal of Scientific Exploration*, vol. 11, no. 4, pp. 435–53.

Dossey, Larry O. 1992. "But Is It Energy?: Reflections on Consciousness, Healing, and the New Paradigm." *Subtle Energies*, vol. 3, no. 3.

———. 1993a. "Healing, Energy, and Consciousness." *Subtle Energies*, vol. 5, no. 1.

———. 1993b. *Healing Words: The Power of Prayer and the Practice of Medicine*. New York: Harper.

Dostoevsky, Fyodor. 1995. *A Gentle Creature and Other Stories,* translated by Alan Myers. Oxford/New York: Oxford University Press.

Downing, Barry. 1993. "UFOs and Religion." *MUFON Symposium Proceedings.* Seguin, TX: Mutual UFO Network, pp. 33–48.

Easterbrook, Gregg. 1998. "Science Sees the Light: The Big Bang, DNA, and the Rediscovery of Purpose in the Modern World." *New Republic* (October 12), pp. 24–29.

Eisenberg, David. 1985. *Encounters with Qi.* New York: W. W. Norton.

Feyerabend, Paul. 1993. *Against Method.* 3rd ed. New York: Verso .

Fowler, James W. 1981. *Stages of Faith: The Psychology of Human Development and the Quest for Meaning.* San Francisco: Harper.

Friedman, Stanton T. 1996. *Top Secret/Majic.* New York: Marlowe & Co.

Greenwell, Bonnie. 1988. *Energies of Transformation.* Cupertino, CA: Transpersonal Learning Services.

Greyson, Bruce, and Flynn, Charles. 1984. *Near-Death Experience: Problems, Prospects, Perspectives.* Springfield, IL: Charles Thomas, publisher.

Grof, Stanislav. 1985. *Beyond the Brain: Birth, Death, and Transcendence in Psychotherapy.* Albany: State University of New York Press.

———. 1988. *The Adventure of Self-Discovery.* Albany: State University of New York Press.

———. 1992. *The Holotropic Mind.* San Francisco: Harper.

———. 1998. *The Cosmic Game: Explorations of the Frontiers of Human Consciousness.* Albany: State University of New York Press.

Grosso, Michael. 2004. *Experiencing the Next World Now.* New York: Paraview Pocket Books.

Guth, Alan. 1997. *The Expansionary Universe.* Reading, MA: Addison-Wesley.

Harpur, Patrick. 1994. *Daimonic Reality: Understanding Otherworld Encounters.* New York: Penguin Books.

Hawken, Paul. 1994. *The Ecology of Commerce.* New York: HarperCollins

Henderson, Hazel. 1997. *Building a Win-Win World: Life Beyond Global Economic Warfare.* San Francisco: Berrett-Koehler.

Herbert, Nick. 1985. *Quantum Reality.* New York: Doubleday Anchor.

Herman, Judith. 1997. *Trauma and Recovery.* New York: Basic Books.

Hill, Paul R. 1995. *Unconventional Flying Objects: A Scientific Analysis.* Charlottesville, VA: Hampton Roads Publishing Co.

Ho, Mae-Wan; Popp, Fritz-Albert; and Warnke, Ulrich. 1994. *Bioelectrodynamics and Biocommunication.* London: World Scientific.

Hopkins, Budd. 1981. *Missing Time: A Documented Study of UFO Abductions.* New York: Marek.

———. 1987. *Intruders: The Incredible Visitations at Copley Woods.* New York: Random House.

———. 1996. *Witnessed: The True Story of the Brooklyn Bridge UFO Abductions.* New York: Pocket Books.

Howe, Linda Moulton. 1993, 1998. *Glimpses of Other Realities.* Vol. 1, Huntington Valley, PA: LMH Productions. Vol. 2, New Orleans: Paper Chase Press.

Hufford, Art. 1993. "Ed Walters, the Model, and Tommy Smith." *UFO Journal,* no. 297 (January), pp. 9–12.

Hunt, Valerie. 1996. *Infinite Mind. Malibu,* CA: Malibu Publishing Co.

Huxley, Aldous. 1970. *The Perennial Philosophy.* New York: Harper & Row.

Hyzer, William G. 1992. "The Gulf Breeze Photographs: Bona Fide or Bogus?" *MUFON UFO Journal,* no. 291 (July), pp. 3-8.

Jacobs, David M. 1992. *Secret Life: Firsthand, Documented Accounts of UFO Abductions.* New York: Simon & Schuster.

———. 1998. *The Threat: The Secret Alien Agenda.* New York: Simon & Schuster.

Jahn, Robert G., and Dunne, Brenda J. 1987. *Margins of Reality: The Role of Consciousness in the Physical World.* San Diego/New York/London: Harcourt Brace & Co.

James, William. 1902. *Varieties of Religious Experience.* Reprinted by New York: Macmillan, 1997.

Jung, C. G. 1959. "On The Psychology of the Trickster-Figure." *Collected Works of C. G. Jung: Archetypes and Collective Unconscious.* Vol. 9, part I. Princeton, NJ: Princeton University Press.

Kaku, Michio. 1994. *Hyperspace: A Scientific Odyssey.* New York: Oxford University Press.

———. 1997. *Visions: How Science Will Revolutionize the 21st Century.* New York: Bantam.

———. 1998. Interviewed by Art Bell on *Coast to Coast* radio program. March 4.

Keeney, Bradford. 1994. *Shaking out the Spirits: A Psychotherapist's Entry into the Healing Mysteries of Global Shamanism.* Barrytown, NY: Station Hill Press.

Larsen, Stephen. 1994. "The Making of a Zulu Sangoma, Vusumazulu Credo Mutwa." *Shaman's Drum,* no. 35 (Summer).

————, ed. 1996. *Song of the Stars: The Lore of a Zulu Shaman* (Vusamazulu Credo Mutwa). Barrytown, NY: Barrytown Ltd.

Lawson, Alvin H. 1980. "Hypnosis of Imaginary UFO Abductees." In *Proceedings of the First International UFO Congress*, edited by Curtis Fuller. New York: Warner Books, pp. 195–238.

Leir, Roger K. 1998. *The Aliens and the Scalpel: Scientific Proof of Extraterrestrial Implants in Humans*. Columbus, NC: Granite Publishing Co.

Levine, Howard E., and Friedman, Raymond J. 2000. "Intersubjectivity and Interaction in the Analytic Relationship: A Mainstream View." *Psychoanalytic Quarterly*, Vol. 69, pp. 63–92.

Lewels, Joe. 1997. *The God Hypothesis: Extraterrestrial Life and Its Implications for Science and Religion*. Mill Spring, NC: Wild Flower Press.

Mack, John E. 1994. *Abduction: Human Encounters with Aliens*. New York: Charles Scribner's Sons.

————. 1995. *Abduction: Human Encounters with Aliens*. Rev. ed. New York: Ballantine Books.

————. 1996. "Studying Intrusions from the Subtle Realm: How Can We Deepen our Knowledge?" MUFON 1996 *International UFO Symposium Proceedings*.

————. UFOlogy: *A Scientific Enigma*. Seguin, TX: MUFON.

Maney, Will. 1998. "Integration: Changes in Perception and Sense of Self." *PEER Perspectives* (Cambridge, MA), no. 2, pp. 7, 17.

Mankiller, Wilma, and Wallis, Michael. 1993. *Mankiller: A Chief and Her People*. New York: St. Martin's Press.

Markides, Kyriacos C. 1987. *The Magus of Strovolos*. Reprint, New York: Viking Penguin.

————. 1989. *Homage to the Sun*. Reprint, New York: Viking Penguin.

————. 1992. *Fire in the Heart*. St. Paul, MN: Paragon House.

McLeod, Caroline, et al. Forthcoming. *Psychopathology, Fantasy Proneness, and Anomalous Experience: The Example of Alien Abduction*.

Meadows, Donella. 1993. Beyond the Limits. White River Junction, VT: Chelsea Green.

Metzner, Ralph. 1994. *Well of Remembrance*. Boston: Shambala.

————. 1997. *Unfolding Self*. Novato, CA: Origin Press.

Miller, John G. 1994. "Lack of Proof For Missing Embryo/Fetus Syndrome," in Pritchard, Andrea, et al., eds. *Alien Discussions*. Cambridge, MA: North Cambridge Press.

Mitchell, Edgar. 1996. *The Way of the Explorer*. New York: Putnam.

————. 1998. Presentation at Star Wisdom conference, Newton, MA, May 9.

Monk, Ray. 1990. *Ludwig Wittgenstein: The Duty of Genius*. New York: Penguin.

Monroe, Robert. 1971. *Journeys Out of the Body*. New York: Doubleday.

————. 1996. *Ultimate Journey*. New York: Doubleday.

Moody, Raymond. 1975. *Life After Life*. Covington, GA: Mockingbird Books.

Mookerjee, Ajit. 1986. *Kundalini: The Arousal of Inner Energy*. 3rd ed. Rochester, VT: Destiny Books.

Morse, Melvin. 1990. *Closer to the Light: Learning from Children's Near-Death Experiences*. New York: Villard.

————. 1992. *Transformed by the Light: The Powerful Effect of Near-Death Experiences on People's Lives*. New York: Villard.

Morton, Patrick. 1998. *Following the Creative Process in Mathematics and Dreams*. Audiotape available from Arthur Associates, Peterborough, NH.

Mullis, Kary. 1998. *Dancing Naked in the Mind Field*. New York: Pantheon Books.

Mutwa, Credo Vusumazulu. 1966. *Africa Is My Witness*. Johannesburg, South Africa: Blue Crane Books.

————. 1986. *Let Not My Country Die*. Pretoria, South Africa: United Publishers International.

————. 1999. *Indaba My Children: African Tribal History, Customs and Religious Beliefs*. Reprint, New York: Grove/Atlantic. (Earlier editions: London: Kahn and Averill, 1985; Johannesburg, South Africa, Blue Crane Books, 1965).

Narby, Jeremy. 1998. *The Cosmic Serpent: DNA and the Origins of Knowledge*. New York: Putnam.

Newton, Michael. 1994. *Journey of Souls: Case Studies of Life Between Lives*. St. Paul, MN: Llewellyn Publications.

Nisker, Wes "Scoop." 1990. *Crazy Wisdom*. Berkeley, CA: Ten Speed Press.

O'Leary, Brian. 1996. *Miracle in the Void: Free Energy, UFOs, and Other Scientific Revelations*. Kihei, HI: Kamapua'a, 1996.

Osis, Karlis, and McCormick, Donna. 1980. "Kinetic Effects at the Ostensible Location of an Out-of-Body Projection During

Perceptual Testing." *Journal of the American Society for Psychical Research*, vol. 74, pp. 319–29.

Pazzaglini, Mario. 1991. *Symbolic Messages: An Introduction to a Study of "Alien" Writing*. Newark, DE: PZ Press.

———. 1994. "Studying Alien Writing." In Pritchard, ed., *Alien Discussions*, pp. 551–56.

Perkins, John. 1990. *Psychonavigation: Techniques for Travel Beyond Time*. Rochester, VT: Destiny Books.

———. 1994. *The World Is as You Dream It: Shamanic Teachings from the Amazon and Andes*. Rochester, VT: Destiny Books.

———. 1997. *Shapeshifting: Shamanic Techniques for Global and Personal Transformation*. Rochester, VT: Destiny Books.

Perry, Mark. 1986. "The Strange Saga of Steve Trueblood." *Veteran*, vol. 6, no. 3 (March), pp. 1, 10–13.

Persinger, Michael. 1989. "The Visitor Experience and the Personality: The Temporal Lobe Factor," in Stillings, Dennis (ed.). *Cyberbiological Studies of Imaginal Components in the UFO Contact Experience*. St. Paul, MN: Archaeus Project.

———. 1992. "Neuropsychobiological Profiles of Adults Who Report Sudden Remembering of Early Childhood Memories: Implications for Claims of Sex Abuse and Alien Visitation/Abduction Experiences." *Perceptual and Motor Skills*, no. 75, pp. 259–66.

Phillips, Ted. 1975. *Physical Traces Associated With UFO Sightings*. Evanston, IL: Center for UFO Studies.

Popp, Fritz-Albert, et al. 1984. "Biophoton Emission: New Evidence for Coherence and DNA as Source." *Cell Biophysics*, vol. 6, pp. 33–52.

Price, A. F., and Mou-Lam, Wong. 1969. *The Diamond Sutra and the Sutra of Hui Neng*. Boulder: Shambhala.

Pritchard, Andrea, et al., eds. 1994. *Alien Discussions*. Cambridge, MA: North Cambridge Press.

Pritchard, David E. 1998. Presentation to PEER's Star Wisdom Conference, Newtonville, MA, May 9.

———. 1994. "Physical Evidence and Abductions." In Pritchard, ed., *Alien Discussions*, p. 279–95.

Puthoff, Harold. 1996. CIA-initiated Remote Viewing Program at Stanford Research Institute. *Journal of Scientific Exploration*, vol. 10, pp. 63–76.

Radin, Dean. 1997. *The Conscious Universe: The Scientific Truth of Psychic Phenomena*. New York: HarperCollins.

Radin, Paul. 1956. *The Trickster: A Study in American Indian Mythology*. New York: Philosophical Library.

Randles, Jenny. 1988. *Alien Abductions: The Mystery Solved*. New Brunswick, NJ: Inner Light Publications.

Reich, Wilhelm. 1949. *Ether, God, and Devil*. Reprint, New York: Farrar, Strauss and Giroux.

———. 1951. *Cosmic Superimposition*. Rangeley, ME: Wilhelm Reich Foundation.

Riess, A., et al. 1998. "Observational Evidence from Supernovae for an Accelerating Universe and a Cosmological Constant." *Astronomical Journal*, vol. 116, p. 1009.

Rilke, Rainer Maria. 1984. *Selected Poems of R. M. Rilke*, edited by Stephen Mitchell. New York: Random House.

———. 1987. *Letters to a Young Poet*. New York: Random House.

Ring, Kenneth. 1980. *Life at Death*. New York: Coward, McCann.

———. 1984. *Heading Toward Omega: In Search of the Meaning of the Near-Death Experience*. New York: Morrow.

———. 1992. *The Omega Project: Near-Death Experiences, UFO Encounters and Mind at Large*. New York: Morrow.

Ring, Kenneth, and Valarino, Evelyn. 1998. *Lessons from the Light: What We Can Learn From the Near-Death Experience*. New York: Plenum Insight.

Roberts, Jane. 1972. *Seth Speaks*. Englewood Cliffs, NJ: Prentice-Hall.

Rubik, Beverly. 1995. *Life at the Edge of Science*. Oakland, CA: Institute for Frontier Science.

Russell, Peter. 1998. "Sciences, Consciousness and (Dare I Say It) God," *Consciousness Research and Training Newsletter*, vol. 21, no. 1 (June), pp. 3–9.

Sagan, Carl. 1985. *Contact*. New York: Pocket Books. The 1997 film of the same name was based on this novel.

Schlemmer, Phyllis. 1993. *The Only Planet of Choice: Essential Briefings from Deep Space*. Oakland, CA: Gateway Books.

Schild, Rudolf. 1994. Presentation at PEER forum, November.

———. 1998. Interview with author, December 30.

Sheldrake, Rupert. 1995. *Seven Experiments That Could Change the World*. New York: Putnam.

————. 1998. "Experimenter Effects in Scientific Research: How Widely Are They Neglected?" *Journal of Scientific Exploration*, Vol. 12, pp. 73–78.

Shucman, Helen. 1976. *Course in Miracles*. Glen Elen, CA: Foundation for Inner Peace.

Skolimowski, Henryk. 1994. *The Participatory Mind: A New Theory of Knowledge and of the Universe*. New York: Penguin.

Smith, Angela Thompson. 1998. *Remote Perceptions*. Charlottesville, VA: Hampton Roads Publishing Co.

Smith, Huston. 1992. "Postmodernism's Impact on the Study of Religion." In *Huston Smith: Essays on World Religions*, edited by Darrol Bryant. New York: Paragon House. pp. 262–279.

Somé, Malidoma Patrice. 1995. *Of Water and the Spirit*. New York: Arkana/Penguin.

Sparks, James. 1996. Interview with author, July 15.

————. 2007. *The Keepers*. Columbus, NC: Granite Publishing, LLC.

Star Wisdom Conference. 1998. "Exploring Contact with the Cosmos. A Native American/Western Science Conference and Dialogue on Extraordinary Experiences." Conference sponsored by PEER (Program for Extraordinary Experience Research), Cambridge and Newtonville, MA, May 8–9.

Stevenson, Ian. 1997. *Where Reincarnation and Biology Intersect*. Westport, CT: Greenwood-Praeger.

Stolorow, Robert, George Atwood, and Bernard Brandchaft, eds. 1994. *The Intersubjective Perspective*. Northvale, NJ: Jason Aronson, 1994.

Strieber, Whitley. 1987. *Communion: A True Story*. New York: Morrow/Beech Tree Books.

————. 1996a. *The Secret School: Preparation for Contact*. New York: HarperCollins.

————. 1996b. Interview with the author, June 16.

————. 1998. *Confirmation: The Hard Evidence of Aliens Among Us*. New York: St. Martin's Press.

————. 1998. Unpublished letter to Michael and Ian Baldwin, June 16, 1998.

Sturrock, Peter, et al. 1998. "Physical Evidence Related to UFO Reports," proceedings of a workshop held at the Pocantico Conference Center, Tarrytown, NY, September 29–October 4, 1997. Published in *Journal of Scientific Exploration*, vol. 12, no. 2, pp. 179–229.

Subtle Energies, peer-reviewed journal published by International Society for the Study of Subtle Energies and Energy Medicine, Golden, CO.

Swimme, Brian. 1996. *The Hidden Heart of the Cosmos*. Maryknoll, NY: Orbis Books.

Tanenbaum, Shelley. 1995. *Mindfulness in Movement: An Exploratory Study of Body-Based Intuitive Knowing*. D. psych. diss., Massachusetts School of Professional Psychology.

Tarnas, Richard. 1991. *Passion of the Western Mind*. New York: Ballantine.

Tart, Charles. 1997. *PSI: Scientific Studies of the Psychic Realm*. New York: Dutton.

Temple, Robert. 1976. *The Sirius Mystery*. Rochester, VT: Destiny Books.

Thorne, Kip. 1994. *Black Holes and Time Warps*. New York: North.

Tintinger, Lesley Ann. 1997. *The KWA Vezilanga Cultural Village at Magaliesburg*. Cramerview, South Africa: Works of Credo Mutwa. Privately published.

Travis, Mary Ann. 1998. "The Z Files." *Tulanian* (Summer), pp. 16–23.

Vallee, Jacques. 1988. *Dimensions: A Casebook of Alien Contact*. Chicago, IL: Contemporary Books.

———. 1990. *Confrontations: A Scientist's Search for Alien Contact*. New York: Ballantine Books.

———. 1992. *Revelations: Alien Contact and Human Deception*. New York: Ballantine Books.

Van der Post, Laurens. 1975. *A Mantis Carol*. New York: Viking Penguin.

Walsh, Roger. 1990. *The Spirit of Shamanism*. Los Angeles: Jeremy P. Tarcher.

Walters, Ed, and Walters, Frances. 1990. *The Gulf Breeze Sightings*. New York: William Morrow & Co.

Warren, Larry, and Robbins, Peter. 1997. *Left at East Gate*. New York: Marlowe & Co.

Washburn, Michael. 1995. *The Ego and the Dynamic Ground: A Transpersonal Theory of Human Development*. (2nd ed.) Albany: State University of New York Press.

Weiss, Brian. 1988. *Many Lives, Many Masters*. New York: Simon & Schuster.

———. 1993. *Through Time into Healing*. New York: Simon & Schuster.

Westrum, Ron. 1978. "Science and Social Intelligence About Anomalies: The Case of Meteorites." *Social Studies of Science*, vol. 8, no. 4, (November).

White, John, ed. 1990. *Kundalini Evolution and Enlightenment*. New York: Paragon House.

Whitehead, Alfred North. 1933. *Adventures of Ideas*. New York: Macmillan.

Wilber, Ken. 1983. *Eye to Eye: The Quest for the New Paradigm*. Garden City, NY: Anchor.

———. 1998. *The Marriage of Sense and Soul: Integrating Science and Religion*. New York: Random House.

Williamson, Duncan. 1992. *Tales of the Sea People*. Northampton, MA: Interlink Publishing Group.

Wittgenstein, Ludwig. 1965. "A Lecture on Ethics." *The Philosophical Review*, vol. 74 (January), pp. 3–12.

Wolf, Fred Alan. 1989. *Parallel Universes: The Search for Other Worlds*. New York: Simon & Schuster.

Woolger, Roger. 1987. "Aspects of Past-Life Bodywork: Understanding Subtle Energy Fields." *The Journal of Regression Therapy*, vol. 11, nos. 1 and 2.

———. 1988. *Other Lives, Other Selves*. New York: Bantam.

Zajonc, Arthur. 1992. Interview by Jane Clark, "Contemplating Nature." *Noetic Sciences Review*, no. 23 (Autumn), pp. 19–25.

———. 1995. *Catching the Light: The Entwined History of Light and the Mind*. New York: Oxford University Press.

Zimmerman, Michael E. 1993. "Why Establishment Elites Resist the Very Idea of UFOs and Reported Alien Abductions." Gulf Breeze UFO Conference, Pensacola, FL, October 22–24.

Zimmerman, Michael E. 2002. "Encountering Alien Otherness," in Saunders, Rebecca (ed.). *The Concept of the Foreign*. Lanham, Maryland: Lexington Books, pp. 153–177.

———. 1997. "The Alien Abduction Phenomenon: Forbidden Knowledge of Hidden Events." *Philosophy Today* (Summer), pp. 235–54.

———. 1998. "How Science and Society Respond to Extraordinary Patterns." *PEER Perspectives*, no. 2, (Winter 1998), pp. 3–4. Cambridge, MA: Center for Psychology and Social Change.

Index

Paperbacks also available from White Crow Books

Marcus Aurelius—*Meditations*
ISBN 978-1-907355-20-2

Elsa Barker—*Letters from a Living Dead Man*
ISBN 978-1-907355-83-7

Elsa Barker—*War Letters from the Living Dead Man*
ISBN 978-1-907355-85-1

Elsa Barker—*Last Letters from the Living Dead Man*
ISBN 978-1-907355-87-5

Richard Maurice Bucke—*Cosmic Consciousness*
ISBN 978-1-907355-10-3

G. K. Chesterton—*The Everlasting Man*
ISBN 978-1-907355-03-5

G. K. Chesterton—*Heretics*
ISBN 978-1-907355-02-8

G. K. Chesterton—*Orthodoxy*
ISBN 978-1-907355-01-1

Arthur Conan Doyle—*The Edge of the Unknown*
ISBN 978-1-907355-14-1

Arthur Conan Doyle—*The New Revelation*
ISBN 978-1-907355-12-7

Arthur Conan Doyle—*The Vital Message*
ISBN 978-1-907355-13-4

Arthur Conan Doyle with Simon Parke—*Conversations with Arthur Conan Doyle*
ISBN 978-1-907355-80-6

Leon Denis with Arthur Conan Doyle—*The Mystery of Joan of Arc*
ISBN 978-1-907355-17-2

The Earl of Dunraven—*Experiences in Spiritualism with D. D. Home*
ISBN 978-1-907355-93-6

Meister Eckhart with Simon Parke—*Conversations with Meister Eckhart*
ISBN 978-1-907355-18-9

Kahlil Gibran—*The Forerunner*
ISBN 978-1-907355-06-6

Kahlil Gibran—*The Madman*
ISBN 978-1-907355-05-9

Kahlil Gibran—*The Prophet*
ISBN 978-1-907355-04-2

Kahlil Gibran—*Sand and Foam*
ISBN 978-1-907355-07-3

Kahlil Gibran—*Jesus the Son of Man*
ISBN 978-1-907355-08-0

Kahlil Gibran—*Spiritual World*
ISBN 978-1-907355-09-7

Hermann Hesse—*Siddhartha*
ISBN 978-1-907355-31-8

D. D. Home—*Incidents in my Life Part 1*
ISBN 978-1-907355-15-8

Mme. Dunglas Home; edited, with an Introduction, by Sir Arthur Conan Doyle—*D. D. Home: His Life and Mission*
ISBN 978-1-907355-16-5

Edward C. Randall—*Frontiers of the Afterlife*
ISBN 978-1-907355-30-1

Lucius Annaeus Seneca—*On Benefits*
ISBN 978-1-907355-19-6

Rebecca Ruter Springer—*Intra Muros: My Dream of Heaven*
ISBN 978-1-907355-11-0

W. T. Stead—*After Death or Letters from Julia: A Personal Narrative*
ISBN 978-1-907355-89-9

Leo Tolstoy, edited by Simon Parke—*Forbidden Words*
ISBN 978-1-907355-00-4

Leo Tolstoy—*A Confession*
ISBN 978-1-907355-24-0

Leo Tolstoy—*The Gospel in Brief*
ISBN 978-1-907355-22-6

Leo Tolstoy—*The Kingdom of God is Within You*
ISBN 978-1-907355-27-1

Leo Tolstoy—*My Religion: What I Believe*
ISBN 978-1-907355-23-3

Leo Tolstoy—*On Life*
ISBN 978-1-907355-91-2

Leo Tolstoy—*Twenty-three Tales*
ISBN 978-1-907355-29-5

Leo Tolstoy—*What is Religion and other writings*
ISBN 978-1-907355-28-8

Leo Tolstoy—*Work While Ye Have the Light*
ISBN 978-1-907355-26-4

Leo Tolstoy with Simon Parke—*Conversations with Tolstoy*
ISBN 978-1-907355-25-7

Vincent Van Gogh with Simon Parke—*Conversations with Van Gogh*
ISBN 978-1-907355-95-0

Howard Williams with an Introduction by Leo Tolstoy—*The Ethics of Diet: An Anthology of Vegetarian Thought*
ISBN 978-1-907355-21-9

Allan Kardec—*The Spirits Book*
ISBN 978-1-907355-98-1

Wolfgang Amadeus Mozart with Simon Parke—*Conversations with Mozart*
ISBN 978-1-907661-38-9

Jesus of Nazareth with Simon Parke—*Conversations with Jesus of Nazareth*
ISBN 978-1-907661-41-9

Rudolf Steiner—*Christianity as a Mystical Fact: And the Mysteries of Antiquity*
ISBN 978-1-907661-52-5

Thomas à Kempis with Simon Parke—*The Imitation of Christ*
ISBN 978-1-907661-58-7

Emanuel Swedenborg—*Heaven and Hell*
ISBN 978-1-907661-55-6

P.D. Ouspensky—*Tertium Organum: The Third Canon of Thought*
ISBN 978-1-907661-47-1

Dwight Goddard—*A Buddhist Bible*
ISBN 978-1-907661-44-0

Leo Tolstoy—*The Death of Ivan Ilyich*
ISBN 978-1-907661-10-5

Leo Tolstoy—*Resurrection*
ISBN 978-1-907661-09-9

All titles available as eBooks, and selected titles available in Hardback and Audiobook formats from www.whitecrowbooks.com

www.JohnEMackInstitute.org

CPSIA information can be obtained
at www.ICGtesting.com
Printed in the USA
BVHW030001021021
617923BV00001BA/4